TECHNOLOGICAL CAPABIL

CW00347377

T. I. Nwan

Manchester 1984.

Also by Martin Fransman
INDUSTRY AND ACCUMULATION IN AFRICA (*editor*)

Also by Kenneth King
EDUCATION AND PAN-AFRICANISM
THE AFRICAN ARTISAN

TECHNOLOGICAL CAPABILITY IN THE THIRD WORLD

Edited by
Martin Fransman and Kenneth King

MACMILLAN

© Martin Fransman and Kenneth King 1984

All rights reserved. No part of this publication may be
reproduced or transmitted, in any form or by any means
without permission.

First published 1984 by
THE MACMILLAN PRESS LTD
London and Basingstoke
Companies and representatives
throughout the world

ISBN 0 333 35294 7 (hardcover)
ISBN 0 333 36062 1 (paperback)

Printed in Hong Kong

Contents

The Contributors

Martin Fransman   Department of Economics, University of Edinburgh

Kenneth King   Centre of African Studies, University of Edinburgh

Ronald Dore   Technical Change Centre, London

Frances Stewart   Queen Elizabeth House, University of Oxford

Gustav Ranis   Economic Growth Centre, Yale University

Jorge Katz   IBD/ECLA/IDRC/UNDP Research Programme on Scientific and Technological Development in Latin America

Raphael Kaplinsky   Institute of Development Studies, University of Sussex

Manfred Bienefeld   Institute of Development Studies, University of Sussex

Colin Leys   Queen's University, Kingston, Canada

Martin Bell   Science Policy Research Unit, University of Sussex

Françoise Caillods   International Institute of Educational Planning, Paris

Sanjaya Lall   Institute of Economics and Statistics, University of Oxford

Ashok V. Desai   National Council of Applied Economic Research, New Delhi, India

Thomas Owen Eisemon   Centre for Developing Area Studies, McGill University, Montreal, Quebec

Larry E. Westphal, Yung W. Rhee and **Gary Pursell**
  The World Bank

Carl J. Dahlman   The World Bank

Paul Bennell   Institute of Development Studies, University of Sussex

Steven Langdon   International Development Research Center,
  Ottawa, Canada

Jens Müller   Institute for Development and Planning, Aalborg
  University, Aalborg, Denmark

Sheena Johnson   Science Studies Unit, University of
  Edinburgh

I. Introduction

Martin Fransman and Kenneth King

This book reflects the new interest in the 1980s in the process of Third World technological change. While formerly research in the area of Third World technology focused largely on issues related to the transfer and choice of technology from abroad, more recently attempts have been made to understand how imported technology is assimilated and changed to suit local circumstances, and how technological improvements of various kinds are brought about. These new concerns are highlighted from the point of view of development economics and education in the first two papers in Section II by Fransman and King. These two papers serve the dual purpose of introducing many of the new research interests, while at the same time highlighting some of the areas of debate and agreement in a number of contributions in the present book. The remaining papers in Section II provide an overview of many of the issues, of both a theoretical and policy kind, which emerge in the examination of technological capacity in the Third World.

In Section III the discussion of technological change is located within the context of an examination of the international economy. Here the major contention relates to the extent to which changes in the world economy help or hinder accumulation and technological change in various Third World countries. Case-study material relates to the implications of microelectronics applications occurring at the world technology frontier. The relationship between learning and work organisation on the one hand, and technological capability on the other, is examined in Section IV, while Section V is devoted to a number of case studies drawn from countries in Asia, Latin America and Africa. One of the aims in the selection of countries was implicitly to consider the implications of the experience of more advanced and technologically sophisticated Third World countries – the so-called newly industrialised countries – for those at a far lower level of industrialisation – countries in Africa for present purposes. Finally, a select bibliography is included containing recent references.

Most of the papers in this book were originally presented at a conference held at the Centre of African Studies, University of Edinburgh, in May–June 1982. This conference continued the Centre's tradition, established over the last twenty years, of organising inter-disciplinary meetings on various themes relating to Africa and the Third World. In the case of this particular conference, one of the organisers' aims was to focus on technological capability from a variety of disciplinary perspectives, and this is reflected in the papers. The editors gratefully acknowledge the generous financial assistance provided by the Education Research Programme and the Science and Technology Programme of the International Development Research Centre of Canada. While the IDRC provided the larger part of the funds, important contributions were also made by the Faculties of Social Sciences and Science and the Centre of African Studies at the University of Edinburgh. Needless to say, none of these bodies bears any responsibility for the views expressed in this book, which are solely those of the authors concerned. The editors also wish to acknowledge the tireless and efficient assistance given by the Secretary of the Centre of African Studies, Neeltje Brady. Thanks are also due to Pravina King, who assisted most ably in organising the conference, and to Tammy Fransman, who also bore many of the burdens.

II. General: Technological Capability in the Third World

Technological Capability in the Third World: An Overview and Introduction to some of the Issues raised in this Book[1]

Martin Fransman

INTRODUCTION

The aim of this paper is to provide an introduction to some of the issues that are raised by the various contributors to this book. As will be seen, there are a number of important differences between contributors with regard to the perspective that is brought to bear on the study of technological change in the Third World and, correspondingly, the policy implications that follow. While it is clearly not possible to raise here all of the important issues discussed in these contributions, some areas where the differences regarding perspective and policy have been notable have been selected for comment. These are: new approaches to Third World technology in historical perspective; the conceptualisation of technological change and technological capability in the Third World; the political economy of technological change; international trade and technological capability; the world technology frontier; and the capital goods sector. It need hardly be added that this chapter is no substitute for a thorough reading of the rich accounts given in the other contributions to this book.

In the following section an attempt is made to situate, in a broader historical context, some of the recent concerns that have been expressed in some of the literature on Third World technology.

NEW APPROACHES TO THIRD WORLD TECHNOLOGY IN HISTORICAL PERSPECTIVE

It may not be entirely incorrect to suggest that there has, since the latter 1970s, been a rather fundamental shift in focus in the study of

Third World technology. While, as will be pointed out, there have been some important continuities, earlier studies tended to focus largely on the problems associated with the transfer of technology from richer to poorer countries. The problems related mainly to the cost, suitability and effectiveness of the technology transferred. For reasons which have by now become familiar, it was suggested that the recipient countries had to pay extremely high prices for the technology that they purchased, largely as a result of their relatively weak bargaining power (it being recognised that technology was a commodity with specific characteristics, which meant that its price was determined in a different way from other commodities, with important implications for social welfare).[2] Furthermore, the technology itself was often unsuited to local resources, conditions and objectives and it often operated in an inefficient way in the recipient countries. The recognition of these important difficulties spawned a large number of significant policy-oriented studies aimed at increasing the benefits of countries importing technology.[3]

An assumption that was rarely made explicit in many of these studies was that Third World countries possessed extremely weak technological capabilities and that the focus ought therefore to be on the import of *foreign* technologies, rather than on local technological capabilities. Clearly this assumption was based on reality, as statistics of the huge imbalance in technology trade between richer and poorer countries showed, and as similar figures on the world distribution of research and development expenditure and science and technology person-power revealed. Accordingly this assumption entered the literature, sometimes in rather extreme form as the following quotation from Cardoso makes clear:

> Basically the dependency situation is maintained because, in addition to the already stated factors of direct control by the multinationals and dependence on the external markets, the industrial sector develops in an incomplete form. The production goods sector (Department 1), which is the centre-pin of accumulation in a central economy, does not develop fully. Ordinarily, economists refer to 'technological dependency' and it means that the economy has to import machines and industrial inputs, and consequently has to stimulate exports (especially of primary goods) to generate the necessary foreign exchange.[4]

While this position follows quite directly from the central arguments of dependency theory, others who would not claim to have been influenced by dependency theory were not immune from similar assumptions. Even the perceptive Rosenberg was of the opinion that the Third World was technologically dormant in many important respects:

> Many of the major innovations in Western technology have emerged in the capital goods sector of the economy. But underdeveloped countries with little or no organized domestic capital goods sector simply have not had the opportunity to make capital-saving innovations because they have not had the capital goods industry necessary for them. Under these circumstances, such countries have typically imported their capital goods from abroad, but this has meant that they have not developed the technological base of skills, knowledge, facilities, and organization upon which further technical progress so largely depends.[5]

In the area of trade theory the same implicit assumptions were often made. From Heckscher-Ohlin type models to technology trade models it was widely assumed, and therefore concluded, that the Third World would be (if not the hewers of wood and the drawers of water) the exporters mainly of unskilled-labour-intensive goods.

From the latter 1970s, however, the assumption about extremely weak technological capabilities in the Third World began to be challenged, as the focus of attention shifted to an examination of technological processes and change in these countries. Increasingly researchers became interested in what happened to technology as it was imported and assimilated. Accordingly, rather than focusing research primarily around issues relating to the costs of importing technology, a greater amount of attention began to be given to the processes involved in the mastering and adaptation of this technology. The shift in attention was substantial and raised a number of important new issues relating to technological *change* in Third World countries. It was increasingly realised (see, for example, the succinct paper by Nelson, 1978) that technology was implicit, in the sense that the seller always possessed more information about its use than could be embodied in the blueprints, training, etc. sold to the buyer, and that its transfer accordingly involved a significant degree of uncertainty. The process of assimilating and reproducing technology both from local firms and from abroad therefore required firms to solve numerous problems, the answers to which were not always given by the seller of the technology. These problems were all the greater when, as in the usual 'north'–

'south' transfer, the conditions under which the technology was developed differed substantially from those in the recipient country. The assimilation and reproduction of technology therefore involved a process of technological *change*, however minor. It did not take long for some writers (see notably the earlier writings of Katz and Lall) to point out that these changes in some cases led to the emergence of a different 'technological trajectory' from that prevailing in the richer countries. In turn this led to the appearance of products and processes that were sufficiently different from those produced in the richer countries to show up in figures of (mainly 'south–south') exports of technology in various forms.

The change in direction accordingly led to the posing of new questions. Whether or not the shift was from a static to a dynamic preoccupation as some writers have suggested,[6] the new focus required an analysis of the process of technological change in Third World countries rather than a more limited consideration of the costs and benefits (the latter usually excluding technological change) of transferred technology. Nevertheless we should not ignore that there were some important continuities between the 'earlier' and 'later' concerns. This is seen most clearly, perhaps, in the studies of the transfer of technology concerned with the 'unpackaging' of imported technology. To the extent that unpacking involved the substitution of local for foreign firms, the issues of the technological capability of the firms and of the requirement for strengthening this capability came to the centre of the discussion. To this extent it may be suggested that the earlier concerns led 'naturally' to the later concerns.[7]

Nevertheless, it may be argued that there was far more to the change in focus than this, and that, to use the Khunian terminology, the changes themselves also owe a good deal to paradigmatic shifts. This requires further elaboration.

While reference has already been made to the change in focus that occurred, it is this change itself that must be explained. In what follows it will be suggested that the change referred to is to be explained in terms of, first, the demise of two hitherto dominant paradigms, second, the effects of the early stages of the rise of a new paradigm and, third, the impact of a new set of crucial 'facts'. These three factors, it will be shown, related in important ways.

The two paradigms that hitherto were dominant in the area of Third World technology were neoclassical economics, on the one hand, and dependency theory on the other.[8] For reasons that are now rather well known, both these paradigms began to lose their dominance in the

1970s. In the case of neoclassical economics one major blow came from the apparent failure of the highly industrialized Western economies, which was not anticipated or readily explained by neoclassical economics, while another came from the attack waged in the so-called 'capital controversy' on the grounds of logical inconsistency. The result was that this paradigm lost its previous dominance and economic theory became engulfed in civil strife as a number of different schools of thought began to contend in the vacuum that was thus created. The displacement of neoclassical economics had important implications for the study of technology in poorer countries since much research in this area had focused on neoclassical-type questions such as: the labour or capital intensity of technology, the substitutability of capital and labour in response to changing factor prices, the use of a production function in the estimation of the contribution of 'technology' to the output and productivity of Third World countries, etc. The undermining of neo-classical economics in the area of technology thus tended to weaken the influence of much research undertaken from the point of view of neoclassical pre-conceptions and, furthermore, opened the way to the posing of the fundamentally different questions referred to above.[9]

In this way, there emerged an increasing receptivity to the new questions that were beginning to be asked as the 'neoclassical blinkers' were removed. The questions themselves, however, were starting to be posed partly as a result of the demise of the other hitherto dominant paradigm, namely dependency theory (or at least cruder versions of this theory). Two factors, it seems, were responsible for the demise of this second paradigm. On the one hand was the emergence of the crucial 'facts' referred to above, namely the rapid rise of the newly industrialised countries like Hong Kong, India, Singapore, South Korea and Taiwan in Asia and Argentina, Brazil and Mexico in Latin America. The experience of these countries apparently proved that successful capitalist accumulation was possible in 'the periphery'. On the other hand, and by no means unrelated to the last point, was the theoretical critique from a Marxist perspective of writers such as the late Warren (1980). These writers argued that it was Marx's view that capitalism would successfully take root when it was introduced into countries like India. Since dependency theory was often associated with left-of-centre thinking, the latter critique had an important impact.[10]

It was this intellectual/theoretical and empirical climate that 'produced' the new questions and shift in focus that occurred. With the 'dependency blinkers' now removed researchers increasingly wanted to understand how and why successful accumulation was occurring in the capitalist periphery and this examination centrally involved a technology dimension. However, a further powerful influence affected the perspective from which the 'new questions' were posed. This influence stemmed from the impact of latter-day Schumpeterian thinking which, while not yet exerting a dominant influence in the theorising of technological change in the richer countries, has already made a decided impact in much of the recent work in the area of Third World technology.[11] With its emphasis on disequilibrium and uncertainty, Schumpeterian thought has had clear intellectual attractions in a world so obviously characterised by similar features. Furthermore, unlike the case of Keynesians and Monetarists, technological change lies at the heart of the Schumpeterian theory of capitalist economic development, and this feature too is appealing in our present world where the speed and consequences of technological change are so marked. Accordingly Schumpterian approaches such as the 'evolutionary theory' of writers such as Nelson and Winter came to exert a decided influence in studies of Third World technology. (Unlike Schumpeter, however, Nelson and Winter stressed the importance of more minor forms of innovation.) However, while not yet nearly so influential, we should also note the attempts to theorise technological change from a Marxist point of view, as exemplified by Leys' contribution to the present book which is discussed below in the section on the political economy of indigenous technological change.

The 'perceptual set' therefore shifted in this way, and the study of technological change within Third World countries was accordingly placed firmly on the agenda. At the same time, as will be made clearer later, links were established with some of the earlier concerns, taking in particular the form of questions about the relationship between the import of technology and local technological activities.[12] In the following section more will be said about the various forms of technological change that have been identified for specific attention.

DEFINING TECHNOLOGICAL CAPABILITY AND CHANGE IN THE THIRD WORLD

For the reasons mentioned above, from the latter 1970s an increasing amount of interest came to be shown in the process of technological change in Third World countries and in how this change related to the import of technology. The purpose of this section will be to clarify what is meant by technological change in this paper and to give an idea of some of the more specific forms of such change that have been identified as important.

In this paper, technology is defined broadly so as to encompass everything pertaining to the transforming of inputs into outputs. Technological change involves change, however minor, in the way in which inputs are transformed into outputs,[13] including changes in the quality of the output.

There are three aspects of this definition that are worth making explicit, since they have a particular bearing on some of the discussion in later sections of this paper. The first is that technology also includes the social organisation of the production and labour processes. A change in the social organisation of production and labour is therefore technological change. Perhaps the best example of such change is an increasing division of labour which changes the way in which inputs are transformed into outputs, although this does not necessarily (and did not in the early period of capitalist production before the introduction of machinery) involve changes in the physical means of production.

Second, knowledge plays a central role in changing inputs into outputs. This knowledge may be embodied in hardware and software, in people and in institutionalised practices and procedures. Experience under some conditions will provide the basis for learning which, in turn, will lead to the acquisition of new knowledge. To the extent that this new knowledge leads to changes in the transformation of inputs into outputs, technological change occurs. The insight that knowledge is highly unevenly distributed at any point in time and that the accumulation of knowledge is a highly specific process (so that, for example, there is no reason to expect the same forms of knowledge to emerge from two identically equipped and staffed plants) has led to an important breakthrough in the way in which technological change is understood. In particular, writers such as Nelson and Winter and Rosenberg have used ideas like these as the basis for an attack on the limitations of the neoclassical analysis of technological change and as a justification for the alternative Schumpeterian approach which they have proposed.

Third, it must be kept constantly in mind that the way in which inputs are transformed into outputs in particular enterprises is intimately influenced by events *external* to them. Competition is the main vehicle through which these external events are brought to bear as constraints on the enterprise. Over time the force of competition will ensure that the technologies in use in the enterprise meet minimal efficiency criteria: failure to meet these criteria will lead, in the longer run, to the undermining of the enterprises and their relatively inefficient technologies. A large number of factors will determine the extent of the competitive pressures exerted on enterprises. Of particular importance in the later section on international trade and indigenous technological change is the extent to which international competitive pressures, emanating from best-practice producers in the world economy, influence enterprises in the domestic and/or export markets. Trade policy may affect the extent of these influences and, as we shall see, a set of critical questions relates to the kind of policies that best facilitate the strengthening of technological capabilities.

From the latter 1970s some of the literature on technological change in Third World countries began to distinguish between different 'capabilities' pertaining to various aspects of the transformation of inputs into outputs that were seen to be important in the context of these countries. These capabilities involved the following kinds of activities: the search for available alternative technologies and the selection of the most appropriate technology; the mastering of the technology, that is its successful use in the transforming of inputs into outputs; the adaptation of the technology in order to suit specific production conditions; the further development of the technology as the result of minor innovations; the institutionalised search for more important innovations with the development of R & D facilities; the conducting of basic research. A number of comments may be made regarding this categorisation of capabilities.

Although the last two capabilities will usually represent more complex (and costly) activities, the first four capabilities are not necessarily presented in ascending order of complexity. The capabilities required, for example, in the search for alternative ways of generating large quantities of electricity might far exceed those required for the modification of agricultural implements in order to adapt them to local conditions. The copying of a complex machine might be a more difficult (and costly) task than the design of a simple new machine. Nevertheless, by distinguishing the last two capabilities as we have done, we are suggesting that there is a fundamental distinction to be drawn between the capabilities involved in 'know-how' and those involoved in 'know-why' (a distinction made in Lall's paper). As Westphal shows, South Korea has, on the basis of 'know-how' to a greater extent than that of 'know-why', successfully mastered imported technology and used it for exports. None the less, it must be recognised that a qualitative jump is required in moving from the former to the latter, and the ability of, and constraints on, firms and countries to make this jump may be important in determining longer-run progress.

We now turn to discuss the political economy of technological change.

THE POLITICAL ECONOMY OF TECHNOLOGICAL CHANGE

Having briefly defined what we mean by technological capability in this book, it will be helpful to situate its study within the context of the broader society-wide factors that influence it. Having done this we will be in a better position to examine in detail some of the more specific factors that have a bearing upon these capabilities.

Technology and technological change are not autonomous forces exerting uni-directional effects on society and neither are they neutral. The widespread belief to the contrary stems, perhaps, from the mistaken view that sees technology as the mere application of science, and scientific progress itself as the result of the sudden flashes of insight of the Great Thinkers transcending existing social and theoretical circumstances. The recognition, however, that science and technology interact in important ways and that both are intimately affected by prevailing social, political, theoretical and economic circumstances[14] has extremely important implications for the way in which we examine technology and technological change.

When some of the recent literature on technology in the Third World is examined from the point of view of this perspective on technology, something of a paradox emerges. On the one hand the 'appropriate technology' literature suggests that imported technology often remains an alien force in Third World countries, impervious to local resource availabilities and objectives. Far from being shaped by societal forces, such technology exerts an independent influence of its own, seriously limiting future possibilities. On the other hand, however, other parts of the literature have stressed the local influences that are brought to bear on foreign technology. The literature has emphasised, along the lines of the Schumpeterian evolutionary approach elaborated upon by writers such as Nelson and Winter, the incremental forms of technological change that take place when technology is imported. Since technology is *always* to some extent implicit, in the sense that the buyer never possesses as complete an information set as the seller, such incremental changes are the rule rather than the exception. Accordingly, local circumstances will come to exert an influence as the foreign technology is assimilated and adapted. In this literature the circumstances usually identified have been either economic (e.g. local prices, size of the domestic market, etc.) or technical (e.g. input availabilities, physical conditions, etc.). In contrast to the 'appropriate technology' literature, therefore, the latter studies have suggested that technology is to some degree responsive to prevailing conditions.

Leaving aside the question of the extent to which foreign technology ultimately responds to local technical and economic circumstances, it is of interest to note that some contributors to the present volume have pointed to the importance of other social determinants of technological change. Dore and Stewart, for example, have stressed, in addition to economic and technical factors, the importance of the backgrounds, interests, motivations and ideologies of those most intimately connected with the process of technological change. Dore, for example, emphasises all these factors in his discussion of the reasons for the weight given to self-reliance in the science and technology chapter of the Indian Sixth Five Year Plan. Similarly, Stewart argues that 'in trying to explain why some societies innovate effectively and others do not, the fundamental and underlying explanation often seems to lie in the realm of history and interests, rather than in particular policies . . . Hence a major element in any work on indigenous technical change should be to trace how the interests and rewards of the major decision-makers relate to a static or dynamic environment and to local and foreign sources of technology.'

However, the analysis of the determinants of technological change must go further than an examination of the factors influencing the decision-makers. Society-wide factors may also be important, though perhaps less directly, in determining technological change. In analysing the effects of such society-wide factors on the process of technological change, Leys, in his contribution to the present book, relies on the all-embracing and elusive concept of the 'social relations of production'. Technology he sees as 'an aspect' of the social relations of production which include relations of ownership, class relations (both in and out of production) and the corresponding form and character of the state. In this way technology is seen as neither an independent force influencing society nor as neutral with respect to that society. From this perspective Leys implicitly challenges the 'appropriate technology' view which, as we have seen, argues that imported technology is an independent influence. On the contrary, Leys

suggests that technology-in-use is a manifestation of the dominant social relations of production, while at the same time it may also influence these relations. Müller's discussion of Tanzania is used to illustrate this point. Here, Leys argues, the substitution of multinational-
controlled technology for the simpler forms of technology used by the
local Asian bourgeoisie resulted from the latter's exclusion from the
alliance established between the Tanzanian dominant class and international capital. In this case we see the technology being used resulting
from the class relations prevailing in the country at the time, even if the
technology narrowly defined is not adapted in any way to suit local circumstances. However, while for Leys technology reflects and incorporates the dominant social relations of production, it also produces
effects of its own. This is seen in the case of machinery which, while it
embodies technology, simultaneously embodies the prevailing dominant social relations in the country in which it is produced. In the case
of advanced capitalist countries, for example, machinery is likely to be
capital-intensive and its use associated with a sharp division between
mental and manual skills with increasing deskilling over time as new
vintages are designed and produced. The transfer of this technology
will produce social as well as economic effects in the recipient society
and Leys points particularly to the problem that this raises for socialist
societies attempting to create socialist relations of production.

The 'social relations of production perspective' also raises further
important questions about the transfer of technology. This perspective
suggests that the prevailing social relations will in the last resort influence both the technology that is transferred in the first place and the
effectiveness of this technology. Accordingly, problems of various
kinds may be expected in the case of technology transfer to countries
where the social relations of production are fundamentally different
from those prevailing in the exporting country. For example, in the
case of countries where labour has not yet been subjected to the
rhythm and discipline required by capitalist production, such requirements being embodied in the technology transferred, it may be expected that the technology will operate at levels of efficiency substantially lower than in the exporting country. Following this line of
reasoning, an important set of questions are raised about the recently
industrialised countries such as Japan, South Korea, Taiwan,
Singapore and Hong Kong which have apparently been extremely successful at incorporating and reproducing Western technology. Have
social relations in these countries, though in some respect dissimilar
from those prevailing in Western industrialised countries, nevertheless

been particularly conducive to capitalist forms of production, or have important changes had to be made in social relations in order to facilitate the import, reproduction and advancement of Western technology? Morishima (1982) suggests that the former was the case in Japan. The Japanese slogan 'wakon yōsai' (Japanese spirit with Western ability) implied that it was possible to 'graft' Western technology onto the pre-existing Japanese society and culture. But why was this society so amenable to Western technology? In answering this question Morishima stresses the importance of Confucianism in the making of the 'Japanese ethos'. He suggests that Confucianism underwent a significant change when it was introduced into Japan via China and Korea. While in China Confucianism emphasised benevolence as the most important virtue, in Japan it was loyalty that was stressed.[15] This ethos of loyalty facilitated the relations of subordination and discipline that were essential for the functioning of institutions such as the Japanese military and capitalist factory.[16] In this way (and together with a number of important preconditions) Japanese firms were able to successfully establish capitalist production and begin to incorporate Western technology which embodied social relations of production that were in many respects similar to those already prevailing in Japan. However, having successfully incorporated and reproduced Western technology, some observers – both inside and outside Japan – have begun to question whether Japanese 'culture' is capable of advancing this technology sufficiently for Japanese firms to become world leaders. This discussion tends to revolve round Western individualism (that is, the Western individual feeling free to creatively break with the socially accepted wisdom) which, it is claimed, is absent in Japanese co-operative society. While these discussions clearly require a good deal of elaboration before more convincing conclusions can be reached, in this section we have suggested that important issues are raised as the result of seeing technology and technological change as being intimately influenced by the prevailing society while at the same time themselves affecting this society.

INTERNATIONAL TRADE AND INDIGENOUS TECHNOLOGICAL CHANGE

In this section the relationship between international trade and indigenous technical change will be discussed.

Of all issues in economic theory and policy, that relating to the costs and benefits of international trade has one of the longest histories and remains one of the most controversial. Accordingly it is hardly surprising that we see in the literature, and in the contributions to the present book, a sharp divergence of opinion regarding the relationship between international trade and technological change. In order to clarify the differences it will be useful, for the purposes of the discussion, to distinguish between two extreme positions. At the one extreme the 'free trade argument' suggests that optimal technical change requires free trade at *all* points in time. At the other extreme the 'autarky argument' proposes that technologically weaker countries must become entirely technologically self-reliant as a necessary (but not sufficient) condition for building up its technological capability.

The latter argument in its extreme form may be easily disposed of. The main reason for this is that there are very few who would argue that the long-run benefits of local technological development will *always* exceed the costs, given the option of importing technology that will do a more or less similar job. Not surprisingly, therefore, there are no advocates in the present book of the 'autarky argument' (what point is there in having to 'reinvent the wheel'?), and even more closed economies such as China and Russia have continually benefited from the import of technology (that is, in the twentieth century).

The 'free trade argument', however, even in its extreme form, is more difficult to dispense with. After all, do not more dynamic interpretations of the writings of Adam Smith and David Ricardo suggest that free trade would facilitate a process of specialisation and division of labour which in turn would lead to a more rapid rate of technological change and productivity increase? By posing the question in this way we begin to raise a number of important issues which will be pursued indirectly here in connection with some of the contributions in the present book.

In his paper, Dore argues that one of the reasons for the low level of productivity and technological competence in many – but by no means all – Indian firms is the high level of protection that these firms enjoy. Ranis makes a similar point in comparing the export-oriented Asian newly industrialised countries with those following import-substitution regimes in Latin America. While the latter, he suggests, are 'typically unfriendly to indigenous technological activity' an important improvement can be made with a shift to an export-orientation: 'If and when the society does shift from domestic market oriented import-substitution to an export-oriented regime . . . the chance for a larger role played by indigenous technological activity is substantially enhanced.'

But what reasons are given for the alleged improvement in technological capability? Of the reasons mentioned by Ranis four will be mentioned here. First, it is suggested that prices under export-oriented regimes will be less 'distorted', leading to static allocative gains. Second, as a result of the greater pressures brought to bear on firms by the force of international competition, cost-reducing innovations will be introduced by maximising rather than satisficing entrepreneurs. Third, entrepreneurial skills including technological capabilities will be used and developed effectively when firms are no longer enmeshed in the tangle of bureaucracy that goes together with the control mechanism under import-substitution. Last, Ranis suggests that the indigenous capital goods sector, which plays a central role in technological change, is often undermined under import-substitution by the entry of foreign capital goods. For present purposes it should be noted that while Ranis emphasises the importance of trade liberalisation and international competition, this is *not* the same as insisting that trade should be perfectly free. We shall return to this point later.[17]

There is a further similarity between the views of Dore and Ranis. Both of them, partly as a result of their examination of the Japanese case, stress the importance of the international diffusion of technology to a far greater extent than an independent ability to produce indigenous technological changes. In defining indigenous technological activity Ranis does not mention the creation of 'new' knowledge, as opposed to the adaptation of imported knowledge, and Dore's distinction between 'independent technology learning capacity' and 'independent technology creating capacity' serves to make a similar point.

Other contributors to the present book, however, have been more forthright in advocating some restrictions on trade. Lall, for example, in his paper argues that 'India's performance suggests that it has the broadest and best developed technological capabilities in the Third World'. However, India also has one of the more trade-restrictive and bureaucratic regimes, and this leads Lall to suggest that 'The essential point of interest is to explain how the regime managed to generate a considerable amount of indigenous technological effort that spilled over into technology exports, while maintaining high and indiscriminate protection of the domestic market and a bias against foreign markets'. While perhaps stressing in his present paper to a greater extent than he had done in previous work the disadvantages of the Indian bias against trade, Lall continues to emphasise the importance of his earlier distinction between the protection of goods and the protection of learning and argues that both have provided important benefits in the Indian case. Although he says that more research is needed, Lall suggests that 'it may be argued that the "know-why" capabilities developed in and stimulated by conditions of artificial scarcities and protection provides a base on which more competitive technologies can be easily grafted, and that in a more liberal environment the basic "know-why" itself may not develop'. However, while the potential is in this way created for future improvements, Lall stresses that in many circumstances the incentives do not exist in India for the successful exploitation of the know-why that has been acquired. Furthermore, some of the know-why may not be socially beneficial (e.g. where it does not result in internationally efficient products and processes).

Others have also distanced themselves to a greater extent from the free trade position. Stewart, for example, points out in the present book that in some circumstances international competitive pressure might be so great that firms will not be able to afford to engage in risky activities designed to strengthen technological capabilities, and she suggests, conversely, that protection has often served to build up a local capital goods sector which is a necessary condition for local technological change. Katz is similarly convinced of the necessity, under certain circumstances, of protecting learning processes. Based on his study of two Brazilian firms he concludes that where the domestic market is sufficiently large to permit internationally efficient scales of operation and where the world technology frontier is moving outwards slowly, 'a public policy of protection, systematically maintained over several decades, seems to have successfully induced the development of highly competitive national enterprises based upon a sound indigenous technological foundation'. While the scale precondition is highly restrictive (how many Third World countries will be able to support industries at internationally efficient levels of output on the basis of the local market?) Katz suggests as a result of the study of firms producing at smaller scales that protection can lead to the establishment of a 'successful learning sequence . . . which permits the firm to complete the creation and strengthening of the whole set of plant engineering skills'. Whether such protection is justified will depend on a number of factors which he details on the last page of his paper.

As the above makes clear, there is a good deal of disagreement regarding the relationship between international trade and technological change. However, it would be a mistake to understand this disagreement in terms of a simple free trade versus protection dichotomy[18] In fact it turns out on closer inspection that there are some important areas of agreement among the authors referred to above which transcend this dichotomy. Three such areas are worth mentioning.

First, there is agreement that in many instances there will be significant net benefits to be gained from the import of technology (although, as we shall see later, there may be differences regarding whether in a particular case imported technology will undermine or strengthen local technological capabilities, and over the form of technology import that will be most appropriate). Lall, for example, argues that there are probably substantial net benefits to be obtained in India from the relaxation of controls on the import of both goods and technology. All the writers agree that there can be (but not necessarily always are) important complementarities between foreign and local technology.

Second, all of the authors have agreed that there are important benefits, including the strengthening of technological capability, to be gained from increased exports.[19] (An exception to this is Leys's suggestion that, under socialism, success will be measured by criteria other than economic growth and growth of exports, and that the attainment of socialist objectives might require the curtailment of the activities of the export sector where there is a trade-off between the efficiency conditions demanded by export for the world market and socialist relations of production. This apparent conflict might be resolved by making it explicit that the discussion here refers to capitalist Third World countries.)

Third, it is possible that some agreement might be obtained on the importance of protecting and promoting learning at least in the earlier stages of the development process. Dore himself points out that before Japan switched to a policy of using foreign trade as an engine of growth, the policy was one of 'minimisation of foreign trade (the minimum necessary for imports of capital goods and technology) plus a vigorous policy of building an independent technology learning capacity and using it for large-scale technology imports'. With the benefit of hindsight we know, in the case of Japan, that these policies have succeeded even if they were not necessarily the optimal policies.[20] Similarly, while Ranis notes that the East Asian countries to which he refers began with policies of import-substitution, he does not consider whether these policies and the industrialisation behind protective tariffs that they implied, were in any way necessary for the subsequent transition to an export-orientation and a more rapid development of technological capabilities. Clearly, to take the 'free trade position' mentioned above it would be necessary to demonstrate that free trade is optimal even in the earliest stages of the development process, and none of the authors referred to has done this.

Accordingly we can conclude that the differences noted above on the question of the relationship between international trade and technological change are not captured by the sharp dichotomy between free trade and protection. A number of further points may be made in support of this contention, drawing on the experience of some of the more successful Third World countries.

The first point goes back to the distinction made earlier between trade in goods and trade in technology. Many of the successful countries which have liberalised trade during the export-oriented phase have selectively restricted the import of technology and have made various interventions with the aim of encouraging local technological capabilities. While Dahlman suggests that Brazil has relied more heavily on the use of foreign technology than other countries such as India, Mexico and Korea, he also shows that in selected areas (notably in the capital goods sector) there were important restrictions on the import of technology accompanied by vigorous state attempts to encourage technological capabilities. Similarly, Westphal shows in the case of Korea that government intervention influenced the forms in which technology was imported, in particular limiting the overall importance of direct foreign investment (although he does not detail here all the controls existing on the import of technology). We can therefore see that liberalised trade in goods has not necessarily precluded restrictions on the import of technology and the promotion of technological capability, thus further blurring the usefulness of the free trade/ protection dichotomy in this case.

Second, as has already been implied above in the discussion of the importance of protecting learning at least in the earlier stages of the development process, it might not be sensible to refer to import-substitution and export-orientation as *alternatives,* as is often done. We have already shown that an export-orientation in goods might be accompanied by the import-substitution of some of the related technology. Furthermore, there are reasons for suggesting that in the case of most of the newly industrialised countries (Hong Kong and Singapore are exceptions), import-substitution and export-orientation *in goods* have occurred *together,* although the relative weight of each has changed with successive stages of the development process. This has emerged clearly, for example, in some important recent studies of Korea. In one

of these studies, Nam (1981) provides a comparable updating of
Westphal and Kim's (1977) figures in order to show the changes in
trade and industry incentives from 1968 to 1978. Nam shows that 'despite the import liberalization attempts since the early 1960s, most of
the import-substitution industries are still highly protected by various
import controls, and export industries receive special treatment such
as preferential loans and tax credits'. Furthermore, 'quantitative import restrictions have been far more important than tariffs as measures
protecting import-substitution industries in Korea'.[21] While the
agricultural sector is highly protected by Third World standards, re-
ceiving a 77 per cent effective rate of protection, Nam observes in the
manufacturing sector 'a roughly escalating trend in the level of protection from lower to higher fabrication for non-food manufacturing products'. More specifically, the consumer durables, machinery and transport equipment sectors received effective rates of protection for
domestic sales of 131 per cent, 47 per cent and 135 per cent respectively. Nam notes that 'domestic markets are highly protected for the
import-competing and export- and import-competing sectors' to the
extent of 35 per cent and 26 per cent effective rate of protection on
domestic sales respectively. Nam's figures therefore show that while
Korea's trade has been export-biased, there have also been industry
biases within the manufacturing sector, in particular in consumer durables, machinery and transport equipment. Accordingly, the Korean
success story further weakens the plausibility of either a free trade/
protection or an export-oriented/import-substitution dichotomy.

NB

This takes us to a further criticism of the usefulness of such
dichotomies in understanding the relationship between international
trade and technological capability. The selective protection of infant
industries implied by Nam's calculations raises the question of the
longer-run costs and benefits of such protection, the benefits being
thought of in terms of increasing technological capabilities and
associated improvements in total factor productivities. To put the
matter in starker terms: can technological capabilities be enhanced
under conditions of protection? The answer to this question, based on
some of the papers in the present book and other material, must be in
the affirmative, although it is perhaps worth stressing that such improvements will not necessarily occur. To return once again to Korea,
Westphal (1981) has shown, on the basis of this country's experience,
that 'infant industry protection can "work" in the sense of fostering the
rapid achievement of internationally competitive levels of productivity'. In his opinion, 'it may not be exceptional for the unit domestic re-

source cost of production in a particular type of activity to fall at an annual rate of around ten per cent during the first five to ten years of production'. Furthermore, those South Korean infant industries that have been protected – not all of them have – have begun exporting 'at a very early stage', notwithstanding the fact that for these industries 'effective incentives . . . are far greater for non-export-related sales than for export-related sales'. Dahlman also provides examples of the successful development of technological capabilities under protection, for example, in the case of the Brazilian automobile industry which he refers to as a 'success story of infant industry development'. Similarly, in the specific case of technology exports, Lall (1982) concludes that '"protection of local learning" in the manufacturing enterprises is the main explanation of India's success in technology markets'. Accordingly, it may be concluded that technological capabilities may be enhanced under conditions of protection, although it does not follow from this either that (a) protection is always needed for the development of technological capability, or (b) that the granting of protection will necessarily be followed by improved technological capabilities.

To conclude this section, we have seen that the experience of many of the newly industrialised countries[22] with regard to trade in goods and technology and the enhancement of technological capabilities, is far more complex than any strict dichotomy between free trade and protection or between export-orientation and import-substitution suggests. We have also seen that there is a degree of consensus among the contributors to the present book which further belies the usefulness of such dichotomies. However, important differences still remain, and these relate largely to whether, in particular cases, technology imports in specific forms (such as direct foreign investment, licensing and the import of capital goods) will strengthen or undermine local technological capabilities, and to the related effects of the import of goods. Although the differences are difficult to resolve because of the inherent complexity of the determinants of the learning process itself and the consequent inability to predict whether successful learning will occur under particular conditions, continuing studies of these and other Third World countries will have an important bearing on the conceptualisation of the effects of international trade on indigenous technological capability and on policy formulation.

THE WORLD TECHNOLOGY FRONTIER

It is clear that the study of technological change in Third World coun-

tries cannot neglect to take account of relevant conditions in the world
economy. Industrialisation itself will be crucially influenced by what is
happening in the world economy, and Bienefeld's paper in the present
book suggests that a large part of the explanation of the near-simul-
taneous rise of the newly industrialised countries must be traced to
favourable events in the international economy (such as growing world
export markets, the increasing internationalisation of capital and the
availability of international credit). Since a successful expansion of industrial activity is a necessary condition for improved technological
capabilities it is clear that an analysis of the world economy is important. But the study of world conditions is also important for local
technological capability in a more direct way in terms of events taking
place at the frontiers of technology.

The importance of the technology frontier has already been
acknowledged in much of the literature dealing with technology in the
Third World, although a different significance has been attributed to it
by various authors. For writers like Dore and Ranis, outward shifts in
the frontier itself signal potential opportunities for those Third World
countries eager to encourage (like Japan did) the international diffusion of technology and to benefit from their 'search and learn'
activities. Other writers like Lall (1982) and Katz have emphasised in
their empirical studies that technological change in even the more advanced Third World countries tends to occur either within the frontier,
or on a stagnant or slowly outward-moving frontier. In his present
paper, Katz points out, in the case of the two most successful Brazilian
firms in his sample, that 'it is striking that . . . they operate in industrial
fields in which the world's technological frontier has not experienced
very dramatic jumps in recent years, thus permitting a gradual narrowing of the relative gap that separated them from international technical
standards'. For Katz and Lall, therefore, the rate of advance of the
technology frontier can constitute an important constraint on Third
World industrial and technological activities, and the same point is
made in Stewart's paper, which emphasises, as one example of this, the
significance of scale economies.

Others, however, have stressed to a far greater extent the binding
nature of this constraint for Third World countries at the present historical point in time. This appears most clearly in Kaplinsky's paper,
which argues that in the present phase of the long-run world economic
cycle, cost-saving innovations (and in particular micro-electronics-
based innovations) have occurred so rapidly that the technology gap
between the highly industrialised countries and Third World countries

has widened substantially. For Kaplinsky this gap is becoming increasingly difficult to bridge, with the result that many 'northern' markets are becoming inaccessible to Third World countries, a view echoed to some extent by Bienefeld. However, this view, it should be added, is not shared by all, and Leys is expressly sceptical about the 'lack of openings' that the analysis implies for the Third World.

Despite the disagreements, it is clear (as the disagreements themselves imply) that an analysis of the world technology frontier is extremely important in any discussion of technological capability.[23] However, in most of the studies the frontier itself is treated exogenously, which is unsurprising in view of the complexity of the factors determining the position and shift of the frontier. Kaplinsky's paper, on the other hand, is able to draw on the extremely ambitious attempt by Freeman *et al.* (1982) to provide a Schumpeterian explanation of the so-called long waves of world economic activity. Given the obvious importance of this analysis in the attempt to explain various features of the changes in the world technology frontier, it is worth making a few brief comments.

While this is not the place to delve into the explanation (or its adequacy) offered by Freeman *et al.*, there is one aspect of their analysis that has important implications for the present discussion of technological capability. This is their contention that while the upswing of the (innovation-induced) long cycle is characterised by dominance of product innovations, the downswing, as a result of increasing Schumpeterian competition, is dominated by cost-reducing process innovations such as those related to the attempts to reap increasing scale economies. Since it is these innovations that shift the technology frontier, we have a number of hypotheses about the kinds of innovations that dominate successive phases of the long cycle, which have, in turn, important implications for Third World technological activity. While a large number of policy-related questions immediately come to mind (which will not be pursued here), an overriding question relates to the issue, already discussed earlier in connection with Kaplinsky's paper, of whether the bursts of innovative activity associated with the long cycle do make it more difficult for Third World countries to remain internationally competitive. While we have already seen Kaplinsky's answer to this question, we should return to the views of Ranis and Dore considered earlier in this section, which stress the opportunities opened up for the Third World through the international diffusion of technology. But will Third World countries, even the more industrially sophisticated among them, be able to 'search and assimilate' given the quantum jumps in the frontier? In some ways this brings us back to the dependency/anti-dependency debates referred to in the historical section above, as reflected in the divergent views of Kaplinsky, Bienefeld and Leys in the present volume. No doubt the debate will continue in this context, but before leaving this issue it is worth noting that Freeman *et al.* (1982) themselves express a view on the implications for the newly industrialised countries. They suggest that the downswing of the long cycle, characterised by the dominance of cost-saving innovations, implies a *slow-down* in the shift of the frontier with positive implications for these countries: 'From their viewpoint, [i.e. the newly industrialised countries] the long cycle may be seen as a welcome pause in the rate of advance of the technological or productivity frontier, opening up possibilities of becoming full members of the select group of economic and technological leaders in the future.' (p. 183)

THE CAPITAL GOODS SECTOR

In contrast to the disagreement that characterises discussions on the role of international competition and the world technology frontier, there is a wide consensus on the importance of an indigenous capital goods sector for facilitating indigenous technological change. Thus, for example, Ranis distinguishes the capacity to make adequate choices from the international 'technology shelf' from the capacity to adapt technology to local circumstances, and relates the latter capacity to the existence of a local capital goods sector which 'undoubtedly plays a very special role in determining indigenous capacity'. The same point is made by Stewart and, in the case studies in the present book, by Dahlman, Fransman and Katz.

However, the degree of consensus regarding the importance of establishing a local capital goods sector should not mask divergences of opinion on a number of related policy questions in setting up this sector. To a large extent these differences are related to the disagreements discussed above in connection with the role of international competition and the importance of the technology frontier. While most writers may agree that an indigenous capital goods sector may provide the conditions necessary to adapt and improve products and processes (since this adaptation and improvement will usually require altered capital goods), the agreement will abruptly cease in cases where, at least in the short run, the local production of specific capital goods is inefficient relative to international best practices. In such cases, if competing imports were to be prohibited this would be tantamount to the imposition of a tax on the users of these capital goods who are denied access to the assumed superior imports.[24] Furthermore, as we have seen, writers such as Dore and Ranis have argued that prohibition, by insulating producers from the efficiency improvements necessitated by international competition, will impair longer-run progress. On the other side of the debate are those who emphasise the possibility (not the inevitability) of a *longer-run* learning process which will eventually result in the attainment of international competitiveness, thus perhaps justifying the short-run costs. Clearly, the further away the country's capital goods producers are from the technology frontier, the larger the short-run costs and the longer the period during which these costs are imposed as the firms 'catch-up'. Other factors, such as size of market and economies of scale, which have been stressed earlier, may also play an important role. To make the whole issue even more complex, in those cases where investment projects in the capital goods sector are still being considered, no firm evidence will be available on the likely degree of success of such learning processes *in the future* (since it is not possible to be certain whether successful learning will or will not occur) and consequently on the productivity increases that can be expected. The latter point, which poses a substantial problem for theories and techniques of investment analysis, compounds the difficulties and makes disagreement all the more likely.

Some empirical evidence on these issues is presented in several of the papers in this book. Katz and Dahlman, for example, point to cases where substantial productivity increases occurred in parts of the capital goods sector that were initially protected in Argentina and Brazil, while as we have seen, Lall suggests that similar changes have occurred in Indian firms. However, as Dahlman points out elsewhere, it is not possible to conclude from the productivity increases that the longer-run benefits of local production outweighed the costs. On the other hand, Fransman documents the forms of learning that occurred in the capital goods sector in Hong Kong under conditions of near-free trade, and provides reasons for suggesting that under these conditions some potential protection-related gains had failed to be realised. However, here too it is difficult to know whether the learning process would have been 'deepened' by various forms of government intervention.

These empirical studies serve to emphasise some of the difficulties that are bound to arise in any concrete attempt to plan the capital goods sector in a Third World country.

CONCLUSION

This paper has done no more than select a few of the areas of debate
(reflected in the various contributions to this book) that have emerged
in some recent attempts to analyse technological change in Third
World countries. As a reading of the contributions themselves will
show, there are many other important areas that have not been discussed in this paper. While it is hoped that the present chapter has
served to highlight some of the differences in theoretical perspective
and policy, and accordingly has made explicit some of the underlying
tensions between the various papers, it does not adequately summarise
the richness of the other contributions in this book.

NOTES

1. The author would like to thank Norman Clark and Sanjaya Lall for
   stimulating discussion and comments on an earlier draft, although the
   usual absolution applies.
2. See, for example, some of the work of Vaitsos and Cooper.
3. These studies included many dealing with choice of technique.
4. Quoted in Warren (1980).
5. Rosenberg (1976) pp. 146–7.
6. Cf. the introduction to Stewart and James (1982).
7. I owe this point to Norman Clark.
8. Hirschman (1982) suggests that these two paradigms were united in a
   'strange alliance' against 'development economics' which he associates
   with the works of writers such as W. A. Lewis. Hirschman suggests that
   while neoclassical economics was monoeconomics (in that it used a unified
   approach in the analysis of both rich and poor countries), development
   economics insisted on the specificity of Third World conditions and therefore on a different way of analysing these countries. In practice, however,
   studies of technology in the Third World tended to be influenced either by
   neoclassical economics or dependency theory. We shall return later to
   Hirschman.
9. It should be stressed that this discussion of the reduced influence of neoclassical economics refers specifically to the area of technology. While
   writers such as Little (1982) have argued that since the 1960s neoclassical
   economics has made a sustained and increasing impact in development
   economics more generally (particularly, but not only, in the fields of trade,
   industrialisation and investment policy), this claim has not gone un-
   challenged – see, for example, Sen (1983) and 1982 Presidential address to
   the Development Studies Association (UK). The discussion below on international trade and indigenous technological capabilities touches implicitly on related controversies. However, it is clear from the writings of
   many development economists working in the area of technology that by
   the latter 1970s neoclassical economics had lost most of the influence it
   once exerted (see, for example, the writings of Katz, Lall, Nelson and

Stewart). The major reason for this was that neoclassical economics said very little about the causes of technological change and, as writers such as Nelson and Winter and Rosenberg have shown, made highly unrealistic and misleading assumptions about the process of such change.

10. Dependency theory was often associated with nationalist interests, particularly in Latin America.

11. The intellectual debt to writers such as Nelson and Winter and Rosenberg is made explicitly clear in the work of authors such as Katz, Lall, Stewart and Westphal. As is shown below in the section on the world technology frontier, Schumpeterian thinking is also influencing development studies through the important work on long waves by Freeman *et al.* (1982).

12. Certainly from the point of view of Third World technology studies it would appear that Hirschman (1982) is premature when he refers to the 'decline of development economics'. On the contrary, there has been a resurgence in this area of research, largely, as has been pointed out, as a result of the demise of neoclassical economics and dependency theory, which Hirschman fails to take into account.

13. In some cases, but not necessarily all, technological change will result in an increase in total factor productivity.

14. See, for example, Barnes and Edge (1982).

15. Morishima (1982) pp. 14, 15.

16. See, for example, Morishima (1982), p. 61. Sen (1983), drawing on the same source, makes a similar point.

17. Although Ranis does not do so here, the 'Smithian' argument could also be put forward, particularly in the case of relatively small countries, that export-orientation, by extending the market, provides the benefits of a greater division of labour.

18. While the 'autarky argument' referred to above proposes a complete ban on foreign trade, the protectionist position would not be all-embracing and would leave room for debate over whether in any particular instance protection is beneficial or not. The free trade/protection dichotomy emerges from much of the literature on trade theory (e.g. Corden, 1971) which has tended to argue for the optimality of free trade. (For a summary of much of this literature and for various attempts at a neo-Ricardian alternative see Evans (1981).) Corresponding to the free trade/protection dichotomy has emerged a similar export-oriented/import-substitution dichotomy. The connection between the two is clarified by Krueger (1981) who notes that, 'At first glance, the superiority of the export-promotion strategy appeared to vindicate the view of trade theorists, who had advocated free trade and who saw export promotion as coming closer to a free trade regime than did import substitution.' (p. 3) However, as this quotation implies and as this insightful article by Krueger makes clear, and as we shall suggest below, the relationship between the two 'dichotomies' is much more complex.

19. In the present book it is Westphal's paper on Korea that deals in most detail with the effect of exports on technological mastery.

20. While many writers (such as Milton Friedman) have argued that Japanese modernisation and economic development *began* with the Meiji Revolution in 1867, Morishima (1982) suggests that protection, including the pro-

tection of learning, played a central role in the Tokugawa period. Protection during this period, which lasted for about two hundred years until the Meiji Revolution, Morishima argues, laid the industrial foundations that made the advances of the Meiji period possible:

> Isolation also functioned as a protection for internal industries. A comparison of Japanese agriculture and industry with those of the Western countries clearly shows that Japan then had a comparative advantage in mining and agriculture. It would have been more beneficial for her to specialise in them and exchange their products for foreign manufactured goods than to produce those goods within the country. Therefore, if free trade had been permitted between Japan and the West, Japanese handicraft manufacturing industries might have been wiped out. Thus this isolationist policy prevented the Tokugawa economy from specialising in primary industries and allowed it to maintain manufacturing industries, though at a primitive level. The relative ease with which the Meiji government succeeded in industrialising Japan was due in part to the [Tokugawa] Bakufu's possession of workshops for the manufacture of gunpowder, shipyards and other Western-style factories during the later years of the Tokugawa period, and the development of these Western-style factories was in turn due to the preservation of handicraft skills throughout the Tokugawa period. (pp. 59–60.)

21. Cf. Corden (1980):

> If the objective is to expand manufacturing on the grounds of protecting infant industries, a tariff or set of import quotas is clearly not optimal. Compared with a direct subsidy to manufacturing output, it creates a consumption distortion by unnecessarily shifting the pattern of domestic demand away from manufactures. In addition, it creates a home-market bias by failing to protect exports of manufactures. The latter distortion could be eliminated by supplementing the tariffs with export subsidies. (p. 64)

22. Hong Kong and Singapore (the latter from the mid- 1960s) are partial exceptions. For further discussion on Hong Kong see Fransman (1982) and the article on Hong Kong in this book.

23. This is particularly apparent in the case of policy-related studies. In criticising choice of technique studies, for example, Bhalla (1981) notes that 'Most empirical case studies are focused on the question of choosing from a set of alternatives at a given point in time, thus largely neglecting the process whereby new technology is developed, applied and diffused.' He quotes Stewart: 'a major weakness of the micro-studies is their static nature. This means that the studies become obsolete as fast as the machines under examination.' (p. 377)

24. In the case where local production is subsidised so as to make it competitive with imports, users will obviously not be similarly taxed. However, it is not clear whether subsidies that retain a significant degree of foreign competition give firms enough 'breathing-space' to invest in and accumulate learning skills. In this connection it may be recalled that the infant industries mentioned by Westphal (1981) – and we saw that the machinery sector in South Korea received a high degree of effective protection in 1978 – were granted protection in the form of high tariffs and quantitative restrictions.

REFERENCES

Barnes, B. and Edge, D. (eds) (1982) *Science in Context. Readings in the Sociology of Science*. Milton Keynes: Open University Press.

Bhalla, A. S. (1981) *Technology and Employment in Industry*. Geneva: ILO.

Corden, W. M. (1971) *The Theory of Protection*. Oxford: Clarendon Press.

Corden, W. M. (1980) 'Trade Policies', in Cody, J. *et al.*, (eds) (1980) *Policies for Industrial Progress in Developing Countries*. London: Oxford University Press.

Evans, D. (1981) 'Unequal Exchange and Economic Policies: Some Implications of the Neo-Ricardian Critique of the Theory of Comparative Advantage', *IDS Bulletin*, vol. 6, no. 4, March 1975, reprinted in I. Livingstone (ed.) (1981) *Development Economics and Policy: Readings*. London: Allen & Unwin.

Fransman, M. (1982) 'Learning and the Capital Goods Sector under Free Trade: The Case of Hong Kong', *World Development*, vol. 10, no. 11.

Freeman, C., Clark, J., Soete, L. (1982) *Unemployment and Technical Innovation: A Study of Long Waves and Economic Development*. London: Frances Pinter.

Hirschman, A. O. (1982) 'The Rise and Decline of Development Economics', in M. Gersovitz, C. F. Diaz-Alejandro, G. Ranis and M. Rosenzweig (eds) (1981) *The Theory and Experience of Economic Development. Essays in Honour of Sir W. Arthur Lewis*. London: Allen & Unwin.

Krueger, A. O. (1981) 'Export-Led Industrial Growth Reconsidered', in W. Hong and L. B. Krause (eds) (1981) *Trade and Growth of the Advanced Developing Countries in the Pacific Basin. Papers and Proceedings of the Eleventh Pacific Trade and Development Conference*. Seoul, South Korea: Korea Development Institute.

Lall, S. (1982) *Developing Countries as Exporters of Technology. A First Look at the Indian Experience*. London: Macmillan.

Little, I. M. D. (1982) *Economic Development Theory, Policy and International Relations*. New York: Basic Books.

Morishima, M. (1981) *Why Has Japan 'Succeeded'? Western Technology and the Japanese Ethos*. Cambridge: Cambridge University Press.

Chon Hyun Nam (1981) 'Trade and Industrial Policies, and the Structure of Protection in Korea', in W. Hong and L. B. Krause (eds) (1981) *Trade and Growth of the Advanced Developing Countries in the Pacific Basin. Papers and Proceedings of the Eleventh Pacific Trade and Development Conference*. Seoul, South Korea: Korea Development Institute.

Nelson, R. R. (1978) *Innovation and Economic Development: Theoretical Retrospect and Prospect* (mimeo).

Nelson, R. R. and Winter, S. G. (1974) 'Neoclassical versus Evolutionary Theories of Economic Growth: Critique and Prospectus', *Economic Journal*, pp. 886–905.

Nelson, R. R. and Winter, S. G. (1977) 'In Search of Useful Theory of Innovation', *Research Policy*, 6.

Rosenberg, N. (1976) *Perspectives on Technology*. Cambridge: Cambridge University Press.

Sen, A. (1983) 'The Profit Motive', *Lloyds Bank Review*, January 1983, no. 147.

Stewart, F. and James J. (1982) *The Economics of New Technology in Developing Countries.* London: Frances Pinter.
Warren, B. (1980) *Imperialism: Pioneer of Capitalism.* London: New Left Books.
Westphal, L. E. and Kim, K. S. (1977) 'Industrial Policy and Development in Korea', World Bank Staff Working Paper, no. 263, Washington DC: World Bank.
Westphal, L. E. (1981) 'Empirical Justification for Infant Industry Protection', World Bank Staff Working Paper, no. 445, Washington DC: World Bank.

Science, Technology and Education in the Development of Indigenous Technological Capability

Kenneth King

INTRODUCTION

In broad comparability with the changes in economic theories and policies of the last chapter, the period 1960 to 1980 witnessed shifts in education and development theory which have resulted now in the beginnings of interest in the notion of indigenous technological capability. The critique of the 1960s' faith in investment-in-education-and-modernisation has been sufficiently widespread that there is no cause to rehearse it here;[1] equally, criticism of dependency theory, which was one of the successors to the modernisation era, has also been effective in undermining the cruder versions of cultural imperialism and of the alleged subordination of the entire education apparatus to the economic system and the international division of labour.[2] The other successor to the short-lived modernisation period was the very wide-ranging concern for equity, employment, income distribution and basic needs, especially in regard to rural and marginal urban populations.[3] This had a much greater impact on educational thinking from the late 1960s than did the dependency literature. Then finally from the mid to late 1970s, research on education and labour markets started turning up evidence of significant autonomy and self-reliance at the national, regional and community level. Within a short period, the literature of the donor agencies was full of the possibilities for endogenous self-reliant development, and the utilisation of indigenous technical knowledge. The independent actions, differing patterns of participation, and cultural heritage of specific countries were widely acknowledged.[4]

These broad changes in the conceptualisation of education and development will only be discussed here selectively in relation to indigenous technological capability. It should be stressed in so doing that

31

frequently changes in the conceptualisation of development have been much more clearly marked in the development literature of Western donor agencies and academics than they have in planning offices of ministries of education or labour in developing countries.[5] It goes without saying, therefore, that an agency retreat from, say, planning the development of high-level manpower à la Ashby, Myers and Harbison need not significantly deflect the philosophy of a country – Nigeria, for example – from massive expansion of its university sector.

Indigenous technological capability was, in a sense, on the agenda during the era of investment in high-level manpower. In Karachi (1961), Santiago (1962) and Addis Ababa (1960), the UNESCO conferences assumed that the creation of scientific and technological manpower was straightforwardly by the creation of polytechnics and universities.[6] The issue was localisation of expatriates where they existed, and the expectation was that the new mechanisms like apprenticeship, technical schools, and agricultural extension would operate not very differently from the way they had historically in the North. The classic illustration of this faith is the volume of papers on education and economic development from the 1963 conference in Chicago on the role of education in early stage development.[7] But even though the mood then was optimistic, there was the first warning shot in Foster's elegant attack on the 'vocational school fallacy in development planning'.[8] Investing in intermediate-level technical capacity via schools was perhaps not as certain an enterprise as had been suggested.

Already in the mid 1960s, the earlier global interest in scientific and technological manpower from school to university, from apprenticeship to agricultural research, had begun to narrow. First, rate-of-return studies, roundly attacked though they were from the very early 1960s,[9] had suggested a focus on primary education as the best investment for resource-poor countries. Second, the worry about over-production of high-level manpower, and about educated unemployment at secondary and university levels hastened the academic and donor agency retreat from policies supporting large-scale increases in university-level science and technology. Indeed the very popularity of engineering, medicine and science at university partly derived from the restrictions on their expansion.

By the early 1980s, the investment approach to education had travelled a long way, and was now principally concerned with the continued justification of spending on basic, primary education. Beyond education being a basic need itself, the investment could be justified in terms of better health, less mortality and reduced fertility.[10] As to increased productivity, there was some evidence that agriculture could be improved by so many years of schooling, but only in special circumstances.[11] As to the effect of education on productivity in industry both modern and traditional, twenty years of research seem to have revealed very little. Thus a very recent review of the literature has to admit:

> We think there *is* some relation between school and productivity but it is difficult to say whether the important contribution of formal education to increased material output takes place in the early years of schooling or at higher levels, where specialised techniques and perhaps more organisational skills are learned. Certainly Psacharopoulos' 'higher rates of return to primary schooling' cannot be used to prove or even suggest that investment in primary schooling contributes more to growth than investment in higher education.[12]

The debate about the significance of investment in primary education, and especially its impact on agricultural and industrial productivity, is potentially of some importance in analysing the education impact on indigenous technological capacity. Although it is alarming that so little still seems to be known about the nature of educational influence on productivity at different levels, a good deal of the uncertainty must derive from the narrow conceptualisation both of education and of productivity. To measure education in terms of mere years of schooling (regardless of quality), and productivity in terms of individuals' or firms' income, would be unlikely to yield data of interest to the study of technical capacity.[13] We shall suggest later the need for much more sensitive measures of learning both in school and without.

We have identified the original investment approach to high-level manpower as a stream that progressively narrowed to a consideration of the impact of primary school. It is noticeable, however, that from a different source a much more comprehensive approach to the investment in scientific and technological manpower began to emerge once more in the late 1970s and early 1980s. Following the concern with equity in school and work, and the discovery of the informal labour market, its technology and learning routines, it became suddenly important to understand local technical knowledge, especially as it seemed possible that a mix of local knowledge and imported could provide the building blocks of what was coming to be called 'endogenous technological development'.

The crystallisation of a new encouragement to science and technology investment came with the UNCSTD conference of 1979. Unlike the early 1960s, it now incorporated a very different notion of endogeneity in technology. But there was no doubt that higher technological education was also once more a respectable goal. The Lagos Plan of Action for the Economic Development of Africa followed in 1980, mapping out a very wide range of human resource issues directly relevant to the stimulation of indigenous technological capability. The combination of absorption and adaptation of imported technology with plans 'to develop technology locally' is typical of the new emphasis, as is the spread of recommendations from motivation, to technical entrepreneurship, to non-conventional technology disciplines in higher education.[14]

At the national level, too, we can expect an increasingly analytical connection between the science and technology system and the entire educational apparatus, as suggested by the Lagos Plan. Though not directly related, an excellent example of the marriage of the science and technology system with the wider political culture, including education, is to be seen in the 1981 study of Tanzania: *Development Strategy and Technological Transformation: the Limits of Self-Reliance.*[15] This is a particularly important study, for it presents the full power of technological dependence in Tanzania and the now rather frail social and political resources to enhance technological self-reliance and indigenous capability. It is a welcome glimpse of the difficulty in marking out a more autonomous response, since the political will required to build on the existing indigenous technological capability is a world away from the easy declarations about endogenous development at international meetings.

It may perhaps be useful to pull together some characteristics of these more recent studies, concentrating especially on those that seem likely to unravel more satisfactorily the education component of indigenous capability.

First, there is a tendency to locate the study of capacity within an analysis of the larger *scientific environment* of the country, including in that the national research environment. This has focused attention not on a quantitative assessment of scientists, engineers, etc., but on the institutional infrastructure supporting technological negotiation, modification and capacity development. This cannot be done without a careful mapping of the endogenous technological base. The specificity of the national research environment makes it essential to sort out different strategies for strengthening research and technological capacity.[16] A natural consequence of an environmental approach is the categorisation of technological capability in different economic and political settings: hence the value of K.N. Rao's work on scales of technological capability in different groups of countries, and the analysis of potential in specific technologies, for example chemical engineering, across countries.[17]

A second increasingly important constituent of new work on science and technology systems in relation to education and development is *historical analysis*. Much more needs to be known about the emergence of scientific and technological capacity over time. Historical studies, therefore, such as Eisemon's in Kenya and India,[18] Müller's in Tanzania,[19] or King's, also on Kenya,[20] illustrate the complexity of making generalisations about strengthening the scientific culture or building on the local technological base. Stretching as they do over several decades, they offer the opportunity to identify the existence of very different science policy regimes even in a group of deceptively similar countries.

A third ingredient of new work drawing together science, technology and education is the attempt to look simultaneously at *the role of the state and of capital in relation to the formation of industrial skills*. Very little analysis has been attempted on the political economy of skill formation – the interest of international capital, local capital and the state in producing certain kinds of skill and not others – what industry is prepared to pay for and what typically gets subsidised by the state. For most countries we presently lack accounts that make sense of the complementary or contradictory nature of the state and industry's training strategies; in other words, the negotiation between the state and private capital over the development of indigenous technical capacity is still virtually a closed book. But we shall be a lot nearer an understanding of the political economy of ITC when we have further industry-specific analyses, such as that on the metal fabrication sector in Kenya being undertaken by Britha Mikkelsen.[21]

A fourth feature of some very recent research that will need to be replicated has been an interest in the examination of *scientific and technical careers*. Quantitative assessment of science manpower and technological potential will continue to be important, but total numbers of technicians or engineers tell us very little about their utilisation.[22] Qualitative analysis of science careers as affected by the nature of their training and the wider industrial or agricultural environment are likely to become an important feature of the mapping of national ITC. This new emphasis, illustrated by Bennell's study of the engineering professions in Kenya, begins to get behind the job title to the nature of the work itself.[23]

A fifth cluster of recent research that touches very relevantly on the learning side of ITC is that associated with separate studies by Caillods,[24] Clayden[25] and Bell.[26] Each takes a particular general issue, like 'skill', or 'learning by doing', or 'work-organisation', and sorts out a categorisation of these loosely-used terms in ways that sharpen their potential for the analysis of ITC very markedly. Given the prevalence of the term 'learning' in much technical-change literature, Bell's elucidation of its very different senses is critical in a volume that seeks to analyse capability from a number of disciplinary perspectives. Similarly, Caillods's work on the variation in firms' employment structures and use of technical labour even within the same sector of economic activity is a useful warning against thinking of ITC in terms of set ratios of engineers, to technicians, to skilled and unskilled labour.

A last feature of new literature on the learning side of technical capacity comes from the unpackaging of skills and knowledge in the informal and traditional craft sectors. Drawing on anthropology, history and sociology, the structure of local knowledge systems, whether on health, agriculture, construction or craft, has begun to be examined for their development and adaptation potential. Work on wayside mechanics and smithies side by side with many other forms of indigenous technical knowledge is suggesting an element of ITC that should certainly be regarded with attention.[27]

These various threads do not yet constitute a comprehensive approach to the analysis of ITC, but they do indicate approaches to conceptualising the formation and utilisation of human resources that, taken together, are very different from traditional investment and manpower analyses. However, research is still being conducted in a very fragmented way and has not been synthesised. To be done well it requires cross-disciplinary skills in education and labour market analysis, and the use of qualitative and historical research techniques, as well as insights from the wider political economy, industry and agriculture. It will not therefore make the analysis and planning of technological manpower any easier than it was in the 1960s, but it does now look as if, for several countries, the research results necessary to that planning are beginning to become available. They include at a minimum the following:

(i) analysis of higher education policy regimes in relation to the scientific research environment;

(ii) historical account of development of state training and technology system in relation to training and technology changes by industrial and agricultural employers;

(iii) outline of local technical knowledge systems, outside the formal sector;

(iv) selective, qualitative description of scientific and technological careers with emphasis on skill and knowledge acquisition and utilisation;

(v) interaction among forms of learning in relation to rural and urban technologies.

The rest of this paper will be concerned with the last of these items, which, although it overlaps with some of the others, looks very broadly at the sources of technical and scientific competence in the home, school, farm and factory. The context of the argument is more derived from Eastern Africa than from other regions, despite reference to India and Latin America. Also it is written in the awareness that other papers relating to Africa offer three case studies of learning and technological change in different production sectors: in the traditional craft sector in Tanzania as it interacts with the modern large-scale metal fabrication (Müller); in the medium-size, predominantly Asian, wood and textile industries as they are affected by state policy and the multinational sector (Langdon); and, finally, in the engineering sector that cuts across public, parastatal, multinational and local firms (Bennell).

INTERACTIONS BETWEEN LEARNING AND TECHNOLOGY

Scientific and technological capacity via education is back on the agenda of African ministries of education, confirmed by their ministers' conference in Harare in mid-1982. As it is just over twenty years since their predecessors met in the historic Addis Ababa conference of 1961, with its powerful faith in investing in education, it may be useful to review progress in conceptualising the impact of education and training on technological capacity and technical change over these two decades. Some things have changed. There is a much greater realism about the likely influence of educational investment upon economic growth, whether in agriculture or industry, than was the case in the heady days of investing in high-level manpower. There is also much greater recognition of the out-of-school sources of skills, experience and knowledge. The educated unemployment crisis that appeared inevitably with the democratisation of education at Independence forced many education policy-makers to look closely at the nature of available work in developing countries. This led in turn to an awareness of work options other than in the formal sector of the economy, and to the schools' role in preparing students for these very different futures. Over the course of the 1970s, consequently, external funds for education have been increasingly directed at interventions that had relevance for improved opportunities for the majority who would not pursue higher secondary and college education. Money has been available for diversifying schools, orienting students to rural skills, pre-vocationalising otherwise academic structures. But all of this has been predominantly institution-based, in schools or in some nonformal training area. Equally, it has been motivated by a concern with *attitudinal* change in students towards different kinds of work, rather than with excellence in work itself, whether in towns or in the rural areas.

Because of the widespread critique of formal education from the late 1960s, research attention has either wandered from the school, polytechnic and university sector altogether, or has focused on the malfunctioning of the system (Diploma Disease, Paper Qualification Syndrome, etc.). Not that the research interests of the North, nor patterns of external aid to education have dictated the general orientation of the education system or local education research. Indeed, education has continued to expand at the primary, secondary and tertiary levels in ways that are little affected by the priorities of the main donors. Yet both local and foreign planners have at one level been exercised about basic relations between education and unemployment, and about changing student aspirations towards certain kinds of work.

Putting it very simply, it has sometimes appeared as if to the policy and planning people the aspirations of too many students were too high in Africa, and would need somehow to be lowered, or modified. Even though none of this has very directly affected parents' determination to organise or pay for more education, it has diverted attention from those aspects of education that could well have a close relationship to ITC. With the emphasis on quantitative expansion and on orientation to productive work, there has been insufficient attention given either to the quality of knowledge and skills acquired or to their utilisation in the work-place. The fact of working was more important than the outcome or productivity of the work.

All this has meant that there is a very serious lack of information about many of the potentially important education ingredients in indigenous technological capability. Arguably, many forces could be operating for and against the development of ITC, including literacy levels, and especially technical literacy; basic primary and secondary education, but especially maths and science education; and finally higher scientific and technological education. Although it is encouraging that the ministers of education in Africa are once more stressing the key role of science and technology education, there is currently a dearth of serious study either of the potential of these several fields or of the quality of what is currently being achieved in them. We shall in a moment briefly look at some of these education sectors, identifying trends that are emerging and research that could be timely in exploring the interactions between educational and economic aspects of ITC, but first it is essential to stand back somewhat from the concept of indigenous technological capability itself. Like many complex notions (for example, 'good' teaching, or 'good' business sense), it is easier to list the attributes and actions associated with it than to get to its essence. It is also somewhat straightforward to list the necessary (but not sufficient) conditions of good teaching or business enterprise, but still be far from making policy recommendations for producing these particular competencies. Thus the attempt to define teacher effectiveness or entrepreneurship has produced enormous quantities of research looking at the wider economic and social environment as well as analysing the attitudes and actions of people or firms that seem clearly successful. Yet the good teacher and the successful entrepreneur still appear to remain well outside the realm of policy despite all the training colleges and small business development programmes. Similarly with ITC. A firm or agency that has ITC is able to carry out preinvestment work, make technology choices, negotiate, purchase, install, maintain, modify, and even diffuse the technology acquired. To carry out these activities, the particular individuals in the enterprise will need to have gained certain levels of expertise, through education, training and experience. But clearly neither the economic activities associated with successful ITC nor the prior mix of education and experience are equivalent to ITC. More broadly, the particular manpower policy of the state and its industrial and agricultural policy are bound to have a direct effect on the condition of ITC, as, in turn, will aspects of the international economy and the pattern of relations between North and South.

The temptation to discover a formula (for example, so much protection, so much technological education, so much attitudinal orientation) remains strong, but the more ITC is itself unpackaged, the more necessary it seems to sort out at this stage more accurately what some of the accompaniments of ITC are. There is such an array of potentially powerful factors operating differently in different countries that it is exceedingly unlikely that an ITC cookbook can be prepared. More valuable will be an understanding of the range of possible educational and economic interactions in particular settings.

Before turning to the disaggregation of some of the educational factors impacting on ITC, one further general point needs to be made about the focus of ITC research to date. At the moment, it is clear that much more attention is being given to the role of ITC in the formal industrial sector, and the typical location of technology studies therefore has been in steel mills or cement factories, automotive plants, or in high-technology industries. Very little attention, however, has been given to the smaller local firms in the urban sector or to aspects of the informal urban economy. Nor has there been much interest in issues of technological capacity either in the small or the large farm sector. There are obviously good reasons for looking at the urban industrial situation of ITC, especially in the relatively urbanised countries of Latin America, and even more obviously in Hong Kong, Singapore, etc.; but in countries where the formal industrial sector touches a fraction of the productive population, and where it is perched somewhat precariously on a large base of urban petty production and smallholder agriculture, the concern with ITC needs to be widened. Of critical importance to ITC must be a consideration of the linkages among the technologies of these somewhat artificially distinct sectors. It is presumably highly unlikely that ITC will be flourishing here and there in, say, some of Africa's modern industrial estates without that having some implication for many other parts of the country. Putting it another way, can we describe a technology as having been indigenised if the capacity and confidence to modify and adapt it is restricted to a handful of people in an industrial estate? Successful indigenisation of a technology must imply something about the *diffused* ability to cope with it, even though there may not be more than a small number of firms making a particular product. The indigenisation of sugar or paper processing must mean more than the capacity embodied in a handful of resident engineers. Is there, in addition, in the smaller provincial towns a series of general engineering workshops which can troubleshoot on the sugar factories as well as on the maintenance and modification of agricultural machinery?

Indigenisation therefore has a quantitative dimension to it, which becomes peculiarly complicated in many parts of Africa, where there are significant groups of non-African indigenes who have traditionally dominated the more advanced technologies of both industry and agriculture. For indigenisation to be effective it has to go beyond the white or Asian communities, as was shown very forcefully in the example of Uganda. Consideration of this angle on indigenisation, of course, implies rather different approaches to the training of high-level local manpower than has been traditional. Firm-specific inquiries about manpower requirements in particular categories will differ dramatically from calculations of manpower derived from a broader definition of ITC. These broader and narrower interpretations of ITC, based separately on industry and on the nation, are what confirm the importance of looking across industry and agriculture at the diffusion of technological capacity.

They also suggest a dynamic historical approach in assessing the indigenisation of technologies. There is presumably a series of interacting technology frontiers in many Third World countries, cutting across smallholder agriculture, the petty workshop sector and the larger industrial areas. For a comprehensive picture of ITC, it will be important to have a sense of movement on the peasant technology front, as much as in the micro-industries of the informal urban economy, or in the import-substitution sphere. A nation's technology system has to take account of the processes of technological change across all these areas.

INFORMAL EDUCATION, LOCAL KNOWLEDGE SYSTEMS, AND
NON-COGNITIVE ASPECTS OF ITC

In examining the impact of many aspects of education upon the indigenisation of technological capability, it may be appropriate to start with that which has received least attention – informal learning. Yet in the reproduction of technical capacities, or, indeed, resistance to new technologies, systems of informal education are quite crucial. It is now widely accepted that there exist among many groups in any national population local agricultural, health and craft knowledge systems that need to be understood if more diversified, and more 'modern' information and technology are to be effectively disseminated to the urban and rural areas. Properly speaking, these peasant and craft technologies are a key illustration of ITC. As knowledge systems they are very widely disseminated; the knowledge and technology are almost exclusively reproduced in the household, and they are not necessarily unscientific or anti-modern. In fact, there have been notable examples of indigenous agricultural technologies being vindicated after being vilified (intercropping is a case in point). Nevertheless, there are concerns about too romantic a view of these local knowledge systems. In Ethiopia at the moment it has been thought necessary to mount a major campaign against non-scientific belief systems. Indeed the highest priority of their science popularisation programme has become the determination and eradication of non-scientific beliefs of Ethiopians.[28]

This campaign points up the conflict between different interpretations to which we alluded briefly – between completely indigenised technologies, and technologies that, having been more or less recently imported, the government is anxious to indigenise. This is not simply an academic distinction. There is plenty of evidence of 'traditional' indigenous technology incorporating dramatic technical change yet remaining in the same broad line of business (the Panchals in India making the transition from blacksmithing and metal work into the manufacture of machine tools, or the scattered examples in Kenya of a similar move from smith to machinemaking).[29] Equally, there are compelling examples in Botswana and Tanzania of the destruction of indigenous bases of technology in wood, metal and clay.[30]

Another crucial aspect of the informal development of ITC must be the technological environment in which young people are nurtured. Little is known in detail of the early formation of scientists and technologists, but the degree of technical literacy at home, in the village or streets must be critical. Just as general reading material is essential to sustain traditional literacy, so is technical literacy supported in the home by the presence of specialised tools, and secondhand machinery – even junk. But what is clear about the informal learning environment of many homes and villages in Africa is how very little there is in the way of technical clutter to stimulate children; and more important still, it has been argued that 'the cultural values of most of the African societies have rigidly conformist attitudes towards the environment; modern science, on the other hand, is usually manipulative'.[31]

Potential sources of informal technical literacy should not be analysed only for pre-school children. The relative poverty or richness of that environment remains important throughout schooling (learning the physics of electricity at school, but no batteries, wiring or electricity in the home), and into working life. For the small businessman, workshop manager or amateur enthusiast, Africa is largely isolated from the 'sci-tech' literature, the specialist journals, and the whole world of cheap do-it-yourself kits and components. In this situation, communication of new technologies informally is impeded, and networking through the media virtually non-existent. Widening the popular base for ITC is obviously a high priority, and it may well be necessary to invest in many varieties of *popular technological education* if the scientific work of the formal schools and colleges is not to be undermined by the milieu.[32]

But creating a richer technical environment is clearly not a sufficient stimulant to independent technological activity. Whatever the skills imbedded in the local knowledge systems, and whatever the environment, there is apparently another element operating on technological capacity – *entrepreneurial* activity. Like the search for 'the effective teacher', the analysis of successful entrepreneuriship has proved immensely problematic, and yet it looks as if family and community cohesion is a vital non-cognitive aspect of ITC. Certainly in case studies of the transition of Asian *fundis* (skilled men) into owners of large engineering workshops, construction companies, and modern factories, it is commonplace to acknowledge the importance of family ownership, small beginnings, original use of appropriate secondhand machinery, and many other aspects of successful ITC firms.[33] What is tantalising, however, in these case studies of appropriate technological mastery is isolating the family, cultural or community aspect of this enterprise. It is relatively straightforward to analyse their technical skills and formal technical knowledge, also their machinery and products at different stages of their development. It is also possible to sort out the wider political economy of colonial East Africa, in which these imported and immigrant communities were afforded an informal monopoly of petty trade and industry. And yet all this leaves unexplained the contribution of the family or community's commercial 'culture' and attitudes towards productive work. These latter are obviously more resistant to quantification than the investment in the firm's human and physical capital, but they appear none the less important to analyse, particularly if ITC is to become an objective of government policy and planning. For example, East and West African economies at the moment have very large numbers of small operators working with secondhand machinery or handtools like yesterday's East African Asians. What is going to determine their movement beyond these present levels of indigenous skill and technology? Apart from training programmes and economic measures, what might be the role of cultural factors in this process? Kenya offers a fascinating case study for any such analysis of the differential response of various communities to new technology, for as waves of Asian skill penetrated into all the smaller towns in the colonial period, some African communities adopted and reproduced these skills rather rapidly and others hardly at all. The result in the 1980s is that there has been a highly uneven indigenisation of these originally Asian technologies. It would seem, therefore, that some research on culture and entrepreneurship is unavoidable in any complete analysis of ITC.[34]

A last point to note about informal education in relation to ITC is that it is peculiarly evident in the expanding activities of the informal sector of the economy. There, where the boundaries between the household and the workplace are often non-existent, a rather rapid assimilation of values and technical skills can be observed. It is clear that the technology is part and parcel of a wider pattern of social relations, which is reproducing very rapidly large numbers of workers with rough-and-ready ITC. These first generations of workers in tin, metal, wood and steel are separated by a wide gulf from most of the remaining rural craft skills, but are equally far from the competencies needed to service the most sophisticated products of the region's modern sectors. Several new initiatives are being attempted to develop this level of technological capability, and gradually expose it to a more knowledge-based technology. But this kind of ITC development strategy needs to be based on a much more thoroughgoing analysis of the changes in the technology of these petty producers. It is easy to talk of the dynamism (or the sweated work conditions) of the informal sector, but it is vital for policy formulation to know what have been the cycles of product change, technical change and skill change.

In summary, informal technological education is an area of study that has been much neglected in the search for the essence of ITC. Perhaps several of the most crucial unexplored spaces of ITC lie in this sphere, and their unravelling could be of critical importance for governments involved in the planning of micro-industrial projects. But the quality of the informal technological environment is not only a vital element in understanding technical change in peasant production and the informal industrial sector; it has been suggested that the early technical environment of many working in scientific occupations needs very careful attention. If this environment is deficient, the formal school and the university may have to compensate for many late-starters in scientific literacy.

FORMAL EDUCATION, SCIENCE AND ITC

The formal school and college system is one of the main objects of recommendation about an improved base for science and technology, whether for rural development or for ITC in the formal agricultural and industrial sectors. Attention is focused on agricultural science, engineering science as well as physics, chemistry, maths and the biological sciences. In many African countries there is now the reappearance of an 'investment' approach to these subjects. They offer the hope of compensating in school for the deficiencies of the technological environment, and are seen to be neglected with peril in the fight against technological dependence. The recent declarations at Harare of the Ministers of Education catches this investment and compensatory rhetoric exactly:

> Science and technology form the basis of industrialisation; the fact that they can be used as such effective instruments and vehicles of development means that the entire population must be associated with scientific and technological advance, that they must be given pride of place in education . . . There was unanimous agreement that it was high time action was taken on all matters concerning the extension and improvement of science and technology teaching at all levels, with a view to mastering and modifying imported technology, putting an end to scientific and technological dependence, and finding solutions to the most pressing problems of development.[35]

In India, by contrast, investment in 'elite' scientific technological education has been much more widespread and sustained over three decades; this has been and still is a vital adjunct to state policy on indigenous technological development in the modern agricultural and industrial sector. Formal science is now held, however, to have done very little for Indian rural areas outside the sphere of the green revolution, nor to have benefited the large number of backward communities. Consequently in many of the more innovative rural development projects of recent years there has been a quite explicit faith in the transforming potential of 'discovery' science through schools and nonformal education. Science is conceived as a weapon in the armoury of conscientisation for the poor and backward.[36]

The situation is different again in Southern Africa with the conspicuous domination of science and technology by the whites, and where, in the view of some, the 'cardinal task of scientific research [for Africans] is to help build a scientific technological base for the socioeconomic development of the liberated zone of Southern Africa'.[37] And it is different again in Latin America, where there are interesting parallels to the Indian attempts to develop a popular science for the transformation of marginal communities.[38]

In many of these areas the formal education system is expected to become involved in what may sound contradictory. Lacking funds, equipment and sufficient talented teachers, it is challenged, nevertheless, to compensate for the technological backwardness of society or groups in society. This is evident in the special treatment of African engineers-in-the-making, who in many engineering colleges get exposure to basic materials-handling and manipulative skills which have not been part of their earlier informal education. Similarly, in schools, there are constant proposals for the introduction of productive work, appropriate technologies, and education for production, to translate the academic subjects into areas of application and transformation.

In many of these ways, the school or college can be seen as tackling some of the observable problems in African economies. But what is much less known and little researched is the capacity of schools to act as carriers of these large aspirations. ITC has been characterised as being partly to do with the confidence to analyse, unpackage, modify and adapt imported technologies. But to what extent can the formal school and college offer the kinds of skills and attitudes to take these initiatives? The science subjects are meant ideally to furnish the experience of reasoning, deduction, trouble-shooting, testing and experimenting, all of which seem akin to ITC activity. But in resource-poor environments does science fulfil these minimum conditions? Equipmentless, and increasingly without any practical component, can it really anticipate the science lab in agriculture or industry? Shorn of all extras, can 'blackboard science' in an examination culture prepare students for confidence and creativity?

It is important in seeking to isolate the particular contribution of science education not to overemphasise the role of practicals, or to place too much reliance on discovery methods, for it is clearly possible to spend hours in the laboratory 'discovering' principles that could be presented by the teacher or read in a book in a matter of minutes.[39] In this connection there is some evidence that Hong Kong and South Korea, for example, have taught their school and university sciences in a highly theoretical manner. Perhaps less crucial than the practical side has been the focus in these countries on high-quality science and maths achievement in an atmosphere of very intense competition. But for countries considering a new 'investment' approach to science it will be very important to sort out what it is that can be expected from science teaching, and what are the minimum essential accompaniments of those outcomes. Science kits, for instance, have been an unquestioned part of the recipe for improving science, especially for external donors, but almost nothing is known about their utilisation.[40] Equally it may be possible to teach science highly theoretically if elsewhere in the economy industrial skills have been acquired by large numbers of the workforce.[41]

By way of contrast, in Africa the problem may be less one of practicals versus blackboards than the quality of science and maths teaching generally. In harsh contradiction to the rhetoric of Harare with its doctrine of liberation through science must be the current status of science and maths in African schools. The failure rates in these subjects at the end of basic secondary school are likely to become a matter of critical national concern, as 75 per cent of the cohort, and above in some countries, are dramatically underperforming. The plans for the schools to compensate for meagre *informal* technology education become quite hollow, if the schools' own business cannot be successfully completed.

In this situation it is tempting for ministries and national examination councils to begin to gear much of science, maths and technology away from the tiny spectrum of formal sector employment and towards what might be termed 'science for self-employment'. But here too very little is known about the potential of such an approach. Can there really be a significant relationship between the very ordinary teaching of science in the many government and self-help secondary schools, on the one hand, and some observable impact through school-leavers, on family life, the farm and workshop? Is there any evidence that science (unless creatively taught, as in some of the Indian urban and rural experiments) can really confront, challenge or build upon the existing indigenous technologies of the farm or firm?[42] If it can, is it simply the scientific processes that are responsible, or are they part of some wider and more amorphous set of 'modern' attitudes and values?

These questions need to be posed and researched in ways that are relevant to the supply side of a nation's ITC. But very different research will have to be undertaken from that which has so far narrowly concerned itself with improving science curricula or that which has tried to isolate what level of education is likely to give the best 'return'. Qualitative analysis of science achievement and its utilisation in different technological settings (including that of women working in the farm and home) will be useful to begin to sort out what can and cannot be expected of science, and in what technological environments. But it will not be easy, and results will not be readily transferable to other national settings.

Research should not, however, be restricted to the sphere of science for rural development. There are highly significant developments going on at the university and college level in the teaching of science, agriculture and engineering, in Africa and elsewhere, that merit the closest attention for their impact on ITC. The trend towards a 'depracticalised' science and technology certainly has its counterpart at university, and it is not uncommon now for students in some countries to be taught engineering by teachers with little or no hands-on industrial experience. From graduation to a research degree and back again to teaching is not an uncommon pattern, but it is one that places a premium on theory; as does the dwindling finance for replacing equipment and ordering materials in many universities, including those in Zaire, Ghana and Uganda.

But the wider political economy of the country has a powerful impact on the university role in the formation of capacities for indigenous technology. The option of orienting university science and engineering to rurally appropriate technologies or to the improvement of indigenous technology is evident here and there, though very seldom stronger than the student and staff interest in the technologies of modern industry, the governments' technical ministries, and the parastatals. Obviously the financial rewards to these two different orientations will continue to affect student and staff preferences, but another factor is critically important to ITC, and that is the differential scope for design and development work in the various industrial and agricultural occupations. If, as has been mentioned above, the confidence to design, develop, modify and adapt are inseparable from ITC, what is the milieu that will facilitate these? If university science and engineering are presented as primarily the verification of the experiments and theories of North America and Europe, it will perhaps not be surprising that design, and project work are not at a premium, nor that engineering graduates gravitate to the quiet waters of the public sector.[43] And yet if modern industry and agriculture afford little scope for LDC scientists and engineers beyond overseeing the purchase, installation, maintenance, and replacement of the products of the North, then is there much point in a design-based syllabus in engineering, for example? It could, by contrast, be argued that a concentration on the mass urban and rural problems of renewable energies, and their exploitation, or on building-materials development, would be more likely to afford a comparative advantage to local scientists in design and development work. Here too, however, it is soon obvious that even research in wind, sun, waves, and biomass is likely to have gone much faster and further in the industrialised countries. The justification, then, for the renewable energy research projects in the Third World must sometimes be that the wheel (or windmill) needs to be reinvented, so that in the poorer parts of the world the experience of discovery and its application can be offered at relatively low cost. In this connection it is interesting to note the number of engineers engaged in the development of energy-efficient cookstoves in East Africa. Here is a niche protected from international competition, offering an opportunity for very-low-cost research and development expenditures. But to many others, these appropriate technologies, though offering some design scope, seem to beckon poor countries towards a different future from the North. The idea that engineers in the 1980s should propagate the pre-industrial revolution technologies, of water, wind, and ox-power, to replace human labour naturally encounters major attitudinal barriers, regardless of the needs in the rural areas.

The engineering college or science faculty in the poorer developing countries has therefore almost to look three ways in producing levels of ITC: backwards to basic technologies that need to be experienced anew in the rural areas, and require massive low-cost dissemination; to the present technologies in the import substitution sector which need to be maintained, as well as modified; and forwards to the many applications of computer technologies. The scope for local modification and adaptation will differ dramatically from the first to the third of these, and yet none can be disregarded with impunity, so great is the range of technological literacy from the subsistence peasant to the urban operators of computer-controlled process industries.

The very range of technologies presents something of a dilemma for the educational planning of indigenous technological capability. What should determine the size of the science and engineering faculties?: the present modern sector technology market with its very small manpower requirements?; the largely unserviced technology requirements of the rural and marginal urban areas? Are there advantages in deliberately overproducing graduates from universities and intermediate technical institutions in the expectation that such people can create their own opportunities? Many of these questions underline the extraordinary discontinuities between education planning and technology planning. Even with the demise of manpower planning, the size of the science, agriculture and engineering faculties may still be more 'planned' than arts or social sciences, but this may often be more a result of the high cost of provision than of any assumptions about national needs.[44] There is a similar lack of research behind the figures in national studies of scientific and technological potential. Numbers are aggregated of different types of science manpower, but almost no attention is given to the patterns of utilisation of these personnel. What does it mean to say that the nation has 5,000 scientists, or 100,000? Such figures frequently appear in statements about a nation's science potential, but they tell virtually nothing about the deployment and capability of these numerical resources.

Just as in the formal school system there is a need to get behind the numbers of people doing science, and ask questions about quality and post-school utilisation, so in industry and agriculture an ITC perspective would lead to questions about the nature of scientific careers, the professional journals and associations that support these careers, and the use of time in different activities. How great a correspondence is there between the formal education of scientists and the later environment and tasks with which they work? Increasingly, an ITC perspective will lead researchers to examine the quality of scientific life in underdeveloped economies, both in education and at work. Such studies should offer very valuable qualitative data to planners concerned with investment in science and technology. Behind the rhetoric of numbers of scientists and scientific potential, it would then begin to be possible to ask about the intellectual consequences of studying, say, chemistry or veterinary science for those ultimately following scientific *and* non-scientific careers. Similarly, case study work on the differing quality of formal science education and of science-based careers in both the informal sector and the formal labour market could begin to elucidate some of the most longstanding questions about the limits of educational reform on the one hand, and the domination of science training by the underdeveloped state of the economy on the other.

There are a few indications that work is just beginning in some of the new directions. For example, research has been asking what lies behind the mere figures of national applications for patents, what can be deduced from this about the creativity of scientific manpower.[45] Work has also been initiated on particular professional groups, in ways that examine the interaction between the ideology of formal training and the nature of the particular job, for example engineering, in an underdeveloped country.[46] But a great deal more will need to be done if the 1980s' concern with investment in science and technology is to be more productive than the investment rhetoric of two decades earlier.

LEARNING ON AND OFF THE JOB IN RELATION TO ITC

It has been suggested earlier that in many countries the major preoccupations of those concerned with training have been with the attitudes of the trainees towards work, rather than with that cluster of characteristics associated with technological capability. Thus, for several decades, the debates on technical and vocational education have circled around the success or failure of different forms of training in aligning young people to agricultural and industrial work. The interest has been predominantly in whether the orientation worked. Did the graduates of vocational schools, or diversified schools, go into jobs that used those skills, or was the investment wasted? A subsidiary concern was with finance. Given that technical and vocational provision is more costly, was it sensible to offer such training during formal education immediately prior to employment, or once employment had been secured? There is accordingly a rather large literature on such matters as 'the vocational schooling fallacy', the use of vocational and technical schools as inferior alternatives to academic schooling, and of polytechnics as backdoor routes to the university.[47] The nearest the available literature comes to the variables connected to ITC is in the contrast between the alleged dynamism of the informal sector of the economy and its training system, on the one hand, and the rigidities and certificate-orientation of the state's formal training apparatus on the other. The informal sector is applauded for its ingenuity, improvisation, adaptability, readiness to make locally what cannot be obtained in the regular dealers.[48] By contrast, the national vocational training system is criticised for its tendency to be used only by the larger firms and government departments, and to be locked in through a series of trade tests and qualifications to the salary structures of government and the multinational firms.

Like other parts of the education system both formal and informal, the vocational training apparatus has been affected and conditioned by the nature of industry and agriculture in the country. In many situations, the very restricted size of modern industry and agriculture has meant that there was little expectation that sufficient training would get done on the job. Consequently the vocational training system is frequently intended to compensate for the lack of apprenticeships and training places in industry, or agriculture. These high expectations for off-the-job learning and pre-vocational training have often not been fulfilled, for reasons similar to the other over-expectations of science in school: a relatively weak institution in terms of staff, equipment, and status has not been able to offer an enriched environment for skill development, in conditions parallel to the best industrial or agricultural practice. Hence there has been a tendency to emphasise theory at the expense of hands-on practical training.

It is difficult to generalise across so many developing countries at different stages of development, but it is clear that the application of an ITC perspective to the analysis of formal technical and vocational education would be valuable. Instead of the concern with attitude and placement, it will become important to sort out the significance of the 'know-why' knowledge picked up in off-the-job training as compared with the 'know-how' knowledge in the firm itself. The former, more science-based knowledge is intended to raise the worker's potential, allowing him to work more intelligently and independently, and to counter in a small way the employer's preference for firm-specific skills. But before recommending this science-based training off the job as having ITC potential, many key issues require close research attention. In several countries in Africa, the firms with a very high ITC record (for example Asian companies in East Africa) have a very poor record in off-the-job training, while the government, parastatal and multinational sectors which patronise the state training system are not considered particularly innovative. In other areas, for example South Korea and Singapore, formal off-the-job vocational training is very widespread, and is considered to have played an important role in the development of technological capacity.

What these few examples suggest (and many more could be adduced) is the need for an approach that involves a more comprehensive account of the relation between training, industry and agriculture in particular countries and regions. The role of Asians in East Africa, or Japanese in relation to South Korea, is so significant in the process of skill formation that generalisations about formal training and ITC derived from these settings could be misleading. But what can be said with some certainty is that the vocational training of skilled workers has very frequently been discussed in isolation. It has frequently neglected the upgrading of the informal economy, and has been little integrated into the planning of technician and management training. As a result a great deal more appears to be known about the training of workers than about the role of the technologists and managers. An ITC perspective on firms, or on farms, however, will have to pay much more attention to the many interrelations of production. In the modern sector, for instance, the attainment of ITC would seem to depend just as crucially upon the technological literacy of the management and higher technical cadres as upon the particular skill mix of the workers. By contrast, in the micro-enterprises of the informal sector where the management may also be the skilled workers, upgrading should perhaps be less concerned with skill development than with production innovations.

The range of research required on formal training off the job may thus be very wide indeed, but a useful start would be case studies of firms or enterprises that appear to be good examples of ITC in action. How have such ITC firms acquired their know-how? From what mix of informal education, and formal education and training has their expertise been gathered? There are equally complex research questions on the institutional side of formal training. Because of the high costs involved there has been a tendency for polytechnic and technological training to be undertaken at the employers' request; thus in many countries students at such institutions are sponsored and already have a job. However, given the small number of available jobs, increasingly students and parents want access to higher technological training without being seconded from employment, but as a way of creating a job opportunity. Indeed, in some cases, institutions are created on the assumption that technological capability can be produced in an institutional setting and find itself work. Here again, therefore, we see the conjunction of ITC with ideas of entrepreneurship development and self-employment coming into play in economies where the formal labour market is small.[49] We have, however, very little information about the consequences of policies that deliberately seek to overproduce middle-level manpower. But it is noticeable both in the South and even in the industrialised countries that deepening unemployment crises produce an interest in further technological capability.

We have noted that learning off the job has become more prevalent as opportunities to learn on the job have shrunk in proportion to the numbers now seeking work in the modern sector. Learning on the job has itself however begun to be examined as an instrument for developing ITC. Attention has focused both on the smaller range of on-the-job learning in the modern sector of industry and agriculture, as well as on the very large number of jobtrained workers in the rural and urban informal sectors. In any discussion of ITC it is crucial to recognise that in most developing countries the majority of skilled labour is reproduced on the job, whether in the household economy, the small farm or the workshop. Even in the modern sector, it is probably true that learning at the enterprise level constitutes a very large proportion of the total skills and competences acquired by workers. What is then perhaps surprising is how relatively little attention these in-firm learning processes have had.

As with every other sector of learning, it is plain that the quality of the educational experience depends a great deal on the wider state of the economy as well as on the range of activity within the firm itself.

Thus, in an underdeveloped economy, we have seen expectations that each sector would compensate for the previous one – the school for the weaknesses in the technological environment, formal training for the weaknesses of the school, and, finally, learning on the job for gaps in previous education and training. But, of course, learning on the job in turn reflects many of the same weaknesses noticed in informal education. Thus, in the case of engineers, their formal university training requires an 'apprenticeship' of several years' exposure to a wide spread of engineering practice before they can be considered qualified. But the problem in many small countries is that the range of engineering practice is so restricted by the nature of existing industry that a thoroughly diversified apprenticeship cannot always be satisfactorily arranged. Hence, paradoxically, the university has sometimes been called upon to offer a master's course to help compensate institutionally for the meagreness of on-the-job training opportunities in engineering.

This example from engineering highlights a very basic problem affecting science and agriculture graduates, as well as technicians, and many tens of thousands of ordinary school-leavers, in countries with a small industrial base. The demands of the work-place are constrained and limited by capital, markets, level of technology, etc., all of which will make it likely that the rewards to science and technology careers will be secured less in research and application of new technologies than in administration. This bureaucratisation of science manpower is a direct counterpart of the theoretisation of science and technology in schools and colleges, and of course reinforces this trend in education.[50] Clearly this situation raises very major questions about the actual utilisation of indigenous technological capability which has been produced at very great cost to the state. Such problems may well appear particularly starkly in countries like Zimbabwe, Kenya or Tanzania where historically 'indigenous' technological capacity has been white or Asian. Despite the higher salaries in the private sector, the local engineering and science manpower will often be drawn into the public sector where the training opportunities and career tracks are more certain than the task of Africanising expatriate ITC in industry and agriculture.

One reason that the effective localisation of industry or large farm agriculture has proved so difficult in many countries is precisely because there are so many crucial aspects of on-the-job learning possessed by the owners, managers and expatriate technicians. Martin Bell's suggestive list of different ITC-related aspects of learning on the job mentions several of these in a general context,[51] but with very rigid distinctions between worker, technician and manager on the one hand, and with the frequency of expatriate ownership, on the other it is obvious that learning on the job will be restricted and defined by the wider social relations of production. Looked at historically, Africans now learn on the job in East and even South Africa skills that were once restricted to Asians and whites, but there are still whole reaches of informal learning at the technological and management levels that are effectively a closed book. Indeed, some of the skills and knowledge that seem to account for successful Asian ITC in East Africa should certainly be thought of as learnt on the job: widespread trade contacts in Africa, Asia and Europe; knowledge networks about new processes and developments; knowledge about the value of business travel to trade fairs, conferences; and of course the family and community support mentioned earlier. Acquiring these is a world away from the possession of a science or engineering degree, even if the latter is a precondition for exploiting this less formal learning.

There are therefore two aspects of on-the-job learning that need to be distinguished for their relation to technological capability; first, the exercise in regular employment of the skills and knowledge partly acquired in formal education, and, second, the acquisition of a mass of corporate knowledge, not necessarily technical, without which the more technical knowledge cannot be grounded satisfactorily. The distinction between types of on-the-job learning in different kinds of firm will be very important. Thus, for instance, new industrial estates intended to develop local entrepreneurs will need to pay as much attention to the non-technological learning needs if the enterprises are to grow beyond their first set of machinery imports. In the less-developed countries, and in the remoter regions of the more industrialised, small industry development corporations have to pay attention to providing some of this more diffuse on-the-job learning, since paradoxically it cannot always be picked up on the job.

Research tasks in the area of learning on-the-job are many, but from an ITC perspective, much more work needs to be done in the many countries that do not have a large industrial sector like India or Brazil, and perhaps particularly in countries where the indigenisation of innovative agricultural capacity is as urgent a task as the localisation of expatriate industrial skills.

CONCLUSIONS ON EDUCATION AND TECHNOLOGY IN RELATION TO ITC

The bulk of this discussion has been involved with teasing out the inter-relations of different parts of the education system as they connect with the technology system. With all the four major modes that have been mentioned (informal knowledge systems and informal education; formal primary, secondary and tertiary education; formal off-the-job training; and learning on-the-job), a main emphasis has been on analysing the range of factors influencing the acquisition of capacity. We have noted a tendency in the planning of technological capacity to put great faith in the formal school and university system, and to emphasise cognitive achievement. Our examination would suggest, however, that in less-developed economies formal education has often inherited obligations to compensate for major gaps and weaknesses in informal technological education as well as to anticipate deficiencies in formal training and on-the-job learning in the work-place. The school or college, however, is not particularly well suited to compensating for lack of exposure to an industrial culture, or to offering a richer experience of, say, engineering tasks than local industry affords. Indeed, under the pressure of expansion of student numbers, and dwindling education budgets, there are clearly major questions to be asked about the quality of basic scientific achievement itself in school and university, apart from any additional tasks attributed to them.

Running through this account also, however, has been the sense that successful technological capability is not solely a question of formal technological skills and scientific knowledge, but of attitudes and values, including some most complex to reproduce in an institutional setting. Curiosity, creativity and self-confidence are not easily provided in formal education, but it is noteworthy that in several countries science teaching is being regarded as a vehicle for producing these and other positive attitudes. Again it is easy to be sceptical about developing a scientific temper in schools that are reduced virtually to no scientific apparatus. But in reality very little has been done at all in developing countries on the sources of intellectual curiosity and work attitudes, whether in school or without.

The third thread running through this account is the assumption that if ITC is a vital policy objective, it cannot be something that happens only in the handful of industrialising countries of the Third World, and only in the large process and manufacturing industries of these countries. If ITC is about capacities to adopt, adapt and modify existing or imported technologies, then it can probably be identified not just in countries that have a toehold on some of the world technology frontiers, but in the many others that are looking at how to organise on a massive scale very minor technological changes in agriculture and in their small-scale industry. It seems conceivable that technological innovation in smallholder agriculture, cottage industry or in the micro-industries of the informal sector is not a totally different phenomenon from the process of technical change in a cement plant or steel mill, even though the scale is dramatically different.

A last element that has been implied here all along has been the need to look at the education side of ITC as constantly affected by the larger economic and political context, of the country and region, its industrial and trade policy, and by the world economy. Changes in, say, the chemistry syllabus may seem rather remote from the larger industrial and political decisions affecting the state. Does it really matter what exposure to innovative industrial self-help students receive in Botswana, if their country's larger political economy is subordinate to the economy of the Republic of South Africa? Is it important to study the dynamism of on-the-job learning in the informal sector if its work and prospects are also subordinated to the priority and protection of the large-scale sector? In reaction to these kinds of worries about the relevance and scope of educational reform in relation to ITC, it could be argued that there is a complex and little-understood set of inter-relations between the economic and political forces operating upon technological capacity, and the social and economic pressures producing educational capacity. But there is certainly a measure of autonomy in the way the education and training system responds to popular and official pressure, as well as to influences from external aid. The history of unsuccessful attempts by colonial and independent states to make education serve certain economic purposes is testimony to this autonomy; it might equally caution planners about the problems of insuring that the education system produced characteristics favouring ITC. But what is clear in this review is that educationists (and economists) are very uncertain about the longer-term consequences of what is taught in school and college, just as they are uncertain about the technological stock on to which development-science or technician skills are being grafted.

Finally, the scope and complexity of relations between education and technology in respect of ITC may perhaps be better appreciated by way of a diagram (see Figure 1). This illustrates international influences impinging on the national educational apparatus as well as on

FIGURE 1 *Interactive model of education and technology*
in relation to ITC

International Education Influences
↕
National Education and Training Apparatus

Informal Learning   ↔ *Formal School*   ↔ *Formal Training*   ↔ *Learning on Job*
in family, group,   *College* and   *learning by doing*
trade association   *University*
                         learning

↕
Possible Science and Technology-related Outcomes of Learning
↕

1. creativity
2. reasoning
3. confidence
4. experimentation   *through LEARNING*
5. modification
6. project design
7. dissemination

↕
ITC
↕

1. Preinvestment decisions
2. Search for and selection
3. Negotiation and purchase
4. Maintenance or repair   *of TECHNOLOGIES*
5. Modification
6. Design
7. Dissemination

↕
Possible Science and Technology Capabilities emerging from work-place
Rural   *Urban*

Peasant	Small, cash	Large-scale	Urban	Modern	Large-scale
subsistence↔crop farm	↔farm, ranch↔informal	workshop,	MNC or
	sector		sector	↔govt.	↔local industry
				small	or govt. sector
				industries	

↕
National Industrial and Agricultural Policy
↕
International Influences on Trade and Technology

national trade and economic policies. In turn there are a series of education and training sectors influencing each other in different ways, just as there are powerful interactions among the technologies of the various employment sectors. There is, for example, no such thing as an urban informal sector technology, separable completely from the technology of the modern workshop sector or from technologies used in the small farm sector. Similarly it is crucial to see the achievement of educational capacity not just as a school or college product, but rather as a school or college product affected by informal learning in family and group, altered by post-school training, and altered again by learning on-the-job. Thus the direction of the technology of Tanzania's rural blacksmiths, for instance, needs also to be understood in terms of technological decision-making at the large-scale urban level,[52] and, in education, university science is influenced by a set of international factors as well as by the local knowledge systems, and the local technological environment.

ITC, however, is not something that is increased automatically by a particular mixture of educational influences, local, national or international, nor is it adequately described as being augmented by a particular trade policy regime – whether free trade or protectionist. Of course, in most cases, comprehensive, cross-sectoral, interdisciplinary work waits to be done; but perhaps enough has been said already to suggest that in Africa, at any rate, understanding and then building on existing sources of ITC is vitally important. Strengthening ITC, however, will require a great deal more than isolated changes in science curricula, the creation of technological universities, or greater international competition. The technological environment as a whole will need to be affected. Hence the battery of recommendations for action in the Lagos Plan, 1980–2000. But even if all that is put into place in the right sequence and with adequate funding, we need to remember that at its most basic ITC is both a simpler and a more complex thing than all the variables we have adduced in this and other papers to facilitate it. Edward Shils, though writing in the very age of quantitative investment in science and technology twenty years ago, underlined the one factor it is vital to secure even for the most humdrum technological modification of imported technology:

Even if there were a judicious choice of those problems which are most important for economic progress and most amenable to economic solution; even if the right numbers of qualified scientists were produced by the most economical methods; and even if the right amounts of money were spent on buildings, equipment, the right selection of problems, and the right training. It is also a matter of activation, of tradition, and of a propitious atmosphere within the research establishment.

The extension and elaboration of this scientific tradition, of the body of inherited scientific knowledge, are, in the last analysis, a product of the scientific disposition of disciplined curiosity and sensitivity. Organization, equipment, financial support, and large numbers of persons are only instruments for the operations of this scientific disposition. It really does not make any difference whether the new states eschew pure research for the time being and concentrate their efforts on applied research. The successful prosecution of applied research is almost as dependent on the scientific disposition as is pure research. It is, therefore, essential for those who administer and promote scientific research for economic development, for the improvement of human welfare, to remember that the vital center of the disposition is formed by immersion into the tradition of creative scientific work.[53]

NOTES

1. For overviews of the changing themes, see A. R. Thompson, *Education and Development in Africa* (London:1981) ch. 4; K. Blakemore and B. Cooksey, *A Sociology of Education for Africa* (London: 1980) ch. 8.
2. Particularly useful in presenting the dependency implications for education is the chapter 'Education for Development or Domination', in M. Carnoy's *Education as Cultural Imperialism* (New York: 1974). For a comment on dependency in education, see, among other papers, M. McLean, 'Dependency Theories and the Urge to Decentralise', workshop on 'Centralised versus Decentralised Control in Education', London Institute of Education, Feb. 1983. Also, Carnoy, 'Education for alternative development', *Comparative Education Review,* vol. 26, 2 June 1982, pp. 170, 174.
3. The ILO Employment Missions to Colombia, Sri Lanka and Kenya are a useful illustration of change in development theory. For some of their educational implications, see Richard Jolly, 'The Judo Trick', in C. Ward, *Education and Development Reconsidered* (New York: 1974) pp. 58–72.
4. D. Brokensha *et al., Indigenous Knowledge Systems* (Washington, 1980). See also issues of *Development Dialogue,* from the mid-1970s.
5. A valuable trio of volumes separated by a decade and illustrating shifts in western academic and donor thinking, would be C. Arnold Anderson and M. J. Bowman, *Education and Economic Development,* conference 1963, published in 1965; C. Ward, *Education and Development Reconsidered,* conferences in 1972–4; and finally, *Financing Educational Development: Proceedings of an International Seminar in Mont Sainte Marie, Canada,* 19–21 May 1982 (IDRC, Ottawa).
6. For a historical assessment of each of these major conferences and their implementation, see *International Journal of Educational Development,* vol. 1, no. 1 (1981): contributions by C. Brock, J. K. P. Watson and A. R. Thompson.
7. Anderson and Bowman, *Education and Economic Development.*
8. P. Foster, 'The Vocational School Fallacy in Development Planning', in Anderson and Bowman, ibid, p. 142 ff.

9. G. Psacharopoulos, *Returns to Education: An International Comparison* (New York, 1973). For a very early critique of this kind of calculation, see T. Balogh and P. Streeten, 'The Co-efficient of Ignorance', *Bulletin of the Oxford University Institute of Economics and Statistics,* vol. 25, no. 2 (1963) pp. 99–107.

10. C. Colclough, 'Primary Schooling and Economic Development: a review of the Evidence', World Bank Staff Working Paper, no. 399 (June 1980). S. Cochrane, 'Fertility and Education: What do we Really Know?', World Bank Staff Occasional Paper, no. 26 (Washington: 1979).

11. M. Lockheed, D. Jamison, and L. Lau, 'Farmer Education and Farmer Efficiency: a Survey', in T. King, (ed.), 'Education and Income', World Bank Staff Working Paper, no. 402 (Washington: 1980).

12. M. Carnoy, H. Levin, *et al.,* 'The Political Economy of Financing Education in Developing Countries', in *Financing Educational Development,* p. 46.

13. K. Lewin, A. Little and C. Colclough, 'Adjusting to the 1980s: Taking Stock of Educational Expenditure', in *Financing Educational Development,* pp. 30–1.

14. OAU, *Lagos Plan of Action for the Economic Development of Africa, 1980–2000* (1980) chs iv, v. See also, development of African Institute for Higher Technical Training and Research, Nairobi, and the significantly entitled paper by its director, M. O. Chijioke, 'The Higher Educational Resources for Industry' (Nairobi, 1981). Also, Lee Thanh Khoi, 'Science et technologie: les choix du developpement endogène' (UNESCO, 1982).

15. Tanzania: *Development Strategy and Technological Transformation in Tanzania: the Limits to Self-Reliance* (Aug. 1981). See also J. Müller, *Liquidation or Consolidation of Indigenous Technology* (Uppsala: 1980).

16. For work on the higher education research environment, see papers of World Bank/Research Review and Advisory Group meeting on Education Research Environments, Nov. 1981. Also Tanzania, *Development Strategy.*

17. K. N. Rao, 'LDC Institutional Infrastructure for Training and Education', paper to 1979 UNCTAD conference. Also, Rao, 'A Scale of Technological Capability', unpublished paper, MIT, Specifically on Kenya, see Rajni Patel, 'Scientific and Technological Capability in Sub-Saharan Africa', unpublished paper.

18. T. Eisemon, *Science in the Third World: Studies from India and Kenya* (New York: 1982).

19. Müller, *Liquidation or Consolidation.*

20. K. King, *The African Artisan* (London: Heinemann, 1977).

21. Britha Mikkelsen, 'Formation of an Industrial Labour Force in Kenya: Participation of State and Capital in Training Labour for Metal Manufacturing Industries', IDS working paper, no. 377, Dec. 1980, Nairobi.

22. K. King, 'Science, Technology and Education Research in Eastern Africa', unpublished paper (Oct. 1982) p. 24.

23. Bennell's work has, however, a rigorous quantitative base; see his 'A Quantitative Assessment of the Utilisation of Engineering Manpower in Kenya', IDS working paper, No. 381, Nairobi.

24. Caillods, in this volume. See also J. Hallak and F. Caillods, *Education,*

Work and Employment, vols 1 and 2 (Paris: IIEP, 1980).
25. J. Clayden, 'Indigenous Technological Capability and the Changing Pattern of Industrial Skill', paper at workshop, 'Facilitating ITC', CAS, Edinburgh University, May 1982.
26. R. M. Bell, in this volume.
27. Brokensha *et al.*, *Indigenous Knowledge Systems.* Also *IDS Bulletin*, vol. 10, no. 2. *Rural Development: Whose Knowledge Counts?*
28. Kebede Teku, 'Nonformal Dissemination of Technologies', Science, Technology and Education seminar (hereafter STE) IDRC, Nairobi, Jan. 1983. See also Brokensha *et al.*, *Indigenous Knowledge Systems.*
29. King, *The African Artisan.*
30. Patrick Van Rensburg, 'ITC in Externally Controlled Societies – Botswana' ITC seminar, CAS, Edinburgh; Müller, *Liquidation or Consolidation.*
31. C. Juma, 'Training for Technological Capacity: Research Priorities', STE seminar, Nairobi, 1983.
32. M. Opondo has argued that this informal education should consist of simplified do-it-yourself manuals on appropriate basic technologies, simplification of technical literature, production of kits of equipment for home assembly and use, exhibitions and fairs: 'Some Current Problems in Technology Education in Kenya', STE seminar. See also T. Whiston, 'Changing Global Requirements: a Continuing Dilemma', ITC Seminar, Edinburgh.
33. See papers by Langdon and Müller in this volume.
34. P. Marris and T. Somerset, 'African Businessmen: A study of Entrepreneurship and Development in Kenya (Nairobi: 1971) esp. chs 2 and 3.
35. UNESCO, preparatory meeting of experts for the conference of Ministers of Education, Harare, 21–5 June 1982, item 5.4.
36. For a discussion of this phenomenon, see K. King, 'Science, Technology and Education Research in India: a Discussion Paper', Aug. 1982.
37. M. Sefali, 'Research Priorities in Southern Africa: the Tasks of Science and Technology Development in the SADCC Region', STE seminar.
38. F. Arbab, unpublished papers on the Rural University, FUNDAEC, Cali, Colombia.
39. W. Haddad, 'Role and Educational Effects of Practical Activity in Science Education', World Bank, 1981, p. 51.
40. See King, 'Science, Technology and Education Research in India'.
41. Note the massive initiation of S. Korean workers to industrial work and organisation at the hands of the Japanese and, later, the Americans.
42. Especially Kishore Bharati in Madhya Pradesh, and the Homi Bhabha Science Education Centre, in King, 'STE research in India'.
43. Bennell, chapter in this volume for an examination of design in Kenya engineering.
44. Until recently, for example, Indian engineering college places were an apparent island of planning in a sea of social demand. Even that, however, is rapidly changing.
45. See Dinesh Mohan, 'Sea of Mediocrity', *Seminar* (New Delhi) Feb 1981; and S. Watanabe, 'Invention and the Patent System in the Third World. Some Policy Issues', WEP research working paper. ILO, 1982, Geneva.

46. Bennell, 'A Quantitative Assessment'.
47. See articles by P. J. Foster, R. Crane and M. J. Bowman, in Anderson and Bowman, *Education and Economic Development.*
48. See ILO mission to Kenya, *Employment, Incomes and Equality* (Geneva: 1971); and King, *African Artisan.*
49. Kenya's many Harambee Institutes of Technology are an interesting illustration of this.
50. Bennell, in this volume.
51. M. Bell, in this volume.
52. Müller, in this volume.
53. E. Shils, 'Towards a National Science Policy', in J. W. Hanson and C. Brembeck, *Education and the Development of Nations* (New York: 1966).

Technological Self-reliance: Sturdy Ideal or Self-serving Rhetoric

Ronald Dore

GLOSSARY

For the purposes of this paper, words are used as follows:

Transfer of technology By 'transfer of technology to developing countries' I understand 'getting knowledge that is only in some foreigners' heads into the heads of one's own nationals'. The learning process may well be largely accomplished by buying and studying some piece of imported capital equipment in which the new knowledge is embodied, as when the Japanese government bought its first Jacquard loom, and had its craftsmen dismantle and assemble it time after time until they had learned its technology and could then begin to think about devising or buying or stealing the technology of making it. And nowadays it may be a sensible shortcut to import both machine and its original devisers in some form of joint venture. But it is entirely possible for technology to be transferred as blueprints or as images in someone's head.

Buying Technology involves buying (a) the right to be taught the technology, (b) exemption from claims under patent laws, not *necessarily,* also, (c) hardware embodying the technology, although that is often the most sensible shortcut.

ITLC and ITCC are independent technology learning capacity and independent technology creating capacity. The first is what the Japanese showed they had by the time they could put their Jacquard loom back together again blindfold; the second was what they had when they worked out which of its metal parts they could safely substitute with wood. One sometimes needs, also, the separate concept, IWTRC – independent world technology reconnaissance capacity; the information-gathering network that can survey what is available in the world, detect new developments, judge what is worthwhile buying and learning in detail. Unless otherwise specified I include IWTRC in ITLC, the other part of which is, of course, the theoretical sophistication to understand what is going on in new technology.

Nationalism A pretty horrible emotion (in all its forms throughout the declension: I am a patriot; you are a nationalist; he is a bloody chauvinist). But some people's nationalism is more forgivable than others. The asymmetry in GATT, allowing protectionism to poor countries and denying it to richer countries seems to me an 'inequity' justified by the objective of reducing international income disparities. For the same reason, the nationalism I would deplore in a rich country I find more condonable in developing countries. Along with other pretty distasteful things, like India's Madamolatry and other cults of the personality, it may provide absolutely necessary cement for growth strategies in which the state (claiming to represent the nation) has to play a central role. This not only sounds, but is, condescending, perhaps. Well, if apologising is any help, I apologise.

SRACI syndrome or self-reliance-as-categorical-imperative syndrome: a condition that requires attention when there is evidence that it inhibits healthy growth; usually the result initially of an excessively high nationalism content in the political bloodstream, but sustained by various self-equilibrating mechanisms to be discussed later. Its main symptom is excessive regard for ITCC and contempt for ITLC (reflected, perhaps, in reference to 'Assimilate, modify and adapt' – two words for ITCC and only one for ITLC – thus clothing the stark indecency of 'learn', 'copy', 'imitate' with the latinate vagueness of 'assimilate'). The expression of the SRACI syndrome in British industry is sometimes lampooned as the NIH syndrome: not invented here. At the conferences on Development Alternatives which look forward to the day when some blacksmith in Bihar will produce a genuine Third World Alternative to the bicycle, NIH can be elevated to the status of high principle. Thus the Monrovian Declaration of the OAU: 'the transfer of technology' is a term that 'should be stricken from the International vocabulary'.[1]

PROPOSITIONS

(1) ITLC needs a dash of humility; ITCC needs a dash of hubris. Still halfway-rational nationalism can promote both in the mix required

(Gershenkron and the advantages of backwardness in the right hands); emotional nationalism inhibits the first and promotes hypertrophy of the second – hence the SRACI syndrome.

(2) Most developing countries need a certain amount of ITCC from the very beginning of industrialisation. Even if, by now, transfer of technology from ITDG can take care of most of their 'appropriate to factor endowments' problems (there must by now be as little payoff in a search for a new winnowing machine as there is for a new corkscrew); 'appropriate to local environment' problems may well require some ITCC – adapting a standard blast-furnace to local lignite, a canning process to local fruits, a waterjet loom to temperatures far higher than where they have been hitherto used, etc.

(3) But, for a long, long while (a while that gets longer and longer for the later developers; it will be longer for Korea than it was for Japan, and longer for Malaysia than it will be for Korea), *ITLC is overwhelmingly more important than ITCC*. Japan, for the best part of a century, put nearly all its effort – with due teeth-gritting humility – into ITLC. They tolerated, though with much discomfort, the stereotype that resulted – 'clever imitators these Japs but nothing more'. ITCC was reserved for marginal adaptation. But now they have got to the frontiers, and ITCC has become central. In 1979, one quarter of all foreign patents registered in the US were registered by the Japanese as, during the 1970s, they climbed ahead, first of the British, then of the Germans, Swedes and Swiss.

They are still paying more for their earlier learning than they are yet earning from their newer venture into teaching, but the balance of payments on *new* technology contracts became favourable in 1973. Between 1950 and 1978, during which time the Japanese bought the bulk of the new knowledge produced in the West between 1940 and 1978 (including the big wartime production), they paid out to foreigners – in royalties, outright purchase, returns on equity participation, etc. – $9 billion. Putting that sum in constant 1978 dollars would increase it, but would not bring it near the $60 billion-odd which was spent on R&D by the US alone in the single year of 1978.

(4) Developing countries differ enormously in their present, and short-term potential, ITLC. This is partly a question of size: 0.05 per cent of Senegal's manpower compared with 0.05 per cent of India's manpower is as a platoon to a battalion. But it is also a question of:

(a) Intellectual sophistication – again technological skill levels in India are vastly superior to those in any African and most Latin American countries;

(b) International contacts to create a technology intelligence network for efficient IWTRC – again, India's brain-drained diaspora is a great potential resource, still utilised only through informal contacts;

(c) honesty – how far one can trust in the (let us call nationalism in this case 'patriotism') of one's technologists – how far, when they are supposed to be negotiating with foreign multinationals on behalf of the country or of a 'national' firm one can trust them to be honestly negotiating with them and not getting into bed with them.

Given the enormous range of difference in these dimensions, any generalised prescriptions for 'developing countries' are practically worthless.

(5) The open-economy stategy versus delinked self-reliance debate, and the technological dependency/self-reliance debates, are different debates. Delinking, minimisation of foreign trade (the minimum necessary for imports of capital goods and technology) *plus* a vigorous policy of building ITLC and using it for large-scale technology imports, is a perfectly viable development strategy if your ITLC is really good enough and your economy is big and resource-endowed enough. It has been basically the Russian strategy (the SRACI syndrome being given only retrospective expression by inventing Russians who invented the submarine, the telephone, etc.). It was, briefly, Japanese stategy until they switched to favour the expansion of foreign trade as a growth-stimulator. The questions whether or not foreign trade expansion leads to faster industrial growth, or whether the costs of taking that route are worth the advantages – the Bela Balassa etc. debate – is not the *same* as the ITLC emphasis *vs* ITCC emphasis debate, except in so far as the expansion of industrial exports does sometimes *require* world class technology for adequate export product quality. It is hard to sell shirtings and sheetings, even in Britain, if you have shuttle-looms that leave a ridge across the cloth every two or three yards. (Though if your IWTRC is good enough, your answer may not necessarily be the obvious one of importing new automatic looms, but a cheap Japanese electronic-sensor add-on device which stops the shuttle for changing before it is empty.)

But, in fact, there does seem to be a correlation between the positions countries take in the two debates. Self-sufficiency in trade and the cult of self-reliance in technology *tend* to go together. One can summarise in a two-by-two table:

Growth Strategy	Technology Strategy	
	Buy/Learn	Be Self-reliant
Expand industrial exports for growth	Viable	Non-viable
Minimise trade	Quite possible but rather rare	Where delinkers tend to gravitate

THE INDIAN CASE

India is a splendid example. India needs much more attention in the technology debate because it is the one country where self-reliance is actually being practised, where there is a well-developed industrial base, and a substantial cadre of highly trained and very bright people to form (interchangeably) her ITLC or ITCC.

What follows are a few impressions picked up in a few weeks in India while engaged on other things. If some of the emotionalism which attends many economic debates in India – and none more markedly than those concerned with matters of self-reliance – has rubbed off onto my feelings in the matter, I apologise in advance. My thesis is as follows:

(1) India has too many desperately poor people multiplying far too rapidly for Indians to be content with the sort of growth rates they are getting. They spell, in fact, mounting disaster.

(2) Faster growth could come (a) from exports of manufactures, (b) from making high-cost manufacturers (both state and private), now guaranteed all modern comforts by their monopoly positions, bestir themselves to create a bit of ITLC and so seek ways of becoming more efficient (and, if they have export potential) even world competitive.

(3) Such policies are inhibited (a) by the self-interest of the monopolists, aided and abetted by (b) the research scientists in government, and (c) the politicians and intellectuals who have the gall, from the vantage point of their homes in the more salubrious parts of Delhi and Calcutta and Bombay, to mix their fanciful rhetoric about self-reliance with the most moving expressions of their deep concern for 'the weaker sections' of society.

To begin, then, with growth. 1980–1 was a good year in India. Growth more than compensated for the bad year of declining output that preceded it. Over the two years taken together GNP rose by 2 per cent (industrial output by 4 per cent). Population, meanwhile, increased by 4 per cent.

K. N. Raj is no alarmist and no enemy of self-reliance, but he could
not find much ground for hope at the ISI anniversary celebration of the
Mahalanobis legacy.[2] The Mahalanobis scenario of self-reliance
should have had India half-industrialised by now. Instead, the same 74
per cent of the workforce is in agriculture as when he was drafting his
first plans. Landless agricultural labourers numbered 31 million in
1961, 55 million in the 1981 census. Growth has been confined to
limited areas. 'Over at least one half of the country, the rate of growth
of agricultural output has lagged significantly behind the rate of growth
of agricultural population.' Raj speaks of an actual decommercialisa-
tion of agriculture and lower living standards over large parts of the
country. There are reports from many districts of agricultural wages
remaining roughly what they were in the 1960s – while the industrial
worker consumer price index went (1960–80) from 100 to 439.

Inexorable population growth absorbing most of the increase in production has meant that 'there could not have been any significant increase in the demand for manufactured consumer goods'. The small-
domestic-demand depressant of industrial growth is, as Raj puts it, not
Keynesian, to be cured by fiscal or monetary tuning, nor curable by income redistribution. It is for real: 'of a more structural nature, connected with the rate of growth of agricultural output and of
population'.

That is the problem. No prospects of significant fertility decline. A
vast increase in the labour force over the next fifteen years already
born anyway. More potential mothers reaching the age of eighteen
than at any time in history. India just cannot *do* with economic growth
rates of 2–4 per cent. Given her endowments of resources and skill,
and the elapsed time for accumulating experience (Tata's steel mill at
Jamshedpur started in the same year as Japan's first at Yawata), there
is no reason why it should not have been India rather then Brazil and
Korea that is beginning to export cars and ships and manages growth
rates of 6–10 per cent.

So what has gone wrong? It is not only restricted domestic demand.
Raj relates how Mahalanobis expected – reasonably – that once the infrastructure of basic capital goods industries was created, industrial
growth would accelerate. In fact it has slowed – lower now than in the
1960s: the inevitable slowdown as the ISI programme of replacing imports comes to an end, not being compensated by new sources of expansion – certainly not foreign trade. India's foreign trade is about half
South Korea's, a country with 5 per cent of its population. The
change in trade structures of the two countries is striking:

Composition of Exports (%)

	Primary Products	Textiles/ Clothing	Machinery/ Transport Equipment	Other
India 1960	55	35	1	9
India 1977	44	20	6	30
Korea 1960	86	8	—	6
Korea 1977	15	32	17	36

And the slowdown has happened in *spite* of a steady increase in investment. Gross savings rose, from 9½ per cent of GDP at the beginning of the 1950s to 22 per cent in the late 1970s, and investment in industrial plant more or less proportionately – a very respectable rate indeed. *But* the industrial plant that these savings financed became steadily more costly (prices rose faster than the general price level) and less productive. Why? Raj suggests, in addition to increased energy costs, 'underutilisation of capacity, inefficient plant utilisation and poor technology built into the existing capital stock'.

All too plausible if the visitor to India only looks around him. But the 'poor technology' needs to be divided into two categories. The envelopes whose surface-coating is so poor that one's pen tears holes, the block-pad made with a perforator with so many teeth missing that every page tears like a Rorschach test, the filing-cards of such wastefully thick lamination that one wonders what rough handling library readers must mete out to their catalogues – all these things might possibly be the result of 'making do' with antiquated equipment lovingly maintained with improvised spare parts, eschewing re-equipment in the interests of saving national capital resources for more basic essentials like steel mills and atom bombs. All very laudable: hurrah for the informal sector.

But the second kind of 'poor technology' is very different. A car called the Ambassador is an early 1960s Morris Oxford: design, technology and tools imported originally for a joint venture, bequeathed subsequently to a wholly Indian firm. At some point in the 1960s India could say: 'import substitution in cars has now taken place'. Period. Have the production engineers at the Ambassador car factory been out there on the shop floor, not just keeping the plant in tiptop museum piece condition, but wondering how they can improve the manufacturing process to get costs down? Have they been staying on after 5 p.m. in the evening working on projects for a design modification? Have they been scouring the trade press, buying foreign cars for dissection,

searching avidly for cheap ways of buying or stealing other people's innovations to make the Ambassador better and cheaper? If they have, it
is strange that there should be no sign of these efforts in the product
which continues to trickle out of the factory, year after year, unchanged, I am told, in shape or performance, as gas-guzzling and
polluting as any early 1960s car ever was, the only change being the
steadily rising price.

And why should they be doing all those enthusiastic improvement
things anyway? Answer: for all the same mysterious reasons as a group
of engineers and managers in TELCO, one of the firms in the TATA
group with a very particular ethos, *have* done all those things, have
kept to world-competitive efficiency levels in trucks and buses, and
by virtue of these efforts displaced Leyland entirely in South East
Asian markets – reasons that (again I rely on hearsay) have something
to do with self-actualisation, liking efficiency for its own sake, feeling
part of a group that can be proud of itself, etc. Certainly, if those
motives are *not* present among Ambassadors engineers, it is hard to
see how they can have any other incentives: certainly not financial
ones. Complete protection against foreign competition, an X-years
waiting-list of customers, controlled cost-plus pricing allowing for
steady increases in wages in real as well as money terms. Stay on after 5
p.m. working on some improvement project? You must be joking.

To move from anecdote to scholarship, an analysis of the accounts of
Indian companies shows clearly, apparently, that the monopoly firms
have high profits and low growth, the firms in oligopoly industries have
lower profits but higher growth.[3]

If the reader senses a certain moralistic judgement here – TELCO
engineers good, Ambassador engineers bad – it is partly because I do
value productiveness and innovativeness and being keen on one's
work as intrisic values; partly also because I cannot forget that figure of
55 million village labourers with steadily diminishing work opportunities, and believe that only a generalisation of TELCO behaviour
can stave off disaster for them.

THE PRIVILEGED SELF-RELIANTS

So the first group of beneficiaries from self-reliance are the managers
and engineers of the protected industries. They can sit back and relax.
'We have *achieved* self-sufficiency in automobiles.'

The system allows them, also, to be generous to their friends. They can, though sometimes the government takes a bit of persuading, mollify the unions with wage increases. They can afford to pay high prices for their steel. So the feathers work through the bedding of the whole organized sector. With labour markets, in particular, insulated from supply/demand pressures coming from the informal and agricultural sectors, the organised sector as a whole can absorb the bulk of the income increase that the economy generates. The privileged island grows more privileged: quite apart from the flesh pots of middle-class Bombay, a recent thesis calculates the wage of the unskilled labourer in the Bhilai steel plant at 5 to 7 times the wage of agricultural labourers in the fields around the plant.[4] Smart union leaders can sell job opportunities in the organised sector for the price of several months' wages.[5]

This state of affairs persists – Ambassador manufacturers can even pose as paragons of self-reliant industrialisation – very largely because of the miasma of self-reliance rhetoric, academic and governmental, which encourages them in their complacency. The sources of this rhetoric are, I suspect, very varied. I say 'I suspect' because what follows should be read as provocative hypothesis, being based on hearsay and inference from hearsay rather than systematic enquiry. I trust that it will, however, serve to open up the issue.

One source of the rhetoric, to begin with, is doubtless all those employed in public sector R&D and government scientific laboratories – or, more exactly, the people who administer them and speechify about them, rather than those who actually do the work. Of course, creating new technology is more exciting than scouting it out, copying it, learning it from elsewhere. And even if you do not feel confident about actually being able to create it, it is much better for your prestige if people *think* that is what you are doing. So, naturally, most of the talk about independent technological capacities sounds like talk about ITCC, not about ITLC.

Moreover, ITCC involves experiments, large budgets for equipment, the building of project empires: ITLC may only involve literature searches, study tours, the chance to be involved in the design of new industrial projects.

It is small wonder that the scientific community is thoroughly in favour of building ITCC. Apparently there are some in government who wonder whether such an emphasis is necessarily in the national interest. In the science and technology chapter of the Sixth Plan, the scientists who presumably wrote it clearly felt under some pressure and wrote defensively about the current emphasis in government on cost-effectiveness, and aversion to taking big financial risks, which 'carried the danger of erosion of the spirit of self reliance and indigenous effort'.

I am sure there are some scientists and technologists to whom this means that engineers building a cement plant, say, should do everything they can to figure out for themselves the best technology to use, and rely on foreign consultants only when necessary – and not to tell them things they could find out themselves by more assiduous search. (And the government's restrictions on the use of foreign consultants, even if they do sometimes have to be circumvented in the interests of efficiency, are probably a sensible way of pushing people in this direction.) But to many others it means that Indians should use their ITCC to create what the Delhi wits would call a really Hindu cement technology.

In point of fact, to stick with cement for a moment, a good deal of imaginative work at the Cement Research Institute in Delhi is going on. A pair of researchers (one of them since brain-drained to Illinois) have published over the last year three papers in *World Cement Technology,* one reporting detailed studies of the properties of pozzolano cement using power-station waste fly-ash (capable of adding up to 20 per cent to the existing cement production capacity very cheaply), one reporting tests of locally available mineralising additives which would allow a 10 per cent reduction in kiln temperature, and another suggesting the use of lignin waste from Indian paper factories to thin the feed slurry, reduce its moisture content and save 4 kWh a ton from the drying process. There is no doubt about the quality of the ITCC displayed (even if it does seem to be all laboratory ITCC, not ITCC centred in the coal face of the production process). But, at the same time, the ITLC job of keeping up with mainstream cement plant technology – with all the energy-saving and capital cost-saving developments of the last ten years – simply has not been done. Krupp–Polysium have had to be brought in to do a turn-key job for Coromandel's new cement plant, and the Modi Group, after two years persuading the government that self-reliance was not possible, have finally negotiated permission to get Blue Circle as consultants (jointly with an Indian firm) for the construction of theirs. (It will take six years from first plans to completion.) Meanwhile it is the Korean firm, Hyundai, which is competing with Blue Circle and Krupp–Polysium for plant constuction orders and which has won the contract to build an up-to-date plant in Indonesia.

One can see pretty clearly the pattern of interests which should have prompted the government scientific establishment (which presumably wrote the science and technology chapter) to take the defensive line in the Plan quote above. But why should a leading civil servant and intellectual like Hakser quote these lines and endorse their sentiment with such warm approval: 'Self-reliance must be at the very heart of science and technology planning.'[6] The question is a little like asking why every Indian intellectual has to be in favour of socialism: it is part of the ambient intellectual climate. But it is possible, I think, to separate out several distinct discrete strands.

(1) One is a purely cognitive matter of economic conceptualisation. Economists have not all absorbed the fact that technological change is far more dynamic than it ever was, obsolescence faster (and it is *not* just a matter of micro-electronics, and that international competition over very large areas is now competition in product type and quality, not price competition for standard products. Raj quotes Mahalanobis as thinking that once India had created its basic industries, it would enjoy enormous advantages of lower costs for capital goods. But that was not to foresee, for example, the very great cost reductions that have been made in steel-making and cement-making technology in the last ten years. Cement can now be produced more cheaply from the big dry-process plants with energy-saving precalciners which make most of Japan's cement, even counting the high capital charges, that it can in most of the fully depreciated older and smaller wet-process Indian plants. The fact that so much of Japan's capacity is in newer processes is largely a function of her high levels of investment leading to a more recent average vintage of capital, and one can hardly blame India's slow rate of investment on the cement industry. But some of the developments of the last ten years do lend themselves to incorporation in retro-fitted modifications to up-grade existing plant. How far the engineers of India's cement plants have been active in learning about these techniques, and seeking ways to take advantage of them, I cannot say. All I do know is that the Indian economists who have told me of the cement industry, its supply and political corruption problems, and suggested that the *only* thing needed was simply to increase capacity, are missing an important dimension. 'We have mastered cement technology', is their assumption – the way Mahalanobis thought one did generally with capital goods.

(2) A second strain is the real difficulty of turning the situation around. Apart from the vested-interest situation, the sheer difficulty of changing the incentive pattern is admittedly considerable. A steady re-

moval of protection, and exposure to the stresses of international competition is the obvious way of making firms improve their competitiveness, but for an industry as far behind international levels as Ambassador cars, the timescale for becoming internationally competitive would have to be a long one. A schedule of decreasing tariffs with the firm promise – or, rather, threat – of zero tariffs imports in, say, ten years' time, would seem to be a possibility, but I am told by a senior bureaucrat who thinks along these lines that the Ministry of Finance sternly sets its face against such schemes. Tariffs are revenue, and it is unsound to tie up your options in revenue sources far in advance. Such is the importance attached to forcing industry into world competitiveness.

(3) There may also be in this a touch of the Brahmin economist's contempt for industry. Agricultural economics flourishes. Agricultural economists rub shoulders easily with Jat and Rajput farmers. Economic historians turn over every clod of agrarian history. But commercial history? Studying the doings of those *low caste* Bania fellows? Of Marwaris?

(4) Another element, perhaps, is a certain self-denying asceticism. Indian intellectuals really are a bit more moral than the intellectuals of most other developing countries, and many, I think, particularly those who have lived abroad, take a certain pride in the fact they do not go lusting after the latest Toyota and Mercedes, and are content to bump along in an Ambassador as the price of their country's following a decent, egalitarian and self-respecting development path. It is a (very, very modified) form of Ghandism one can sympathise with, even if it has consequences that are far from egalitarian.

(5) And, finally, nationalism, of course. It is not only that scientists want to think of themselves as part of ITCC not of an ITLC; every patriotic Indian wants to think his scientists creative. But that is a less important part of it than the xenophobic part. The brave posture of scorning any help from foreigners (from the foreign multinationals who have the property rights in a lot of the technology) is appealing. In reality it takes more patriotism *and* self-confidence to grit your teeth in all humility, negotiate with the multinationals, drive an intelligent bargain and be damned to those who impugn your integrity. But it is easier and more comfortable to be purer and to have no truck with foreign devils. The academic economist can empathise with an engineer who feels that way. The admixture of paranoia with rational argument in the Indian reaction to the recent IMF loan is a striking indication of the strength of feeling involved. (When a popular economist needs a very

difficult operation, however, all his friends momentarily forget their insistence on technologial self-reliance and club together to send him to a foreign surgeon.)

I hope I have made my case that India's situation requires more attention to ITLC and less to ITCC. I have tried to guess at the forces that sustain an ideology that overwhelmingly favours the latter over the former, which ideology both justifies and reinforces policies and practices that seem inappropriate.

AND EDUCATION

The cognitive abilities necessary for an effective ITLC vary, of course, as between fields of specialisation. In metallurgy, chemical engineering, electronics, I suspect they are much more considerable than in, say, construction technology, and the requirements both for theoretical training and for on-the-job accumulation of experience are that much more demanding. An effective ITLC in, say, steel-making technology, requires far higher levels of ability than effective ITCC for agricultural implement engineering.

But this paper has not been primarily about cognitive abilities, but about values and attitudes as they express themselves to task definitions and work performance. I come, finally, to the hobby-horse I am accustomed to riding. The difference between a developing country technologist who can grit his teeth and set out on the inglorious task of mastering somebody else's technology, and one who is preoccupied with asserting the right to be an innovator, is a difference:

(a) between concern for substance and concern for status;
(b) between someone who gets some intrinsic satisfaction out of doing an efficient job of work and someone who is more concerned with the rewards of money or prestige that what he can represent as achievement will bring him;
(c) between those who have learned at school to *enjoy* learning, to enjoy the experience of mastering some new technique or body of ideas, and those who have not;
(d) between those who have the confidence to admit their inferiority by learning from those who know more (a confidence springing from a belief in their power eventually to remove the inferiority by learning), and those who lack that confidence and seek instead

fields of 'creative' endeavour where they can avoid being placed in the humiliating (because they see it as *in*curable) situation of learning inferiority.

I do not propose, yet again, to say why I think that the examination-centred secondary and higher education which predominates in the developing world works precisely to produce people who are more concerned about getting status (initially the status of graduates) than about learning anything, people for whom 'learning' is associated with drudgery and anxiety rather than enjoyment, people whose only source of confidence in themselves is the judgement of examiners who admit them or refuse to admit them as qualified to become conforming members of the system of privilege, people who have been trained for many years to put all their efforts into self-promotion rather than into trying to 'do a good job'. I cannot prove any of this, but research we are starting in Sussex, Tokyo, Colombo, Kuala Lumpur and Madras might eventually produce some evidence.

But one final thought from India. Self-confidence is perhaps the central key: confidence in one's ability not to be cheated by foreigners, confidence in one's imperviousness to any condescension or arrogance which foreigners might take advantage to display their superior position in the teacher–learner relationship. (Or, at least, enough imperviousness to stick with the task: read some of the diaries into which nineteenth-century Japanese poured some of their suppressed resentments.) That key element of self-confidence is more likely to be bred in elite secondary schools than in the secondary schools of an aspiring lower middle class, especially in those elite schools whose student body is both an *achievement elite, the nation's top examination scorers, and also* predominantly drawn from elite families – as is the case in France, as is slowly becoming the case in Japan, as will become more and more the case in Britain as Oxbridge admissions are rationalised and made fairer without any change in the proportions coming from independent schools. And as is already the case in India. The reasons why such schools breed confidence are obvious. The assurance that they are bound for top positions in society, the fall-back position of family privilege, their long experience of being at or near the top of the class in their previous schools, all create the possibility that, in good hands, they can develop not only confidence, but also zestful curiosity and pleasure in mental activity however much the system in which they operate emphasises the mindless routines of examination preparation – mindless routines that *do* have an inhibiting effect on the zest and learning capacity of the strugglers and plodders of lesser ability. In a recent interview the deputy secretary-general of OPEC complains about 'the whole socio-economic attitude towards learning and the philosophy of learning' in Arab universities. 'I have had my children raised partly in England and the system is entirely different. You know, a schoolboy in England has a chance to think. A schoolboy in the Arab world . . . is asked to simply cram a lot of information – some of it useless – and when it is unstructured through the process of human enquiry and human curiosity which is innate in every child it becomes a burden to learn. And it becomes meaningless. They just repeat what they hear.'[7]

It is not just schools that make the difference. The 'socio-economic attitude towards learning and the philosophy of learning' which prevails in the home is also enormously important. If the pupils in elite schools come from a home environment created by parents who have had just such a privileged education themselves (and if those parents' schooling was *also* reinforced by similarly educated grandparents), there is even stronger likelihood of producing the sort of people who can create good ITLC – men and women who are not content to take their salary to operate black boxes whose inner workings do not excite their curiosity, people who have the confidence to be more concerned about matters of substance than about matters of status, and people who can deal with foreigners as equals even while accepting the learner role.

This cumulation of intellectual sophistication over the generations is an important part of the matter: there are far more people who fit the profile of a good ITLC recruit in India with its longer traditions of Western education than in Africa. Most people after a few weeks in India can distinguish those Indians who are only one generation away from the villages from those who are already at three or four generations distance.

And with that, what seems distressingly like an argument for the functionality of elitism in developing country education, I had better end my paper. If I have written a number of things that are acceptable when said over a drink, but not when written down on paper, I apologise for my gaucherie.

NOTES

1. OAU, *What Kind of Africa in the Year 2000* (1979) p. 21.
2. K. N. Raj, 'Problems of Plan Implementation: Resource Mobilisation', *Mainstream,* 26 January 1982, pp. 24–8.

3. N. S. Siddharthan, 'Industrial Stagnation: A Study', *Mainstream*, 26 December 1981.
4. A. Saha, *Cultural Influences on Industrial Productivity: India and Japan* (Karaghpur, Indian Institute of Technology).
5. U. Ramaswamy, *The Textile Workers of Coimbatore*, Delhi (Oxford University Press, forthcoming).
6. P. N. Hakser, 'Reflections on Science and Technology in the Sixth Five Year Plan', *Man and Development*, vol. iii, no. 3, September 1981.
7. *South*, February 1982, p. 101.

Facilitating Indigenous Technical Change in Third World Countries

Frances Stewart

What is *indigenous technology*? I take it to be a local capacity to create/ adapt/modify technology. In other words, as well as the creation of some completely new technology, it includes the local development of technology already known elsewhere and the local modification of imported technologies.

What are the *reasons* for LDCs trying to establish indigenous technical capacity? The nature of the justification for the creation of indigenous technical capacity is of importance, since it is relevant to the type of capacity it is desired to create and consequently to the policies/conditions conducive to its creation. It is also relevant to determining how much effort countries should devote to it. There are four distinct reasons:

(i) in order to use imported technologies efficiently – since in very many cases some adaption, or at the least trouble-shooting, is necessary. Some have argued (for example, Maxwell, 1977) that *any* efficient use of imported technology requires some local technological capacity;

(ii) in order to create technology with appropriate characteristics, in view of the inappropriate nature of much of the technology imported from developed countries;

(iii) because of the learning effects of doing it yourself, which become cumulative, eventually creating a dynamic comparative advantage in more sophisticated and often more remunerative lines of production;

(iv) in order to reduce technological dependence on advanced countries. Near-complete technological dependence tends to involve loss of local control over many aspects of production (since these form part of technology contracts), and it reduces a country's ability to bargain toughly on the terms of technology transfer, as

81

well as having adverse effects in terms of self-respect and self-reliance.

Most countries in the Third World would be concerned with these objectives. Perhaps (ii) (appropriate technology) is least widely adhered to, but the other reasons apply almost universally as a justification for creating indigenous capacity for technical change. While we can be confident that local technological capacity will contribute to these objectives, we know very little about the quantitative effects – for example, how local capacity affects the terms of the technology bargain. More careful research into these relationships would be helpful in suggesting how much effort it is worth countries putting into the development of technological capacity and the type of effort that produces most results.

POLICIES

Much of the rest of this note briefly considers some of the major policy areas relevant to the creation of indigenous technology.

TRADE POLICY

One needs to distinguish policies towards the import of goods and services, and policies towards the import of technologies.

Policies towards goods and services

There are fairly complex relationships, depending, among other things, on the stage of development, which do not make it easy to come to simple conclusions.

(1) Production of the relevant goods and services is a necessary precondition for technological activity. In the very early stages of development, protection/import substitution is a necessary condition (in most cases) of production. Hence in the early stage of development, protection is necessary for local technological activity. But while it is necessary, it is not sufficient. It is quite possible – and indeed is often observed – that production takes place behind a heavy protective barrier on the basis of imported technology with no local technological change. Bell *et al.* (1982) describe one case. See also Pearson (1977).

(2) After the initial IS stage, countries may choose between further IS or moving into export orientation (or some combination). India, broadly, provides an example of the first; Taiwan and S. Korea of the

second; while Brazil has followed combination policies. For this stage of development economists have put forward strong arguments on each side, for a relationship between the strategy chosen and technological development. On the one hand, it is argued that a capital goods sector is necessary for local technological development and that this can only be achieved behind protective barriers. In addition, the goods produced with local technology may not be internationally competitive initially and may require protection. An export orientation would put such emphasis on market success that entrepreneurs could not afford to experiment with local technology. On the other hand, it has been argued that protection permits firms to prosper without innovating or adapting to local conditions. For example, it can be argued that a higher level of X-inefficiency is associated with more protection (and/or less competition). The competitive pressure to adapt to local 'factor endowment' is, it is argued, less with a more closed economy.

The work of Katz has shown technological activity occurring behind protective barriers, as has the work of Lall on India. Fransman (1982) has suggested that protection is necessary in Hong Kong for further development of the capital goods industry, while the 'counter examples' (especially S. Korea and Japan) turn out not to be all that open as economies, after all, but to have a quite substantial element of protection. From the empirical evidence so far, it seems protection is associated with the build-up of local industry, and especially capital goods industry, necessary for local technological activity. But protection alone is not sufficient. Moreover, the more open economies have also innovated, though so far they appear to have been more successful in the international market for goods than the international market for technology (see Lall, 1981). Any successful industrial expansion is likely to be associated with some local technological activity, because adaption to local conditions is part of the process of successful industrial activity. Thus, the effectiveness of industrial strategy may be more important to (industrial) innovation, than its nature (protection or export-orientation). But it is quite likely that the trade strategy will influence the *type* of innovation that occurs. It seems plausible to hypothesise that local *product* innovation will occur more often behind protective barriers, while the export-oriented economies will tend to take product design from their main developed country markets. On the other hand, *process* innovation (reduced costs, greater labour-intensity) may be more likely under the pressure of international competition and endowment reflecting factor prices. More systematic empirical evidence is needed on this issue.

Policies towards import of technology

It seems to be established that local technological capacity is an infant industry requiring protection in the initial stages: this conclusion is independent of any reached about trade policies towards goods. This does not mean that all technology imports should be kept out. That would be an absurd conclusion, with the implication that each country needs to re-invent everything. Moreover, much local technological activity takes the form of adapting and modifying imported technology for which – by definition – technology imports are essential. It is clear then that what is needed is a *selective* policy towards the import of foreign technology. Devising and executing an appropriate selective policy is the central problem. The appropriate policy depends in part on the type of local technology it is intended to promote.

Three types may be contrasted. First, a strong 'appropriate' technology orientation may suggest exclusion of most advanced capital-intensive technology and inappropriate products. Hence the technology imported will be only that necessary to help develop local appropriate technology. Second, countries may wish to adapt foreign technology to local conditions, and to use foreign technology to learn to produce it for themselves. Historically Japan and, in the 1960s and 1970s, China followed the policy of importing the initial technology and then trying to reproduce it locally. With this policy, technology will be only imported if it cannot be produced locally, and in each case will be imported only once. Local R&D will be directed towards learning from and adapting the imported technology. S. Korea – on paper anyway – has been following this type of policy. Third, the aim may be to master the most advanced technologies. Here restrictions on technology imports may be mild and take second place to the aim of technological mastery. This appears to be the Indian policy.

As with policies towards goods, more research is needed in this area. But it does seem established that countries can learn a lot from Japan's historical experience and, in particular, from the dual policies of selective technology imports and heavy and well co-ordinated local R&D efforts.

INDUSTRIAL POLICY

There are many types of local technological activity – ranging from minor 'blue-collar' improvements to productive techniques, to design of new products and new processes. Requirements *vis-à-vis* industrial policy may vary according to the type in question. Broadly, industrial expansion of any kind, especially in a competitive environment, is likely to bring about some blue-collar innovation. The 'competitive environment' is not necessarily a matter of international competition, but may be a product of local competition. But as the dimension of innovation gets more ambitious, then industrial policy becomes significant. First, the capital goods industry, especially the machine-tool/engineering sector, is a vital element. In addition, some sectors are more dynamic, technologically, than others. In some research-intensive industries, technological change is fast and continuous. In other sectors, technology may remain unchanged for decades. The fast-changing sectors obviously are more likely to be associated with technological change, but it is also more likely that much of this change will be imported and not local. LDCs face a real problem today, arising from the massive technological change in some sectors, often associated with very substantial economies of scale. These changes may render obsolete existing know-how and learning, and make it difficult, often impossible, for countries with small markets to compete. (See the analysis of lathes in Argentina by Jacobsson, 1981). At best, the huge economies of scale in some areas mean that LDCs can generally only hope to be able to enter a few of these areas, and the policy of advancing on all fronts (balanced growth) becomes impossible. It follows that *selection* of areas in which to specialise is very important and needs to be based on (a) likely technological trends; (b) learning effects; (c) export possibilities; as well as the more conventional (d) country factor endowment. In general, the desire to generate local learning effects and a capacity to produce technology is an important additional criterion in selection of industry and one that is completely excluded from most cost-benefit analyses.

ECONOMY WIDE POLICY

(1) *Incentives for local technical change* Various financial incentives may be given for R&D but these may not be very effective in that (a) they often simply result in a reclassification of expenditure rather than any real change; (b) local innovation often results from 'blue-collar' efforts outside formal R&D departments. A very important area is to increase the acceptability and use of locally designed products. (In India there is considerable evidence of underuse of local technology as compared with foreign.) One major area of policy here is policy towards *products* and *brand names*. Disallowing foreign brand names (or

brand names altogether), and limiting advertising, reduces the market power of foreign technology. Another powerful tool is the use of government purchasing to promote local technology. In practice, partly as a result of aid-tying, government purchasing also often exhibits a bias in favour of foreign technology.

(2) *Mechanisms of technology transfer from abroad* The more packaged the transfer (for example, subsidiary of MNC), the less government control and the more likely that foreign technology will be used. Governments can negotiate with MNCs to promote and use local technology. They also need to negotiate to outlaw clauses and conditions that inhibit local technology development – for example, MNCs taking out patents and then not using them; clauses that prevent other local firms from using technology generated within an MNC. A general bias towards 'unpackaging' tends to help local technology capacity, as a first step in developing such capacity is the ability to put a technology package together (see Mytelka, 1978).

(3) *Macroeconomic policy* Technology change and learning is more likely in an environment of continuous industrial expansion. Argentina provides an example of a country that has lost much in this respect through government policy depressing industrial activity, leading to closing-down of firms and the loss of much learning.

(4) *Local linkages* A major inducement for technological change (see Rosenberg, 1976) comes from demands imposed by one firm on its suppliers. If firms receive their supplies from overseas, this important inducement and source of change is lost. This, of course, has bearing on the question of protection discussed earlier, and also on the choice of industry. Industries with strong natural local linkages are likely to have greater technology change effects than those (for example, assembly plants) where most inputs are imported.

(5) *Monopoly/oligopoly versus competition* On the one hand, scale economies plus the need for some 'protection' of local innovation might suggest that large-scale and oligopolistic firms would best promote local technological change. On the other, the incentive to innovate will be less. Moreover, in so far as the large firms produce foreign-designed products, they will tend to innovate on the basis of changes imported from abroad, and will in so doing make it difficult for small local firms to compete on the basis of their 'local' products. Innovations carried out by large firms are less likely to be appropriate than those carried out by small. In some areas, because of scale economies, large firms may be the only feasible solution. But in many others, small

firms may have more to offer, but there may need to be some co-ordinated research and training efforts to counter the disadvantages of small-scale.

INSTITUTIONAL POLICY

A major institutional problem lies in the area of science and technology policy, R&D institutions, and the most appropriate relationships between these and the productive sector. There is plentiful evidence of expensive and ineffective science institutions (see, for example, Ranis, in Beranek and Ranis, 1978) and of complex technology plans with few results. In general, the links between science and technology institutions and users tend to be weak. In LDCs, firm R&D normally forms a small proportion of the total in comparison with DCs. These weak links with users of technology might be offset by (a) locating more R&D in firms; and (b) trying to change the nature of the relationships between firms and institutions by different contractual arrangements. But in addition there is the vital question of interests and motives among the scientific community and local economic decision-makers – both currently may often be served by the 'marginalisation' of science that has been observed. The various links and interests need further exploration (see, for example, Biggs, 1982, and Clark, 1980). In the light of more knowledge, some quite minor changes might produce results, although for a complete change a revolution in political economy may be at issue.

TRAINING/EDUCATION

The supply of people with appropriate qualifications in significant quantities is obviously a necessary (though equally obviously not a sufficient) condition for local technical change. But what meaning can we give to this statement? What are the right qualifications or the right quantities? In so far as blue-collar innovation has been established as an important source of innovation, then the 'right' qualifications are those at the level of skilled blue-collar worker. Primary education has been suggested as an important determinant of agricultural innovation (see *World Development Report*, 1980). I have seen little research on the educational/skill qualifications associated with industrial blue-collar innovation. This is an important area for research. Undoubtedly, while formal educational establishment can make a contribution towards the provision of the appropriate skills, learning on-the-job plus firm training schemes play an important part. But because of externalities, special schemes may be necessary to promote firm training. The private interests of firms may be to develop specialised skills that are most likely to remain within their province. But the social interest may be better served by a more general and flexible training. Hence government intervention may be needed to see that relevant general skills needed are created, either by government training schemes or by subsidies to firm training.

THE POLITICAL ECONOMY OF CREATING LOCAL TECHNOLOGY

Some classes, in some environments, get their major rewards (in status as well as money) from a static environment. A classic historic case of this is the absentee landlords in nineteenth- century Ireland. In other contexts, status and remuneration arise from innovation. Industrial entrepreneurs in Britain in the eighteenth and nineteenth centuries realised their rewards through technological dynamism, but in the twentieth century the situation has been reversed and innovators in Britain have little status and rather low rewards. The effects on the rate of innovation in Britain are well known. In LDCs, similarly, some classes in society form dynamic elements and some static, while some societies reward dynamism, while others at best tolerate it. In each society it is possible to trace these influences – which are the effects of the interactions between class formation, culture, education and the economic environment – to establish the dominant forces and how they affect the rate of innovation. In the context of present-day LDCs, there is the further factor of foreign interests which can become so intertwined with local interests and local decision-makers that the dominant class of decision-makers favour the use of foreign innovations as compared with local ones. In trying to explain why some societies innovate effectively and others do not, the fundamental and underlying explanation often seems to lie in the realm of history and interests, rather than in particular policies. The policies may often be the proximate cause of one outcome rather than another, but they are also the reflection of these deeper influences. Hence a major element in any work on indigenous technical change should be to trace how the interests and rewards of the major decision-makers relate to a static or dynamic environment and to local or foreign sources of technology.

It is much easier to explain the dynamism of some economies (for example, Japan) in these terms, than with reference (only) to the effects of particular policies and institutions. Similarly with respect to explaining technical change in LDCs; changes that reinforce the politi-cal and economic power, status and rewards of dynamic elements in society (which may include particular economic policies, or particular institutional change) may be critical in creating indigenous technical change.

ALTERNATIVE THEORETICAL APPROACHES TO TECHNICAL CHANGE

Recent analyses of technical change form four distinct groups. (In large part this grouping follows that of Biggs (1982), who analyses approaches to agricultural innovation into three groups – induced innovation, structuralist and institutional.)

(1) *Empirical case studies especially at a micro-level* In this approach, rather detailed case-studies are explored on innovation within particu-lar firms. For the most part the studies are approached with few theoretical preconceptions, and the story of major influences over in-novation emerges from the investigations. For example, Maxwell's (1977) study of innovation in a steel firm in Argentina shows how par-ticular events – for example, shortage of capacity, the presence of a dynamic entrepreneur – led to particular innovations. The absence of theoretical preconceptions tends to be both a strength and a weakness of these studies. It is a strength to the extent that all sorts of facts are collected that might be overlooked in so far as they do not fit into any particular theory; some of these facts may turn out to be the critical ones. It is a weakness in so far as general influences can get lost in the detailed story – the proximate influences are recorded more readily than their underlying causes. Moreover, while the micro-historical basis of the approach generates considerable insights into the innova-tive approach, it tends to make the results particular to the cases re-corded and difficult to generalise. While no authors fit uniquely into any one category, both the Katz (1978) studies and Lall's (1981) work fall mainly into the empirical approach, with the Katz studies being primarily based on micro-case studies, and Lall's consisting of analysis and collection of data across a broader front.

(2) *Neoclassical approach* Here the main focus is on the effects of prices in 'inducing' technical change; the inducement may work directly on economic decision-makers (firms or farms), or indirectly through in-fluencing the activities of technology institutions. The theoretical

aspects of this research show how one would expect prices (especially factor prices) to influence innovation of profit-maximising (and other) types of decision-maker. The empirical element of the work tests how this works out in practice. Binswanger and Ruttan's (1978) work is a leading example of this approach. The Yale project fits broadly into this category, especially with respect to the 'profits function' approach.

(3) *A political economy approach* (of which the Marxist is a special case). According to this view, it is the interests of those classes or interest groups responsible for carrying out research and development and initiating technical change which is the main determinant of the rate and direction of technical change. The Marxist version of this approach would put emphasis on class interests, defining class with reference to mode of production, while other versions would include more particular interest groups. The 'marginalisation' of science in the Third World has been explained with this type of approach, as being the result of the dominant interests among decision-makers (multinational firms, local interests who have become 'compradors', whose interests have become allied to foreign interests) being best served by the use of foreign and inappropriate technology. The biases in the Green Revolution – benefiting the larger and richer farmers, with the net effect in some cases of impoverishing further the poorer elements in society – have also been explained by class interests dominating the direction of research and innovation. Herrera (1973) and Sunkel (1973), on the role of science and technology in the periphery, and K. Griffin (1974), on the green revolution, provide examples of this type of approach.

(4) *Institutional explanations* Two types of institutional approach should be distinguished:

(a) *descriptive and politically neutral* Here science and technology institutions are taken to have an independent and dominating influence on technical change. Failures in innovation are attributed to institutional deficiences. This is pre-eminently the approach of the UN institutions, which emphasise the significance of institutional change and technology planning to bring about technical change. (See, for example, the recent UNCTAD document: 'Planning the Technological Transformation of Developing Countries' (TD/B/C.6/50).)

(b) *analytic with a political economy element* In this approach, scientific and technical institutions are taken to have a major influence on innovation – as in the first institutional approach – but the workings of the R&D institutions are seen to be the products of the influences/interest groups associated with them, the financing groups, the scientific community itself and the groups for whom the technologies are designed. Hence 'failures' of R&D institutions are not explained by failures in design of the institutions, but by the interactions of the various interest groups. The work of Clark and Biggs provides examples. Work in this area has been primarily directed at agricultural research institutions, but in principle a similar approach could readily be adopted with respect to industrial research.

In a very simple way, the various approaches are summarised in the diagrams below. The arrows indicate the assumed direction of causality. The first three diagrams represent the neoclassical, the political economy and the institutional approaches, each involving a single type of causality, working in a unidirectional way. A in Figure 2 shows factor prices determining technical change; Diagram B class interests; and Diagram C institutions.

Each of the views represented in these diagrams seems to be a much oversimplified representation of reality. (In fact these representations are a much oversimplified view of the various authors mentioned,

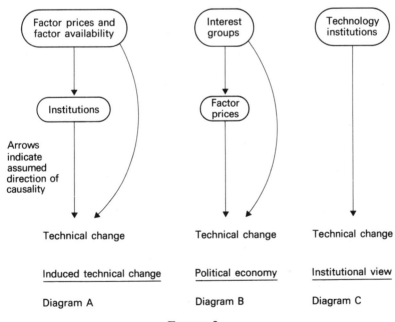

FIGURE 2

which encompass more of the elements of other views than is allowed for here. None the less, I believe this oversimplification is derived from significant differences between these groups.) The major value of the empirical case-study approach has indeed been to show how oversimplified the single-cause type theory is, as it is apparent in particular cases that there are myriad causes for technical change; that causality is not unidirectional, but the nature of technical change itself influences the environment – including interest groups, and factor prices. All the major factors picked out by the various theories and depicted above do it seems, from both *a priori* reasoning and case studies, have some influence on technical change, both directly and through the way in which they influence the other major variables. For example, tractorisation is encouraged by subsidised prices for tractors and low cost of credit (the factor price explanation), but these low prices are themselves, in part at least, the result of class forces (the influence of the large farmers and tractor producers), that is, the class explanation. In this case it might seem that class interests play the dominant role, but this is not entirely correct because factor prices are rarely completely dominated by interest groups, but (as they do in this case) contain a 'natural' element, representing the opportunity costs of the resources.

Figure 3 shows a more complex set of relationships than in the approaches described. In this representation each of the major factors is shown as influencing technical change; in addition each influences the other main variables, while the nature of the technical change itself helps determine the variables. In this comprehensive approach, class interests, for example, in the form of foreign interests, an industrial bourgeoisie with foreign connections and an urban 'elite' working class, would contribute to the determination of factor prices (low capital prices, relatively high urban wages) and would directly, and indirectly via these factor prices, help determine the nature of technology change. But the factor endowment would also play some independent role in that the price of labour would still be relatively (compared with developed countries) low. Technology institutions are themselves influenced by the conglomeration of class interests and by the prevailing factor prices. Yet they may also have some independent role, depending on their own logic, itself a function of their design, the interests they serve and the training and objectives of the scientific community. The outcome of this complex interaction is a certain type of technical change, which is of significance in determining the configuration of variables in the next period – what class interests emerge, for example, how factor availability is influenced, and so on.

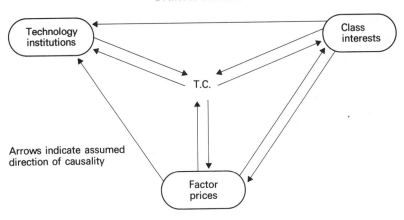

A Comprehensive/Eclectic Approach

FIGURE 3

A major contribution of the theoretical and empirical work on technical change has been to indicate the presence of this multiplicity of causal factors, and interactions between them. While, in the past, most work has been based on one or other of the various approaches, at this stage of our knowledge it would be more valuable if empirical work could be designed to explore the interactions represented in the comprehensive approach. At this stage we know that such interactions exist, but we know little about their precise nature or magnitude, nor about which relationships are dominant.

REFERENCES

Bell, M., D. Scott-Kemmis and W. Satyarakwit (1982) 'Limited Learning in Infant Industry: a Case Study', in F. Stewart and J. James (eds), *The Economics of New Technology in Developing Countries*. London: Frances Pinter.

Beranek, W. and G. Ranis (1978) *Science and Technology and Economic Development*. New York: Praeger.

Biggs, S. (1982) 'Institutions and Decision Making in Agricultural Research', in Stewart and James, *Economics of New Technology*.

Binswanger, H. P., V. W. Ruttan *et al.* (1978) *Induced Innovation, Technology Institutions and Development*. Baltimore: Johns Hopkins.

Clark, N. (1980) 'The Economic Behaviour of Research Institutions in Developing Countries – some Methodological Points', *Social Studies of Science*, 10.

94   *Facilitating Indigenous Technical Change*

Fransman, M. (1982) 'Learning and the Capital Goods Sector Under Free Trade: the Case of Hong Kong', *World Development*, vol. 10, no. 11.
Griffin, G. (1974) *The Political Economy of Agrarian Change*, London: Macmillan.
Herrera, A. (1973) 'Social Determinants of Science in Latin America, Explicit Science and Implicit Science Policy', in C. Cooper (ed.), *Science, Technology and Development*, London, Frank Cass.
Jacobsson, S. (1981) 'Strategy Problems in the Production of Numerically Controlled Lathes in Argentina', paper for Workshop on Comparative Methodology in Studies of Technological Change, Research Policy Institute, Lund.
Katz, J. (1978) 'Technological Change, Economic Development and Intra and Extra Regional Relations in Latin America'. IDB/ECLA/UNDP/IDRC Regional Program of Studies on Scientific and Technical Development in Latin America, Working Paper No. 30, Buenos Aires: Economic Commission for Latin America.
Lall, S. (1981) *Developing Countries as Exporters of Technology*, London: Macmillan.
Maxwell, P. (1977) 'Learning and Technical Change in the Steel Plant of Acindar SA in Argentina', Buenos Aires, IDB/ECLA Research Programme in Science and Technology Working Paper, no. 4.
Mytelka, L. (1978) 'Licensing and Technological Dependence in the Andean Pact', *World Development* 6.
Pearson, R. (1977) 'The Mexican Cement Industry: Technology, Market Structure and Growth', IDB/ECCA/UDNP/IDRC Working Paper no. 11, Buenos Aires. Economic Commission for Latin America.
Ranis, G. *et al.* (1980. 'International and Domestic Determinants of LDC Technology Choice: Contrasting Agricultural and Industrial Experience', Economic Growth Centre, Yale.
Rosenberg, G. (1976) *Perspectives on Technology*. Cambridge University Press.
Sunkel, O. (1973) 'Transnational Capital and National Disintegration in Latin America', *Social and Economic Studies*, 22.
World Bank (1980) *World Development Report*, Washington, D.C.

Determinants and Consequences of Indigenous Technological Activity[1]

Gustav Ranis

Our basic premise is that to the extent that any one dimension is 'key' to the successful application of technology in the development context, it is the quality of indigenous technological activity that counts the most. Moreover, though demonstrably more difficult, we hope to be able to maintain this premise even as we descend from generalities to address the more specific linkages with other dimensions of the complicated technological 'ball of wax'.

Section I will present some definitions and suggest one way of viewing the key relationships among the many concepts floating about the literature. Section II will focus on the supply- and demand-side determinants of indigenous technological activity. Section III, finally, will discuss the potential and actual consequences for LDC societal objectives of putting indigenous technological activity in its proper place and briefly summarise the policy implications of this view.

I. INDIGENOUS TECHNOLOGICAL ACTIVITY: DEFINITIONS AND RELATIONSHIPS

The profession, as well as most real world actors, needs little convincing today – in contrast to the situation in the early post-war era – that the black box labelled 'technology' contains all variety of 'goodies' which, if we could just unlock it and sort it out, is more likely to make the difference between success and failure than most other prescriptions, certainly including those relying heavily on the brute force of capital accumulation, with or without assistance from the outside.

It is our contention that 'the' basic key to unlocking that box is the twin recognition that (i) the co-existence with more advanced countries and more advanced country technologies – in both product and process dimensions – represents an overwhelmingly important dimension of an LDC's environment – for better or worse and whether we like it or not – and that (ii) the nature and extent of indigenous technological activity will, in fact, determine whether it indeed is 'for better' or 'for worse' – or, at least for 'not as good as it should be'.

The first part of this contention is based on the premise that, no matter how 'closed' or 'self-reliant' the developing economy, the existence of a backlog of accumulated knowledge of 'how' to produce and on 'what' (attributes) to produce, across countries and across time, dominates all technological activities. Thus 'technological dependence' in the broadest sense of that much abused term is an incontrovertible and inescapable fact of life. The second part of the assertion is based on the premise that nothing can ever be efficiently transferred to a particular place at a particular time without having to be modified to make it fit the always peculiar local circumstances; this applies as much to essentially turn-key projects as to the 'rediscovery' of old ways of doing things within the developing country itself. In other words, the wheel cannot be imported as is and it cannot be 'reinvented' either; to some extent it has to be adapted or modified if it is going to fit in with always different and ever-changing local circumstances.

It is the capacity to make those changes continuously, rather than to invent something emerging full-blown 'from the brow of Zeus', that constitutes, we believe, most relevant technological activity. In these terms all technological activity is indigenous almost by definition; but it is the quality of an LDC's indigenous technological capacity that determines how 'well' or 'appropriately' – in terms of a changing endowment – technology choices, adaptations and modifications are being made on a continuous routinised basis.

Unfortunately, the stock of indigenous technological capacity can only be identified in its use; thus, as with entrepreneurship, it is difficult to define capacity independent of the occurrence of indigenous technological activity. As a consequence, one is forced to settle for tangible evidence of demonstrated indigenous technological activity appearing in association with presumably relevant dimensions of capacity.

Demonstrated indigenous technological activity may be defined in three related ways: one refers to the initial choice of the technology as embodied in blueprints, salesmen's handbooks, machinery patents and commodity trademarks, foreign or domestic; a second refers to the required modifications of that technology for effective local application; a third focuses on the diffusion of best practice, with appropriate modifications, across agricultural and industrial establishments. Add to this the fact that the accumulated storehouse of human knowledge –

that is, the potential 'shelf' or technology space – is constantly being added to as a consequence of the march of science and technology in the mature industrial countries, and we begin to see the outlines of the formidable conceptual tiger we have by the tail.

The quality of the indigenous technological activity actually observed is thus partly a function of the capacity to choose wisely (and cost-effectively) from among the shelf technologies, partly a function of the capacity to tinker and adjust, and partly a function of the capacity to channel and diffuse. While these capacities are clearly neither fully independent in concept nor empirically identifiable in isolation – for example, the capacity to diffuse relevant information and the capacity to tinker are usually closely associated – it is nevertheless worthwhile to try to distinguish among them. They may well depend on somewhat different human and/or organisational and institutional abilities on the supply side and be critically affected by different dimensions of the economic environment determining the demand side. Together they add up to a certain quality of indigenous technological performance the level of which has to be assessed in terms of the system's total responsiveness to the economy's underlying endowment conditions as well as its flexibility to changes in those conditions over time. We intend to take a closer look at these underlying supply- and demand-side determinants of indigenous technological activity in what follows.

II. SUPPLY- AND DEMAND-SIDE DETERMINANTS OF INDIGENOUS TECHNOLOGICAL ACTIVITY

Activity of any kind is based both on the capacity to carry it out, a supply-side concept, and on the desire to carry it out, a demand-side concept. Indigenous technological activity is no exception. While a division into supply and demand factors is necessarily at times somewhat artificial, it remains useful for expositional purposes. Accordingly we intend to discuss the various ingredients of each consecutively, bringing to bear the relevant evidence as appropriate to the case.

The most obvious and yet also the most important ingredient of indigenous capacity resides, of course, in the quality of the human resources available to the developing society. The qualities that affect the nature and direction of the process of search among 'known' core techniques and product choices, and the qualities that affect the process of modification and adaptation, may not be precisely the same, but they are very likely to be closely related, that is, to have their roots in differing or the same combination of formal and informal learning experiences to which the economically active population has been exposed.

Economic historians and historians of science have been puzzled for some time about the precise origins of a basic technological capacity embedded in a society's entrepreneurial population at large. Such capacity is obviously related to some extent to general literacy, especially in the agricultural sector,[2] and very likely also to the extent of the overall primary educational system's emphasis on general cognitive processes and on empirical problem-solving capacity using locally informed cases. Historically, the USA, for example, borrowed heavily from England in the last half of the nineteenth century, but the key to her subsequent success resided in the mechanical engineering industries which facilitated new production with interchangeable parts and was based on a wide-spread tinkering capacity. As Rosenberg saw it, the Americans borrowed freely and extensively, with very little genuine inventive activity of their own, even during the colonial period. The role of widespread general education provided for a substantial measure of technical literacy at all skill levels and created a substantial problem-solving capacity which undoubtedly helped the USA to be both 'highly discriminating in borrowing patterns and highly selective in the uses to which imported technologies were put'. While the USA produced few contributions to frontier science and even frontier technology, the improvement of imported technology in a labour-saving direction as part of the 'American system' responsive to the more labour-scarce endowment situation à la Habakkuk, required not only engineers who had at least a grounding in 'high technology' and its use, but also large numbers of polytechnic-level technical personnel imbued with an extremely pragmatic attitude towards technology. The USA as a frontier society with virtually unlimited natural resources and therefore not inclined to invest heavily in indigenous basic innovations, stands in some contrast to Germany, the other beneficiary of England's loss of technological leadership. In the USA, infrastructural investments by government, in education as well as in agricultural research and extension services, helped create a broadly based technological literacy to improve and diffuse technology; natural-resources-poor Germany, in contrast, focused on government-supported basic science and science-intensive industries and a much more elitist, general as well as technical, educational structure.

Most contemporary developing countries find themselves in situations with a natural resources endowment likely to be much less plentiful than that of the nineteenth-century USA and a skilled human resources endowment much less plentiful than that of Germany. The reliance on the embodiment of unskilled but literate labour is thus likely to be much more important. Historical Japan, with her poor natural resources but abundant human resources endowment, in fact, might be viewed as the most relevant for LDCs. After early Meiji government mistakes in attempting to apply Western-style, land-abundant methods in agriculture, mainly developed for wheat, to a small-scale, land-scarce, rice economy – and similar errors in industry via importing inappropriate 'turn-key technology' for use in public-sector plants – it took the Japanese relatively little time to recognise the importance of selecting imported technology relatively carefully and then adapting it substantially to local conditions. Both in agriculture and in industry, trial and error led to greater reliance on private-sector decisions regarding technology choice. The enhancement of indigenous technological capacity through education, through demonstration farms and extension, and through the efforts of travelling veteran farmers, had their counterpart in more informal private diffusion activities in the non-agricultural sector. The empirically based response of Japanese industrial as well as agricultural actors to the changing availability of a technology potential, would not have been possible without a strong and well-dispersed educational base, both general and technical, which has been a part of the Japanese scene from the very beginning.

Neither nineteenth-century USA nor Japan were thus pioneers either in science or in basic technology, but they both developed a definite capacity to absorb science and imported technology as a basis for their own very substantial achievements. The capacity of each to respond successfully to very different endowment conditions is related to the nature and reach of the educational system, as well as to the quality and strength of other infrastructural interventions.

No actions of government can, of course, legislate 'against' the basic, drastically different, initial endowments. They can, however, play an important role in the educational and institutional sphere to overcome supply-side constraints on indigenous technological activity. The substantial adaptations on top of imported technology in Japanese industry, as well as the almost instantaneous diffusion of the improved technology in both industry and agriculture in nineteenth-century Japan, are but a case in point. The emphasis on primary education, the role of the agricultural extension service, the land policy and the expansion of the railroad and rail-repair network played a similar role in the USA. The engineering-intensive technology that was adapted to the wide-open spaces of the United States is hardly less relevant than that of Japan, which took a more capital-stretching path.

The causal direction does not, of course, always run from science to basic and then to applied technology. As Kuznets, among others, has pointed out, technology continuously gives rise to as many puzzles that require a further response by the scientific and technological community, as the other way around. Thus the USA and Japan, over time, built their own science capacities partly in response to such demands, partly because they could increasingly afford a scientific establishment marching to a different (longer-term) drummer. But at an earlier stage, relevant, say, to most contemporary African societies, the capacity to utilise or modify international technology and adapt it to different environments depends on the extent to which tinkering can become routinised within a substantial proportion of the entrepreneurial and engineering-cum-polytechnic population.

The capacity to pick intelligently from an international shelf in full awareness of the costs of search, adaptation, etc., may be more of a white-collar task of information-gathering plus R&D activity, while the capacity to solve puzzles and adapt further is likely to be a mix of white- and what might be called blue-collar R&D and information-diffusion capacities. It takes a certain amount of wisdom, for example, to choose initial foreign technology to be at least in the 'vicinity' of a system's domestic capacity so that it acts as a stimulus to the problem-solving capacities of the indigenous population, not as a discouragement. It takes a somewhat different set of talents to make the crucial adaptations to meet peculiar local conditions. Whether these are equally dependent on general literacy, or on more formal engineering education, is beyond my ken. What seems clear is that the second capacity needs to be much more widely diffused throughout the population and may be very much related to the existence of a capital goods industry, especially in mechanical engineering, repair shops, etc. in developing countries. Such a capital goods sector undoubtedly plays a very special role in determining indigenous capacity in the sense that it provides a given quality of human resources a chance to have a multiple impact. We are dealing here not only with so-called 'compulsive sequences' – that is, new ideas at one processing stage forcing appropriate changes in techniques and attributes up or down the line – but also in terms of the simple proposition that 'tinkering' requires complementary resources which must themselves be adjusted and modified in the course of development. The extent to which simple repair and mechanical engineering industries are developed is bound to have a wider multiplier effect in terms of the ability to modify products and processes in a wide range of client industries. This has been demonstrated through the examples of blacksmiths in Sri Lanka, tube-well repair shops in the Punjab and metal-mechanic industries in Peru.

Other supply-side dimensions affecting indigenous technological activity, of course, relate to the organisational/institutional infrastructure which the public sector may or may not create, or may or may not channel in appropriate directions. We have in mind here the extensive science and technology institutional infrastructure which often favours export cash-crops while discriminating against food crops in agriculture. These institutions focus on the relatively advanced end of the science and technology spectrum, giving short shrift to more modest problem-solving capacities in the engineering and metal working industries.

It is, of course, difficult to fashion hard-and-fast decision rules which might tend to eliminate any frontier-type, publicly funded research activity, whether it is basically science- or technology-oriented; but the burden of proof clearly should be on the allocation of very scarce budgetary and human resources in that direction, when the most elementary private-sector adaptation and diffusion capacities are relatively underdeveloped and could be given substantial assistance through modest public-sector contributions. There can be little doubt, for example, that a society's information-gathering and adaptation capacities need to be viewed as of one cloth, even though we may differentiate them conceptually. We also know that there exist startling gaps in knowledge about existing technological choices, domestic and foreign, within any given developing country, along with the well-known absence of the capacity to make the necessary modifications. Thus the best network for diffusing information, while probably in the private sector, can be helped by government actions, for example, by utilising the same resources now in traditional science and technology institutes to support a network with built-in information cum problem-solving capacity available to the crucial private actors in both the agricultural and non-agricultural sectors. We are not referring here to 'question and answer' services, which usually don't make too much sense because of the unlikely ability of the final customer to be able to formulate the proper question, but rather to public-sector support for an essentially private network, which permits information and problem-solving capacities to be combined and enhanced by encouraging 'doing' and gaining confidence by 'doing'.

The specific public-policy changes required for such an information/ diffusion/adaptation network cannot, of course, be spelled out, certainly not for all country types and stages of development. But once we recognise that these capacities are indeed of one type and must be accessible to a large number of small blue-collar actors, we can examine possibilities such as rural industrial extension services along the lines of the more successful farmer associations and introduce such changes into decentralised credit institutions as development banks or commercial banks which have many rural branches. There is often a need in such cases for this particular function to be subsidised, at least initially, preferably on a declining scale over time. To a modest extent, a change in the reward system within the so-called science-and-technology-institute community can also be of help by focusing scarce entrepreneurial scientific and intellectual energies in the direction of a strengthened indigenous technological capacity, rather than the ability to participate in the invisible college of the international engineering and scientific establishment.

There are undoubtedly important institutional and organisational choices that affect the quality of a society's indigenous technological capacity over time. One of these clearly includes the issues of subcontracts *vs* more integrated firms in industry, as well as the related issue of how soon modern inputs produced outside of agriculture replace traditional inputs. The simple minimum-cost choice answer may not include the dynamic effects in terms of encouraging indigenous technological competence outside the large firms. The Japanese record of doing a good deal of industrial subcontracting early on, and enforcing enhanced quality standards by encouraging quality as well as price competition among a number of would-be suppliers, is a case in point. We are not suggesting the encouragement of subcontracting via subsidisation, or any other selective government policy actions: only that a policy of at least even-handedness, with respect to the allocation of infrastructure to rural areas, would seem to constitute an important supply-side action to strengthen the opportunity for a more decentralised growth of indigenous technological capacity. Most often the existing LDC allocation of public overheads in the industrial sector positively encourages the integration alternative: for example, power rates are often lower in the large cities, and the construction of roads and other overheads tends to favour industrial concentration. This is also true in the agricultural sector, where irrigation and other overhead allocation in favour of local elites is often quite blatant as a consequence of the relative weakness of decentralised rural organisations, both public and private, in most of the developing countries.

Another organisational dimension relevant to the supply side of the indigenous technology capacity canvas refers to the choice between batch and continuous production lines, which may have differential dynamic consequences that are often not included in private-sector calculations. Episodal accounts certainly seem to indicate that, very much in the vein of the modern Volvo story, a batch production process encourages the search for product and process change much more so than the continuous assembly line. Such dynamic dimensions would, of course, have to be weighed against static comparative cost calculations, but sensitising the private sector to such issues, including incorporating this dimension within a network which enhances information and R&D capacity, which might be partially encouraged by public-sector action (see above), should be included in the consideration of how to strengthen supply-side factors.

A quite distinct dimension of the supply-side infrastructure that may assist in the development of indigenous technological capacity is related to the legal side. As we have already noted, in the more successful developing countries we witness a good deal of so-called blue-collar R&D activity, with problem-solving going on in unconventional locations and carried out by unconventional actors. Such 'minor' innovative activity can be encouraged through worker incentive systems, suggestion-box approaches, etc., as traditionally in Japan, but also through the legal device of establishing a so-called utility model or 'petty patent' as an alternative and supplement to conventional patenting legislation. Such an alternative, interestingly enough, exists in both Japan and Germany, the latecomer countries, as well as in some of the more successful contemporary developing countries. The system encourages application for the protection of smaller innovations with a lower 'novelty' requirement, protected at lower financial and bureaucratic costs, in exchange for a shorter period of protection – that is, five to seven years as opposed to fifteen years. In such contemporary LDCs as South Korea and Brazil, petty patents seem to be granted primarily to nationals and individuals, in contrast to regular patents which go predominantly to foreign corporations. The history of the Japanese textile industry, for example, indicates that, historically, such utility models were very important, especially in weaving, which relied heavily on domestic innovations based on traditional handlooms, improved with the help of imported Batten and Jacquard related ideas. Petty patents played a lesser role in cotton-spinning, which relied more heavily on adaptations from fully developed inventions 'embodied' in imported machinery. It is, moreover, interesting to note that petty patenting seems to have been concentrated in mechanical engineering activities.

Moving beyond the utility model, the patent system as a whole, including design patents, trade marks, licensing systems, etc., has not been carefully examined in this century with respect to its encouragement or discouragement of indigenous technological activity. We are all aware of episodal evidence to the effect that foreign patents introduced into LDCs are often used for blocking rather than transfer of technology purposes, and that licensing payments often do not reflect the technology content of the transaction. It is quite possible that a fuller reconsideration of the trade-offs between the appropriability of private-gains function of patents and its function as a conveyor of information, if utilisation can be enforced, could point the way to substantially enhancing indigenous technological activity, given a certain level of human and institutional/organisational capacity within the LDC.

In addition to typological differences in the initial conditions among countries – for example, size, resource endowment, etc., – policies crucially affect the intensity of the search for indigenous technological activity on the part of individual actors, both in the public and private sectors. A developing country in early transition growth, for example, typically adopts a policy environment for purposes of primary import substitution industrialisation which is typically unfriendly to indigenous technological activity. This is, in general, a period that focuses on 'getting things done', providing a warm environment for a new industrial entrepreneurial class including obtaining the necessary physical tools or technologies from the outside. It is a period that emphasises physical accumulation as opposed to efficiency, and places much less heavy emphasis on the refined calculus of choosing appropriate technologies, either in terms of the careful search of international shelves or in terms of the effort necessary to make the appropriate adaptations or modifications domestically.

These regimes, in other words, discourage the coming-into-play of substantial indigenous technological activity, partly because they typically distort product and factor prices away from the endowment picture, and because they usually create windfall profits for the private entrepreneurial class which make them much less interested in seeking out indigenous technological opportunities. It is, of course, also a period that typically encourages free entry of foreign capital goods while protecting intermediate as well as final goods via the normal cascading of tariffs, which policy may have a long-term deleterious effect on the establishment of an indigenous capital goods sector, so often an essential ingredient, as we have seen, for the construction of indigenous technological capacity on the supply side. When government interventions especially favour, as in the India of the 1950s, Ghandian khadi and its associated traditional technology, on the one hand, and Mahalanobis steel mills based on imported technology, on the other, what is squeezed out is the vast array of indigenous technological activity likely to be most appropriate to changing endowment conditions.

The problem of distorted relative factor and product prices is too well known to require much attention here. Underpricing capital, imports, and skilled labour, and overpricing unskilled labour of course affects static technology choices. For our purposes even more important is how it affects the nature of the search for new technologies over time. This is also a subphase of transition during which, for a number of reasons, great expectations abound with respect to the power of the imported process and of the internationally specified product, which apparently every developing country seems to go through, although the extent, severity and length of the import substitution policy syndrome of course vary substantially.

Perhaps more important than the relative factor price and relative product price dimension is the intensity with which normal entrepreneurial functions are likely to be carried out. The more that scarce entrepreneurial energies are spent on playing the controls game, obtaining the slips of paper required for assuring oneself of the windfall profits available in various controlled markets, the less energy left for concern with indigenous technological activities. One can find this to be true in the agricultural sector where prices are often set artificially, as well as when there exist restrictions on entry and on access to scarce resources for new and small entrepreneurs in nonagricultural activities. This typically leads to 'invisible handshakes' between elitist capitalists and elitist workers, and a narrow growth path that excludes the majority of potential entrepreneurs who could substantially contribute to a successful search for indigenous technological activity.

If and when the society does shift from domestic-market-oriented import substitution into an export-oriented regime via substantial reform in the various relevant policy areas, the chance for a larger role played by indigenous technological activity is substantially enhanced.

We have certainly observed this in the East Asian cases which graduated from import substitution to export substitution in the early 1960s. When such graduation does not take place, however, and countries persevere in import substitution, as in most of the Latin American countries and some of the ASEAN countries, an accelerated tendency for the noncompetitiveness and satisficing rather than maximising behaviour inimical to the demand for indigenous technological activity must be noted.[3]

Countries like those in Sub-Saharan Africa, still largely in early import substitution, are of particular interest here. They still have a fateful choice before them, that is, whether to persevere in import substitution, shifting from primary to the more technology and capital-intensive secondary type, or to shift into an export-oriented policy stance.

The size of a developing country represents an important demand-side typological characteristic quite aside from its effect on the availability of particular human and physical endowments already referred to. Among other reasons, such size determines the relative importance of domestic versus international markets regardless of the policy regime in vogue at a particular time. In other words, even in the most successful case we would expect the domestic market insulated from international prices to be much more important in the large than in the small country case. In the case of smaller countries, the pressure for maintaining competitiveness by finding new labour-using products and processes will come relatively more from abroad. For larger LDCs it will come mainly from the demands of a broadly based balanced growth process in domestic markets. In that connection we should remind ourselves that the demand for indigenous technological activity has two components: one focused on the continued search for more appropriate processes, the other on more appropriate products. Successful technological activity of the process type is likely to be more relevant to the export sector, with its emphasis on price competitiveness in international markets, while success in the search for appropriate technological activity on the product attribute side is likely to be more important with respect to the domestic blade of successful development, that is, via balanced growth in domestic markets. Thus, assuming that supply-side elements are well dispersed across the country, depending on its size and the dispersal of its population, the contribution of indigenous technological activity to each of these major blades of development will depend very much on the policy mix determining the intensity of the demand.

The important typological dimensions thus include size, the extent of labour surplus, etc., as well as the initial geographic density of the population, the kind and extent of the existing transportation system, the level of initial agricultural productivity, which together indicate the ideal static degree of industrial decentralisation for any given product mix. While we must assume that such initial characteristics setting the parameters for demand as well as supply-side elements are not readily amenable to policy, the factors that determine the strength of the motivation of the individual entrepreneurs can be directly influenced by policy. LDC governments can affect the extent of the monopolistic or oligopolistic control of industries by internal measures as well as by the extent of effective protection granted. A reasonably competitive environment is the best insurance for creating the requisite demand-side pressure for indigenous technological activity. Without a shift from satisficing to maximising behaviour on the part of individual economic actors, there is very little chance that much indigenous technological activity will be in evidence. Exclusive attention to the supply side is very much like pushing on a string. If millions of individual decision-makers don't have the 'bit between their teeth', little else will follow.

It is, of course, true that the rest of the world can also be very helpful or harmful in terms of the environment for indigenous technological activity in a given developing-country context. Foreign aid, for example, to the extent it is tied to particular commodities or sources of technology, clearly provides an obstacle instead of an asset. On the other hand, by inducing a country to shift its policy mix it can also be of important help in the creation of a better environment for indigenous technological activity. It can do this both by helping create supply structures, a good example being the CIGYAR organisation in agriculture, an international network of supply-side information on foodcrop technology choices, as well as by encouraging a shift to more endowment responsive policies and the erosion of windfall profits, on the demand side. Similarly, with respect to multinationals, greater willingness to participate in a flexibly phased development programme rather than obstructing it by export prohibitions, cartelisation and market-sharing arrangements, may make an important contribution to the domestic environment in which indigenous technological activity can flourish. The already-referred-to use and misuse of patents for transferring technology rather than obstructing market access is another case in point, as is the willingness to unbundle various components of the multinational package. Public policy can affect MNC behaviour at least by making the provision of subsidised investment guarantees, surveys, tax benefits, etc., discretionary rather than automatic or dependent only on financial flow criteria.

III. INDIGENOUS TECHNOLOGICAL ACTIVITY: CONSEQUENCES AND POLICY CONCLUSIONS

Obviously it takes both favourable supply and demand conditions to evoke adequate levels of indigenous technological activity. The question we may still want to ask ourselves is what difference does it really make in terms of the underlying development performance indicators we are most familiar with, including some combination of growth, employment and equity, with the diminution or elimination of conflict among these objectives a high priority. In other work comparing the performance of East Asian and Latin American NICs[4] we have been able to conclude that, in fact, it is possible to avoid seemingly inevitable conflicts between employment and growth, on the one hand, and the distribution of income, on the other, mainly by affecting the way in which growth is generated. This work, moreover, indicates that the extent to which a society's own changing endowment is effectively utilised in the course of transition represents the most important single ingredient of that performance. This, in turn, is by definition, in large part determined by the society's ability to fully harness its indigenous technological capacity as it moves through various subphases, from infant-industry-dominated import substitution to an export substitution subphase characterised by much greater market orientation.

It is by now well known that the East Asian countries such as Japan, historically, and Taiwan and Korea, more recently, have done much better than the Latin American cases such as Mexico or Colombia, in terms of this ability to husband indigenous technological activity to the development process. This, we believe, is directly related to differences in supply conditions, as well as the different courses taken by the two systems – that is, the perseverance of import substitution in Latin America, and the shift to export substitution in East Asia. Different income-distribution performance, along with growth, result directly from the differential role of indigenous technological activity in determining product and process mixes.

While there is no need here to present the details of the differential performance in terms of the mopping-up of labour surplus, growth rates, Gini coefficients, etc. in the two types of NICs as a demonstration of the point being made, it is possible to assert that the favourable distribution of income in the context of rapid growth in a place like Taiwan was related not only to an initially favourable distribution of assets, particularly land, but also to the fact that substantial indigenous technological activity was in evidence, making small farm holdings more productive, inducing land to be used more intensively for such labour-intensive crops as mushrooms and asparagus, activities that attracted especially the poorest or smallest farmers and thus simultaneously improved the distribution of income.

Similarly, with respect to non-agricultural activities, both rural and urban, the decentralised nature of the industrial structure, made possible by the equitable allocation of public-sector infrastructure on the supply side, as well as the relatively mild form of primary import substitution plus an early shift to export substitution on the demand side, led to an industrial structure that was highly decentralised and labour-intensive in technology both from the product and process points of view. The fact that 50 per cent of rural families' incomes was generated in non-agricultural activity represents an important ingredient of the demonstrated large role of indigenous technology activity. Such decentralised industrialisation provides higher employment and higher incomes for the same poorest families; at the same time, urban infrastructural requirements are lower, and equilibrium market areas, reflecting a compromise between economies of transport costs and economies of scale, move in favour of relatively smaller market areas. This, in turn, favours output bundles, permitting more scope for indigenous technological activity of the product as well as of associated labour-intensive process variety. With the poorest families often profiting from the by-employment opportunities offered by decentralised rural industry and services, such a combination of appropriate goods and processes leads to an extraordinary absorption of unemployment labour hours in an efficient fashion, making a substantial contribution to the improvement rather than the deterioration of the distribution of income during rapid growth.

Indigenous technological activity contributes to the efficient labour intensity of agricultural and non-agricultural production in the labour surplus economy. While the functional distribution of income does not tell the full story of the family distribution of income, it makes a substantial contribution to it, as we have explored elsewhere.[5] We can, for example, point to the sharp gap between the typical relative share of labour in Latin American industry (that is, 0.4 falling to 0.3 over time) and that of the East Asian case (0.6 and rising to 0.7) as one indication of the differential level of indigenous technological activity. A growth strategy that permits the relatively greater penetration of foreign markets by labour-intensive nondurable consumer goods is much more able to induce indigenous technological activity, by permitting the absorption of workers and the forging of a strong link between indigenous technological activity and the improving distribution of income. In Latin America, on the other hand, the much lower resort to labour-intensive technology and output choices caused by the perseverance of import substitution policy, had the important consequence of resulting in continued high levels of income inequality that we are now observing in places like Mexico and Brazil. There can be little doubt that how output is generated and what growth-path is selected is the single most important consequence of the quality of indigenous technological activity. In the East Asian case, increased sensitivity to changes in factor endowment permitted indigenous technological activity to come to full bloom, and incorporate its results in what is being produced, and how. In the case of the Latin American growth-path, the veil between endowments and prices has thickened, while entrepreneurial energies have been ever more focused on obtaining a favoured place in the queue for directly allocated goodies, rather than deploying indigenous technological activity in the search for the construction of the 'better mouse-traps'. The search for indigenous technological activity, we must remember, is also a function of the requisite human capacities as well as the extent of help from information and network capacities created by public-sector actions. As Rosenberg put it, 'economic forces and motives do not act in a vacuum but within the changing limits and constraints of scientific and technical knowledge.'[16]

The conclusions for public policy that follow from all this are sufficiently self-evident. The combination of supply and demand conditions must be rendered sufficiently favourable for indigenous technological activity of the requisite quantity and quality to take place. In such an event we can be quite confident that it will produce the desired effects in terms of the bottom line, the society's development objectives.

Levels of overall competitiveness and, specifically, the impact of macro policies which distort price signals have the effect of inhibiting the demand for appropriate technology, and may be viewed as the most serious obstacle to the generation of adequate indigenous technological activity. On the supply side, the *sine qua non* is the joint or separate capacity to pick from the full storehouse of human knowledge that which is appropriate and to modify it at the same time. The high private-search costs involved in this effort can be assisted by public-sector contributions to the educational and institutional network, to enable tinkering to take place across the entire landscape. Constraints on patenting, licensing and trade-marks from outside must be re-examined. Current R&D allocations must be directed to enhancing the capacity via government extension services or selective subsidies on a declining basis through private banking channels. The role of the Japanese-style trading company or the trade-association case on the model of the Japan Cotton Spinners' Association, which assisted the almost instantaneous diffusion of new technology, should also not be underestimated.

In general, given our review of the determinants and consequences of indigenous technological activity, it is clear that the emphasis must be on the functioning of an internal decentralised network and the capacity to sustain it, rather than on the transfer of hardware from the outside. While we are *not* arguing for the preservation of outdated handicrafts, we *are* arguing for the recommendation that indigenous Z goods industries, perhaps in disuse for some time, may provide the basis for modernised efficient production activities based on indigenous technological capacity. It must be emphasised that we are dealing here with the generation of alternative modern production processes in search of new attribute combinations, not the artificial preservation of outmoded techniques and products. Nor is the latest technology always inappropriate, or the most basic good invariably appropriate; but the gap between the social and private calculus can be reduced, if not eliminated, with the help of changes in macro policies. Thus the most important resource of all, namely broad-based entrepreneurial and innovative capacities, can be harnessed.

A society's full participation in experimentation and tinkering lies at the heart of the required confidence to make appropriate technological choices. Such increased confidence should not take the extreme form of tending towards technological autarky since, as we have pointed out above, the presence of advanced-country technologies will continue to be overwhelmingly important as a stimulus and as a point of departure. Developed countries, whether they like it or not, will continue to make key catalytic inputs, both on the human and on the physical resources side, in helping to develop and enhance a science and technology capacity that permits individuals to ask the right questions, to choose more appropriately, and to adapt more effectively.

In some instances, however, it may also mean that less-developed countries may have more to learn from each other than from the more advanced countries. The centre of gravity for inducing indigenous technological activity clearly rests with the mobilisation of thousands of nonspectacular adaptive responses and modifications of modern processes across a vast number of applications and landscapes. Given both differentiated endowments and objectives, the individual actors in the typical developing country must be given the widest physical opportunity to choose among alternatives and to have the maximum pressure, combined with the fullest possible information, to achieve the objective of a diminished conflict between growth and distribution, by virtue of their active pursuit of indigenous technological activities.

NOTES

1. The author wishes to thank members of the Workshop, especially Martin Fransman, as well as Robert E. Evenson of Yale, for their comments.
2. For example, see Christopher Colclough, 'The Impact of Primary Schooling on Economic Development: A Review of the Evidence', *World Development,* March 1982 ('The evidence . . . from studies of farmer productivity suggests that individual behavioural changes that result from schooling are stronger when literacy is widely spread.')
3. For some concrete examples, see the author's: 'Industrial Sector Labor Absorption', EDCC (April 1973), as well as 'International and Domestic Determinants of LDC Technology Choice', (with G. Saxonhouse) in *Technology Choice and Change in Developing Countries: Internal and External Constraints,* Barbara Lucas and Stephen Freedman (eds) (Dublin: Tycooly International Publishing Ltd, 1982).
4. G. Ranis, 'Challenges and Opportunities Posed by Asia's Superexporters: Implications for Manufactured Exports from Latin America', in *Export Diversification and the New Protectionism,* ed. W. Baer and M. Gillis (NBER, 1981).
5. J. Fei, G. Ranis, S. Kuo, 'Growth and the Family Distribution of Income by Factor Components', *Quarterly Journal of Economics,* Feb. 1978.
6. Nathan Rosenberg, 'Science, Invention and Economic Growth', *Economic Journal,* March, 1974.

Technological Innovation, Industrial Organisation and Comparative Advantages of Latin American Metalworking Industries[1]

Jorge Katz

INTRODUCTION

During the course of the past decade I enjoyed the rare opportunity of conducting a vast exploration into the economics of technological change in manufacturing firms of the six largest Latin American countries. Jointly with a team of economists and engineers we examined from a historical perspective – that is, covering various decades of operation – the technological and overall economic performance of well over fifty industrial firms, carefully recording and studying their behaviour both from an economic and an engineering point of view.

Our purpose throughout the enquiry has not been that of attaining statistical representativeness. Pin-factories are not known in the profession for their representativeness, but they none the less have been the source of one of the most powerful insights ever in the history of economics. Instead, our purpose has been that of throwing a fresh and new look at manufacturing plants in different LDCs and, thereafter, to produce some initial building-blocks for a future more-ambitious construction. We found justification for such a venture in the vast amount of *a priori* normative literature which normally overflows our desks providing notions of conventional wisdom that very seldom are borne out by surrounding facts.

In the large majority of these case studies we enjoyed ample firm collaboration over a long period of time; thus, the explorations are based on a vast amount of otherwise unavailable information concerning the determinants and consequences of entrepreneurial behaviour in general, and of technological actions in particular – that is, change in the overall set of technical knowledge and information used by any given enterprise, as far as product design, process engineering, and production organisation are concerned.

The studies cover a wide array of underlying circumstances in terms of size, nationality, type of industry, patterns of industrial organisation, etc. In other words, we looked both at small-size family enterprises as well as at large incorporated firms; we approached both national and foreign-owned firms; we examined producing steel, cement and petrochemicals – that is, continuous-flow standarised commodities – as much as we looked at plants producing agricultural machinery, machine tools and other such mechanical engineering products, where production runs tend to be small and production organisation normally is 'discontinuous' – that is, 'shop-wise'. Similarly, we also paid attention to 'individual-order' plants, such as shipyards or other such firms specialising in the production of hydroelectric turbines, large and complex boilers, heat-exchangers, electrical generators, and so forth. Here too, production organisation is 'discontinuous' and 'shop-wise', like in the previously mentioned group.

The purpose of the present paper is that of presenting a few preliminary generalisations emerging from the huge package of empirical evidence obtained from the above-mentioned research programme. The second section deals with the idiosyncratic nature of LDCs' manufacturing plants. Reasons emerging on the one hand from various peculiar features of technical knowledge or information as an input to the production process and, on the other, from the highly particular circumstances that normally obtain in the production environment of almost any LDC, account for the idiosyncratic nature of the original choice of technique and production organisation chosen by any given firm, as well as for the subsequent technological search path followed by such company in order to operate the original technology in any evolutionary fashion.

The third section examines the micro and macro determinants of the search process for new technical information that develops at the individual plant level. Any given firm has to be looked at as producing two different flows of output; the first one (obviously the more important one) a flow of goods (or services); the second one, a flow of incremental units of 'new' technical information or knowledge: 'new' here meaning for the company itself. The discussion in this section will follow and expand the notions of 'localised search' and 'natural trajectories' advanced in recent years by J. Stiglitz,[2] N. Rosenberg,[3] and others.[4]

The fourth section will briefly look at the structure and sequential nature of the learning process emerging at the individual firm level. Product engineering capabilities seem to appear first, followed later on by production and process engineering skills. Our evidence shows production planning and industrial organisation capabilities developing at a much later stage, in many cases during the second (or even third) decade of company operation. Nationality, size of company and general macroeconomic atmosphere seem to affect the time dimension and the nature of the learning sequence hereby described. A model of somewhat similar features has been examined by J. Utterback[5] and W. Abernathy in various different papers.

Finally, and on the basis of ideas and empirical evidence advanced in sections two to four, in section five, we pay a short visit to the old argument of learning, infant-industry considerations and protection. The case seems to be strong for 'made to order' actions which would closely reflect the specificity of the learning path followed by any given company, rather than for unique and across-the-board measures of the sort currently argued in the main stream of the trade and development literature.

THE IDIOSYNCRATIC NATURE OF MANUFACTURING FIRMS IN LDCs

Two different sets of reasons account for the fact that manufacturing plants in LDCs significantly differ from their counterpart in mature industrial societies. On the one hand such differences result from the very nature of technical knowledge and information as a factor of production. Various different special properties of such factors of production preclude the notion of a perfect transfer of production technology from one firm to another. There is no such thing as two perfectly identical manufacturing plants in the world, even if one of them is intended to be a close replica of the other.

On the other hand, LDCs possess a vast number of social, organisational and economic characteristics which either preclude, or make highly uneconomic, any attempt at straightforwardly replicating 'from-the-shelf' technology previously used in developed countries. Among such features, we notice the following: domestic markets are smaller, rates of tariff protection are much higher, the competitive atmosphere is much weaker, distortions in technical information and market imperfections appear much stronger, shortages of skills and levels of uncertainty much more dramatic, etc., than those prevailing in developed industrial societies.

Both sets of reasons have been previously discussed in the literature and we do not need to spend much time reviewing them here. Concerning the first one, that is, peculiar features of technical knowledge and information as a factor of production, R. Nelson has, a few years back, pointed out that:

> To the extent that technologies are tacit, firm production sets are fuzzy around the edges. To the extent that imitation is not trivial, the idea of an industry wide production set the elements of which are accessible to all firms is a misleading abstraction. To the extent that technologies are not well understood, sharply defined invention possibility sets are a misleading concept and interaction between learning through R&D and learning through experience is an essential part of the invention process. These aspects – tacitness, inimitability, and low level of understanding – clearly are not orthogonal but may well go together. I have used the term 'tacit' to refer to uncertainty regarding the range of available techniques for production, and 'low understanding' to indicate lack of a reliable R&D activity; the phenomena here are very close and not readily separable in practice. Difficulties in imitation can stem from lack of explicitness about what is being imitated or lack of understanding to enable the imitator and teacher to distinguish essential from inessential elements; these aspects sound different but may be close to the same thing. However, I propose that for modelling purposes it is useful to think of three different dimensions in characterising particular technologies: explicitness, inimitability, degree of understanding.[6]

Turning now to the idiosyncratic nature of the production environment of most LDCs, it is quite clear that LDCs differ from DCs in aspects such as market size, degree of tariff protection, availability of skills, market imperfections, information distortions, etc.[7] Such differences continuously flash out specific price and non-price signals which, to a greater or lesser extent, reach the entrepreneurial community and induce particular responses. As far as technology is concerned, the response to such signals takes place on at least two different levels: on the one hand, in relation to choice of technique – that is, in connection with the technological package originally chosen by industrial firms to begin their operation in an LDC environment; on the other hand, the above-mentioned distinctive structural features of LDCs greatly affect both the rate and nature of the locally undertaken technological search efforts – that is, the generation of new technical knowledge and information. In neither case – that is, choice of original technology, and domestic technological search efforts – is the behaviour of manufacturing firms in LDCs likely to replicate actions previously undertaken by industrial firms in more developed countries.

Consider first the case regarding choice of technique. Let us begin by looking at the incidence of market size. With very few exceptions, industrial firms operating in LDCs are far smaller – between 1–10 per cent – than their counterparts in developed nations. For example, a 'representative' Latin American firm producing automobiles could produce anything between 20 and 100 thousand units per annum. A machine-tool manufacturer would produce from 100 to 500 lathes per year, whereas a petrochemical plant producing polyethylene would manufacture anywhere between 10 and 200 thousand tons per annum. Industrial firms producing similar products in mature industrial societies would normally be five to ten (or more) times larger.

Such differences in plant size induce very many differences in the technology initially chosen by any given company. Continuous-flow, highly automated technologies, which would normally be the technology of choice for a new industrial undertaking in a developed country environment, are frequently ruled out right from the beginning by firms operating in LDCs. This is so for at least two different reasons. On the one hand, such technologies normally involve a rate of output that is well beyond the size of the local market. On the other hand, such plants frequently embody a level of operational and maintenance complexity that cannot be adequately handled by the locally available engineering and technical skills.

Instead of such options, LDCs' manufacturing firms usually settle for a discontinuous technology, and for a much lower degree of automation. Moreover, in those particular cases in which continuous-flow operation is almost compulsorily enforced by prevailing engineering design habits, as in the case, for example, in the production of automobiles or autoparts, LDCs' firms usually end up with the worst of all worlds – that is, with a small continuous-flow 'line', turning out a highly diversified output mix, intended for various small individual markets. Here the firm not only picks up the highly negative effects of the much smaller plant size. It also picks up a very high incidence of down-time resulting from an abnormally diversified output mix.

The choice of a discontinuous, not highly automated technology, certainly has major consequences not only for the plant 'lay-out', the type, nature, etc. of the machinery and equipment to be employed, and the overall production organisation, but also affects the size and nature of the economies of scale which can eventually be captured by the firm, as well as the type of technological search efforts the company would find profitable to undertake through time. In other words, not only will the initial physical configuration of the plant be rather different, but also the organisation of production and the sources of efficiency growth the company can exploit through time will be dramatically at variance from those underlying the operation of comparable manufacturing plants in developed countries.

Scale is by no means the only variable on account of which the original choice of technique in LDCs is normally based on logical considerations that are fundamentally different from those underlying investment and plant-construction decisions in DCs. Lack of, or highly imperfect, subcontracting markets, also play an important role in this respect, in as much as they induce a much higher degree of vertical integration at the individual firm level.

Obviously a much higher degree of vertical integration than that in DCs has strong consequences for plant design, type of equipment and labour force to be employed, etc., as well as for market organisation.

A high 'make/buy' ratio normally means 'inhouse' provision of goods or services that are technologically dissimilar to the company's major activity (for example, a metal-mechanic plant having to produce rubber or plastic components, which demand a rather different set of scientific, engineering and production principles from those that are demanded for the production of metalmechanic products). A high degree of technological dissimilarity necessarily means lower technical specialisation, and many more difficulties concerning production planning and industrial organisation. A higher likelihood of idle capacity is to be expected in situations in which firms are forced by environmental circumstances to overextend their degree of vertical integration.

Yet a third and final set of reasons accounting for differences in original choice of technique between DCs and LDCs, is to be found in conventional factor price differentials which induce the utilisation of techniques less intensive in the use of relatively expensive production factors, raw materials and so forth.[8]

So much, then, for original choice of technique. An idiosyncratic start calls for an equally idiosyncratic path of successive improvements and technology upgrading efforts. Our next section will examine the micro and macro variables that influence the rate and nature of the domestically generated technological search efforts.

Before doing so, however, it is important to notice that the available evidence suggests that such efforts respond to a variety of objectives, among which that of lowering production costs is only one, and not necessarily the most important one. In a less competitive environment than the one prevailing in developed countries, the search for cost reductions may well be less important than other alternative strategies, such as, for example, stretching the output yields of the existing plant and equipment. Thus, the technological path followed by manufacturing firms in LDCs will most likely differ in a rather substantial way from the one described in the mainstream of the literature on induced innovation emerging from DCs' writers.[9] This is so not only for the highly specific features of local manufacturing plants, but also for the rather different competitive atmosphere in which such plants are forced to operate.

MICRO AND MACRO DETERMINANTS OF THE RATE AND NATURE OF DOMESTIC TECHNOLOGICAL SEARCH EFFORTS

Four major sets of variables act upon domestic enterprises in LDCs, affecting both the rate and direction of their technological search efforts. Such sets of determining forces are: (i) Strictly microeconomic circumstances emerging from the product and production technology originally available to them. These are firm-specific forces, mostly resulting from physical bottlenecks and imbalances in the original product design and/or plant 'lay-out'. (ii) Signals emerging from the changing competitive atmosphere prevailing in the market(s) catered for by the firm. (iii) Changes in macroeconomic parameters affecting firms in general, such as the rate of interest, the exchange rate, tariffs, etc. And, finally, (iv) new technical information emerging from the international technological frontier.

All four of these sets of forces continuously flash out specific signals that reach the entrepreneurial community and trigger off reactions on their part. The relative weight of these sets of variables obviously changes through time in a complex way, inducing firms to search in different directions or with different intensity. Let us examine each of them individually.

FIRM-SPECIFIC VARIABLES

Manufacturing plants in LDCs very seldom constitute the result of a careful and detailed production and investment programme. More often than not, product designs and plant 'lay-out' start off from highly imbalanced initial 'blue-prints', which are later on steadily upgraded and improved upon. Secondhand and self-produced equipment usually are found within the initially available machinery, while the initial product design very frequently replicates models and specifications far outmoded in the international scenario. In both such spheres – product design and production engineering – physical bottlenecks and imbalances appear rather frequently, inducing company personnel to search for tailor-made solutions. 'From-the-shelf' technical knowledge might be useful as a reference point, but scarcely 'ready-to-use'; what is needed is *ad hoc* solutions which need to be worked out once again at the company level.

The present point can be found in the received literature. March and Cyert, N. Rosenberg and others have suggested that 6 search is 'problem-oriented', in the sense that it is stimulated by a particular symptom which in itself defines the neighbourhood in which the search effort is conducted. In Rosenberg's words: 'My primary point is that most mechanical productive processes throw off signals of a sort which are both compelling and fairly obvious. Indeed, these processes, when sufficiently complex and interdependent, involve an almost compulsive formulation of problems. These problems capture a large proportion of the time and energies of those engaged in the search for improved techniques.'[10]

THE 'COMPETITIVE CLIMATE' PREVAILING IN THE SPECIFIC MARKET SUPPLIED BY THE FIRM

A second, and very important, set of forces affecting both the rate and nature of the domestic technological search efforts is the competitive climate prevailing in the particular market(s) supplied by the firm. The empirical evidence collected during the course of our case studies suggested that technological search efforts are clearly influenced, both in their rate and in their nature, by the dynamics of the market's competitive atmosphere. Monopolistic situations have been seen to be relatively more associated with technological search efforts of the 'output-stretching' variety. By the time the monopolistic advantage evolves into an oligopolistic confrontation, product-differentiation search efforts, as well as a stronger interest in cost-reducing innovations are likely to develop as well. Contrariwise, other things being equal, more competitive environments have been observed to lead to cost-reducing technological search efforts as well as to product-differentiation strategies.

It is important to notice here that as much as individual firms change through time in organisational structure, in the ratio of skilled to unskilled personnel, in the size and complexity of the equipment and production technology they can handle, etc., markets also experience significant changes in structure and competitive atmosphere. 'In-house' technological search efforts closely reflect the evolving nature of the market's competitive climate.

MACROECONOMIC DETERMINANTS OF THE TECHNOLOGICAL SEARCH EFFORTS

We have thus far mentioned the role of micro and market-specific variables in inducing particular technological search efforts on the part of manufacturing firms in LDCs.

It can be scarcely surprising to know that firms also react to changes in macroeconomic parameters. Magnitude of such changes and company's degree of perception seem to be crucial determinants of the pattern of reaction. The following relationships have been observed to prevail:

(1) An increase in the cost of capital equipment very often induces entrepreneurs to postpone major investment decisions. Simultaneously, output-stretching technological search efforts become more likely.

Conversely, a lower cost of capital increases the internal rate-of-return of a given investment project, thus enhancing the likelihood of the firm modernising its plant on the basis of new equipment. Anticipated plant-scrap decisions as well as over-extensions of the life-cycle of outmoded plants have both been detected during the course of our field work, resulting from government policies affecting the actual cost of capital as perceived by the entrepreneur.

(2) A rapid rate of demand expansion – resulting, for example, from different policy actions related to aggregate demand management – will most probably trigger off favourable expectations among entrepreneurs and therefore induce optimistic investment programmes. A buoyant business 'climate' will probably reduce the pay-off of search efforts of the output-stretching variety, making the physical expansion of capacity more likely.

(3) The rate of interest also has a strong influence upon technological behaviour. An increase in the rate of interest, other things being

equal, can be expected to induce search efforts directed towards the reduction of the production cycle. Such efforts could be of the product-engineering sort – simplification of product design, standardisation, etc.; but could also involve process-engineering aspects – for example, reduction of handling-time as between 'stations' of a discontinuous process plant; or production-planning questions – such as, say, a more adequate management of inventories of raw materials and components.

Other such examples of macroeconomic forces acting both upon the rate and nature of the local technological search efforts undertaken by any given firm are by no means difficult to find. In particular, cost and availability of R&D and engineering personnel, government support to an individual company's engineering efforts, etc., seem to be specially important when we want to understand both the size and composition of any given firm's technological search budget.

A fourth, and final, set of forces influencing firm behaviour in the search for new technical knowledge and information emerges from the scientific and technological 'state of the art' and its world-wide changes through time. Let us briefly look at it.

TECHNICAL KNOWLEDGE AND INFORMATION EMERGING FROM THE
INTERNATIONAL 'STATE OF THE ART' FRONTIER

The rate of expansion of the 'best practice' technological frontier, and the legal, economic and technical ease of imitation of the emerging new knowledge, appear as crucial forces affecting in a direct, as well as in an indirect, way the technological behaviour of any given company.

Direct influences come from intra-industry technical progress. Various different agents in any given trade have as their responsibility that of 'producing' new technical knowledge: 'engineering departments of participating firms, public R&D laboratories, process engineering and consulting firms, etc. Part of the emerging new knowledge is secret and remains so for an indefinite period of time. Yet another part finds its way into the public domain through professional journals, trade fairs, plant visits, etc.; also through patent files.

Indirect influences derive from changes in science and technology in general. Advances in, say, fundamental physics, metallurgy or biology which eventually find their way into better machines or new product designs, etc. belong in this category. The current eruption of CAD/ CAM systems across the industrial spectrum constitutes one of the more impressive forms of indirect influence upon company behaviour, this time deriving from developments in microelectronics, solid state physics, computer sciences, and so forth.

Concerning both categories – direct and indirect new technical knowledge and information – the greater or lesser extent of company exposure to new information as well as the ability and skills of each firm's technical personnel to pursue the most promising leads within the broad spectrum of ongoing events, will jointly determine the relative weight and influence of these variables upon company technological behaviour. Channels for the reception of technical information must be set up and operated, and the inflowing information needs to be decoded with a view to the particular importance attributed by the company to the emerging new knowledge. Both these actions are highly firm-specific and will to a large extent decide the degree of a company's technological updateness.[11]

Having thus far examined each one of the four different sets of variables influencing both the rate and direction of the domestically performed technological search efforts, it is important to notice at this point that the relative role and incidence of each one of them is certainly due to change over time. Periods of overall macroeconomic stability, steady expansion of demand and low uncertainty will presumably induce firms to pay more attention to company-specific variables, searching for a more balanced utilisation of the available plant production capacity, for a more thorough de-bugging of product designs, etc. Contrariwise, periods of higher macro instability probably reduce the relative pay-off of domestic technological search activities and simultaneously increase the expected benefits of alternative courses of action.

After briefly dealing with the micro and macro variables that influence both the rate and nature of individual firm efforts in the field of domestic technical knowledge generation, let us now examine in more detail the structure of the learning process itself which obtains at the company level as a consequence of such efforts.

THE SEQUENTIAL NATURE OF THE LEARNING PROCESS

Technological search efforts in the area of product design seem to appear rather early in the technical history of many of the manufacturing firms examined throughout this programme. Only a few years after start-up, firms seem to begin developing 'in- house' technical skills related to product engineering. On the basis of such skills they, first, adapt and improve the original design and, second, start playing product differentiation strategies as part of their competitive behaviour. The 'life-cycle' of industrial products as well as the relatively low incentive to search for cost-reduction innovations, given the rather extreme degree of protection granted to industrial firms, appear as major explanations of the fact that product design engineering capabilities seem to develop at a somewhat earlier stage. We have observed that firms begin with such search efforts long before they can exhibit significant technical strength in other technological areas. Prototypes and plant experimentation for product design purposes seem to appear on the stage much before time-and-motion studies, or other such tools of production engineering and production planning.

The previous statement should not be taken to mean that technological search in areas related to process engineering are entirely absent during the initial years of a firm's life. Rudimentary forms of search in the field of productivity and organisation are almost invariably present during the 'start-up' period. Also, substitution of one raw material for another, the introduction of secondhand or self-produced machinery, etc. necessarily call for some limited amount of search concerning both the production process and the organisation of production.

However, a certain discontinuity could be uncovered in the technical history of most of the firms examined by the present research programme. Such discontinuity, which has frequently involved a major change in attitude concerning process engineering and production planning activities, and was associated with a new approach towards questions of quality control, limits of tolerance, preventive maintenance, and other such technical matters, was related both to a significant reorganisation of the firm's administrative structure (with the creation of a number of new departments such as Quality Control, Research and Development, Tooling, etc.), and to a major increase in the size and complexity of the firm's output mix. These changes frequently demand a rather different way of handling Inventories, Machine Loading Programmes, Quality Control, Transport Operations within the plant, etc. Process engineering and organisation skills generated in an informal way during the initial years of company operation are found to be insufficient at that point, thus necessitating a radical change in organisational structure.

A new approach towards engineering efforts frequently sets in after such discontinuity, a rapid change being noticeable in the ratio of indirect to direct labour inputs.

Summarising, our studies suggest that (i) product design efforts tend to develop rather early in company history, only to be followed at a later stage by process engineering and by production planning engineering capabilities; (ii) more competitive environments seem to induce a stronger drive in the direction of product differentiation and cost-reducing search efforts; (iii) on the contrary, monopolistic market situations seem to induce search efforts of the output-stretching variety rather than search activities related to quality improvement and/or product differentiation.

Obviously we should not take the above-mentioned 'trends' in a restrictive way, as indicating that always, and as a matter of logical necessity, firms behave as hereby suggested. There is nothing compulsory leading monopolistic firms into output-stretching innovations and more competitive ones into product differentiation efforts. Cases can be found where such 'trends' do not obtain, and yet our generalisation seems to rest on rather strong empirical foundations.

A sequence of somewhat similar features seems to underlie both the 'product cycle' literature and the dynamic model of company behaviour developed by J. M. Utterback and W. J. Abernathy in various recent papers.[12] A point not yet explored in the recent literature is that both the rate and specific nature of the technological learning sequences seem strongly to depend upon nationality, size of company and general macroeconomic atmosphere underlying firm operation. Subsidiaries of multinational firms can sometimes do without extended product design departments in as much as they can rely more heavily than local firms upon pre-existing designs from their respective headquarters. Similarly, large firms appear to be more capable than small firms of financing large and specialised engineering teams in all of the three areas under examination – that is, product design, production engineering and production planning and organisation. Finally, an expanding economy characterised by buoyant expectations about the future seems to be more conducive to long-term R&D investment than a contracting economy that quite frequently sets into motion more cautionary strategies.

Having so far examined various idiosyncratic features of the technological behaviour of LDCs' manufacturing plants – that is, their choice of original technique, their particular technological search trajectory, the rate and nature of the learning sequences involved in their evolutionary operation, etc. – we now turn to a set of more general analytical and policy questions which our results seem to illuminate.

PROTECTION, LEARNING SEQUENCES AND THE INFANT-INDUSTRY ARGUMENT

The material so far presented describes a typical enterprise and a competitive scene far different from conventional textbook descriptions. In the neoclassical tradition:

> The firm is the principal agent of production. It transforms inputs into outputs in accordance with a certain production function. The production function, which defines the maximum product attainable with a certain amount of inputs, is determined by the state of technological knowledge. The latter is public, or something like it must be assumed in models that describe the production function of an industry or of an economy as a whole. Enterprises select a point in their production functions such that the rate of earnings is the maximum, given the demand for the product and the factor supply conditions. As a rule, these markets are assumed to be perfectly competitive, so that the enterprise treats prices as parameters . . . over time the product increases as the inputs increase and the firms move through successive production functions when technology progresses . . . Obviously there are strong assumptions behind all this. The image of the firm and of the market is extremely stylized and leaves little room for entrepreneurial incapacity . . . for oligopolistic confrontation. Technological progress, even when it is accepted as a basic factor of growth is treated very simply and Schumpeter's proposition that technological progess and competitive equilibrium cannot coexist is completely ignored.[13]

Unlike so stylised a microeconomic world, our empirical evidence suggests that the industrial sector we have examined throughout the present programme is characterised by: (i) disequilibria, and periods of 'digestion' of such disequilibria, which are relatively longer or shorter depending upon the general macroeconomic context; (ii) firms that are highly innovative and improve their relative position in the market, while others fail to innovate and lose ground, or simply disappear; (iii) entrepreneurs that are better informed and financed than others; (iv) different technological strategies, even within the same market – firms that systematically innovate as opposed to others that systematically imitate; (v) technological and engineering teams of different quality and skills acting in different competing firms; (vi) radical changes over time in the relative position of firms within the market as well as in the competitive climate prevailing in it, etc.

Whereas, in the neoclassical world, as R. Nelson tells us in the previously cited article: 'few interesting issues can be explored or solved by studying the behaviour of individual firms', in the world described by the ideas presented so far, the issues that must be examined by studying the differential behaviour between firms are many and complex.

In short, the neoclassical toolbox appears to us to be far too simplistic to help in understanding entrepreneurial behaviour in the Latin American metalworking field. Several different 'types' of firm within the sector – that is, family enterprises, subsidiaries of MNCs, public companies, etc. – with different objectives, organisation and constraints, with different access to technical information and factor markets, as well as a competitive atmosphere that changes over time, together with a macroeconomic scenario loaded with imperfections, physical scarcities, etc. seem to us to be essential features of reality that need to be taken into account for the purpose of further exploring the expansion path of this industry.

On the basis of this reappraisal of the conceptual framework in which to approach the long-term expansion process of the Latin American metalworking sector, we shall now return to the subject of technological change, its origins, nature and consequences. In other words, given the observed differences among company types within the sector, and also given the type of competition and the evolutionary nature of the growth path of a typical metalworking firm, let us now return to the old but still unsettled question of protection, dynamic comparative advantages, and the pattern of industrialisation. In our view, the empirical evidence emerging from the present research programme enables us to say something new about the extent and purpose of protection policy, as well as about the criteria with which the public authority could monitor the maturity process of an 'infant' firm or industry.

Although the received literature does not prove that the pattern of industrialisation is in some way explained by the pattern of protection, there is little doubt that protection *per se* has induced the process of industrial development. J. Bhagwati and T. N. Srinivasan clearly express this idea in their well-known article on 'Trade Policy and Development' when they say: 'Although it is true that to protect the manufacturing sector as a whole is to support the industrial development of the LDCs, it does not follow that the pattern of industrial production is explained by the pattern of protection, as this is measured in the LDCs' (these authors refer to the case studies on effective protection made by the NBER Project in 1975 and 1976, which cover Turkey, Israel, the Philippines, Ghana, South Korea, India, Egypt, Colombia and Chile).[14]

Once it is accepted that protection eventually induces the creation of an industry where there formerly was no industry, several new questions arise. They include: On what conditions is it justified to protect in order to promote the development of a new industrial sector? How much and for how long should we protect? To achieve what? All these questions take us back to the infant-industry argument as it originally appeared to J. S. Mill and from there onwards in all the classical school.[15] We shall base the following analysis on two types of writings: on the one hand, those associated with the theoretical case for protection derived from the classical economists; on the other hand, the empirical evidence collected during the present research programme, which will be used as a point of reference for the discussion that follows.

Under what conditions is it justified to protect in order to promote the development of an industrial branch? The reply given by Mill is: 'In order to "naturalize" a foreign industry.'

> But this industry should be perfectly adapted to the circumstances of the country. This country should preferably be a young and expanding country and protection should be temporary. The principle is valid when the only difference between the country in which industry already exists and the country that desires to acquire lies in the experience and the level of training of its citizens so that the superiority of the country is only a matter of the acquisition of such experience or level of training, for which it is assumed that there are no obstacles other than the cost of learning itself.[16]

What is meant by an industry's 'perfect adaptation' to the circumstances of the recipient society? According to Mill's argument: a country that accepts the new productive branch should eventually become more suitable for this activity than the society that originally practised it.

The initial sections of this paper have provided us with ample information concerning the main features – technological, organisational, and other – of the industry concerning whose naturalisation in Latin

America we are speaking of, that is, the metalworking sector. We know, for example, that within metalworking production there are areas in which production organisation is continuous, in 'line', and designed to produce large quantities of standard items such as, for example, automobiles. Side by side with the above we also have metal-working production organised in discontinuous workshops, producing small lots of quasi-standard items or even individual orders, custom-made for a specific client. We also know that between these two forms of production organisation, there is an enormous difference in economies of scale, in the relative incidence of down-time, in the nature of the relative factor inputs, etc. On the other hand, we have learned that the metalworking industry is composed both of a large group of family-type enterprises, as well as of domestic subsidiaries of multinational enterprises that operate on the basis of a technological and information package received from the respective parent company, to some extent adapted to the conditions of the host country through locally performed engineering efforts.

It is this sort of industry – and not a hypothetical 'industry' emerging from the neo-classical toolbox – which is being examined in terms of the protection argument. We should therefore ask ourselves: on what conditions can such an industry become 'perfectly adapted' to the circumstances of the host societies, so that once the cost of training and technological learning has been covered – that is, once the domestic technological capacity has been developed – the resulting industrial firms can continue to operate in a competitive environment without requiring additional support?

The material collected during the course of this research programme has enabled us to describe in an evolutionary framework the expansion path of a typical metalworking plant. We believe that, on the basis of such a framework it should be possible now to give a concrete meaning – and therefore a useful one for the purposes of public policy – to the concept of domestic technological learning – as the received theory so requires – by a particular industrial firm (or branch of production). We have argued that a successful learning sequence is one that permits the firm to complete the creation and strengthening of the whole set of plant engineering skills – that is, product design engineering skills, process engineering skills and production organisation and planning engineering skills. A number of studies show that a complete learning sequence of this sort calls for the incorporation into the firm of a large number of professional and technical personnel of different specialities and training levels, ranging from design engineers to time-

and-motion specialists. The same studies show that two or more decades have often been necessary for a given firm to complete the cycle.

Now, neither all the countries studied in the framework of this programme nor all the organisational forms made possible by metalworking technology appear to have been equally successful in completing the above-mentioned learning sequence within the Latin American scenario. There are, on the one hand, those metalworking industries in which production is continuous, organised 'in line', both in DCs and in Latin America. Within this subgroup of metalworking industries the firms examined throughout our exploration exhibit an extremely uneven performance when looking across nationalities, Brazilian companies being much more successful than those operating in, say, Argentina or Colombia. On the other hand, we find metal working plants organised under the form of a discontinuous array of 'shops', producing small batches of quasi-standard goods or even individual orders. This form of production organisation is structurally different from the foregoing one, and therefore the analysis of whether or not it is worth protecting it in order to permit the gestation of a domestic learning sequence should be carried out by using other variables and arguments.

Let us first look at the case of continuous flow, in 'line' production of metalworking products. Of the several cases of this sort studied in the programme, two Brazilian firms stand out as those that most closely support the case for protection. They are Romi and Metal Leve, respectively producing conventional lathes and pistons. Both these firms have (i) moved towards international plant scales, (ii) dramatically expanded their R&D efforts, significantly approaching the international technological frontier, and (iii) increased their exports, actively competing in DCs' markets.

Three factors appear to have helped the above-mentioned firms to achieve a greater relative success than equivalent firms in, say, Argentina. On the one hand, because of the large size and dynamism of the Brazilian domestic market, these firms could count on at least two decades of a large protected domestic market upon which to base their expansion. On the other hand, and perhaps as the consequence of the foregoing, in both cases they developed a clear propensity towards the installation of international plant scales – a propensity that is absent in most other countries of the region; this has permitted both firms to capture large economies of scale. Finally, it is striking that in both cases they operate in industrial fields in which the world's technological frontier has not experienced very dramatic jumps in recent years, thus permitting a gradual narrowing of the relative gap that separated them from international technical standards.

In other words, in those cases in which simultaneously the size of the domestic market has permitted the erection of plants of international scale – that do not have disadvantages of size *vis-à-vis* establishments in the developed world – and in which the world's technological frontier has not experienced significant leaps over time, a public policy of protection, systematically maintained over several decades, seems to have successfully induced the development of highly competititve national enterprises based upon a sound indigenous technological foundation.

It should be noted that, as the traditional infant-industry argument requires,[17] our own analysis of the previous paragraphs presupposes as given the state of the art at the international level. If we accept that the state of the art is in fact constantly changing – in the above cases, numerically controlled lathes partially substituting conventional lathes in metalworking processes and the same being true for pistons made from new alloys – the situation becomes somewhat more complex and calls for a dynamic analysis that explicitly incorporates such changes in the 'state of the art'. On the one hand, if the new product is not a perfect substitute of the old one – that is, if enough demand for the mature product is likely to continue – its future production need not encounter difficulties even if the 'state of the art' changes quite significantly. In other words, the local firm could continue to exploit its achieved technological learning even within the framework of a mature product. In terms of our previous Brazilian example, while the demand (national or international) for lathes and pistons of the conventional type persists, we believe that the justification of protection continues to be a valid one.

A different dynamic question appears if sooner or later the mature product is due to disappear, being completely substituted by the new one. In this case, the domestic technological capabilities arising from the production of the mature product may, or may not, be the most appropriate ones for successfully following (or even leading) the movement of the international technological frontier. To follow the frontier may well require a different set of technological skills, which the production of the mature product may not have provided (or even required), or may have done so only in a partial and insufficient way.

Something of this sort may actually be happening in one of the previously mentioned Brazilian firms and its transition from conventional lathes – an area in which the firm has given evidence of having successfully completed its learning sequence – to numerically controlled lathes; the company has now felt the need of signing a licensing agreement with a large multinational firm, which is due to supply technical knowledge in electronic fields which the previous – entirely mechanical – production experience did not in fact provide. As we can see, the case is somewhat more complicated than the one argued by classical economists. Should society take upon itself to protect a second, or even a third, round of indigenous learning in order to prevent the technological gap from widening once again, or should the returns from the first learning sequence finance the dynamics of the evolving process? This is a major theoretical and policy issue which has thus far received little attention in the literature.

None of the other large-scale 'in-line' metalworking plants in our sample can be regarded as equally successful examples. In each and every one of them, we have uncovered different forms of indigenous technological learning. However, and in spite of that, they are all far from constituting examples of successful naturalisation of metalworking production in the Latin American environment.

The situation changes significantly when we leave large-scale, continuous-flow production and move on to examine 'shops' that produce in small batches or custom-made orders.

Let us first take the case of individual order production, which is carried on in plants of a discontinuous, 'shop-wise' organisation both in DCs and in LDCs. We have seen in previous pages of this paper that this type of metalworking plant turns out a much more heterogeneous group of products, is less subject to conventional economies of scale, and enjoys a certain degree of 'natural' protection which arises from the idiosyncratic nature of the customer. It is in such sort of framework that we must examine whether or not it is worth protecting metalworking firms of this kind in the expectation of 'naturalising' them to the Latin American environment.

While market size appeared as the crux of the matter in large-scale continuous-flow metalworking operation, here 'in-house' engineering design capabilities and availability of modern and updated numerical control equipment become crucial; also, the human skills adequate to operate and maintain this type of machinery. We are speaking, for example, of metalworking firms capable of producing complex equipment for nuclear or hydroelectric plants, large turbines, generators, heavy boilers, etc.; establishments of this sort must have significant engineering design capabilities and the possibility of handling and machining parts and components of great complexity and size.

The likelihood of successfully 'naturalising' metalworking plants of this sort in Latin American countries depends to a critical degree upon the availability of a large number of highly skilled technicians and engineers, as well as specialists in 'software', computing sciences and the like.[18] Countries like Argentina, Brazil, Mexico and Colombia are those in which metalworking plants of this sort have already appeared and where the likelihood of their future successful development seems brighter.

A further observation appears to be justified at this point. The main customer for metalworking products emerging from this type of metalworking firm is the public sector through its various infrastructure works. It is the public sector that should provide stable long-term demands capable of keeping in operation project-engineering departments of sufficient size and level of specialisation as well as stable R&D and production programmes, which would ensure close-to-capacity utilisation of the available skills and machinery. This is an issue of public policy that should be carefully considered by Latin American governments that are interested in sustaining a healthy learning sequence in this type of metalworking firm.

A third type of metalworking industry, the advisability of whose installation in the Latin American context warrants examination, is that in which production in the region is organised in small lots and under the form of 'shops', while the production of developed countries increasingly tends to be organised in 'line'. As in the foregoing cases, it is worthwhile evaluating the extent to which it is worth protecting these types of ventures in order to bring about their 'naturalisation' to the local environment.

Two different facts seem to play an important role in this case, in addition to conventional relative factor price differentials that can *per se,* partially or totally, offset the underlying initial scale disadvantages.[19] On the one hand, we have already pointed towards the existence of a certain amount of natural protection in many metalworking items such as, for example, a machine tool or a harvester. These products usually demand a relatively important effort of technological adaptation to the domestic environment, this obviously accounting for a certain advantage in favour of the local producer who carries out the adaptation efforts. On the other hand, in recent years, considerable progress has been made in the Latin American region in the application of techniques and methods of production planning and industrial organisation like the study of 'families' of parts, or the reorganisation of plant 'lay-out' in 'cells' or 'technology groups', which make it possible to capture significant economies of scale even within the framework of a discontinuous-production organisation.[20]

In certain specific metalworking branches, the simultaneous impact of a certain amount of 'natural protection' plus a proper exploitation of economies of scale attained through the use of the above-mentioned production planning and organisation techniques, may result in a successful 'naturalisation' of metalworking plants producing in small lots, even in fields where DC plants operate in large scale, with highly automated production 'lines'.

Of course, there is no logical necessity for this to be so. Since we are here speaking about a relative difference between two different production functions – that is, that of a plant organised in 'line', which is the one operated in DCs and the one corresponding to a discontinuous, 'shop-wise' organisation, as is employed in LDCs – the actual difference appears to be a matter of empirical nature capable of being significantly different across industries. The feasibility of successfully 'naturalising' these types of industries in the Latin American environment cannot be ruled out *a priori*. Conversely, where the scale differential is really large, an attempt to force the naturalisation of industry will lead to clearly suboptimal situations from the social point of view.

To sum up, having shown that, on the one hand, metalworking industries belong in at least three different types of industrial organisations – in-line production, small-lot production and to-order production – and, on the other, that the feasibility of 'naturalising' a specific type of metalworking industry by inducing its installation and development through protection depends upon (i) the relative gap between the production function employed by DCs' and LDCs' plants, (ii) the rate of technological learning and productivity growth attained by both DCs' and LDCs' plants, (iii) conventional factor price differentials, (iv) the degree of natural protection enjoyed by the product, etc., our empirical evidence seems to support the idea that, except for specific examples inherent in the Brazilian case, large-scale 'line' production of standardised products operates in the Latin American region behind international standards. Conversely, the relative success appears to be much greater in metalworking branches that produce individual orders, and small series, particularly where the underlying disadvantages are counteracted by significant domestic engineering efforts in areas of product design and production planning and organisation.

Perhaps the most important conclusion emerging from the present discussion is that no general statement concerning public policy in the field of protection can be made on the basis of a simplistic specification of the production function. 'Tailor-made' policy actions appear to be needed that would closely reflect the specificity of the learning situation of each particular form of production organisation.

NOTES

1. In the preparation of this paper the author makes use of ideas and research results obtained by him and his fellow colleagues from the IDB/ECLA/IDRC/UNDP Research Programme on Scientific and Technological Development in Latin America which he directed from 1975 through 1982. The use of the above-mentioned material is kindly acknowledged.
2. A. B. Atkinson and J. Stiglitz, 'A New View of Technological Change', *Economic Journal,* September 1969.
3. N. Rosenberg, *Perspectives on Technology* (Cambridge University Press, 1976).
4. R. Nelson and S. Winter, *An Evolutionary Theory of Economic Change* (Cambridge, Mass.: Belknap Press of Harvard University Press, 1982).
5. J. M. Utterback and W. J. Abernathy, 'A Dynamic Model of Process and Product Innovation', *Omega,* vol. 3, no. 6 (1975). Also, 'Innovation and the Evolving Structure of the Firm', Working Paper of the Graduate School of Business Administration, (Harvard University, June 1975).
6. R. Nelson, 'Innovation and Economic Development. Theoretical Retrospect and Prospect', Working Paper no. 31, IDB/ECLA/UNDP Research Programme on Science and Technology (Buenos Aires, April 1979).
7. For a more detailed treatment of this topic, the reader can see, S. Teitel, 'Towards an Understanding of Technical Change in Semi-Industrialised Countries', Working Paper no. 34, IDB/ECLA/UNDP Research Programme on Science and Technology (Buenos Aires, April 1979) revised version.
8. That conventional factor price differentials tend to play a less crucial role than market size and degree of vertical integration, has also been pointed out by other researchers in recent years. See, for example, S. Morley and G. W. Smith, 'Adaptation of Foreign Firms to Labour Abundance in Brazil', in J. H. Street and D. D. James (eds), *Technological Progress in Latin America. The Prospects of Overcoming Dependence* (Boulder, Colorado: Westview Press, 1979).
9. A clear-cut example of the present point is the pathbreaking study by W. E. G. Salter, which greatly influenced a whole generation of European researchers working in the field of innovation and productivity growth. See, from the above-mentioned author, *Productivity and Technical Change* (Cambridge University Press, 1960).
10. Rosenberg, *Perspectives on Technology.*
11. K. Arrow, *The Limits of Organization* (New York: N. W. Norton, 1974).
12. These two authors write, 'The technological development of a plant will be evolutionary in nature and it will proceed from conditions which are described as fluid towards a highly developed specific state'. Also, product-cycle authors seem to have such a conceptual framework in

mind. See W. J. Abernathy, 'Production Process Structure and Technological Change', *Decision Science,* vol. 7 (1976) p. 607. Also, from the same author, *The Productivity Dilemma: Roadblock to Innovation in the Automobile Industry* (Baltimore: Johns Hopkins University, 1978).

13. R. Nelson, 'Research on Productivity Growth and Productivity Differences. Dead Ends and New Departures', *Journal of Economic Literature,* September 1981, p. 1031.

14. J. Bhagwati and T. N. Srinivasan, 'Trade Policy and Development', *World Bank Reprint Series,* no. 59, reprinted from R. Dornbusch and J. Frenkel (eds), *International Economic Policy. Theory and Evidence* (Baltimore: Johns Hopkins University Press, 1978).

15. R. Soifer, 'Some Aspects of Trade, Development and Protection', mimeo, (London, 1978).

16. J. S. Mill, *Essays on Some Unsettled Questions of Political Economy* (London, 1844).

17. M. C. Kemps, 'The Mill-Bastable Infant Industry Dogma', *Journal of Political Economy,* February, 1960.

18. It should be noted that a contemporary trend in metalworking plants of this sort in the developed world is to introduce computer-aided design (CAD) systems that substantially modify the work of the design office and substitute microelectronic technology for skilled design personnel. This raises a number of interesting questions relating, on the one hand, to the convenience of substituting capital for labour in countries in which different relative factor prices prevail. On the other hand, the incorporation of CAD raises questions relating to the design time required by any given engineering team dealing with new product development, and the effect this has upon the competitive edge of a given firm. Finally, it should be borne in mind that CAD is beginning to spread in Latin America, as we are told by R. Kaplinsky in a recent study: see, 'The Technological Gap between DCs and LDCs. Computer Aided Design' (Institute of Development Studies, University of Sussex, 1981) mimeo; and 'Trade of Technology. Who, What, Where and When?' (Institute of Development Studies, University of Sussex, 1982) mimeo.

19. H. Pack, 'The Capital Goods Sector in LDCs. A Survey', mimeo (Washington, 1979).

20. E. A. Arn, *Group Technology* (New York: Springler-Verlag, 1975).

III. The International Economy and Technological Capability

Trade in Technology – Who, What, Where and When?

Raphael Kaplinsky

I GETTING TECHNICAL CHANGE IN PERSPECTIVE

INTRODUCTION

It is tedious, and unnecessary, to dwell on the relatively recent accept-ance by economic theory that technical change is an important factor underlying the rate and nature of accumulation, and that it is not some-thing exogenous to the economy, arising as manna from heaven. If anything, the balance has swung too far in favour of highlighting the role which technological capability *per se* can play in stimulating economic activity in analyses which fail to situate technical change within relations of production. However, in my view, it is not only with respect to the failure to locate technical change in a political economic context that much of contemporary research in this area falls down. Equally disturbing is the ahistoricism underlying many of the ana-lytical and presumptive conclusions which are drawn from various empirical studies.

There is now a burgeoning literature on the extent to which some LDCs have managed to develop a technological capability which is re-flected in the changed nature of their manufactured exports. In the context of earlier analyses of technological dependence in import-substituting industrialisation and the limited spill-over from TNC-dominated export-led growth, this emerging phenomenon has been surprising. The key to its understanding (as argued in the pioneering studies of Katz, Lall and O'Brien, among others) lies in a specifica-tion of what is meant by R&D and technical change. Thus Lall, for example, is at pains to contrast the Indian experience with the

> unfortunate tendency in the innovation literature of the Schum-peterian school to concentrate on discrete jumps in technology as

the major source of technical change. This 'breakthrough syndrome' has detracted from a proper appreciation of minor changes made in the process of diffusion, imitation and adaptation.

Lall, in summing up the implications of his study on Indian engineering exports, puts himself firmly in this camp of incremental, but substantive, technical-change theorists.

In brief, the manifestation of technological activity by developing countries in the form of technology exports has important and sweeping implications for theory and policy. It induces us to look further to 'evolutionary' theories of innovations for explanations of technical change. It challenges a general belief that developing countries have little capacity for independent technical development, and it calls for a rethinking of conventional theories of trade which assign poor countries a role at the bottom of the skill and technology ladder. (p. 6)

It seems to me that these various studies, often starting from different positions, are drawn to the common position reflected in Lall's comments. This is that despite contrasting circumstances (protection, foreign investment, integration in world markets, expansion of education systems, etc.), a significant number of LDCs have begun to climb up the technological ladder and to close the gap between 'world technology' and 'domestic technology'. The prescriptive conclusion is that what is needed is more of the same, a bandwagon recognised by many other LDCs.[1]

The purpose of this paper is to introduce a wider historical dimension into the discussion. The 'closing' of the technological gap, I will argue, reflected the upswing of the most recent long-wave cycle: as its heartland technology begins to diffuse downstream in the rationalising phase of the cycle, so the technological gap between 'world technology' and 'LDC technology'[2] will begin to reopen. At the same time 'LDC technological capability', with an indisputable momentum of its own, will be generating techniques that are increasingly inappropriate for DC environments, but highly relevant to other LDCs. The consequence of this, in the context of a world of narrowing trade-frontiers, will be to change 'the who', 'the what' and 'the where' of trade in technology. But I believe that, without a more historical dimension than most contemporary studies are blessed with, the significance of these altered structures will be mistaken.

LONG-WAVE CYCLES, HEARTLAND TECHNOLOGIES AND
MICROELECTRONICS

Unfortunately constraints of space limit this discussion of long-wave
cycles, heartland technologies and microelectronics.[3] The essential
points are as follows:

(1) Reviewing the last three hundred years of economic history, his-
    torians have observed a series of long-wave cycles of approxi-
    mately fifty years' duration. Each of these is characterised by an
    expansionary upswing and a downswing of economic contraction.
(2) Various explanations are offered to explain the existence of these
    cycles; a particularly convincing one is that each cycle is charac-
    terised by the development and diffusion of a major heartland
    technology. In the most recent cycle microelectronics have played
    the role of the heartland technology.
(3) The latest post Second World War cycle was characterised by an
    expansionary upswing which passed through its peak in the 1971–3
    period – the downswing speeded up at the turn of the decade. LDC
    economic progress (particularly with regard to manufactured ex-
    ports), and the closing of the technological gap between LDCs and
    DCs, was a phenomenon of the upswing. As the world economy
    becomes engulfed in the downswing, so LDC export-led growth is
    threatened with the diffusion of microelectronics to DC industry
    reopening the gap in technology.

II. A REOPENING OF THE TECHNOLOGICAL GAP

There is no need, here, to recount the progress made at a
macroeconomic level by individual LDCs in moving up the technological ladder in the pre-microelectronic era[4] (in a later section I will draw
out progress made at a specific sectoral level in a particular LDC). As
pointed out in section 1, this has led some observers to conclude that
there has been a narrowing of the technological gap between 'world'
and 'LDC' technology. In this section two sets of observations will be
made. First, as illustrated by a particular sector (computer-aided design), the gains occurring from the introduction of electronics into
established industries are substantial; and the evidence suggests that
these new technologies are diffusing unevenly in the world economy.
Second, the emergence of automation technologies is dependent upon

the widespread diffusion of electronics in a series of separate activities; and the synergies that are involved point to the importance of systems gains. These two sets of observations will be used to illustrate my two basic contentions that the technological gap between DCs and (almost all) LDCs will reopen in the coming decade, and that there will be an increasing trend towards the separation of DC technology and LDC technology.

COMPUTER-AIDED DESIGN: AN EXAMPLE OF THE GAINS ACCRUING FROM THE USE OF MICROELECTRONICS[5]

The technology
CAD is a particularly good example of a software intensive industry. Building on a fairly standard set of microelectronic hardware (predominantly minicomputers) and peripheral components (television screens, computer memory, drawing devices and digitising boards)[6] systems are available to undertake a wide range of tasks to assist designers and draughtspersons in their work. The price of these systems starts from around $30,000 for a single-terminal system which is only suitable for drawing, to around $1.5m for a 30-terminal system which provides both a wide variety of analytical applications programmes and a capability to undertake numerous, unrelated batch processing tasks such as payrolls and customer billing. Of these prices, around 30 per cent is hardware; the rest comprises overheads and a considerable input of software.

The growth of this sector has been quite remarkable. Having reached around $80m in 1976, the sector 'took off' with the value of output reaching around $1b in 1980. Projections of sales value for 1984 are between $4b and $8b. By comparison, the projection for global sales of robots is only $2b by 1990, and only $4b for colour TVs in the USA in 1984.

Benefits arising from the use of CAD[7]
It is particularly difficult to assess precisely the benefits arising from the use of CAD.[8] The most we can do in this study is to illustrate the types of benefits that individual users have realised and attempt to classify these in some preliminary way. On the basis of an interview conducted with users in the UK and the USA it is believed that the benefits arising from the use of CAD can be classified into three major areas, namely CAD as a draughting tool (that is, the choice of technique), CAD as a design tool (that is, both the choice of technique and its influence on

products) and the downstream benefits that it allows (that is, CAD as a key to systems gains). We will briefly discuss each of these in turn as well as a series of other benefits relevant to the impact of electronics on LDCs.

CAD as a draughting tool A number qf users visited had actually computed the overall average productivity of their CAD systems. On average, most of these users were realising productivity gains of over 3:1 over manual systems. Given the sorts of productivity ratios observed, the costs of using CAD equipment and the salaries of draughtspersons, it is possible to compute some of the economic benefits arising from the use of CAD. One US user in the aerospace/ defence sector had undertaken a detailed internal study of matching CAD and manual systems involving an equivalent workload of 43 persons–years of manual-draughting in 1980. Using the productivity ratios generated in this study (2.5:1 in 1979 and 3.32:1 in 1980), and the costs of using turnkey CAD systems which were primarily purchased for design rather than draughting (and were hence more expensive than low-cost draughting-aids), the economics of choice are as follows. With the 1980 productivity ratio of 3.32:1 and working on a double-shift basis, the payback period was less than 10 months. Thus, given the 1980 productivity ratio and the cost of the CAD equipment, it would pay to use CAD equipment when gross salary costs (that is, including overheads) exceed $10,000 per annum. Yet these calculations – derived from actual observation – arise from the use of expensive CAD design equipment, rather than the emerging low-cost basic draughting tools.[9] These financial benefits which we have calculated only cover savings attributed to the productivity of designers and draughtspeople. However, there are a range of other financial benefits which arise from better-quality drawings, and drawings which have fewer errors. For example, certain drawings are characteristically revised eight to twelve times – in manual offices this implies a messy and error-prone product; with CAD these problems are largely removed. Almost all of the users visited felt that the benefit of more accurate drawings was one of the major advantages of its use.

Other relevant benefits from CAD There are numerous benefits arising from the use of CAD, of which two in particular stand out in relation to our interest in the impact of electronics in LDCs. First is the ability it gives management to control proprietary information and the pace at which a hitherto independent labour force works. Specifically from the viewpoint of LDCs, one British heavy electrical manufacturer was able to take advantage of CAD technology to the detriment of LDCs. In manual-drawing days, drawings provided to subcontractors in developing countries frequently contained more information than was necessary, and it was too expensive and time-consuming to produce a specific set of drawings for each subcontractor. Consequently, the firm observed, there was the inadvertent transfer of technology to LDC firms who subsequently became effective competitors. In this case, CAD had given this British firm greater capability to control the amount of information contained in drawings passed to LDC subcontractors and hence to limit the growth of potential competition. A second area of benefit arises from the use of CAD as a marketing tool. A large number of users, in all sectors of production, remarked that their CAD systems were frequently used as an effective marketing tool.

The future diffusion of CAD by sector
The benefits of using CAD are therefore substantial. But if we are to assess the impact of CAD technology (and by extension, microelectronics-related technologies in general) on LDCs, we need to form some view on how rapidly the technology is diffusing and to which sectors. It is clearly impossible to know what the rate of diffusion of CAD technology will be, since there are so many imponderables in the equation. It is, however, possible to make a reasoned guess. If Henwood (1980) is accurate in his assessment that penetration of US industry in 1980 was 'less than 5 per cent' (say 4 per cent), and if CAD sales to manufacturing industry continue to grow at 40 per cent per annum, then assuming no growth in the absolute size of the US industrial sector, penetration will be around 20 per cent by 1985 and around 100 per cent by 1990. These estimates are of course extremely crude, but they do suggest that under seemingly conservative assumptions,[10] penetration of DC manufacturing industry by CAD will become fairly widespread over the coming decade.

While it is reasonably clear that CAD technology has diffused from the electronics to the mechanical engineering industry, and is now moving into the civil engineering sector, defining the *detailed* path of diffusion of CAD technology is not an easy task. In general we can only generate a perspective on the likely paths of diffusion, by examining the economic sectors affected most significantly by each of the three areas of benefit discussed in the previous section.

Two criteria can be used to determine the detailed path of the diffusion of CAD technology, namely draughting intensity and design intensity. The striking conclusion is, as can be seen from Table 1, that CAD looks like diffusing most rapidly precisely to these non-traditional-manufactures sectors where LDC exports grew most rapidly in the 1970s, where LDCs hope to increase further their manufactured exports in the 1980s, where value-added is highest and where the technological spin-off is likely to be greatest. Thus, unless LDCs utilise CAD technologies (and by extension other microelectronics-based technologies), then they will fail to realise the large productivity gains, and will introduce 'lower-quality products' with slower lead-times. It is important therefore to determine whether CAD technology is actually diffusing to LDC producers.

TABLE 1   DC Imports of Manufactures from LDCs in Relation to Design and Draughting Intensity

	Value $m		Growth		Rankings (N = 15)		
	1970	1978	1978/1970	Value (1978)	Growth	Draughting Intensity	Design Intensity
Traditional Manufactures							
Semi-finished textiles	1815	9610	5.3	1	13	11	11
Leather	183	950	5.2	9	14	13	12
Clothing	1181	9502	8.1	2	10	12	14
Shoes	151	2033	13.5	7	6	14	13
High Technology Manufactures							
Chemicals	588	2282	3.9	5	15	9	6
Metals and metal products	319	2223	7	6	12	10	9
Machinery except electrical and business	81	1136	14	8	5	4	3
(Farm machinery)	2	29	14.5	15	4	7	7
Electrical machinery	372	4463	12	3	7	1	1
Business machines	81	600	7.4	12	11	2	5
Scientific instruments	24	359	15	13	3	3	4
Motor vehicles	23	603	26.2	11	2	8	10
Aircraft	18	737	40.9	10	1	6	2
Shipbuilding	40	355	8.9	14	9	5	8
Consumer electronics	214	2391	11.2	4	8	*	*
Total Manufactures	5493	40195	7.3				
Total Traditional Manufactures	3330	22095	6.6				
Total Higher Technology Manufactures	2163	18100	8.4				

* The 1960 data are not comparable. In general, design is high in this sector and so is draughting.

Source: Calculated from US Dept of Labour (1979), which provides information on ISIC sectors and US Central Intelligence Agency (1980), which provides information on Standard International Trade Classification (SITC) sectors.

The geographical diffusion of CAD

It is not my intention here to chart the diffusion of CAD through the 'developed world': suffice to point out that the diffusion is probably greatest in the USA, but that recent market growth-rates have been substantially higher in Japan and Europe than in N. America. What is of relevance here is the degree of diffusion to LDCs. From a survey of machinery suppliers of turnkey interactive systems, a number of relevant observations can be made about these sales to LDCs. First, in total they comprise around 44 systems, or around 32 if South Africa and Yugoslavia are excluded. This is in the context of a global installed base (of the turnkey systems investigated in this study) of over 8,000 systems. Second, most of the vendors had lost track of these sales to LDCs and were unable to service them; in one extreme case, hardware had been shipped to Zaire some years ago without any supporting software and the equipment was obviously useless. Third, the cost of servicing LDC markets is usually high. One firm which is making an effort to penetrate the Brazilian market due to the future expansion of the automobile sector, is having to specifically train a software and a hardware engineer to support the sale of an initial system; in another case, the purchasing TNC petroleum company has specifically trained supporting staff at its own expense. Fourth, most LDC applications are for mapping, which is generally used in petroleum fields or has strategic counter-insurgency imperatives underlying its use.[11] Fifth, many of the CAD suppliers reported a significant degree of *general* interest from LDCs (especially China, Hong Kong, Taiwan and Singapore) concerned with the purchase of state-of-the-art technology, but without any *specific* knowledge of the uses of CAD, or even its nature and cost.

The evidence also suggests that only a very limited capability to produce CAD-system software exists within LDC themselves. To the best of my knowledge only one set of LDC CAD equipment exists, and that emanates from the Tata Institute of Fundamental Research in India. It is worth emphasising the technical excellence of the Tata Institute, which already in the 1950s built its own digital computer and was, then, abreast of technological developments in the US.[12] There are currently four imported turnkey systems in India, three of which are installed for predominantly electronic applications. Working with the basic graphics software of their turnkey systems, the Tata Institute has assembled four further systems, two of which have been sold to research institutes. One of these runs off a minicomputer (with two terminals) using bought-in software from the UK, and the other two run off small mainframe computers largely using Tata application programs. These programs are predominantly for the electronics sector and do not appear to have the sophistication of their turnkey counterparts. Nevertheless, despite these deficiencies, the Tata systems do work – the major obstacle to wider diffusion probably relates more to lack of demand from an unsophisticated industrial base than the inadequacy of their own software.

AUTOMATION: THE IMPORTANCE OF SYSTEMS GAINS[13]

Having analysed the gains arising from the use of electronics in a particular activity, I will now consider the implications that the technology holds for the wider diffusion of electronics to other types of automation technologies. Two things stand out from the literature on automation. First there is the definitional ambiguity in the literature between the wide meaning of the term (which refers to mechanisation in general) and the more narrow perspective (which confines the term to cybernetic feedback-control mechanisms). I choose to use the concept in its widest context, incorporating both mechanisation and feedback control. And, second, it is important not to get too carried away with respect to the pace and extent of automation, as was the case in the 'automation scares' of previous eras. However, despite this cautionary note, I believe that DC technology is making an important qualitative transition in its move to the 'factory of the future', the phrase used by General Electric in its attempt to climb back up the technological ladder.

In order to fully understand the significance of the new automation technologies that are beginning to emerge, it is necessary to develop a perspective on the history of the modern industrial enterprise. Over the last three centuries the industrial enterprise has become increasingly specialised. Beginning from the archetypal 'informal sector' firm where the owner was responsible for everything from design to marketing, firms grew in size and tasks became increasingly specialised. The result was that already by the 1920s three different spheres of production had begun to emerge, each with its own set of *activities*. The first of these spheres is design, with the following basic activities – schematic design, detailed design and drawing. The second sphere is production/distribution where the process of manufacture actually occurs. Here the particular activities involved are influenced by whether it involves process or batch production, and whether the product is assembled or formed. But in all cases the following types of activity are involved: setting up equipment, feeding raw materials/ components, processing/assembling/forming, inspection, storage, handling and distribution. The final sphere is that of control, in which (stratified) management performs four major sets of functions – purchasing, production planning, sale, and financial planning and control. In each of these four functions the following types of activities are involved: information-gathering, information storage, information manipulations, the presentation of information and its transmission.

Having recognised the existence of these three spheres – each with its attendant activities – it is possible to characterise three major forms of automation. The first is *intra-activity* automation – for example, nineteenth-century copying lathes, desk calculators and photocopying machines. The second is *intrasphere* automation in which various activities within a single sphere are linked up – for example, a moving production line, or a CAD system that is used for both drawing and design. And, finally, there is *inter-sphere* automation in which activities in different spheres are linked up – for example, a CAD system that automatically produces a parts list (in the control sphere) and that automatically sets up machine-tools and testing equipment (in the sphere of manufacture/distribution).

The history of automation is largely confined to the first of these types, although the move to mass-production lines also saw the limited development of some intra-sphere automation in the manufacturing sphere. The introduction of *electronics* into each of the individual spheres has really been a phenomenon of the 1970s, and it provides the potential for a quantum-leap in the degree of intra-sphere and inter-sphere automation. This is largely because of the fact that the control algorithm in all of these various, individual activities is reduced to the same binary building blocks that are the currency of electronics-based devices.

This is an extremely important point to grasp. For example, as we saw in the case of CAD equipment, the average intra-activity gains were in the region of $3:1$.[14] Yet these are considered by most innovating firms to be short-run gains: the real potential of the equipment will emerge, as most firms who were interviewed realised, when the downstream synergies with other sets of electronic equipment could be realised. These include parts-listing, inventory controls, estimating, billing, machine-setting and mechanical control. A similar point can be made with regard to intra-sphere automation in the control sphere. Here most empirical studies show that productivity gains with word-processors are substantial, but only in relation to a fairly restricted set of activities (such as amending texts, or mail-order typing). However, when word-processors are linked to electronic filing systems, intelligent copiers and other word-processors, then productivity gains realised will increase significantly. (This is the real importance of the 'integrated work station'.)

I believe that this distinction between these types of automation helps us to understand the paradoxical situation in which, despite the recent downstream diffusion of electronics, there has been a slowdown in productivity growth in all OECD economies. This is due to the combined effect of a not-quite-mature automation technology in information-processing activities[15] and the 'breathing space' involved in the setting-in-place of individual components of the electronic jigsaw. Once they are there and linked up, it seems to me that the pace of productivity growth will begin to speed up once more.

In many sectors the various elements of electronics-based intra-activity automation are in place. The cutting edge of technical progress lies in joining these together – this underlies, for example, the recent moves by IBM into satellite transmission, into CAD, and now into the manufacture of industrial robots. IBM's strategy is being emulated by many other firms, including Philips, General Electric, ATT and Xerox. However, to be implemented, intra-sphere and inter-sphere automation necessitates two major preconditions: the first is the widespread existence of individual components of this electronic jigsaw; the second is the ability to reorganise enterprises in such a way as to take advantage of these systems gains (an ability in which the Japanese seem to excel and the British seem to lack).

Here lies the major point I wish to make. Previous eras of automation were largely of an intra-activity nature. They were relatively easy to introduce and could be done so gradually, often in isolation from the technique used in other activities. But to gain the benefits of new forms of automation, a much wider depth of intra-activity automation is required, with an ability to take advantage of the relevant synergies. It enormously ups-the-odds for LDCs.

Compounding the difficulties for LDCs, in my view, is the fact that, unlike non-electronic control devices which have a moving-part control system, the 'black-box' type solid state electronic devices make it considerably more difficult to pursue the Japanese-style policy of reverse-engineering (that is, learning by undoing, a phrase coined some years back by Frances Stewart).

For all these reasons I believe that not only is the pace of technological change in DCs beginning to increase but the technologies that are emerging are increasingly inappropriate for LDCs and make it inherently more difficult for ITLC ('independent technology learning capacity' – Dore) (this book) to take place.

Lest it be argued that LDCs could circumvent the new technologies by continuing to utilise pre-electronic vintages (a choice of technique perspective) but with reduced wages to make up for productivity rates, it is important to recognise that the new automation technologies offer cost reductions as only one of their many benefits. More significant in some sectors is their ability to produce higher-quality products (for example, semiconductor memories – see Rada, 1982) with significantly reduced lead-times (one of the major factors inducing the use of electronics in the automobile sector). Without the use of electronics-based technologies it will be increasingly difficult to produce high-income goods for DC markets in a competitive environment. And despite the greater ease with which electronics-based technologies can be operated (see Kaplinsky, 1982b), there are at least some compelling reasons to argue that LDCs are less likely to utilise these technologies efficiently,[16] particularly those that are heavily reliant on software. This is because it appears that software-intensive technologies require a close, interactive link between the users and suppliers and between different sets of users.

Accordingly, when it comes to the production of high-income goods for DC markets, or the production of capital goods to be used by DC producers, the gap between 'world technology' and 'LDC technology' is beginning to reopen again.

III WHAT OF LDC TECHNOLOGICAL CAPABILITIES?

So where does this leave LDC producers who, as observed by many commentators, have over the years built up a substantial technological capability of their own. There is no necessity to document this rise in technological progress here – others have done so more ably, particularly in the macroeconomic context as reflected by emerging LDC exports of technology and technology-intensive goods. Rather, in this section I propose to recount the experience of a single LDC in a particular sector, and by so doing to illuminate the qualitative characteristics of this technological capability. The country in question is India, the technology is that which produces crystal sugar.

The story of sugar is long and complex; here I will only draw out the major issues that are relevant to the concerns of this paper. Sugar is uniquely indigenous to India, where it was produced for many centuries before the technology (and products) were transferred to China, Persia and then the West. However, from the latter half of the nineteenth century, a number of innovations were introduced by DC plantation owners[17] which improved the quality of the product (making it whiter) and increased the sugar/cane yield from around 5 per cent to current levels of 10–12 per cent. (This is in the context of a maximum attainable recovery rate of around 14–15 per cent). Thus this stream of technology – referred to as Vacuum Pan (VP), since the water in cane-juice is drawn off by being boiled under a vacuum – is now mature. The most modern factories in DCs (processing beet rather than cane) are process-operations in which the production-sphere is almost fully automated through distributed processing by hierarchies of electronic control systems. As observed in the previous section, technical progress in these firms is now concentrated in the control sphere and in reaping the gains of inter-sphere automation through procedures such as automatic stock control and invoicing.

The first Indian VP sugar-cane factories were established in the late 1920s, after which sugar production grew at a compound growth rate until 1980 of over 7 per cent p.a.; of the major producers only Brazil (and this in the last decade) has registered such a high growth-rate for any significant period of time. Currently though, Indian VP mills (all new-built indigenously) are between 20 per cent and 40 per cent of the size at which full-scale economies can be reached; moreover they are very labour-intensive with none of their control systems involving electronics. Thus while Indian VP plant manufacturers now actively compete with DC suppliers in supplying similar equipment to other LDCs, there have been no cases of them supplying plant for DC markets, partly because these generally process beet rather than cane, but mostly because the Indian suppliers are unable to meet the demand for the automated processing systems used in DC economies.

Around 1955 the Indians set out to upgrade the traditional khandsari technology. This was done by focusing on two of the six different subsystems involved in processing. These were crushing, where mechanical rollers were substituted for traditional bullock-crushing,[18] and boiling, in which the juice was boiled in open-pans – hence leading to the name open-pan-sulphitation (OPS). The remaining four sub-systems–clarification, crystallisation, centrifuging and drying/packing – were not given undue emphasis, since they were not critical, and had already benefited from the gradual introduction of mechanised equipment (for example, the substitution of centrifugal separators for the traditional pressing processes).

By the late 1960s the attainable sugar recovery in OPS plants had increased from 5 per cent to around 7 per cent. Yet, largely because of the disparity between even the improved rate and the 10–12 per cent of VP plants, OPS remained unviable from the private viewpoint and could only be justified from the social viewpoint with relatively high premia on foreign exchange, wages and discount rates. It thrived, as Baron (1975), Forsyth (1977) and others pointed out because of government protection or because of the natural protection afforded by small pockets of cane which were a peculiar characteristic of Indian operating conditions.

On the other hand the Indian engineers recognised the key point that precisely because OPS technology was sub-optimal (whereas VP was close to the achievable maximum), the returns to marginal inputs of R&D would be very high. Thus Garg, a key figure in the development of OPS technology, responded with the argument that

> The large scale technology took about 125 years to develop to the present efficiency. Most of the present-day resources are on its side, viz, rich infrastructure, capital and finances, political influences and demarcation of market. The mini-sugar of OPS Khandsari is only 22 years old. Even if a small part of these resources and development facilities are provided to mini-sugar technology, it can even compete with the large scale sugar complexes having their own cane cultivation. (Garg, 1979, p.12)

Leaning partly upon the experience of DC technical institutions, a traditional molasses-expelling technology from Quebec was modified and significant improvements were made in the crushing technology. At the same time, a key bottleneck was eroded by redesigning furnaces used in the boiling stage. The consequences are that OPS technology can now stand on its own feet, without any government subsidy or protection, in relation to the sorts of VP plants currently used in India. It is a striking example of indigenous technical capability (Kaplinsky, 1982c).

Yet, when compared to the most modern large-scale technology, OPS plants remain sub-optimal. In the context of actual plant sizes the 200 tons of cane per day (that is, crushing capacity) of the OPS plants compares favourably with the 1,250 tcd VP plants (the median plant size in India), but unfavourably with the large-scale DC alternatives (over 5,000 tcd). The important point here is that few LDCs can develop the cane supply and infrastructure to feed these very large-scale plants at economic costs. For example, two Sudanese plants of 6,500 tcd each operate at only 15 per cent capacity due to cane shortages: the infamous 20,000 tcd Kenana plant is even more disastrous; Sri Lankan plants, too, have difficulties in obtaining cane supplies for even the 1,250 tcd level; and so on.

So the point is that OPS technology, while unviable in relation to the most modern technology, is peculiarly suitable to other LDCs. It represents a particularly 'deep' form of LDC capability. Indian VP technology, while 'shallower', in that it leans directly on DC designs (partly still involving licensing agreements), is competitive in other countries, *but* only in those in which sophisticated electronic control devices are not required. Two other points are relevant in illuminating the discussion in section II of this paper. The first is that OPS is a clear example of the product/process link, in that it produces a different type of sugar (brownish, with inconsistently sized granules). This sugar is not attractive to high-income consumers and will almost certainly not produce sugar exportable to DC markets. And second, OPS remains a batch process, whereas VP is almost entirely a process technology. Hence improvements to OPS are largely of an intra-activity nature (for example, in boiling, or crushing) and can be implemented on an *ad hoc* basis. By contrast, automation of VP plants is increasingly reliant on electronics and is linked in with other activities (for example, new controls for centrifuge machines – see *Food Engineering International*, June 1981). It is consequently more of an intra-sphere and inter-sphere nature and is uniquely provided by DC firms.

To round off the discussion in this section, therefore, I would like to point to the relevance of the sugar case-study. While it might appear that India is an unusual country, given its size, its skilled labour-force and the depth of its industrialisation, its advances in technological capability are not unique: similar stories could no doubt be told for China, Brazil, South Africa, South Korea, Taiwan, Argentina, and other economies. But what the sugar case-study indicates is that, in the microelectronics era, this technological capability is increasingly inappropriate for DCs; it also produces products that are unacceptable for DC consumers. However, by contrast, whereas the drift of DC technology away from batch and towards continuous production makes it less appropriate for LDCs, the growth of LDC technology is particularly relevant to other LDCs.

IV WHO, WHAT, WHERE AND WHEN?

The discussion so far has perhaps been too simple in that it has been couched in sweeping terms, using grand phrases such as heartland technologies, microelectronics-related innovation and so on. The contrast between such generalisations and the detailed analysis of many microelectronic studies of indigenous technical change is striking, and it is tempting to dismiss sweeping conclusions of the sort drawn in this paper. After all, not all LDCs are comparable; sugar and CAD technologies have particular characteristics that make it difficult to generalise to other sectors; it is dangerous to underestimate the difficulties in moving to intra-sphere and inter-sphere automation and so on. Nevertheless I clearly believe that the various points made in this paper are worthy of generalisation, particularly those that draw us away from a continuous incremental technical change perspective (which I believe ahistorical) to the recognition that there are discrete jumps in technologies and that we are now at a minor turning-point in economic and technical history. If this is indeed the case then it is important to briefly turn our attention to the implications that the preceding discussion has for LDC technological capability, and for the who, the what, the where and the when of trade in technology.

WHO?

Parthasarathi, in his analysis of electronic capabilities in LDCs (UNCTAD, 1978), draws the distinction between those countries who pursued an in-depth form of industrialisation such as India and Argentina, and those with a much thinner veneer of industrialisation based upon low-value-added export processing zones. The point of this distinction was to argue that the former groups, with a well-developed industrial base in the electrical-goods sector, had a much better chance of capitalising upon the potential of microelectronics, whereas the latter was more likely to flounder in a sea of radical technical change.

The 'facts' have, however, pointed to a different conclusion – ironically it has been the latter group who have been more able to take advantage of microelectronics, particularly in relation to the production of electronic consumer goods for DC markets (see Clarke and Cable, 1982). But clearly it *is* important to distinguish between the small group of countries (especially Hong Kong, Taiwan, S. Korea and Singapore) who have been able to develop some sort of indigenous capability in the use and (to a lesser extent) the production of micro-electronics components, and the rest. (Incidentally neither set as yet shows much evidence of being able to incorporate electronics into capital goods, a capability that requires more substantive inputs of applications-based software.)

Those countries with a capability to use electronics in final products are generally the same economies as those which are involved in sub-contracting in the electronic-component industries. Here, continued success in both sets of activities is likely to be undermined by two sets of factors (see Kaplinsky, 1981, 1982). First, markets are rapidly closing off and producers are being forced to locate in final consumer markets (this includes both Goldstar of S. Korea, who have built a TV plant in Alabama, and Tatung of Taiwan who have taken over an ailing UK TV manufacturer), and second, changes in technology (such as automation of component-insertion and the availability of powerful microprocessors which, by reducing the number of components, lessen the demand for labour), particularly those that enhance quality and reduce lead-time, are undermining the significance of lower costs in export processing zones.

Those LDCs without a capability in electronics will clearly be affected by the same factors; but, in addition, they will be confronted by their relative inability to use microelectronics either in final products or in production processes. They too, therefore, will also find that they are less competitive in increasingly closed DC markets. However, for reasons discussed in section III of this paper, they will produce technology that becomes increasingly appropriate for other LDCs as the course of DC technological change takes a different route (I return to this point below).

It should be clear from these points that MNCs will be faced with a similar world, in that LDCs become increasingly unattractive as production sites for DC markets. But, in addition, their LDC subsidiaries will be less able to transfer their technology from one LDC to another if they make use of the new technology being utilised in their home countries. So unless they are able to develop their own 'LDC technology', which their indigenously owned competitors will be doing as a matter of course, they will find themselves increasingly cut off from the LDC trade in technology. Overall, therefore, I believe that indigenous LDC firms will become increasingly significant participants in the trade of technology.

WHAT?

From the above it is clear that I am referring largely to capital goods (often referred to as technology-intensive trade), where the 'DC technology' has increasingly become systems-based.[19] In particular, not only does the incorporation of electronics put the emphasis on systems gains (which in turn depends upon the widespread diffusion of electronics in intra-activity automation), but its incorporation in capital makes large demands on applications software. And despite the repeated suggestion that LDCs should excel in this area, given their abundance of unutilised skills, the evidence points to an opposite conclusion. This is that applications software requires close interaction between users and suppliers and between different users (Kaplinsky, 1982b), and consequently LDCs have shown little evidence of developing this type of capability in electronics. Finally, the other three main divisions of electronics – military goods, consumer goods and electronics components – are also unlikely prospects: the former being closed-off for technical and strategic reasons, consumer goods because of closing markets and reduced comparative advantage, and the latter because of changes in technology described earlier. Consequently I think it unlikely that LDCs will develop a capability in any of the major subdivisions of electronics, except for some countries (Hong Kong, Taiwan, S. Korea and Singapore) in restricted sectors of activity (for example, black-and-white TVs, and radios). This is a conclusion shared by other observers (see Kaplinsky, 1982b). Of course it is important to develop a temporal perspective here – in the long run, LDCs will undoubtedly develop these, and other, capabilities; it's the next ten to fifteen years that are relevant to this discussion.

By contrast, as argued in section III above, LDCs are likely to develop a growing relative capability in producing non-electronic capital goods, suitable for other LDCs and producing products acceptable to low-income consumers. As mentioned, it is likely that these will largely be automation *within activities* as defined in section II, allowing for decomposition of technology and the 'unpackaging strategies' which were so popular in the 1970s.

WHERE?

The centralising tendencies within and between economies are likely to be no less evident on this emergent restructuring of world trade in technology than they were in previous phases. A number of countries already stand out as sources of LDC technology, namely India, Brazil, Argentina, Taiwan and S. Korea (Hong Kong and Singapore, being small processing economies, and more dependent upon DC markets for a narrow range of products, are more likely to become financial centres than sources of industrial technology for LDCs). How far the web of contacts of these countries spreads depends largely on wider geo-political events which are currently in the process of 'evolution. For example, some observers predict a growing tendency for trading spheres to emerge, with the US dominating S. America, Europe controlling the ACP countries, and Japan exercising influence over Asia and Australasia (Bienefeld, this book). Clearly the division of such trading spheres (as depression is reflected in the growth of trade barriers) will reflect the nature and extent to which these spheres are delineated.

Nevertheless, despite these uncertainties it is possible to hazard some guess. Africa, particularly East and Central Africa, will continue to import appropriate technology from India; West Africa, while also building such links with India, will also draw technology from S. America, especially from Brazil. S. America will be dominated by Brazilian and Argentinian techniques, although the higher sophistication of their industrial structures will also provide scope for technology exports from Taiwan and S. Korea. Asia is likely to see a developing specialisation with higher-technology goods coming from Taiwan and S. Korea, and more basic ones from India and perhaps Pakistan.

WHEN?

Perhaps, because of the dangers of generalisation, all this seems excessively 'futuristic' and open to the vagaries of uncertainty. Yet we are not referring to the world of the 1990s, for these likely events are already occurring. For example, faced with a closing-off of markets in DCs, Brazil has already begun to reorient its exports to other LDCs in Latin America and W. Africa. Similarly, as observed in sections II and III of this paper, the tendency for indigenous LDC technology to be increasingly appropriate to other LDCs (and similarly for DC technology to be appropriate for other DCs) is already reflected in the 'real world'. Three examples can be given. First, as O'Brien (1981) points out, there is evidence for Argentina that the technology-intensive goods go to LDCs and the basic, traditional manufactures go to DCs. Second, as illustrated in the case-study on CAD, the new systems-based technology has so far not had much appeal to LDCs, despite the significant gains it offers to users. Third, as I tried to show in the sugar case-study, electronics control-systems have not been adopted by Indian machinery suppliers who have concentrated on 'basic' pre-electronic equipment; yet it is precisely because Indian firms have stood back from these process improvements that its technology has proved to be attractive to other LDCs.

IN CONCLUSION

I restate (once again) my major point: I am convinced that much of the discussion on indigenous technical change, based as it is on an incremental process of learning-by-doing supplemented by inputs from the Science and Technology System, is ahistorical. It fails to recognise what Lall refers to as Schumpeterian leaps in technology. While this inadequacy may have been not too damaging during the upswing of the most recent long-wave cycle, the downstream diffusion of microelectronics that we are now experiencing points to the need to requestion some of the conclusions that are now emerging. In particular, the assertion that LDCs can continue to assimilate DC technology at an unchanged rate, and that they can continue their penetration of DC markets in increasingly technology-intensive manufactures, must be open to question. In contrast I offer a view that suggests that the gap between DC and LDC technology is reopening, but at the same time DC technology is becoming increasingly inappropriate for LDCs. The consequence of this I believe, particularly when viewed in the light of restructuring channels of trade, will be for an increase in intra-Third-World trade in technology, with a concomitant decline in the share of technology trade occurring between DCs and LDCs.

NOTES

1. For example, the number of export processing zones increased from 220 in 1978 to over 350 in 1980.
2. For the moment we refer to LDCs as a reasonably homogeneous entity. This assumption is related in section IV of this paper and subsequent discussion is built around a differentiated view of Third World economies.
3. However, interested readers can refer to Barron and Curnow (1979), Clark *et al.*, (1980), Freeman (1977, 1981), Kaplinsky (1981, 1982a, 1982b) and Rada (1979, 1982).

4. By 'microelectronic era' I refer to the use of microelectronics in downstream manufacturing industries – a characteristic of the rationalising downswing of the long wave – rather than in the form of new products which occurs on the expansionary saving.
5. This section is based on my book on Computer-Aided-Design (Kaplinsky, 1982a).
6. These are flat surfaces which are used to convert drawing specifications to the digital format utilised by electronic systems.
7. This sector is based on visits to 13 CAD suppliers and 24 CAD users in Britain and North America.
8. For a discussion of the reasons why these difficulties arise, see chapter 6 of Kaplinsky (1982a).
9. Cheaper equipment is already available and prices are declining as microcomputer and data-storage costs decline – the software component of these systems is minimal and static.
10. The real growth of sales to industry in the US has been well in excess of 40 per cent per annum since 1976. However, the assumption of zero growth of US manufacturing industry over the coming decade is probably too restrictive.
11. In one of these cases the purchase was aided by funds from the US AID.
12. Which built the first digital electronic computer in the 1950s. The Indian version, however, was non-electronic and worked with vacuum tubes.
13. For an elaboration of the ideas in this section, see my forthcoming book on the subject (Kaplinsky, 1983).
14. Leaving aside for the moment the additional benefits of better-quality and shorter lead-time which the interviewed firms generally found to be of greater significance.
15. Perhaps Leyland Motors is not the best example, but it is significant that around 60 per cent of their total labour-force is involved in information-processing activities. Equally relevant is the repeated observation (by Rada, 1979) that the capital/labour ratio in manufacturing activities tends to be more than ten times that invested in information-processing activities.
16. The reasons why LDCs are less likely to use electronics-based technology efficiently are only schematically presented here; but see also the various articles in the *IDS Bulletin* ('Comparative Advantage in an Automating World'. Spring 1982), and Kaplinsky (1982, 1983).
17. This occurred predominantly in the West Indies – only in the 1920s were these technologies introduced into India.
18. In fact, mechanised crushing of a primitive nature had already begun to diffuse since the 1930s when Khandsari plants began to face competition from VP mills.
19. However, I have also commented on the implications for LDCs in the consumer-goods and electronic-component sectors.

REFERENCES

Baron, C. G. (1975) 'Sugar Processing Technologies in India', in A. S. Bhalla (ed.), *Technology and Employment in Industry*. Geneva: ILO.

Barron, I. and Curnow, R. (1979) *The Future with Information Technology*. London: Frances Pinter.

Clark, J., Freeman, C. and Soete, L. (1980) 'Long Waves and Technological Developments in the 20th Century', mimeo, Brighton.

Clarke, J. and Cable, V. (1982) 'The Asian Electronics Industry Looks to the Future', in Kaplinsky (1982b).

Forsyth, D. (1977) 'Appropriate Technology in Sugar Manufacturing', *World Development*, vol. 5, no. 3, pp. 189–202.

Freeman, C. (1977) 'The Kondratieff Long Waves, Technical Change and Unemployment', in *Structural Determinants of Employment and Unemployment*. Paris: OECD, pp. 181–196.

Freeman, C. (1981) 'Some Economic Implications of Micro-electronics', in D. Cohen (ed.), *Agenda for Britain I: Micro Policy (Choices for the Eighties)*. London: Philip Allan.

Garg, M. K. (1979) *Project Report and Feasibility Study of Appropriate Technology in Mini Sugar (OPS Khandsari)*, a Project Report and Feasibility Study No. 2. Lucknow: ATDA.

Henwood, T. D. (1980) *Computer Graphics Industry: In Its Early Growth Stages*. New York: First Boston Research.

Kaplinsky, R. (1981) 'Radical Technical Change and Export-Oriented Industrialisation: The Impact of Micro-electronics', *Vierteljahresberichte*, no. 83.

Kaplinsky, R. (1982a) *CAD in a Dynamic World*. London: Frances Pinter.

Kaplinsky, R. (ed.) (1982b) 'Comparative Advantage in an Automating World', *IDS Bulletin*, vol. 13, no. 2, March.

Kaplinsky, R. (1982c) 'An Economic Evaluation of Recent Improvements made in OPS Sugar Technology', Rugby : Intermediate Technology Industrial Services.

Kaplinsky, R. (1983) *Automation in a Crisis*. London: Pluto Press.

O'Brien, P. (1981) 'Third World Industrial Enterprises as Exporters of Technology – Recent Trends and Underlying Causes', *Vierteljahresberichte*, no. 83, March.

Rada, J. F. (1979) 'Microelectronics, Information, Technology and its Effects on Developing Countries', paper prepared for the Conference on Socio-economic Problems and Potentialities of the Application of Micro-electronics at work, The Netherlands, 19–24 September.

Rada, J. F. (1982) 'Technology and the North–South Division of Labour', in Kaplinsky (1982b).

UNCTAD (1978) 'Electronics in Developing Countries: Issues in Transfer and Development of Technology', Geneva, UN.

US Central Intelligence Agency (1980) *Developed Country Imports of Manufactures from LDCs*, ER-80-10476, Washington.

US Department of Labour (1979) *Tomorrow's Manpower Needs*, Dept of Labour Statistics Bulletin No. 1606.

International Constraints and Opportunities

Manfred Bienefeld

This brief note is intended merely to pose some questions concerning the importance of the international context as the essential background against which the development of 'indigenous technological capability' must be pursued in practice, defined in discussion and understood in theory. It will seek to establish those aspects of the international situation that are most likely to have a direct bearing on the effectiveness or the significance of any particular set of activities and policies, designed to enhance 'indigenous technological capabilities' (ITC).

Posing the question in this way means an emphatic rejection of the national *vs* international debate. It is not sensible to discuss whether the one or the other is more important, when the fact is that neither can be understood or discussed except in relation to the other. It is as illusory to believe that policies for ITC can be devised without any explicit indication of the way in which the international situation is perceived to be developing, as it is to believe that international forces effectively and decisively determine both the nature and the success of nationally defined policies.

Posing the question in this way also means drawing attention to the need to see the issues in a dynamic manner, since the relevant characteristics of the international situation change over time, and the critical task is to come to a view concerning the way in which they are evolving. For this we need empirical evidence and a theory to tell us what facts to look at and how to interpret what we see. We also need both the humility to recognise the tremendous uncertainty involved in coming to any such conclusion and the courage to reach some conclusion, nevertheless.

What the rest of this paper will seek to do is to suggest that the way in which we view the evolution of the global system since the late 1960s, and, more important, the way we therefore see its evolution in the

1980s, should have a central bearing on the way we discuss the question of ITC policy. Specifically, the paper will suggest that the dominant perception of this process, from which policy prescriptions are often directly derived by the most powerful international agencies, is one that is rooted in an economistic, individualistic and excessively static equilibrium theory which almost certainly provides an inappropriate and misleading picture of reality. There are important implications for ITC policies which follow from such a rejection. Just what these are depends of course in part on the alternative view adopted, although, as we shall see, even then the precise implication is not always clear.

First we must, however, turn to a problem that, if not clarified, could undermine the whole of the discussion – namely the meaning that is to be attached to the concept 'national'. Technical change is *indigenous* to a *nation*. The policy discussion centres around *national policies,* and my concerns revolve around the interplay between the *national* and the *inter-national*. There can be little doubt, then, that the definition of 'national' is of central importance.

TOWARDS A WORKING DEFINITION OF NATIONAL TECHNOLOGY

This is not the place to embark upon a deep philosophical discussion of 'the nation state', or of the deep ambiguities of the concept of 'the national interest'. I shall merely identify some important implications of this concept in the context of this particular debate.

At the root of the matter lies the concept of 'the economic unit', which refers to a social unit that allocates its available resources to productive uses in such a way as to maximise the unit's collective or aggregate income (here including psychic income, for simplicity). This unit may be the individual, the nuclear family, the extended family, a collective, or arguably, a nation state. In every case (but the first) there is necessarily some conflict regarding the extent to which different individuals see their membership of such a unit as desirable and, in all cases, their attitude will be influenced by both material and ideological/cultural factors.

Furthermore, it must be stressed that the existence of a unit in this sense does not imply anything about the internal distribution of that collective income, although the way that occurs may well have a direct impact on the stability, and thus on the effectiveness, of the unit's operations – or even on the likelihood of its survival.

The question is, why and to what extent is it sensible or desirable to consider the nation state as an economic unit in this sense? This is important, because only in so far as that is sensible is it also sensible to speak of an indigenous technological capacity, and to be concerned about its development.

The most obvious economic aspect of nationality relates to the state's more-or-less extensive role in distribution which, like a tied pension fund, links its members to the nation through their contributions (investments), and their consequent conditional claims on services or on direct financial payments. Where the claims are minimal (as in UDCs), or where the payments disproportionately exceed the claims (as in the case of tax refugees moving to their favourite tax-havens), or where the claims are honoured across borders (as increasingly within the EEC), this particular material inducement to national identification may be sharply reduced.

If a definition of nationality based on its distributional role is relatively straightforward it is much more difficult to establish the significance of nationality with respect to production. Generally, producers or owners prefer to sell their products or assets (coffee, transistor radios, technical skills) against a convertible currency, because that gives them the ability to purchase the widest possible range of international goods and services with their income. In a full-employment world, with mobile capital and labour, there would be few grounds for standing in the way of this desire. As producers, all microeconomic units would be linked to each other simply and solely through a world market. The need for macroeconomics would disappear and so would the main rationale for nationally defined policies on industrialisation or technology involving intervention in production or trade. Furthermore, while the case for national policy on education, training and research would remain strong, even there, high levels of international mobility would raise issues connected with the 'free rider' problem, familiar from the debates within national economies, drawing attention to the competitive disadvantage suffered by firms who invest heavily in training in the presence of a high level of inter-firm mobility among skilled workers.

This takes us back to the concept of the economic unit as one that pursues certain collective economic objectives by allocating or investing resources in the pursuit of those objectives. Obviously such behaviour requires a reasonable assurance that some real benefits will result and that they will accrue to the unit in question – although even if those conditions are met, the subsequent internal distribution of benefits may be such that it erodes political support for the policy.

For purposes of this discussion the nation will be considered a significant economic unit in so far as it engages in national investment of this type, or rather in so far as its policies are not simply intended to facilitate the relative advancement of the individuals who happen to be its citizens or residents, in order to facilitate their advance 'as individuals'. In short, this definition distinguishes between the nation as a simple sum total of its individuals, and the nation as an economic unit in its own right. The question to be considered generally concerns the impact that certain changes in the international context are likely to have on the feasibility or the desirability of the nation state acting as such an economic unit – especially with regard to the development of an indigenous technological capability. More specifically we shall consider the impact that the international changes of the past fifteen years have had on this issue.

Before turning to consider these questions it is important to clarify that neither the above attempt to reach a clearer definition of the nation as an 'economic unit', nor the following attempt to speculate on the circumstances that are likely to increase the potential benefits to nations from behaving as 'economic units' thus defined, should be interpreted as implying: that such potential benefits are equally available for all nations; that nationalist policies would necessarily reap these potential benefits; that nationalist policy, or rather rhetoric, is always genuinely intended to generate such benefits; or even, if such benefits are plausible, that all members of the society should therefore support them. There is no doubt that nationalism is potentially dangerous and divisive, and that it is frequently a device, not for the pursuit of some common interest, but rather a vehicle for the pursuit of certain sectional interests at the expense of others. But although that is true, it does not warrant the extreme conclusion that the phenomenon is necessarily reprehensible.

In fact, the above definition of the nation as an 'economic unit' is designed to draw attention to the relativity and the political ambiguity of the concept, since it implies the taking of decisions contravening in different ways, the short-term self-interest of various individuals and groups. By definition, this therefore creates a basis for potential conflict and ambiguity, especially since the benefits of such sacrifice are necessarily uncertain and not easily measured.

With these caveats we can now answer the question posed in the heading to this section, which was: What is indigenous technological capability? It is the technological capability pertaining to a nation defined as an economic unit in some significant sense. It is therefore differentiated from technological capabilities that merely happen to be located within the geographic boundaries of a nation.

THE INTERNATIONAL CONTEXT

The three international economic circumstances, which create the strongest inducements for nations to behave as economic units by seeking to capture dynamic benefits for themselves, through nationally defined strategies, are: the absence of full employment; the existence of relatively wide gaps in technological capabilities between different economies; and a high level of uncertainty and instability internationally. These were, of course, the conditions on which was based the claim that developing countries faced economic policy options that were substantially different from those associated with the 'special case' of the industrialised economies. It is ironic that at the end of a decade when all three of these conditions have been strongly reinforced for the vast majority of developing countries, there should be a strong resurgence of the claim that the economics of 'the special case' is, after all, broadly appropriate and desirable in the developing world. What this argument amounts to is a claim that there are few grounds for nations to behave as economic units, and that national policy should merely facilitate and encourage the technical evolution and the international integration of the microeconomic units of which the nation is made up. What follows will suggest that this is an inappropriate conclusion to draw from the 1970s, and that the proper conclusion would emphasise, more than ever, the essential need for developing countries to create, through their national policies, long-term oriented enclaves of relative economic stability in which a cumulative process of investment, production and technical change can be fostered and implemented, albeit that this had better be with a view to catching up with international technological developments.

The argument will proceed in three phases: first it will suggest why global disequilibrium, increased uncertainty and large technological disparities should generate a *prima facie* case for potential benefits from 'national' policy; second, it will suggest why the currently dominant interpretation of the 1970s is fatally flawed; finally, it will sketch in the barest outlines of an alternative explanation that leads to quite different, though not necessarily more optimistic conclusions.

INTERNATIONAL CONDITIONS THAT FOSTER
NATIONALIST POLICIES

It is no accident that nationalism has flourished in underdeveloped countries, in the early stages of the late developers, and in all countries during times of depression, when economic disequilibrium and instability increase massively. Far from nationalism being the cause of these problems it is essentially a response to them, though it is also true that it is a response that in turn creates its own problems.

That international instability and uncertainty should push economies in the direction of nationalist policies is almost self-evident. When prices, exchange rates and interest rates become volatile, and when government policies and the animal spirits of investors or speculators are amplified and given expression through large flows of international finance, then the slow and painful processes of restructuring real economies in accordance with long-term changes in resource availabilities, factor costs and demand patterns, are simply swamped by the rapidity of changes in the signals given by prices. Under such conditions, investment in real production tends to be discouraged by virtue of its essential inflexibility, as against the flexibility inherent in dealings in more liquid assets. *A fortiori,* investment in the really major changes implied by a major restructuring of real economies will be slow to emerge under such circumstances. Indeed it will very probably not emerge, except in the context of some clear, comprehensive and effective national policy – as in the case of Japan, South Korea, France and Germany – where it is made possible through the fact that the three big banks control 70 per cent of large-scale industry.

Widening disequilibria in the international economy have somewhat similar effects. Whether they are identified on the basis of growing rates of unemployment, falling rates of profit or growing levels of excess installed capacity (in relation to the demand possible, given current incomes and costs of production), the effect is much the same. In essence this creates a situation where the rules of the restructuring process are dramatically changed. Instead of the benign principle of comparative advantage guiding these processes, the much harsher and intransigent principle of absolute advantage rules the roost. Indeed the concept of comparative advantage describes the competitive process under full employment, and derives its 'power' from the fact that in that case the harshest sentence ever imposed on a protagonist is to be forced from the production of commodity *x*, into that of commodity *y*, with the added 'sweetener' that it can be shown that commodity *y* was the better thing to produce in any event.

When, however, full employment is not assumed to exist, to be imminent or to be the 'natural' state of the market, then the reality of substantial levels of unemployment will transform the Dr Jekyll of 'comparative advantage' into the Mr Hyde of 'absolute advantage'. Now the competitive process also allocates unemployment, and the advice to simply allow competitive forces to operate becomes impractical, unrealistic and politically untenable – except possibly on the basis of progressively increased repression.

Finally, the existence of wide disparities in technological capabilities increases the desirability of 'national' policy in industry and technology, but, at the same time, constitutes a major obstacle to the satisfaction of that need. The desirability is increased by the fact that under such conditions the relatively backward economies will suffer the largest part of the unemployment allocated globally through the competitive process, while being variously constrained in their ability to move their general technological capabilities forward, by the difficulties associated with their relatively high level of dependence on international markets and on relatively very advanced technologies employed in specific operations. The problems broadly associated with inadequate linkages, with dualism and with the potentially conflictive relationship between the technologically advanced and the much less advanced sectors, all reflect the consequences of relative technological backwardness. These represent real problems, even if not insurmountable or universally homogeneous ones. They represent problems that are generally exacerbated by increased instability and disequilibrium in the global economy, even though such circumstances may also provide important positive openings for particular nations in their attempts to close that technological gap.

There is one final point, which I have not addressed, largely because it is the subject of another paper, by Kaplinsky. This concerns the speed of technological advance internationally. Since in a competitive world 'success' – or even 'survival' – depends upon the *relative* efficiency of production, an acceleration of technological progress internationally creates critical problems for those countries seeking to escape from a position of relative technological backwardness.

On the one hand these changes reduce the competitive capacities of the developing economies and hence increase the need for nationally defined policies to facilitate cumulative indigenous accumulation and resource mobilisation. On the other hand such developments threaten to undermine the ability of such national policies to close 'the gap' and may well argue for the adoption of different means for seeking to do so. The implication for 'national' policy is therefore significant but ambiguous.

This is also related to the notion that technological backwardness not only makes it more desirable for the nation to act as 'an economic unit' (as defined), but also makes it more difficult. The difficulty is political, since the size of the disparity determines the degree of sacrifice required if those who could currently integrate themselves directly into the international economy (that is, sell their products or resources there) are to be asked to 'pool their resources and their economic interests' with the rest of an economy that is not in that position. As that difficulty increases so the likelihood of a genuine national perspective emerging is reduced. The way is opened for comprador bourgeoisies, comprador bureaucracies and comprador labour aristocracies. It is also opened for secessionist pressures and for political instability. One might well suggest that it is the size of that gap that makes the Japanese model so difficult to emulate. The centrifugal pressures are now such that the national consensus that Ron Dore, in his paper, called the 'necessary cement' for an effective policy for indigenous technical change has to be more and more powerful. Unfortunately the cultural factor which once added strength to that cement is also being diluted, further reducing the likelihood that it could be recreated in that form. Now, as a result, it is increasingly direct repression that plays that role, although it remains to be seen whether the current deepening of the international crisis will not threaten the international position of enough groups to induce them to turn to a more genuinely national orientation, on the grounds that the relative attractiveness of the international economy is more than offset by its risks and dangers. This will happen, but in most cases it will simply be a shrinking portion of the society that will cling to its international stakes, and standard of living, by the use of increasing repression, ostensibly made necessary by the intensified need to avert instability so as to meet the increasing competitive pressures abroad.

THE ORTHODOX INTERPRETATION OF THE PAST FIFTEEN YEARS

It is in this context of the increasing politicisation of international markets, of increasing disequilibrium in labour, financial and industrial markets, and of increasing protectionism everywhere, that the experience of the Newly Industrialising Countries has been presented as the basis for a strong reassertion of the doctrine that a strong market-orientation involving the direct exposure of economic units to competitive pressures, is not only a necessary, but, in some versions, virtually a sufficient condition for effecting the restructuring required to reproduce a dynamic equilibrium growth path in the international economy, or at least to produce an effective accommodation of individual economies to the changes occurring in the international economy.

The implication is effectively that nations should not act as economic units in any far-reaching sense, but that they should act primarily to facilitate the development and international integration of the micro-economic units operating within their borders.

Although the serious versions of this argument are both complex and nuanced in their presentation, their effective summary and implication is nevertheless to inveigh strongly against the inefficiencies associated with inward-looking or nationalist strategies which 'distort factor prices', and to assert the efficacy and the adequacy of outward-looking policies which focus on the expansion of exports and the attraction of international capital in an environment where competitive pressures are used to ensure efficiency and where any distribution/welfare objectives, as well as objectives regarding technological development, are primarily regarded as derivative from the rapid growth objective, if accompanied by an appropriate policy on education and training.

In essence, this view denies the relevance or the need for a separate analytic or policy perspective for developing economies by asserting the possibility of full employment even in these economies, given the above policies along with sufficiently 'downward flexible' wage structures. With this possibility asserted, it is possible to argue that labour market pressures will produce both trickle-down and, in the context of the resulting real wage increases, a gradual shift up the international technological ladder.

It is a view that requires a global perception of a gradually expanding full-employment core, which moves steadily up the technology hierarchy, slowly drawing peripheral economies in through the production of unskilled-labour-intensive products and then raising these gradually to make room for the next generation of NICs.

The experience of the past fifteen years does indeed provide some empirical evidence for this position. It is true that new countries have begun to industrialise in this way. It is true that they have begun to move up the technological ladder. It is true that a few of them have generated labour scarcity which has raised real wage rates even of un-skilled labour. It is also true that they have grown rapidly, have ex-panded manufactured exports even more rapidly than GDP, and have drawn very heavily on international finance to achieve these results.

But in spite of all these 'truths', it is incorrect to draw the conclusions that have been suggested, especially when these are drawn relatively indiscriminately to apply both to the least-developed economies, as in the recent IBRD document on 'Accelerated Development in Sub-Saharan Africa', and to the advanced industrial economies, as in re-cent statements emerging out of Thatcher's Economic Policy Review Board, suggesting that if only Britain could get downwardly flexible wages it could attain the dynamism the NICs had in the 1970s.

AN ALTERNATIVE VIEW

While the explosive growth of the NICs was an important development that is not in essence being disputed here, it is the interpretation of those developments that is at issue.

An alternative view of these developments is worth considering, since it has rather different implications for the policy debate. This view argues that the NIC phenomenon emerged as a response to a cer-tain set of international economic contradictions which at one and the same time produced: relatively favourable access to certain industrial-country markets; dramatically increased access to international finance, which could now be borrowed directly by NIC governments, and over which they then had direct control; a sharp increase in multi-national firm interest in relocation of production for third-country markets; and a growing sensitivity to the importance of aid to deal with various emerging geo-political issues.

The emergence of the NICs was conditioned by these factors, al-though these did not determine which countries would seize the oppor-tunities thus presented. This was determined partly by location and geo-political significance; partly by the existence of a strong, 'interna-tionally' reliable regime; and partly by the existence of a significant in-stitutional technological infrastructural and skill base build-up in the context of earlier import substitution policies.

It is true that, building on that base, it was possible for the NICs, under these particular international circumstances, to pursue a growth and export-oriented policy which involved a reduction in the extent to which there was discrimination against exports and in favour of imports. Because the dynamism generated was sufficient to produce a rapid increase in jobs and employment, these 'more liberal' policies could be sustained in these particular circumstances.

Furthermore, even with all of these factors to be considered, it must be emphasised that in a number of critical respects the NIC economies – with the exception of the very small entrepots of Singapore, Hong Kong and possibly Taiwan – were not the liberal, market-oriented economies they sometimes appear to be. If we take the South Korean case as illustrative, we find that: its liberalisation of import restrictions has been extremely careful and gradual, suggesting that they have been well aware that liberalisation must reflect the competitive strength of the evolving indigenous producers; its restrictions on direct foreign investment have been extensive and have been sustained to date, in a manner strongly reminiscent of the Japanese experience; its heavy-industry policy has again been strongly reminiscent of the Japanese pattern, with major decisions taken on the basis of longer-term technological objectives and in clear disregard of short-term efficiency criteria as indicated by existing prices; research and technology have been strongly encouraged and financed by the state and in general the state has played an active and central role in the allocation of investment and in the supervision of its operation.

A recent study has concluded that, in South Korea:

> with high discretionary control over investment and export decisions able to be exerted via the capital market, the government could afford to establish a set of relatively liberal foreign trading policies. The neo-classical focus on the link between trading policies and growth has thus been misleading, for it has obscured the significance of capital market controls as means of state direction of economic activity.
>
> (R. Wade, *Irrigation and Agricultural Politics in South Korea*, 1982, pp. 146–7)

The conclusion that suggests itself in the light of these remarks is one that (a) emphasises the various international circumstances that created the opportunity for the NIC phenomenon; (b) shows quite clearly that the NIC policies that attended their explosive growth were, in fact, in many cases, policies very much developed from the point of view of the nation as 'the effective economic unit', and (c) shows that this behaviour was in any event possible only because of the fact that earlier inward-looking strategies had built the necessary base for these. Using this experience to urge Sub-Saharan African economies in 1982 into export promotion, import and capital liberalisation, and a withdrawal of governments from economic activity, is not only inappropriate, but borders on the incredible.

In the 1980s, markets will be more difficult to find; finance will be more expensive and much more difficult to get; technical change will be more rapid; real wages will be falling in most developing countries; terms-of-trade prospects for traditional primary exports must be rather bleak; and there is no possibility of full employment even in the industrial economies. There is no chance that under these circumstancess a headlong integration into the international economy would provide a hope for trickle-down in the context of a full employment sustained during a move up the technological ladder. The pursuit of policies pretending that this was a possibility would merely represent a smoke-screen for a 'false nationalism' through which a shrinking minority of those owning internationally saleable skills or resources could escape having their interests and circumstances 'pooled' with those of their less fortunate compatriots.

For those countries able on either a right or a left wing basis to generate a policy genuinely concerned with the long-term interests of the nation as an economic unit, there will be a greater need than ever to formulate policies that set in motion a dynamic process of accumulation together with the effective and cumulative development of an indigenous technological capability. This will require policies that are nationally defined and oriented. While it will require national control to continue to be exercised over the formulation and implementation of policy, there can be no clear-cut answer to the question of what degree of foreign involvement is compatible with that objective. This will vary from place to place and from time to time, but it is, and remains, a critically important objective none the less.

Finally, it is important to remember that it is not only foreigners who can threaten such a policy base. There are always groups and interests within an economy that will be more than happy to espouse a premature liberalism in trade.

The final conclusion must be that, for the 1980s, the bulk of developing countries, and especially the relatively weak sub-Saharan economies, will have only two choices: either to espouse liberalism and export-orientation at the cost of increasing social and political polarisation and instability; or to espouse a nationalist strategy that builds with some urgency on the base they now have, and seeks to use foreign exchange and foreign technology in so far as that is compatible with the maintenance of a national process of cumulative growth and technological development – even where that technology may be far, and in some cases even increasingly, behind those used internationally. Unfortunately this second alternative is discouraged strongly by international financial structures, is difficult to sustain in the face of domestic political opposition, and, in any case, may not be viable – depending on its dynamism, the rapidity of population growth and its exposure to external fluctuations. Even so, it is important to look in this direction, since no other is effectively available for any but the most advanced NICs.

Relations of Production and Technology

Colin Leys

The following seeks to make two main points. First, the point often made but often forgotten again, that technology is never neutral but is intimately related to the social relations of production; indeed it is an aspect of those relations. Second, in considering indigenous technological capacity as a problem of development strategy the constraints presented by the international economy must be analysed in a way that also focuses on the primacy of production relations.

TECHNOLOGY AND THE SOCIAL RELATIONS OF PRODUCTION

The perception that technology is not neutral goes back at least to Babbage's *On the Economy of Machinery,* of which Marx made memorable use in *Capital.*[1] Marx, however, tended to think of machinery as having in itself no class character: 'Machinery is *misused* in order to transform the worker, from his very childhood, into a part of a specialised machine',[2] 'machinery *in itself* shortens the hours of labour, but when employed by capital it lengthens them . . . *in itself* it lightens labour, but when employed by capital it heightens its intensity . . . *in itself* it is a victory of man over the forces of nature but in the hands of capital it makes man the slave of these forces.'[3] Engels argued, in 1872, that 'factory slavery' was inescapable even under communism.[4]

However, as the Maoists argued in the debate over 'reds' versus 'experts' during the Cultural Revolution, a given technology – including machinery – reflects or embodies the relations of production in which it develops.[5] This is true both of the products produced, and of the machinery and the labour process by which they are produced. A given item of machinery may be capable of being used within different relations of production from those in which it was produced. But systems

175

of machinery are designed for specific sets of production relations: relations of production are specific 'relations of ownership . . . including, I think, class relations and the corresponding form and character of the state'.[6] Removed from those relations even a machine is apt to become inefficient, unreliable or even worse. In some cases this is self-evident (for example, assembly-line equipment), in others it is less obvious but still apt to be so.

The point becomes politically important when it is a question of transferring technology systematically between countries. In general, it will only be practicable if the relations of production appropriate to it exist or are established in the importing country. For this reason the issue of technology can become the focus of a political struggle, as happened, for example, in Tanzania over the proposed establishment of a big tourist sector.[7] Those who argued against it saw that not only would the demonstration effect of the presence of foreign tourists increase domestic pressures for individualism and consumerism, but the facilities that tourism would require or generate (airports, restaurants, hotels, shops, travel agencies, banking facilities, taxi services, prostitution, etc.) would all enhance the 'logic' and seeming inevitability of a capitalist development path – and enlarge the social forces with a vested interest in it.

Where the dominant relations of production are in conflict with a given technology, the technology is replaced. Müller's examples from Tanzania, in this volume, illustrate this point. The social relations of production that produced the technology of the traditional rural blacksmiths were in conflict with those that were being promoted by the classes represented by the state; the old rural relations in which this technology had developed were undermined, and it progressively disappeared (see p. 377). Similarly with the technological capacity of the indigenous Asian entrepreneurs (p. 380): its consolidation and further extension would have necessitated the inclusion of the Asian manufacturers in the dominant class alliance. The African leadership, however, sought, for various reasons, to exclude the local Asian capitalists, and instead an alliance was made (in practice though not in theory) with international capital, leading to the importation of technology corresponding to a much later period in the development of capitalist manufacture.[8]

The reason why Marx seems to have thought that machinery itself has no class character is that he saw in every technological advance a step towards the 'realm of freedom', emancipation from toil, for humankind; and the phenomenal increases in the productivity of labour finally achieved by capitalist technology in some sectors of production have had the same effect on the way we tend to look at it today. But it is important to confront the social character of capitalist technology, especially if, unlike Marx, you see reason to think that capitalism will not make it possible to emancipate from toil *all* the peoples of the world, if any.

Before trying to illustrate this in relation to other papers, two last general points perhaps deserve to be made. One is that notwithstanding the unique historical success of capitalism in developing productivity-raising technology, it is not impossible to imagine a non-capitalist society that did so, as well or better (for instance, by removing any incentive for workers to oppose innovation by guaranteeing them the full benefits of it). It is also possible, on the other hand, to imagine a society in which raising labour productivity ceased to be the chief criterion of technological excellence. Indeed this seems to be implied by Marx's conception of the 'realm of freedom', in which the new needs produced within communist relations of production would presumably not be needs for more consumption (which under capitalism they must be), but needs for creative activity, society, enriched culture, etc. The technology corresponding to the production of such needs would presumably be considered advanced in so far as it maximised such things as collective decision-making about production, individual or collective creativity, rewarding working relationships, a cleaner or quieter environment, etc. Such a technology could not compete easily, if at all, with capitalist technology in world markets. For a country that must do this to a significant extent, therefore, it seems that a strategy of 'technological dualism' would be necessary, using productivity-maximising technology in sectors which must compete, while seeking to insulate other sectors from the impact of the relations of production which this would require. This would obviously be difficult. Although the case envisaged here is purely formal, its relevance to proposals for 'alternative' technological strategies seems evident.

'INDEPENDENT TECHNOLOGICAL-LEARNING CAPABILITY' VERSUS 'INDEPENDENT TECHNOLOGY-CREATING CAPABILITY'

Dore's paper in this volume stresses the necessity of matching the capacity to create new technology in an underdeveloped country with a capacity to discover and learn the technology developed elsewhere. The key presupposition in Dore's discussion of the Indian case, however, is that India is a capitalist country, and as such must compete in world markets (including its own). Given this, and given the speed of technological change, India must learn to learn, as Japan did. Dore's argument on this point seems entirely convincing.

However, the presupposition is not stated. Dore seems to argue that technology is a universal good which the proponents of technological self-reliance wish to deny their countries, out of, at best, a misguided nationalism. This is made clear when he argues that even a strategy of 'de-linking', reducing trade in world markets to a minimum, can and should be combined with a strategy of learning foreign-invented technology. The implication is that this strategy can only be a strategy for 'catching up' and 're-linking' later on, and that the relations of production necessary for the successful assimilation of the available foreign technology are not problematic in any way. But it is possible to question, for many underdeveloped countries, whether any such strategy is really realistic; and for them, the absorption of capitalist technology which requires capitalist production relations may be strongly contra-indicated.

This is the sort of country to which Bienefeld's arguments are particularly addressed, and his paper might at first seem to reflect the approach to technology that I have advanced. But this is not altogether clear. The nationalist development strategies which he envisages as an alternative to the market-oriented 'liberalisation' doctrines being urged in World Bank reports and elsewhere must, he says, set in motion 'the effective and cumulative development of an indigenous technological capability', using foreign technology only selectively in so far as it is compatible with 'a national process of cumulative growth and technological development – even where that technology may be far, and in some cases increasingly, behind those used internationally' (p. 173). Moreover this sort of alternative strategy may be pursued on 'either a right or a left wing basis' (p. 172): what matters most is that it should be national. This leaves the impression that the essential feature of the technology used in such a strategy is only that it should be comprehensible by the indigenous population. Its social character is not seen as a problem.

However, while it is possible to imagine a right wing nationalist regime following a strategy of selectively using imported, if obsolete, capitalist technology, the problems involved for a left wing one seem too substantial to be ignored. Short of being able to confine the imported technology in a segregated enclave, problems seem bound to be posed by the social relations implicit in the design and quality of the products; the machinery for producing them (for example, assembly-line technology and the Taylorist separation of knowledge and control from execution on which it rests); the accounting system (such as that which, according to Müller (p. 384) led to the Ubungo Farm Implement Manufacturing Company in Dar es Salaam becoming a two-product factory and subsequently a factory organised on Taylorist principles); the mode of appropriation of the imported technology (joint-ventures would be excluded, for instance); and so on. Examples abound in the literature on Tanzania.[9] Solving such problems is theoretically possible and presumably this is part of what is meant when people refer to 'adapting' and 'modifying' imported technology. But it implies a very high degree of clarity about the social relations of production implicit in technology, and a sophisticated ability to disengage what is acceptable from what is not, to ensure that only the former is adopted and assimilated, and to neutralise the contradictions that will inevitably arise in spite of all efforts. In the real world one of the results of underdevelopment is that progressive forces lack skills and experience in precisely this area; and the progressive regimes to which they give rise are relatively weak in face of internal and external pressures which make such a controlled, discriminating approach to technology even harder. For these reasons I think the thrust of Bienefeld's argument is more realistic for a right-wing nationalist strategy of technological development than a left-wing one.

THE NATURE OF THE INTERNATIONAL CONSTRAINTS

These remarks are not intended to cast doubt on Bienefeld's analysis of the general implications of the world economic crisis for development strategy in underdeveloped countries. Yet there are also some difficulties involved here which relate to the conceptual issues discussed earlier. The structure of Bienefeld's argument is that because liberalisation will be destructive to many if not most UDCs, and in particular will not lead to a new generation of Newly Industrialising Countries (NICs), the alternative to be explored is a strategy of development designed to strengthen 'the nation as an effective economic unit'. I would like to examine some of the steps in this argument.

First of all, there is Bienefeld's own recognition that while the world recession will be destructive for most UDCs in so far as they are integrated into the world economy, it 'may also provide important positive openings for particular nations in their attempts to close [the] technological gap'. What is the force of this qualification? The point presumably is that some countries may offer particular attractions to capital, or to imperialist states, in the course of the recession. It is indeed difficult if not impossible to know what will prove important in this respect. In general, the increased mobility of capital, once 'external economies' have been 'internalised' in multinational corporations 'by taking over external suppliers and by codifying and routinising skills',[10] makes the attractiveness of particular physical locations to particular capitals a good deal less determinate than used to be the case. In the early 1970s Emmanuel was confident that capital was always attracted to locations in high concentrations of mass consumption;[11] in the early 1980s it is conventional wisdom that it is attracted to countries with cheap and well-policed supplies of labour. The truth seems to be that it is no longer possible to say what is decisive in the location or re-location of 'capital' in general. Natural resources, transportation, shifting patterns of growth in regional markets, 'security', military-aid spending and much else are involved, and affect different branches and forms of capital differently in a situation of worldwide production planning. The concept of 'regimes of accumulation' developed by Aglietta, Lipietz and others seeks to respond to this.[12] A wider variety of different 'regimes' now exists from which various forms of capital may choose. Bienefeld's proviso about the 'positive openings' that may exist for some UDCs is potentially a significant one.

This means, second, that the fact that there are not likely to be any new NICs during the world depression is less decisive than it might first appear. The new 'positive openings' may not be openings to industrialisation based on effective competition in world markets for manufactures, but they might be either significant steps towards that, or alternatively steps along a different path such as services or primary product processing. In other words there may be significant capitalist 'success stories' among UDCs without there being any new NICs: the development alternatives are not necessarily as stark as his account might tend to make them appear.

Bienefeld's explanation of the uniqueness of the NIC phenomenon is also related to this point. He argues that: (1) world conditions in the 1960s and 1970s afforded a unique historical 'door' through which a limited number of UDCs could pass (key conditions being especially favourable access to first-world markets and to international capital which the NIC governments could control; increased relocation of capital by MNCs; and geo-politically-determined aid programmes): I have already suggested that this 'door' was and is not as narrow or as closed as Bienefeld's paper tends to imply. (2) The NICs owe their industrial breakthrough not to liberalisation of trade but to carefully sequenced, government-directed investment and R&D, and long-term carefully managed trade strategies. This argument is, I believe, entirely correct. The question I want to ask, however, is how these *states* (rather than governments, of which there were many different ones during the long period of time to which Bienefeld draws attention) came to pursue these strategies.

Speaking generally, states are an expression of relations of production. State power is indeed used by dominant classes to bring the relations of production into conformity with the requirements of the forces of production with which they are identified; but states do not act autonomously to change the relations of production (they have some autonomy, but only *within* the framework of an established system of production relations). To understand the process of state-directed development of production relations we must first understand the class forces of which the operation of the state is an expression. In relation to the NICs, this means that we cannot explain the emergence of a class of industrial capitalists and the rapid expansion of manufacture by reference to the operation of a 'strong state'; on the contrary, we must seek an explanation of the operation of a 'strong state' in the prior strength of the class of capital.

This has been discussed extensively in relation to the older industrialising countries, including Japan, but not yet as much as might be expected in relation to the newly industrialising countries. A glimpse of what is involved is provided by not merely South Korea and Taiwan but also North Korea and Manchuria which, in the view of U. Menzel, would probably be considered NICs if they were 'market economies' and Manchuria were independent.[13] As Menzel points out, what all four have in common is not that they have liberalised their economies but that their social relations of production were drastically reorganised by the Japanese between 1910 and 1940. Combined with cultural 'legacies' of the previously obtaining production relations this reorganisation resulted in infrastructures, and the development of new class forces, which were critical for industrial development in the 1960s and 1970s. These regimes disposed, by then, not only of large 'free' wage labour forces and a 'class of capital', but a highly educated labour-force and a class of capital with accumulated technological, market and organisational knowledge. The *resulting* state apparatuses also disposed of technical, ideological and administrative capacities to direct and supervise the accumulation process, as well as to repress opposition to it.

If we bring this line of thought together with the earlier point about the 'positive openings' that will exist for some countries in spite of (or because of) the depression, we can see that what is really involved is a broad and multi-dimensional 'field' of possibilities for many UDCs to make *some* advance along *a* capitalist development path. The absence of a complex of conditions, such as those that brought certain countries to the threshold of 'world manufacturing industrialism' in the last two decades, does not mean that the conditions are necessarily absent for a given country to take a different, less dramatic but still significant step towards capitalist development – even though Bienefeld is correct in insisting that this will not come about through 'liberalisation'.

The point is by no means to 'advocate' capitalist development. But it seems important not to pose the options in terms of *either* becoming a NIC, *or* turning to a 'national' development strategy based on 'de-linking'; and not to pose the latter as an alternative without more explicit attention to the social character of what is likely to be involved. In particular, it is potentially misleading to speak as if it does not make much difference whether a 'national' development strategy has a 'left-wing' or a 'right-wing' character; ultimately this seems as significant a choice as that between a 'de-linked' or an 'integrated' path of capitalist development. In relation to a proposed 'left-wing' option, the question needs to be posed whether the social forces necessary to make a reality of it exist in the country concerned. Otherwise it is likely to result in a regime of stagnation, not a regime of accumulation, which may be called 'socialist' but which in fact retards the development of the productive forces with few if any compensating social benefits.[14] And in relation to a proposed 'right-wing' national strategy, the class implications of what is proposed should be frankly stated, so that they can be openly compared with the class consequences of development under an 'open' strategy. Perhaps the actually available right-wing 'national' development option will be preferable for the mass of the population to an 'open' strategy, but this should not be regarded as axiomatic. A 'false nationalism' which benefits only the privileged strata seems as great a risk in this case as a strategy of 'openness'.

NOTES

1. *Capital,* vol. 1 (Harmondsworth: 1976) pp. 466–70; and 544–64.
2. Ibid, p. 547 (italics added).
3. Ibid, pp. 568–9 (italics added).
4. In 'On Authority', Marx–Engels *Selected Works,* vol. 1 (Moscow: 1962) pp. 633–6.
5. See, for example, R. Rossanda, 'Mao's Marxism', *Socialist Register,* 1971, pp. 53–80.
6. G. A. Cohen, *Karl Marx's Theory of History: A Defence* (Oxford: 1978) pp. 34–5; the extension to classes and the state is not authorised by Cohen, though I think it must follow.
7. I. G. Shivji (ed.), *Tourism and Socialist Development* (Dar es Salaam: 1973).
8. In both cases, however, it seems more accurate to describe what happened here as the subordination of the technology corresponding to one set of production relations to the technology corresponding to a different set, than to speak of the 'liquidation' or decline of 'indigenous technology'. At least in the case of the Asian entrepreneurs, they were themselves indigenous, but their technology was imported. Whether they would have independently developed this technology subsequently may be doubted (although they would probably have developed their understanding of it and of more advanced imported technology); as capitalists, their interest would have lain in using the most profitable technology available, rather than in creating new technology themselves. And even if they had made an independent technological contribution it needs to be shown why this should in itself be desirable. It might be less productive, or more import-consuming, or have other prima-facie negative features from the point of view of the economy and society as a whole. It could be argued that the Tanzanian state's 'command' of the indigenous Asian entrepreneurs' technological competence – to use Bienefeld's helpful specification of the respect in which it is valuable that technological capacity should be 'indigenous' – was more complete than its command over the MNC-owned technology imported in the late 1960s and 1970s, because the technology imported by the Tanzanian Asian capitalists was simpler; but this was not a consequence of the *nationality* of the importers.
9. See, for example, A. Coulson (ed.), *African Socialism in Practice* (Nottingham: 1979) chs 6 and 12–14.
10. A. Brenner, *Marxist Theories of Imperialism* (London: 1980) p. 24. Pages 23–4 of Brenner's introduction are a remarkable synthesis of a complex and confused theoretical itinerary on the left in this field.
11. A. Emmanuel, 'Myths of Development versus Myths of Underdevelopment', *New Left Review,* 85 (1974) p. 77.
12. M. Aglietta, *A Theory of Capitalist Regulation* (London: 1979); A. Lipietz, 'Towards Global Fordism?', *New Left Review,* 132 (1982) pp. 33–47.
13. U. Menzel, 'Imperialism, East–West Conflict and Neo-Imperialism in East Asia', paper presented to the German Historical Institute Confer-

ence on Imperialism after Empire, Bad Homburg, September 1982, esp. pp. 1–15.

14. See, for example, G. Kitching, *Development and Underdevelopment in Historical Perspective* (London: 1982) ch. 5; also C. Leys, 'African Economic Development in Theory and Practice', *Daedalus,* April 1982, pp. 99–124.

IV. Learning, Work Organisation and Technological Capability

'Learning' and the Accumulation of Industrial Technological Capacity in Developing Countries

Martin Bell

'LEARNING' AND THE ACCUMULATION OF TECHNOLOGICAL CAPACITY[1]

Discussion of the role of 'learning' in the process of technological development is made difficult by the fact that the term is used to refer to a range of quite different concepts. In common use, the term refers to various *processes* by which skill and knowledge are acquired by individuals or perhaps organisations. In the context of discussion about technological development, it is often used in this way – for example, to refer to the processes by which individual enterprises acquire technical skills and technical knowledge.

However, there is a tradition of quite different usage in the economics literature about technical change. The term is used in that context to refer to patterns of change in the *performance* of production activities. For example, in the classic case of rising productivity with apparently 'fixed facilities', the path of performance improvement is simply referred to as 'learning' – hence, 'learning curves'. Other kinds of performance improvement over time have also been described as learning.[2] In the literature on technological development in industrialising economies, the term is sometimes used in this way. For example, rising productivity in infant enterprises is often described as learning.

What seems to be involved in this second type of use is the presumption that some kind of skill and knowledge accumulation process lies behind the observed performance trends. Such trends are therefore supposed to be the observable *effects* of 'learning', in the first sense, having taken place. Effect is thus terminologically associated with presumed cause *because* additional skill and knowledge has been acquired, the efficiency of task performance rises. This identification of cause and effect is potentially quite misleading. For example, falling unit costs (or rising productivity) with apparently unchanged production facilities may have absolutely nothing to do with increasing skill and knowledge. A quite constant and unchanging stock of skill and knowledge may simply be used to implement a series of minor changes and incremental improvements which over time give rise to falling costs. Thus 'learning' in the second sense may occur without any 'learning' in the first sense having occurred. Alternatively, even if there has been learning in some form of the first sense, that may not have occurred at the point where improved task performance is measured. For example, labour productivity may increase in firm A because the quality of its intermediate inputs has been improved by firm B. This non-coincidence of the location of the two kinds of 'learning' may well stretch across international boundaries. For example, improved productivity in UK rubber-goods plants has increased because of improved product quality and standardisation in the primary processing, natural rubber industry in Malaysia.[3]

Thus, evidence about learning in the second sense in industrialising economies is not necessarily evidence about learning in the first sense. Indeed a question of some importance is about the relationship between the two.

In this paper we shall be concerned with 'learning' in the first of the two senses outlined above – namely, to refer to the acquisition of additional technical skill and knowledge by individuals and, through them, by organisations. More generally, then, the term will be used to refer to the acquisition of increased 'technological capacity'. This, however, merely opens into a second level of possible confusion. The term 'learning' seems to have been used to refer to two quite different kinds of process whereby technological capacity is acquired.

(1) It is often used to refer to a process of acquiring skill and knowledge that depends largely or entirely on experience: learning-by-doing. The execution of production tasks in one period generates a flow of information and understanding which allows execution to be improved in a subsequent period. This flow of 'learning' is therefore seen as a feedback process which operates within production activity. It also seems to involve two distinguishable components. One is a flow of information which stimulates search for improvement. This is usually information about system performance; it consists of information about problems encountered or opportunities perceived. The second is a flow of understanding and knowledge about *how* change might be made. The execution of production activities generates a flow of

knowledge about how the particular system 'works'. The increments of knowledge enable better methods to be defined. In trying out such methods, further flows of stimuli and understanding may be generated to allow the change to be perfected – or at least made profitable.

(2) In more recent studies, the term 'learning' has been used to refer much more generally to the acquisition of increased skill and knowledge by any means at all. This seems to encompass various 'by-doing' kinds of learning, but also various other mechanisms that do not rest on experience accumulation. Thus, 'learning' has come to refer to any way in which a firm increases its capacity to manage technology and to implement technical change.

This distinction may seem a little pedantic, but it probably has important practical implications. The two kinds of learning process function in quite different ways, and probably have quite different implications for policy

As treated in most economic analysis, doing-based learning has three remarkable properties. First, it arises quite *passively*. Little or no explicit action is required to capture the increased knowledge/skill and whatever benefits flow from that acquisition. Second, the learning process is virtually *automatic*. Given a period of 'doing', some quantum of learning will take place. Third, it is *costless*. Learning is acquired simply as a free by-product from carrying on with production. No expenditure beyond that needed for production is required to generate the increased knowledge and skill.

This 'something-for-nothing' model of the learning process leads inevitably towards certain kinds of policy prescription. Increased 'learning' requires increased 'doing', and hence various forms of protection for doing are seen as appropriate means for enhancing learning – the benefits of the learning gained will offset the inevitable costs of protection. Beyond that, the role of policy intervention is limited. Since experience accumulation is simply a function of time or of cumulated total output, questions about policy intervention designed to raise the rate of learning derived from a given stream of production activity are largely irrelevant.

This perspective has long characterised discussions of infant-industry policy in developing economies. More recently it has been applied to the production of technological services that are used for investment in new facilities – protection of domestic supply against imported equivalents has been seen as important in order to generate 'learning' relating to those activities (for example, Cooper and

Maxwell, 1975). More recently still, protectionist arguments have been advanced in relation to more general concerns about enhancing technological development in industrialising economies (for example, Lall, 1980; or Fransman, 1981).[4]

Other learning mechanisms do not have these passive, automatic, and costless properties. They are likely to involve explicit effort and *investment* in the acquisition of technological capacity. Protectionist perspectives on policy may therefore be inappropriate if these non-doing-based learning processes are important sources of increased technological capacity. Some degree of protection, together with the costs of that, *may* be a necessary condition for some kinds of learning – where the benefits from learning will exceed the costs of protection – but may well not be sufficient. Indeed in some circumstances protectionist measures may be counter-productive.

It is important therefore to identify the extent to which doing-based learning, as opposed to other mechanisms, has contributed to the kinds of increased technological capacity and significant technological progress reported in recent studies.[5]

Only a preliminary attempt at this can be made here. This will be organised around Figure 4, which indicates six different kinds of information or knowledge flow that have been described as contributing to 'learning'. Although it is shown in the diagram, the flow of knowledge that is generated by R&D activities will be excluded from the discussion. With the concept of learning defined broadly to encompass all forms of knowledge acquisition, this is somewhat arbitrary. If one defines R&D in the conventional manner, it does not produce technical change as such. It produces the *knowledge* upon which technical change can be based. In principle, then, R&D, and the flow of knowledge it generates, might be considered a 'learning' mechanism that is equivalent to all the others outlined below. Indeed in Katz's discussion of 'learning by spending' (Katz, 1973), it is explicitly treated in that way.

LEARNING BY OPERATING

This flow of experience, which is derived from actually doing production tasks, constitutes one kind of feedback mechanism as described above. It consists of a combination of change-stimuli and increased understanding which enables individuals to improve their own execution of given production tasks. Such individuals may be direct production workers, supervisors or managers who, by implementing micro-alterations to the way they carry out their own operating tasks, generate improved enterprise performance.

The details of this task-specific type of learning-by-doing process are almost unobservable except by the most painstaking investigations. Nevertheless, it does seem that this process is relatively 'passive' and 'automatic', in the sense that it will occur at some rate with the passage of time or with increasing cumulative output. However, as noted in a number of studies,[6] there is a limit to the performance improvement that can be generated from this source, and that limit is often reached very quickly. Even in industrialising economies, this is probably not a significant source of improved production performance over the longer term.[7] Few of the recent studies of technical change in those economies suggest that this kind of learning has made an important contribution to the technological progress reported.

Different learning mechanisms involved in
infant enterprise maturation

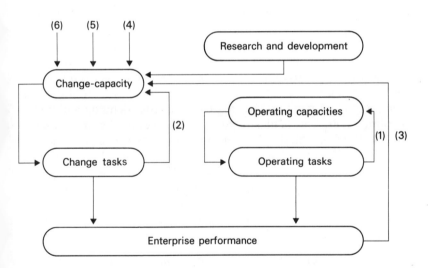

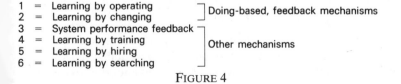

1 = Learning by operating ⎤
2 = Learning by changing ⎦ Doing-based, feedback mechanisms
3 = System performance feedback ⎤
4 = Learning by training ⎥
5 = Learning by hiring ⎥ Other mechanisms
6 = Learning by searching ⎦

FIGURE 4

LEARNING FROM CHANGING

Much of the 'learning' described in those studies seems to have been generated not by doing the operation of existing plants, but by doing various kinds of technical change activity. Although perhaps obvious in principle, this is difficult to substantiate in detail since few of the studies clearly indicate who learned what by doing what. The most explicit emphasis on the point is provided in Maxwell's study of the Acindar steel company in Argentina.[8] Much of the growing technological capacity of the firm was generated from actually undertaking the series of technical changes and improvements made in the plant. In other studies one has to read much more 'between the lines' to identify what was actually involved in the 'learning' to which so much is attributed. Repeatedly, however, the impression given is that it was involvement in *technical change*, not involvement in *technique-operation*, that augmented the technical knowledge and skills of the firms involved.

This, of course, is inherently probable. Opening the 'black box' of a particular production technology and manipulating its contents is much more likely to generate additional knowledge and understanding than is continued operation of a given production system. One probably learns little from facing problems (and even less from ignoring them), but a great deal from solving them. One may learn little from using improved methods, but a great deal from defining and implementing them. This is illustrated, for example, by the brief descriptions in Katz and Ablin (1978) of some of the components of the 'significant process of technical learning' which lay behind the exports of industrial plants from Argentina. One case involved the development of innovative bakery equipment by a firm which originated as a bakery-equipment user. However, it was not the experience of simply using and operating bakery equipment that generated the firm's learning. Rather,

> in the course of production, *it found solutions to various technical problems* which affected its performance . . . in the course of these typical 'trouble-shooting' activities it designed special equipment for the sector. (p. 24, our emphasis)

In another case, a firm that produced and exported chemical plants had adapted an original plant design to use a locally available vegetable oil which was cheaper than the previously specified imported material.

The experience accumulated *in the course of this adaptation* enabled it later on to undertake a new process using fish oil, which proved of interest to a Peruvian firm. (p. 24, our emphasis)

At least three kinds of 'learning' seem to occur when these types of 'minor' technical change are undertaken. First, greater understanding of the *particular form* of the technology is acquired. Second, greater knowledge of the more general principles involved may be acquired, allowing perception of possible wider applications of those principles, or of possible alternative ways of applying them to the particular production situation. Third, increased '*confidence*' in manipulating the technology may be gained. All these kinds of addition to technological capacity seem potentially greater when the technological 'black box' is yet more open during the implementation of major investment projects – for example, when a new industrial plant is created, or when large additions to existing capacity are undertaken.

A number of studies, some empirically based but many not, have emphasised the importance of such 'major' technical changes as opportunities for significant learning. For example, with access to imported technology being blocked during the early 1940s, the Acindar steel company in Argentina had to draw entirely on local technological resources for designing and building its first small plant at Rosario. When it came to expanding the plant in 1947,

Acindar was able to draw on its previous experience in the design, construction and operation of the original furnace so as to introduce several improvements . . . the learning efforts that went on during the initial plant investment helped lower the costs of and improve the efficiency of the subsequent plant expansion.

Yet there was a still more important later benefit to Acindar from its early learning in Rosario – an intangible benefit. This was the psychological boost to all the firm's personnel which resulted from the great success with which they brought the plant into being . . . one still senses the confidence and pride of those involved in this project [and] a definite technological optimism both as regards the development of 'home-grown' adaptations and improvements when required, and also as regards advancing into technological fields completely new to the company.[9]

Participation and involvement in the technological aspects of investment in successive petrochemical plants in Korea seem to have contributed in similar ways to the capacity for undertaking subsequent improvements and modifications (Seoul National University, 1980). However, the evidence of this Korean study indicates a significant circularity in the relationship between learning and participation in major investment projects. On the one hand, there probably are valuable opportunities to augment technological skills by various kinds of 'doing' during the course of such projects. On the other hand, both the extent of participation and the value of learning derived from it depend on the *prior* existence of capacities to undertake the 'doing' and to capture any new knowledge in the process. Nevertheless, stretched through successive investment projects which incorporate related technologies, this circularity may generate a cumulative learning process whereby change-capacity is built up in successive increments.

Thus, the rate of learning-by-changing is unlikely to be linked systematically to the passage of time or the growth of cumulative total output. It is much more likely to depend on (i) the rate of experienced 'minor' changes and on (ii) the rate of investment in major new units of capital-embodied technology, combined with the degree of participation in those projects. However, given the importance of prior capacities to engage in the doing involved in either of these types of change, the rate is also likely to depend on other channels of learning which do not depend on doing.

SYSTEM PERFORMANCE FEEDBACK

As outlined in an earlier paper (Bell *et al.*, 1980) learning from the experience of production depends, at any level above that of the individual task, on institutionalised mechanisms for generating, recording, reviewing and interpreting that experience. Without such a systematic feedback mechanism, the ongoing operation of production will, for practical purposes, generate little or no experience, and the process of technical change in the firm will lack a critical driving force. Dahlman and Fonseca (1978) illustrate the importance of such a feedback system. The USIMINAS steel plant introduced a package of organisational reforms; which included a new standard cost system. The authors note that this was 'the most important part of the reforms from the point of view of the future technological development of the firm'. This cost system provided the firm with systematic information about its own performance. This contributed to generating important stimuli for change – information about problems upon which the firm's problem-solving capacities were then focused.

It is important to emphasise that this kind of mechanism can also generate elements of knowledge and understanding about the technology itself. Regular monitoring of system performance can provide a basis for understanding how and why performance varies. It can generate the kind of 'understanding of why certain things work and others not', which Nelson (1979) suggests is often absent for particular production systems. It can reduce the 'considerable vagueness regarding what new techniques can be developed'. However, there is little that is passive or automatic about this learning mechanism. An industrial plant can run for years without generating any of this kind of understanding, or any systematic stimuli for change. This flow of information is not a function of time or of cumulative output. Rather, it depends on the allocation of resources to generate that flow. Moreover, even if mechanisms exist to generate feed-back information about production performance,[10] this provides only a *potential* contribution to technical knowledge and understanding. As stressed by Dahlman and Fonseca (1978),[11] the extent to which such a flow does actually augment the change-capacity of firms depends on the *prior* availability of skills and knowledge to analyse and interpret the information generated.

LEARNING THROUGH TRAINING

Close examination of a number of studies suggests that various kinds of formalised training were often far more important as sources of technological capacity than were forms of doing-based learning. This distinction will often, of course, be blurred; but the difference is adequately clear in a number of case studies. For example, Dahlman and Fonseca (1978) emphasise the importance of the massive technological training efforts undertaken by the USIMINAS steel company in Brazil. Even during the earliest investment stage, when Brazilian engineers were allocated to work alongside the Japanese engineers, the mechanism involved seems to have been much closer to active and explicit training effort than to learning which was 'passively' acquired through that participation.

A similar picture can be derived from the case studies of Korean firms reported in the Seoul National University (1980) study. Although various kinds of 'doing' played some role in augmenting the technological capacity of the firms involved, the effort made to undertake explicit training was probably much more significant. For example, in the case of one petrochemical plant, the initial foreign technology supplier was required not merely to provide training in the efficient operation and maintenance of the plant. Rather, it was laid down

> that the Korean engineers would be trained by Dow in the application of all the aspects of Dow's current technology – basic process design, detailed equipment design and procurement, construction, testing, start-up, operation, and maintenance – and in the techniques employed in securing improvements to any petrochemical technology.

Similarly, in the case of the highly successful Pohang Iron and Steel Company, the initial technology supplier was required to provide training for engineers in the construction of an integrated steel mill, and not merely in its operation. The scale of the effort involved was remarkable:

> POSCO has sent in total 1,308 engineers and technicians to other developed iron and steel mills for on-the-job training. After several months of field training, they returned . . . to POSCO and actively participated in the construction and operations. They have played a significant role in transferring the imported technology to the other engineers, resulting in the remarkable improvement in productivity.

This kind of explicit investment in the acquisition of technological capacity can be contrasted with other experiences. For example, in the case of a steel galvanising plant in Thailand where virtually no technical change occurred over nine years (Bell *et al.*, 1980), the authors note that:

> Little effort seems to have been made over the thirteen year history of the plant to accumulate a stock of technical resources beyond those needed for basic *operation* of the plant. All training seems to have been undertaken with only that as an objective . . . Most of the training was provided 'on-the-job' in the Thai plant, and was carried on in any systematic way for only 18 months. Three technicians were trained in plant operation for only six months in Japan.

This was not an isolated instance. Table 2 describes features of the training activity undertaken by a sample of larger industrial firms in Thailand during the 1960s and early 1970s. During the technology transfer process by which their production facilities were established, very few of these firms carried out any kind of training across a range of functions concerned with technical change. Very few altered that pattern is subsequent years.

TABLE 2   *Selected Aspects of Training Activity of Industrial Firms in Thailand*
(1960s and early 1970s)

Proportion of firms carrying out:

Types of Technological Training	No Training at all %	'Marginal' Training Activity* %	Some Training During Initial Transfer Process %	After Initial Transfer Process %
For Process R&D	100	0	0	0
For Process Engineering	98	0	2	0
For Process Maintenance	78	12	6	4
For Product R&D	98	0	0	2
For Product Design	96	0	0	4
For Product Quality Control	86	10	4	0

* Indeterminate interview responses suggesting the possibility that limited types of training had been carried out.

Source: Preliminary results, ongoing SPRU study.

LEARNING BY HIRING

Firms need not accumulate their technological capacity only by *creating* it. If the skills and knowledge are available in their environment, these may be acquired through the simple mechanism of hiring the people who embody those resources. In many cases, 'ready-made' technological capacity may not instantly produce efficient technical change for the specific needs of the hiring firm. The acquisition of further experience and/or the undertaking of specific on-the-job training may be necessary. Nevertheless, hiring more or less ready-made technological capacity seems to have been a significant mechanism within the 'learning' process that is reported in some plant studies.

For example, periods of technical change activity in the Ducilo rayon plant in Argentina were associated with distinct peaks in expenditure on technicians and engineering staff (Katz *et al.,* 1978). This was achieved by drawing on the technical staff who were available in other units in the company. In turn, the company as a whole seems to have been able to expand its technological resources relatively easily by hiring 'locally trained professionals coming from the Chemical Engineering School in the province of Santa Fe – a renowned educational centre in chemistry'. Hiring readily available resources also appears to have been an important component of the overall 'learning' process for a number of machinery-producing firms in Brazil and Argentina.[12] Periods of evolutionary experience-acquisition in almost all these firms were interspersed with 'step-jumps' in capacity accumulation when the required resources were acquired 'ready-made'. In some cases experienced design engineers were hired to augment the firms' product-changing capacity which had hitherto been limited to the artisanal experience of the founder-owners. In others, particular phases of evolution were marked by the firms engaging trained technicians for the first time. In one case, an identified need to introduce more systematic production planning and control procedures was met by engaging an engineer with the appropriate skills and experience.

In other words, although the technological evolution of these firms may be described as a 'learning' process, that should be interpreted carefully. Learning-by-hiring seems to have been perhaps just as important as intra-firm accumulation of experience – although some time and some experience were obviously a necessary requirement for integrating hired resources into the enterprise, and for adding the important components of firm-specific experience and knowledge to those acquired resources.

LEARNING BY SEARCHING

Externally acquired additions to the technological capacity of firms will often arrive in the form of 'disembodied' knowledge and information – rather than being (i) already embodied in hirable 'human-capital', or (ii) transferred by a reasonably explicit training process.[13] In fact, however, such knowledge and information very seldom just 'arrives'. Almost always it has to be searched out and acquired by the firm itself. In other words, the flow depends on active effort by the firm, and that in turn requires the prior accumulation and deployment of resources to make that search effort.

Dahlman and Fonseca (1978) emphasise this point in the case of the USIMINAS steel plant. They also indicate the magnitude of the flow of externally acquired technical knowledge which lay behind the technological development of the firm. This knowledge was often acquired as one component within a 'package' which combined the acquisition of particular goods and services, explicit training, and flows of disembodied knowledge and information. For example, much of the knowledge from external sources seems to have been acquired through a succession of technology contracts with foreign consultants, steel producers, and equipment suppliers. More than 200 specific contracts were undertaken between 1965 and 1975. Most of these seem to have centred on the provision of specific services by the foreign organisations, but they also included a substantial component of explicit and implicit training together with a flow of disembodied technical knowledge.

The company also made major efforts to seek and acquire technical information outside the framework of such contracts. Much of this seems to have been information *about* technology:

> information on the performance and technology of other plants and on the development of the technology frontier . . . information to define correctly which are its technological needs . . . This requires obtaining information on modern techniques of production and control, productivity and quality indexes achieved by other firms, trends in the steel product markets, etc.

Very few other firm-level studies provide systematic information about the nature or significance of these external search mechanisms within the overall 'learning' processes that they describe.[14] That may simply reflect the relative unimportance of this mechanism for the particular firms (and technologies) examined. Alternatively, it may reflect underinvestment by those firms in active search for external knowledge. This, in turn, may arise because of undervaluation of the probable returns to such efforts, or because those returns are indeed low *in the context of* markets which generate limited pressures for undertaking change – or both. However, one thing is reasonably clear. As yet, none of these studies seems to have unearthed empirical evidence showing that monopolisation of technical knowledge in the industrialised economies was a significant constraint on learning in peripheral economies. Certainly much knowledge is appropriated by commercial organisations. That indicates that effort and expenditure may be needed to acquire it. It does not suggest that it cannot be acquired.

What then can be said about the relative importance of the two broad categories of learning mechanism? To recapitulate, these are:

(a) Mechanisms where learning is a costless 'by-product' of doing (that is, learning by operating and learning by changing);

(b) mechanisms where learning depends on the allocation of resources (that is, system learning, and learning by training, by hiring and by searching).

Much of the recent literature *appears*[15] to emphasise the importance of the first of these categories. Within that it suggests that learning-by-operating is a relatively unimportant source of increased technological capacity for enterprises. However, one wonders whether the emphasis on the other doing-based mechanism is not overstressed.

Many of the studies that provide the most useful information about how firms acquire their technological capacity have been designed (or at least presented) as firm-specific studies. For at least two reasons these are inherently likely to lead towards overemphasis on the importance of 'doing-based' mechanisms of learning.

(1) If firms survive long enough to provide an adequate basis for observing their longer-term evolution, various kinds of 'doing' will *inevitably* precede observed phases of technical change and/or capacity accumulation. Only a short, slippery slope lies between there and the conclusion of implication: post 'doing' ergo propter 'doing'.

(2) Even if detailed analysis reveals the connections linking 'doing' to the process of technological development, the firm-specific study may still overemphasise the role of 'doing'. At various stages during the evolution of many of the studied survivor firms, there were, one may presume, other firms with equivalent or even larger accumulations of past doing. If any significant number of these firms ceased to exist or progressed less rapidly than the firms observed, it would be difficult to claim overwhelming importance for doing in the process of technological development. Without such comparisons, the single-firm study is at the top of another short slope towards possibly erroneous conclusions about the importance of doing-based learning.

Some 'quantum' of technical change experience clearly is necessary for accumulating technological capacity. But even that limited conclusion must be qualified. The relative significance of different types of learning mechanism probably changes quite radically during the technological evolution of firms and industries.

A priori reasoning, and some evidence, suggests that progress through particular points in the path of infant maturation cannot be effected at all by doing-based learning. Explicit investment in technological capacity becomes at those points a necessary condition for *any* further progress. This arises because of qualitative discontinuities in the path of technological development. These seem to take two forms:

(1) Ongoing technological development periodically requires firms

to shift to qualitatively different types of *technology*. At these points, continuing competitive performance requires the use or production of much more 'sophisticated' or 'complex' processes or products that embody a class of technical knowledge that is substantially different from what is embodied in existing products and processes.

(2) Ongoing technological development may involve shifting between qualitatively different *tasks* in relation to a given general type of technology. For example, product-centred technical change may move through phases based successively on replicative copying, the specification of 'minor' improvements and modifications, formalised overall re-design, and R&D-based innovation. Similarly, increased self-reliance in the supply of technological inputs for investment in new facilities will involve progression through the mastery of different types of task (for example, for pre-investment studies, through detail engineering and more basic engineering, to the development of new knowledge to incorporate in production systems).[16]

In principle, doing-based learning is likely to be an inadequate means for acquiring the capacity to cross these kinds of discontinuity. Experience with one type of technology – however intensive and prolonged – is unlikely to provide the capacity for changing to another type; and doing one kind of technological task is unlikely to contribute much to the capacity for carrying out quite different kinds. Thus, despite the evident importance of experience in some phases of the maturation process, that process may grind to a halt if 'doing' is the only mechanism used for augmenting change-capacity. Two types of evidence are consistent with this view.

First, some studies suggest that more-or-less exclusive dependence on doing-based learning is inadequate for crossing such discontinuities. Amsden (1977), for example, stresses the technologically closed nature of the Taiwan machine-tool industry. Although the industry developed new products for the export-oriented industries in Taiwan, no technical knowledge was acquired from these customers. Knowledge-flows into the industry from other potential sources were apparently also totally absent. 'Learning' in the industry seems to have been totally 'doing-based'. 'The technical know-how of Taiwanese machine tool builders was acquired painfully and pragmatically'. Far from being a source of strength this 'clearly had a retarding effect on the industry'. Moreover, the industry came to face the need for a qualitative technological 'jump' by the mid-1970s – a requirement to shift both product and production technology on to a quite new basis. In Amsden's judgement the existing industry was incapable of making that transition. It could not learn its way across that discontinuity by 'doing' more of what it already did. Continued accumulation of experience of its existing mode of production, provided no basis for ongoing technological development. If that was to occur, new elements of technological capacity had to be injected into the industry. Amsden suggests that such elements might be provided, *inter alia*, by 'vocational and management training and technical assistance'. Fransman (1981) presents a similar picture of the machine industry in Hong Kong. Technological evolution up to the late 1970s had been based almost exclusively on internal knowledge accumulation and doing-based learning. Faced with the need to make a similar qualitative 'jump' in the technological basis of production, the industry had the same kind of limitation. A new knowledge base for further evolution had to be acquired from *outside* the existing industry.

Second, other studies indicate that explicit investment in acquiring change-capacity from outside the firm was associated with making these kinds of transition. This emerges most clearly, for example, from the studies of machinery-building enterprises in Brazil and Argentina.[17] The evolution of these enterprises was periodically punctuated by pressing stimuli for change – usually threats of severe loss of output volume as product markets changed, but also, in some cases, strong pressures to reduce production costs. In many instances the solutions to these problems required a qualitative 'jump' in technology. Often this involved a shift into a distinctly novel type of product technology. In other cases the requirement was to introduce a novel (to the firm) basis of production technology – frequently a novel approach to the planning and organisation of production rather than a novel form of 'hardware'.

A striking feature of these historical records is that the firms seldom learned their way through these discontinuities by 'doing' what they already did. In very many cases these punctuations in the evolutionary 'trajectory' of firms were marked by the acquisition of new change-capacity from outside the firms. As noted above, these acquisitions usually consisted of knowledge and expertise that was already embodied in 'human capital' – in hired design engineers, production engineers, and teams of technicians.

In other words, while one can describe the evolution of these firms as involving 'learning', it is important to note that critical steps in the process were very often effected through learning-by-hiring, and not learning-by-doing. At the same time, although doing-based learning seems to have been an important mechanism in the phases of change lying between these discontinuities, without any comparative analysis in these studies we do not know whether this contributed to anything resembling an optimal rate or direction of technological progress in these situations of protected production. As in the Taiwan machine-tool industry, exclusive dependence on doing-based learning during these phases may also, for all we know, have had a retarding effect on the industry.

The apparent significance of learning by hiring almost ready-made technological capacity has important implications for the less industrialised developing economies. In the third quarter of the twentieth century, economies like Brazil, Argentina and Korea are already well endowed with institutions for creating very many kinds of technological capacity. At the firm level, learning by hiring is a relatively feasible proposition, and does not involve the firm in creating that capacity – although it may have to carry the costs of adding firm-specific and technology-specific elements. In less industrialised economies learning by hiring may be much less feasible. The prior step – creating hirable technological capacity – may have to be undertaken. That will involve the more deliberate effort and more evident costs of what we have called learning by training and learning by searching.

CONCLUSIONS

It is perhaps misleading to suggest that clear conclusions can be drawn from this selective review of fragmentary empirical evidence. Nevertheless, a number of terminal remarks are probably in order.

(1) Recent empirical studies have made a significant contribution by throwing into question some of the unsubstantiated excesses in earlier discussions of 'technological dependency'. They have shown quite clearly that various forms of technical change do take place in at least the most industrialised of the peripheral economies. They have also shown that this technical change is generated by the active deployment of stocks of technical skill and knowledge – by the deployment of 'technology-capital' or 'indigenous technological capability'. However, they also suggest that doing that technical change by having learned was as common as learning by having done it.

(2) Doing-based learning is *one* mechanism for augmenting technological capacity. To some extent it is evidently a necessity in many phases of technological development. However, it does not seem to be sufficient to maintain progress through all phases.

Moreover, there is not evidence to show that it is sufficient to maintain technological progress in the 'easy' phases at a rate or in a direction that makes the most efficient use of resources. Crucially important for transition through discontinuities, and perhaps also for achieving efficient technical progress overall, is investment in the acquisition of technological capacity, and often also investment in the creation of that capacity. Much of the existing empirical literature conveys a pervasive impression that such explicit investment in the human capital component of change-capacity is often a faltering, intermittent and low priority use of resources.[18]

(3) Although the issue has not been covered in this review, the recent empirical literature also provides grounds for thinking that protection of production may be counter-productive with respect to learning. One virtue of many of these studies is that they show technical change not simply as a supply-side phenomenon. It is also shown to be a response to particular stimuli in product and input markets. Most often, these appear to be negative stimuli (for example, threats to existing markets, disruptive increases in input prices, etc.) rather than positive ones (for example, perception of opportunities to open into new markets or to use different inputs, etc.). In other words, demands for technical change seem to have been as important as the availability of capacities to supply it. Moreover, the emergence of demands and the development of supply capacities do not seem to have been independent. The arrangement of the evidence does not always allow clear conclusions about the nature of the relationship between the two. However, in a significant number of instances, effort to acquire additional technological capacity (that is, explicit learning effort) seems to have been induced by the need to respond to stimuli (demands) for technical change. Protection for doing is likely to decrease the incidence and/or intensity of those stimuli, and hence to reduce, not increase, the rate of learning.

(4) One other feature of the technical change process emerges from some of the studies.[19] Considerable institutional change and inter-enterprise mobility of resources seem to characterise the evolution of industries through certain phases of technological development. Larger, more progressive firms come to dominate industries and achieve the scale and other conditions for technological progress. Change in the basic ownership structure and top-level management of firms appears in some cases as a pre-condition for the acquisition of new kinds of technological capacity.[20] The movement of human-embodied skills from less progressive to more progressive firms seems to

be an important component of the overall change process.[21] Protection is likely to raise the profitability of existing resources within existing institutional structures – for example, within small, market-fragmenting, untransformed and relatively less progressive firms. To that extent it is likely to inhibit both the demand for learning and the effectiveness with which available technology-capital is deployed.

(5) It may be useful to ask whether inefficient doing is always the least-cost means of acquiring additional technological capacity, even when some form of experience is necessary for that. Sercovitch (1980), for example, has suggested in his examination of the petrochemical industry in Brazil that (i) relatively passive doing and experience acquisition may be a slow and ineffective means of accumulating certain types of technological capacity; and (ii) the costs and risks of inefficient doing may be very high. On the other hand, as the PETROBRAS initiative illustrates, it may be possible to devise arrangements for acquiring technological capacity that have two characteristics. First, they are explicitly and deliberately focused on that as a distinct objective, and hence are likely to be more effective. Second, they may be run in parallel with efficient doing in a way that allows various forms of experience to be accumulated, but that insulates efficient doing from temporarily inefficient doing, and hence from the substantial costs and risks of the latter.

(6) It is probably important to bring an historical perspective to bear on the processes involved in learning and technological development. As noted earlier, the recent studies that show significant learning, technical change and 'technological self-reliance' in industrialising economies have almost all been generated out of the recent experience of economies that have been doing industrial production in a substantial way for at least 60–70 years. So far, the policy implications drawn from these descriptive studies seem to have been limited to varying degrees of advocacy of the types of policy that appear to have been associated with the observed technical change, technology exports, etc. Other industrialising economies may find less than persuasive the implication that they should proceed along these lines for another 40 or 50 years before making significant dents in the structure of conditions and symptoms that characterise what might still legitimately be called 'technological dependence'.

(7) In seeking an alternative to that prospect, some forms and degrees of protection are likely to be necessary to break existing patterns of technological behaviour, and some accumulation of doing will be necessary to generate particular types of learning. However, it is also

likely to be necessary to recognise more clearly than in some current policy-oriented literature the costs and risks of protection and the limitations of doing-based learning. It may also be important to make much more aggressive and imaginative efforts to acquire and accumulate technological capacity than has been characteristic both of those economies themselves and of the past experience of the more industrialised developing economies. It is not at all clear what this might actually mean in practical situations. However, insights into possible approaches may be gleaned from case-studies like those of Sabato (1973), Sercovitch (1980), Enos (1982), and Dahlman and Fonseca (1978). These emphasise the role of deliberate, aggressive investment in the accumulation of technology-capital – investment that is made in the context of coherent, long-term strategies, and in the light of 'hardnosed', but social rather than private, perspectives on the returns to that investment.

NOTES

1. This paper draws heavily on the preliminary draft of a study carried out by the author for the World Bank. However, the views and interpretations are those of the author and should not be attributed to the World Bank, to its affiliated organisations, or to any individual acting on their behalf.
2. For example, falling per unit capital costs in successive power plants has been described as 'learning' (Mooz, 1978).
3. In this case, however, 'learning' is not even an apt term to describe the improvement in the Malaysian rubber industry.
4. In this context, it is also interesting to note the protectionist arguments advanced by the Cambridge Economic Policy Group as a remedy for the weak competitive position of UK manufacturing industry (see various issues of the *Cambridge Economic Policy Review*).
5. The apparently trivial issue of terminological distinction may also be important. Presumably research in this area is intended to have some kind of link to policy and action. One matter of unavoidable fact is that many people in positions of more direct influence on policy associate 'learning' with 'learning-by-doing'. Distinctions between the two which are embodied in the fine-print of academic studies may pass unnoticed. As increased discussion of the important role of learning percolates through the system, it will inevitably become clothed with the long-standing 'by-doing' connotations.
6. For a review of some of these studies of learning, see Scott-Kemmis and Bell (forthcoming).
7. Improvements in labour productivity may, of course, persist for a long time, but these probably derive much more from inputs of education and training, etc., than from costless 'doing' – except perhaps in a few occupations where effective performance is peculiarly experienced-based.

8. Both here and below, I draw with gratitude on Philip Maxwell's draft D. Phil. thesis.
9. See note 8.
10. This feed-back flow may incorporate more than information from *within* the firm itself (for example, about production costs, product quality, etc.). It may also include systematic information about product performance generated by customers. The importance of this 'learning-by-using' mechanism in industrialised economies has been stressed by Rosenberg (1979). Westphal *et al.,* (1981) note its importance in the case of Korean exporting firms.
11. See also Bell *et al.,* (1980).
12. See, for example, Castano *et al.,* (1981) da Cruz (1980); and da Cruz and da Silva (1980).
13. As with all the categories of learning mechanism, these distinctions will often be very blurred in practice.
14. Miscellaneous anecdotal fragments, and the author's experience in Thailand, suggest that various kinds of overseas visit, study-tour, temporary overseas employment, etc., may be important forms of search activity which contribute significant elements of knowledge and understanding to a firm's technological capacity. See also Langdon's paper in this volume.
15. The difficulty in interpreting much of this literature is not only the paucity of clear definitions of quite what is meant by the 'learning' discussed, but also the lack of clear conclusions about the relative importance of the different mechanisms.
16. A number of recent studies have elaborated such 'stages' of technological evolution in industrialising economies. Progression through those stages is variously described as 'learning', or as being due to 'learning'. See, for example, Lall (1980).
17. For example, Castano *et al.,* (1981), da Cruz (1980), da Cruz and da Silva (1980).
18. As one recent example, Enos (1982) suggests that the explicit Korean effort to extract various forms of technological learning from transfer-based investment in petrochemical plants was not matched in other countries.
19. See, for example, Amsden (1977). Also, if prepared to add a little extrapolative guesswork, see Fransman.
20. See, for example, some of the studies of Latin American machinery producers.
21. See, for example, Kim (1981).

REFERENCES

Amsden, M. A. (1977) 'The Division of Labour is Limited by the Type of Market: The Case of the Taiwanese Machine Tool Industry', *World Development,* vol. 5, no. 3, pp. 217–34.
Bell, R. M., D. Scott-Kemmis, and W. Satyarakwit (1980) 'Learning and Technical Change in the Development of Manufacturing Industry: A Case

Study of a Permanently Infant Enterprise', mimeo, Science Policy Research Unit, University of Sussex.

Biggs, S. D. (1982) 'Institutions and Decision-Making in Agricultural Research', in Stewart and James (1982).

Castano, A., J. Katz, and F. Navajas (1981) 'Etapas Historicas y Conductas Technologicas en una Planta Argentina de Maquinas Herramienta', IDB/ECLA/UNDP/IDRC Research Programme on Scientific and Technological Development in Latin America, Working Paper No. 38, Buenos Aires.

Cooper, C. M. and P. Maxwell (1975) 'Machinery Suppliers and the Transfer of Technology to Latin America', mimeo, Report to the Organisation of American States, Science Policy Research Unit, University of Sussex.

Da Cruz, H. N. (1980) 'Mudanca Technologica no Setor Metal Mecanico: Un Estudo de Caso de Maquinas para Processor Cerais', mimeo, IDB/ECLA/UNDP/IDRC Research Programme on Scientific and Technological Development in Latin America.

Da Cruz, H. N. and M. N. Da Silva (1981) 'Mudanca Technologica no Setor Metal Mecanico: Relatorio Parcial, Parte II', mimeo, IDB/ECLA/IDRC Research Programme on Scientific and Technological Development in Latin America; Fundacao Instituto de Pequisas Economicas, Sao Paulo.

Dahlman, C. J. and F. V. Fonseca (1978) 'From Technological Dependence to Technological Development: The Case of the USIMINAS Steel Plant in Brazil', IDB/ECLA Research Programme on Science and Technology, Working Paper No. 21, Buenos Aires.

Enos, J. (1982) 'The Choice of Technique Versus the Choice of Beneficiary: What the Third World Chooses', in Stewart and James (1982).

Fransman, M. (1981) 'Learning and the Capital Goods Sector Under Free Trade: The Case of Hong Kong', mimeo, Paper presented at the European Association of Development Research and Training Insitutes Conference, Budapest, November.

Katz, J. M. (1973) 'Industrial Growth, Royalty Payments and Local Expenditure on Research and Development', in V. L. Urquidi and R. Thorpe (eds), *Latin America in the International Economy*. London: Macmillan.

Katz, J. M. and E. Ablin (1978) 'From Infant Industry to Technology Exports: The Argentine Experience in the International Sale of Industrial Plants and Engineering Works', ECLA/IDB Research Programme on Science and Technology, Working Paper No. 24, Buenos Aires.

Katz, J. M., M. Gutkowski, M. Rodrigues and G. Goity (1978) 'Productivity, Technology and Domestic Efforts in Research and Development', IDB/ECLA Research Programme in Science and Technology, Working Paper No. 13, Buenos Aires.

Kim, L. (1980) 'Stages of Development of Industrial Technology in a Developing Country: a Model', *Research Policy,* vol. 9, pp. 254–77.

Kim, L. (1981) 'Technological Innovation in the Korean Capital Goods Sector: A Micro Analysis', mimeo, Korean Advanced Institute of Science and Technology.

King, K. (1974) 'Kenya's Informal Machine Makers: A Study of Small-scale Industry in Kenya's Emergent Artisan Society', *World Development,* April/May

Lall, S. (1980) 'Developing Countries as Exporters of Industrial Technology', *Research Policy*, 9, pp. 24–52.

Leff, N. H. (1968) *The Brazilian Capital Goods Industry 1929–1964*. Cambridge, Mass: Harvard University Press.

Mooz, W. E. (1978) *Cost Analysis of Light Water Reactor Power Plants*, Santa Monica: The Rand Corporation.

Müller, J. (1980) *Liquidation or Consolidation of Indigenous Technology: A Study of the Conditions of Production of Village Blacksmiths in Tanzania*. Scandinavian Institute of African Studies, Uppsala.

Nelson, R. (1979) 'Innovation and Economic Development: Theoretical Retrospect and Prospect', IDB/ECLA/UNDP Research Programme on Science and Technology, Working Paper No. 31, Buenos Aires.

Rosenberg, N. (1979) 'Learning by Using', mimeo, Stanford University.

Sabato, J. (1973) 'Atomic Energy in Argentina: A Case History', *World Development*, August.

Scott-Kemmis, D. and R. M. Bell (forthcoming) 'Industry Learning and Experience Curves: A Review of Empirical Evidence', mimeo, Science Policy Research Unit, Unviersity of Sussex.

Seoul National University (1980) 'The Absorption and Diffusion of Imported Technology in Korea', mimeo, Institute of Economic Research.

Sercovitch, F. C. (1980) 'State Owned Enterprises and Dynamic Comparative Advantages in the World Petrochemical Industry: The Case of Commodity Olefins in Brazil', Development Discussion Paper No. 96, Harvard Institute for International Development.

Stewart, F. and J. James (eds) (1982) *The Economics of New Technology in Developing Countries*. London: Frances Pinter.

Westphal, L., Y. W. Rhee and G. Pursell (1981) 'Korean Industrial Competence: Where it came from', World Bank Staff Working Paper No. 469.

Education, Organisation of Work and Indigenous Technological Capacity

Françoise Caillods

This short paper will try to address itself to the question of what are the implications for education and training of a policy aiming at developing indigenous technological capacity. We understand indigenous technological capacity (ITC) as being the local capacity to create, adapt, diffuse and use technology. We will not enter into the discussion of whether the transfer of technology equals increased dependence or whether appropriate technology equals 'cheap technology' or a technology for underdeveloped countries. We will assume that each country would like to reach an equilibrium between the import of certain techniques necessary to accelerate growth and productivity in some sectors, and the creation of a local technology which is more adapted to the country's specific needs in other sectors. The creation of any new technology or the adaptation of an imported one to local economic or social conditions requires a certain indigenous technological creativity and has some important implications for education and training. In the following paragraphs we shall purposely restrict ourselves to the problem of middle-level manpower training, leaving aside the problem of research policy and higher education. We shall try to summarise some of what we know, but in this new complex area much remains to be investigated.

TECHNOLOGY, ORGANISATION OF WORK AND ITC

The choice of technology has important consequences for the organisation of work, the structure of employment and the types of skills required. Whenever the process of production changes, moving, for example, from mechanical work to assembly line, the content of the work changes. This implies changes in the skills required and the process of acquiring such skills.

211

Researchers on the organisation of work have identified three main systems of work which correspond to different levels of techniques and mechanisation of the work (CNRS, 1980). The first system, called 'man-product', corresponds to handicraft. The workers intervene directly in the production of the output and normally use very simple tools (each tool can be used to perform different production tasks). Their work is a succession of fairly simple operations, but the worker has a high degree of independence in its implementation. Skills are principally acquired through apprenticeship. This is what can still be observed in many small firms in developed countries and in the informal sector in developing countries. Technical skills *per se* can be taught in various short vocational courses or in technical institutions, but it seems that the required attitudes, the entrepreneurial spirit, the 'feel for the work' is better taught on the job, in the work-place. In the informal sector, craft skills include not only knowledge of raw materials, tools, and the techniques involved in the craft, but also knowledge of marketing and simple accounting, where to buy materials, how to fix the price, etc.

> The workshop has a low level of mechanization and minimal division of labour, with much of the work being done by hand. Consequently it tends to have a tightly-knit group structure with a high degree of group belongingness and a face-to-face pattern of social relationships between superiors and subordinates. Within this structure of social relationship, skill acquisition constitutes a long-term intensive period of interaction in which the apprentices not only pick up the techniques of their crafts, but also the associated norms (Oyeneye, 1980).

The second system is called 'man-machine'. The workers use machines and various appliances that are adapted to one specific technical operation in a series of operations. The work is normally standardised. With the techniques of scientific organisation of work, the process has been broken down in a set of simple specific tasks, norms being introduced for the accomplishment of each task. Thus, production techniques are associated with a form of work organisation (standardisation) in such a way that the majority of workers – those who are directly involved in the production process – are marginalised.[1] They perform segmented standardised tasks planned by the research and development office. The level of qualification required is very low. It requires nothing more than on-the-job training to become accustomed to the machines and catch the 'operational know-how'. One study on

French enterprises has shown how this on-the-job training takes place, how it develops into a 'collective operational know-how' (Troussier, 1981). When a worker starts working, he is normally given some indication but little explanation by the supervisor on how to operate the machine. The know-how is acquired through an interaction with other workers, particularly the more experienced ones. Later on, the sum of those individual know-hows develops, at the workshop level, into a collective know-how, through interaction with engineers during trials, with maintenance workers and technicians, with the staff of the research and development office, etc. This helps to solve the 'dysfunctioning' that occurs on various occasions in the production process: unplanned variation in the form of the product, errors, misfunctioning of the machine, which do not justify the intervention of the maintenance team, etc. This operational know-how may or may not be taken into account and valued by the employers; it depends very much on the specific pattern of work organisation and social relations within the firm.

Besides those workers directly involved in production, there are a number of others who perform much more complex tasks, such as maintenance of the machinery and equipment. Those require a fairly high level of technical knowledge. In addition, there are supervisors who control the work and a growing number of technicians and engineers who are in charge of quality control, fixing norms, product design, design of new machines, etc. Compared with the first system of work, the man-product system, the man-machine system, based on mechanisation and an ever-greater division of labour, has also introduced a division of knowledge between workers who perform the tasks and need less and less technical knowledge, and those who do the conceptual work and require more and more sophisticated technical knowledge.

In the third system, 'machine-product', the machines have been conceived and adapted to carry out all the production process as well as directly elaborate the product or semi-product. Mechanisation dominates the whole production process and man only has to check the good functioning of the equipment. According to Braverman and Freyssinet, automation is basically down-grading, since it requires no specific skill for the worker apart from a capacity to receive and transmit quickly the information given by the machine. All the know-how, whether conceptual or operational, has been incorporated in the machine. For others (CNRS, 1980), automation can be upgrading, since it can call for the combination of various functions that are normally performed by different persons: combination of production and maintenance or even combination of the preparation of work, production proper, and maintenance. This depends, however, on the work organisation and the willingness to enrich certain tasks.

We could summarise this discussion by saying that, on the whole, the more mechanised the production process becomes:

(a) the greater the division of tasks, and also the division of knowledge between those who execute/operate and the technical and professional staff who plan and conceive (work, machine, product, etc.);

(b) the fewer workers necessary – mechanisation leads to the suppression of many jobs which are only partly compensated by increasing the number of technical staff required;

(c) various systems of work organisation are coherent with one system of work and one technology.

Very often in developing countries, the work organisation system is imported with the equipment and machinery as one big 'technological package'. This is particularly obvious in the case of the purchase of factories 'product-in-hand'; the firm who is selling the equipment is in charge of everything, including the recruitment and training of personnel, until the production starts. Several studies have shown, however, that there is no absolute technological determinism in the organisation of work, nor in the structure of employment. IIEP studies (Hallak and Caillods, 1981a; Caillods and Briones, 1981) analysing firm-employment structures in Panama, Colombia and Indonesia have shown that:

(a) the variation in firm-employment structures within the same sector of activity can be as great as between firms of different sectors of activity;

(b) very few indicators of employment structure (percentage of skilled workers, technician/operator ratio) are significantly correlated with production process variables;

(c) many other variables are as important as the process of production in explaining the variation in employment structures: firm size, its share of the market, the national origin of capital, the existence of trade unions in the firm, etc. For example, the percentage of skilled workers can be correlated to the existence of trade unions in the firm. The ratio of professional staff on the one hand, of technical staff and supervisors on the other, over production operators, is often higher in trans-national firms than in national ones. This may be due to the fact that they have a larger staff involved in research and development, but it is also explained by the fact that they have a much more complex hierarchical structure, and a high number of heads of departments and divisions to control the activity.

Across countries of similar industrial and technological levels, there are significant differences in the occupational structures. A typical example is given by comparing employment structures of firms with similar characteristics in France and in Germany (Maurice, Sellier and Silvestre, 1977). The ratio of supervisors and technicians to productive workers is about twice as much in France as in Germany. For example, in order to produce the same product, it would be necessary to have 450 workers and 20 professional technical workers in Germany, whereas in France it would be necessary to have 400 workers and 40 professionals and technicians. This difference is partly explained by the different historical development of industry in France and in Germany, but it corresponds also to different educational systems: vocational training is given much more importance in Germany than in France. Training is organised in sandwich courses, partly in the school, partly in the firm, while in France training is mainly organised as a full-time course in the school and many less workers receive some training. This contributes to giving more value to the work and know-how of production operators in Germany than in France.[2] The relative lack of importance given to the vocational diploma in France goes together with a process of skill production in the firms which favours the job more than the worker, and the acquisition of specific skills more than that of general professional knowledge; it goes together also with a fairly narrow definition of skills and a heavy supervision. On the contrary in Germany, production workers with their more general vocational training can take up some of the tasks of supervisors.

What conclusions can we draw from these few remarks? Different forms of work organisation are certainly coherent with similar production processes. Are there some systems of work organisation that are more conducive to the emergence of indigenous technological capacity? It seems that certain systems tend to favour more than others the creation of a team spirit, the desire to make full use of the technical equipment, and the innovative capacity of workshop level: the 'learning-by-doing' defined by Bell (1982). Provided workers have a good general and vocational education, greater democracy in the workplace and a broader definition of skills can lead, in the long run, to a reduction of workers' turnover and absenteeism, to a greater identification with work organisation, to an increased professional integrity and to the adoption of innovative behaviour. This may not bring about an immediate increase in productivity,[3] but could do so in the medium or long run. Obviously we do not really know whether the learning-by-doing on the innovation at workshop level brings significant technical change as opposed to other types of learning – 'learning by searching or by hiring' (Bell, 1982). If we decide, however, to enlarge the definition of indigenous technological capacity to include such important dimensions for developing countries as the possibility of making full use of local manpower (multinational firms may be very productive and even adapt technology to local conditions, but if their research and development is carried out elsewhere, much of the gain is lost to the country), the formative capacity of jobs, and skill production in the firm, then any form of work organisation which (a) tends to give more responsibility to workers, (b) would facilitate worker promotion, and (c) fight against segmentation of tasks in the workplace and between occupations, would contribute to raising ITC. To go beyond and identify specific patterns of work organisation that might be associated with firms that successfully adapt or create technology, would require further research, since there is very little evidence of this.

EDUCATIONAL SYSTEM AND FIRMS' PERSONNEL POLICIES

The second question that we can ask is: to what extent does the actual educational system contribute to building indigenous technological capacity? One way of checking this is to analyse how the products of the educational system are being used and by what type of firm.

According to many authors, aid agencies, etc., the main problem that developing countries face, when it comes to making use of or adapting new technology, is not so much the problem of lack of qualified engineers or professionals, but much more a lack of good middle-level personnel: technicians, foremen, etc. Consequently, and along the lines of the analysis given above of the impact of modern technology and mechanisation on skill requirements, many countries have developed their technical education system and created new technical diversified streams, either at secondary or post-secondary levels, in order to train middle- and higher-level technicians. Various studies seem to show, however, that many of those who have been trained in formal technical schools are not really working in jobs for which they have been trained.[4] Many of them, for example, are working as skilled workers. This reflects partly some dissatisfaction on the part of employers with the training system, but it is also the result of the way labour markets function in many developing countries.

From the employer's point of view:

(1) When recruiting a technician, many of them declare that they prefer to recruit technical-school graduates, but they also point out that the initial training offered at those schools is not a sufficient preparation to perform the task they are expected to perform; additional training is therefore required or previous experience in another firm.

(2) Cognitive criteria are not the only ones considered when employers select their middle-level staff: supervisors, foremen, technicians. Many other criteria are taken into account, such as sex, age, attitudes and behaviour. For a technician, the following qualities are required: sense of responsibility, initiative, dedication. A foreman has to have also a sense of leadership. Having gone to school is not a sufficient guarantee that one has those qualities. It is much easier to evaluate the qualities of somebody who is already working in the firm than those of a school graduate.

(3) As a consequence, many employers do not recruit their technicians immediately after school, but they promote the best of their skilled workers.[5] An IIEP employer survey on the use and profile of technicians in Colombia (Caillods and Briones, 1981), shows that 65 per cent of firms say they recruit their supervising staff through promotion of skilled workers or from other firms, and 45 per cent of them recruit their technicians this way.[6]

(4) In order to compensate for the lack of initial training – or in order to complement it – the enterprises send the people they have selected to various vocational courses. The larger ones organise the course themselves. Others send them to courses organised by various institutions, such as the Ministry of Labour. Smaller firms may prefer to recruit technicians who have already acquired experience in other firms. The same study on Colombia shows that 54 per cent of the technicians had to follow some sort of vocational courses before getting access to their jobs.

(5) The educational profile of technicians is extremely varied. Some have nothing more than primary education, while others may be university graduates. (Indeed, given the large number of university graduates who do not find jobs, some employers have found it easier to

recruit young graduates as technicians: for one thing they are 'less expensive' than experienced technicians, and second, they are less likely to 'create problems', since a 'professional' never belongs to a trade union.)

(6) The larger and more dynamic the firm, the higher the amount of technicians who have undergone some sort of formal vocational training. Oddly enough, multinationals do not seem to give as much importance to vocational training as national firms, but they tend to recruit their technicians – as well as other personnel – with higher educational levels (post-secondary technical schools or even university).

(7) The variables that best explain the variations in technicians' salaries in Colombia are, first, the type of firm they are working for (economic sector, nationality of capital), second, their age, and third, the type of vocational training they have pursued. This is not enough, however, to conclude that experience (as measured by age) and vocational training have a bigger impact on their productivity than education.

(8) In the informal sector, education is certainly not a criterion for access to employment. In fact, it is those who have the lowest educational level and who cannot enter the modern sector, who end up in the traditional sector (Hallak and Caillods, 1981b). It is possible also that social relations which exist in formal education (selection criteria of pupils, teaching methods, type of teacher, modes of evaluation) are in contradiction with the working atmosphere of the traditional sector and do not contribute towards developing the spirit of entrepreneurship. In this regard, apprenticeship is much more appropriate. However, there is some evidence that general education above a certain basic threshold allows a real increase in the entrepreneur's productivity. No such evidence exists concerning the effect of apprenticeship versus institutional vocational training.

From the pupil/student's point of view:

(1) The emphasis put on academic certification in several LDCs contributes towards lowering the prestige of technical and vocational schools. Entering those schools is very often a negative choice, thus it is not the brightest who enrol in these schools.

(2) The difference in salaries between technical-school graduates and university graduates is often such that the best students of these institutions try to pursue their studies at higher-education level. A tracer

study of ESEP [IIPE-ISEEA 1982][7] graduates in Peru shows that 69.5 per cent of them did not work, and 48 per cent continued their studies (1982). Of those who work, only half of them declare that they have a job that corresponds to their level of specialisation. The same was found to be true of INEM graduates in Colombia.

The first conclusion that we can draw from these types of studies is that although everybody agrees that middle-level personnel are crucial for the technological development of firms, technical studies are not always very highly considered, either by the educational system which does not push its best elements into those streams, or by the employers who do not select their technicians primarily among their school-leavers and do not reward them significantly. The second conclusion is that there are various ways of making sure that middle-level personnel get the necessary technical competence to perform the job: the first way is obviously to recruit a school or university graduate and give him the required firm-specific training; the second is to hire an experienced technician who has proved efficient in another firm. The third way is to identify the person who seems to have all the qualities to perform the job and then give him the necessary training. Firms train their own technical personnel much more than is usually assumed. The third conclusion is that ITC requires probably more than simple technical competence, but rather a mixture of other attributes: imagination, initiative, etc., a whole set of qualities that are not necessarily developed in the educational system.

In order to conclude on the relationship between ITC and education, probably more research is needed: research on what types of firms do in fact favour ITC – small/large, national/multinational, etc.? Who, in those firms, is mainly responsible for technical change and innovation? How is technological capacity accumulated and acquired in the firm?: through basic education, training in the firm, on-the-job training, etc.? Only when we have an answer to these questions will we be able to design a training and educational strategy for ITC. In the meantime, we can make a few suggestions to favour a technological environment in the school.

CONCLUSION: SOME SUGGESTIONS FOR INCREASING THE TECHNOLOGICAL COMPONENT IN THE SCHOOL

(1) As we have seen above, a great deal of the training of technical personnel takes place outside the school system, either in formally or-

ganised vocational courses, in courses organised by the firm itself, or on-the-job. Firms, however, have a tendency to favour the production of skills that are specifically linked to the production process and that can be of immediate use. They are not so much interested in financing the acquisition of general scientific and technological culture, although in the long run it would help the person to adapt him/herself to new technical environments or even innovate and modify the technical process. The responsibility of developing such general scientific and general knowledge lies, therefore, in the school system. Given the rapid change in the techniques of production and in the content of work, the education and training provided in the general educational system should avoid being too specific and have, on the contrary, a polytechnical character.

(2) Technical and technological studies do not have a very high status in the educational system of most countries. Even when productive work or other technological subjects have been introduced in the curriculum of secondary schools, very rarely have they been given much importance in the evaluation of students. As a consequence, neither teachers nor students pay much attention to them. In order to avoid having two parallel systems, one general academic stream leading to higher education and therefore attracting the best students, and one technical stream with low prestige, science and technology should be introduced in both streams which could thus be integrated. In other words, all students should be given a good scientific and technological culture, and the same one, no matter what specialisation they may opt for afterwards.

(3) Technology should not be introduced as an additional subject in the curriculum, but it should be integrated as much as possible with other subjects such as mathematics and physics. The methods of teaching should emphasise scientific methods of experimentation and inductive approach to technological problems.

(4) Specialisation for very specific jobs would be offered in a network of extremely flexible and diversified courses, outside the formal school systems. These courses could be organised jointly with firms in sandwich courses. They should allow not only the specialisation of workers or technicians, but also their constant retraining whenever necessary.

(5) Scientific and technological education should not be restricted to secondary and higher education. In fact, the generalisation of a

technological culture, from a very early age to higher education, is one of the conditions for mastering techniques. Some initiation to technology should be included in the curriculum of basic education, literacy courses and other non-formal programmes. It should start with the simple observation, description and analysis of the problems of the environment, trying to solve them using all the resources of the community (Le Thanh Khoi, 1982).

NOTES

1. The extreme example of this is the assembly line.
2. This is reflected in the differences in salary between workers and technical staff, which are much less in Germany than in France.
3. With the economic crisis and the priority given to competition, the debate on job enrichment and other autonomous work units seems to have lost much of its strength.
4. According to some studies on various Latin American countries, about one-third only of technical-school graduates work in jobs corresponding to their training [Rama].
5. No matter what their initial training, they only give slight preference to technical-school graduates.
6. At the engineering level, a similar conclusion about on-the-job acquisition is reached by Bennell's chapter in this volume.
7. Schools of higher vocational studies.

REFERENCES

Bell, R. M. (1982) '"Learning" and the Accumulation of Industrial Technological Capacity in Developing Countries', paper prepared for the International Workshop on Facilitating Indigenous Technological Capability, Centre for African Studies, Edinburgh University, May.
Caillods, F. and G. Briones, *Education, formation professionnelle et emploi: Le secteur industriel en Colombie,* IIPE/Ministère colombien de l'éducation, Paris.
CNRS (1980) *L'évolution des systèmes de travail dans l'économie moderne: Conséquences sur l'emploi et la formation,* Acte des journées nationales d'études DGRST-CEREQ-CNRS. Paris: CNRS.
Desarrollo y Educación en América Latina – Síntesis general, Proyecto Desarrollo y Educación en América Latina y el Caribe. [G. Rama (edit.)].
Estudio de segiumiento de egresados de las escuelas superiores de educación profesional (ESEP) en el Peru. IIPE–ISEEA, 1982.
Hallak, J. and F. Caillods (1981a) *Education, Work and Employment,* vol. 1. IIEP.

Hallak, J. and F. Caillods (1981b) *Education, training and the traditional sector*, IIEP Fundamental of Educational Planning.

La France en mai 1981: L'enseignement et le développement technique (1982) Etudes et rapports de la Commission du Bilan. Documentation française.

Le Thanh Khoi (1982) *Science et technologie: Les choix du développement endogène. Etude illustrée de quatre expériences concrètes dans les pays en voie de développement.* Division for the Study of Development, Unesco.

Maurice, A., F. Sellier and J.-J. Silvestre (1977) *La production de la hiérarchie dans l'entreprise – Recherche d'un effect sociétal: Comparaison Allemagne-France, LEST.*

Oyeneye, O. (1980) 'The Nature and Process of Human Resource Development in Nigeria's Informal Sector', *Labour and Society,* vols 3 and 4, October.

Troussier, J. F. (1981) Travail individuel et collectif dans quelques industries, Colloque Formation-Emploi, Toulouse, Dec.

V. Case Studies

India's Technological Capacity: Effects of Trade, Industrial, Science and Technology Policies[1]

Sanjaya Lall

INTRODUCTION

In some recent research I have conducted on exports of technology by developing countries, I have argued that India's performance suggests that it has the broadest and best-developed technological capabilities in the Third World.[2] This presents a paradox: India combines an impressive performance in exporting its technology with a poor one in terms of industrial growth, the expansion of manufactured exports, the absorption of industrial labour, and the introduction of genuinely innovative products in domestic or foreign markets. Could it be that the same set of policies which have held back growth in general have simultaneously prompted the development and export of indigenous technology? Are the two completely unrelated? Or is there a mixture – have some of the restrictive policies promoted technological growth while others have prevented the exploitation of the resulting capabilities in terms of industrial and export growth?

This paper attempts a preliminary answer to these difficult questions, by examining the main features of some policies in India that may have affected the development of technological capability in manufacturing industry (note that defence, nuclear and space technologies are excluded). Since it would have been impossible to tackle all the possible policy intervention that may affect technological change, this paper is restricted to three major fields: trade policies, industrial policies, and science and technology policies. The argument draws mainly on published data and analysis, but it directs the available material along this previously unexplored path.

TRADE POLICIES

IMPORT CONTROLS

Indian trade policies have been extensively analysed in the 1970s[3] and the essential structure of the system has remained intact till today, despite some recent moves to liberalise some capital goods imports and stimulate manufactured exports. As far as imports are concerned, the basic principle has been to ban the imports of all consumer goods, and of all those intermediate and capital goods that were produced in the country (largely regardless of cost, quality and performance) and that were considered 'non-essential'. This quantitative strait-jacket has been supplemented by hefty tariffs on various intermediate and capital-goods imports which were permitted, but the use of tariffs has been mainly for revenue purposes. The 'essentiality' of imports was judged on erratic and *ad hoc* criteria, but within the broad framework of the needs for investment laid down by the Five Year Plans. These Plans laid down various targets for production derived from a Soviet-type planning model, with a heavy bias in favour of 'self-reliance' and little regard for economic efficiency and comparative advantage. This autarkic approach necessitated an early and pronounced emphasis on the domestic production of investment goods and basic intermediates, and to this day the government adheres to the notion of a 'core' sector which is somehow regarded as more important to development than sectors containing most consumer goods.

Bhagwati and Srinivasan comment that the 'import control system worked on (i) incomplete and unsystematic information and (ii) lack of any discernible economic criteria'. And 'whatever limited allocational aims it may have had were frustrated, in varying degrees, by the corruption that inevitably arose from the large premia on imports under the control system'.[4] They go on to describe the various sorts of delays, inflexibilities and inefficiencies that resulted from this system, the main ones being the adverse influence on export performance and the wasteful inter-industrial and inter-firm allocation of resources by permitting and encouraging expansion of excess capacity and by blunting competition (and hence incentives for cost-consciousness and quality improvement).[5]

This system of import controls and unlimited protection of domestic industry naturally resulted in a battery of disincentives to exporting. Export activity is, at the best of times, risky and expensive, especially where new and increasingly sophisticated manufactures are concerned. In India, the trade regime was heavily biased against export activity both in terms of the effective exchange rates faced by exporters *vis à vis* import substitutes, and of the inadequacy of the subsidies which were offered to offset high input costs, small scales of production, bureaucratic delays, technological lags, and the expenses needed to cultivate foreign markets.

It should be obvious from the above résumé of trade controls in India that the highly regulated regime would have exercised pervasive and significant impact on the nature and pace of technological development in the country. The essential point of interest is to explain how the regime managed to generate a considerable amount of indigenous technological effort that spilled over into technology exports, while maintaining high and indiscriminate protection of the domestic market and a bias against foreign markets.

A regime such as India's has several features that may be expected to retard technological development. As Bhagwati and Srinivasan put it, 'There is . . . some *a priori* and empirical support, of different degrees of firmness, for the view that the Indian trade regime *in toto* led to, or accentuated, the lack of attention to quality, design and technical change.' (p. 218) When they set about testing some propositions derived from these general considerations, however, Bhagwati and Srinivasan found that:

(a) 'Clearly, the process of import substitution itself led to the encouragement of research and development activity in Indian industry, primarily through the creation of the need to adapt processes to the use of new, indigenous materials in many cases, thus supplementing the normal establishment of research and development-type cells for quality control and customer-service operations.' (p. 223)

(b) 'Export orientation did not seem to have led to any significant acceleration in research and development expenditures or to a more sharply focused research effort. This was because most research and development expenditure had in fact originated in response to the problems raised by the adaptation of processes to locally available materials and spares.' (p. 224)

(c) Nevertheless, 'the general incentives to reduce costs and to maintain quality cannot but have been reduced by the sheltered markets provided by policies of automatic protection and strict control over domestic entry'. (p. 226)

Bhagwati and Srinivasan, drawing upon Ashok Desai's pioneering empirical work in the field of Indian R&D, succeeded in highlighting one important aspect of technological activity stimulated by India's trade regime: the adaptation of processes to indigenous raw materials. However, they missed out some other equally important aspects which are of more direct concern to technology exports and which are in fact remarked upon by Desai in a more recent paper.[6] In the engineering industry in general, and the capital goods industry in particular, a great deal of technological effort is stimulated by:

(a) the need to engineer the products to specific local customer needs (Indian tractors are a good example)[7] or to each turnkey plant operation (for example, heavy electrical equipment);
(b) the need to bring bought-out components up to the requisite standards and to keep suppliers abreast of new technologies; the suppliers, in turn, transmit know-how back to the buyer;[8]
(c) the powerful protection given to manufacturers against competing capital goods imports, which provide an inducement to innovate (especially in sectors where domestic competition increased) within a relatively low-risk environment where the costs of learning basic design and development could be absorbed;[9]
(d) the need to diversify and grow even within domestic markets, the classic Marris-type of growth-promoting strategy that any modern corporation adopts.

Both the last two arguments implicitly assume that Indian manufacturers resort to their own R&D efforts, rather than to the presumably easier strategy of importing 'ready-made' foreign technologies, because government policies somehow tilt the balance in favour of local technologies. This is in fact the case, as will be discussed in a later section in this paper.

Bhagwati and Srinivasan also hint at a crucial characteristic of Indian technological development: since the trade regime protects inefficient as well as efficient firms, and since it eliminates pressures to keep abreast of development abroad, it also leads to:

(a) the prolonged co-existence of a few firms that are innovative, quality-conscious and dynamic overseas, with a multitude of others that are inefficient, technologically slothful and tied to domestic markets. This means that technological development (and, by implication, technology exports) is bound to be highly localised in a few firms, and may not reflect the capabilities of industry at large;

(b) the progress of technology in a number of dynamic firms at some distance behind the world frontiers (that is, technological progress locally combined with much more rapid progress abroad). This means that Indian technology may only find a market in other LDCs with similar small scales and relatively primitive environments (though there are some process and capital goods industries in which Indian know-how is at international levels). Thus, even technologically progressive industries may need to import new technologies if they are to make a dent in major international export markets.

It is also possible, *à la* Teitel,[10] that a great deal of technological progress occurring in the sort of 'distorted' economy that India possesses has been socially wasteful. Against this, it may be argued that the 'know-why' capabilities developed in and stimulated by conditions of artificial scarcities and protection provide a base on which more competitive technologies can be easily grafted, and that in a more liberal environment the basic 'know-why' itself may not develop. Clearly this is a question that needs much deeper examination, and we cannot pretend to know the answers yet.

In sum, then, the Indian trade regime has certainly stimulated a great deal of innovation because of the industrial environment it has created. However, a substantial part of the observed technological activity may have occurred in *any* regime, given the need for technological activity to implement and adapt an imported technology in a new setting. And much of the remainder is strongly coloured by the specific conditions imposed by government controls – that is, no direct need to keep up with international frontiers, small size of operations, a relatively poor and unsophisticated consuming market, various input scarcities, only sporadic pressures to improve quality, and various industrial licensing policies which inhibit sustained build-up of technology (see below).

INDUSTRIAL POLICIES

LICENSING

Indian industrial policies cover the whole gamut of a manufacturing firm's experience, from the activities that it is allowed to enter, the size of the plant it can install, the source of its equipment, technology and its raw materials, to the remuneration it can offer its executives, the expansion it can undertake, the amount of foreign capital it can invite or borrow and, often, the final prices that it can charge to its customers.

The broad directions of industrial expansion are set under the Five-Year Plans which, as we noted, have traditionally been based on closed-economy assumptions with a heavy bias towards heavy engineering and chemical industries. The licensing authorities follow the priorities and specific capacity targets laid down in the Plans, and this has two important opposing effects on technological development.

First, since little attention is paid to the country's comparative advantage in production or in technology generation, it forces investments into a number of sectors that are commercially unviable (and perhaps socially wasteful), or where Indian conditions cannot sustain an efficient technology over time; this leads to waste of technological resources.

Second, on the other hand, it forces investment into sectors where there may be large potential 'learning' gains, but where investment would not enter under more market-oriented regimes. This leads to faster technological development than would occur under liberal policies.

The licensing authorities also observe a number of other rules:

(a) They do not readily permit expansion by a firm that has a 'dominant position' in any particular market (an MRTP firm),[11] even though the firm may be the most efficient producer and the most dynamic innovator;

(b) They do not permit entry or expansion by a FERA firm[12] (that is, one with over 40 per cent foreign equity) unless it is in some very tightly defined areas of high technology or high export orientation;

(c) They reserve a large number of products (over 800) for production solely by the small-scale sector (capital equipment of under Rs 2 million);

(d) Certain 'core' and infrastructural industries are not open to the private sector at all, in pursuance of the objective that the 'commanding heights' of the economy be gradually taken over by the public sector.

These rules have been slightly relaxed in the past two years, as noted earlier, but by and large the social aims they are supposed to fulfil – containment of monopoly and of concentration of wealth, promotion of indigenous enterprises, promotion of employment generating small-scale units, and 'socialism' – are still professed by the government.

The effects of such rigid and (from the viewpoint of market efficiency) arbitrary investment controls on the performance of Indian industry are too numerous to discuss here. As far as the narrower issues of technological development are concerned, we may note the following.

(i) MRTP controls prevent the natural exploitation of technological dynamism through growth in competitive manufacturing industries. They induce large industrial firms to diversify into completely unrelated activities which are assigned priority in the relevant Plans, where they may have no technological advantage or experience, and so spread resources very thinly and induce a lack of specialisation. This holds down the absolute size of undertakings in many industries to scales tiny by international standards, and so prevents the firms from launching R&D efforts on scales that allow the absorption of new technologies. There are, of course, some exceptions (TELCO is a large truck-producer by any standards, while public-sector firms like HMT and BHEL, not constrained by MRTP, are among the world's leading ten manufacturers in their fields), but by and large the regulation has crippled the growth of specialised firms of viable size.

(ii) FERA regulations have led to a substantial dilution of foreign equity shares in Indian manufacturing. It is likely that such a reduction has also constricted the inflow of new technologies into the country and/or has raised its costs. In sectors where Indian capabilities are inadequate to keep up with world frontiers, therefore, this has increased the technological gaps afflicting Indian industry. It is arguable, on the other hand, that the tight restrictions placed on foreign direct investment in India have promoted the growth of Indian technology. Several instances have been observed where the constriction of foreign technology following equity dilution has induced the firm to expand its own R&D activity and develop its design capabilities (for example, Ashok Leyland in truck manufacture).

(iii) The technological costs of arbitrarily reserving a large number of activities for the small-scale sector (and backing this up with substantial fiscal concessions to them *vis à vis* the large firms – for example, 40 per cent price differences in dyes) are too obvious to enumerate.[13]

(iv) While there is no necessary reason for public-sector enterprises in India to be technologically less dynamic than private ones, only very few of them have proved their technological mettle. In part this may be due to the fact that they were wrongly conceived, and have been set an essentially impossible task (of absorbing very complex, fast-changing or large-scale technologies). In part it is due to their well-known managerial deficiencies and political interference.

On balance, the licensing policies of the government seem to be designed to create and preserve large areas of inefficiency, and must be considered inimical to technological development.

CONTROL ON CAPITAL EQUIPMENT PURCHASES

We have already remarked on the pervasive impact of import controls. As far as capital goods are concerned, the protection given to indigenous manufacturers has resulted in a broad-based, diverse and complex capital goods sector. This sector has enjoyed a certain degree of technological progress over the years and has started to respond to particular customer needs with new innovations. However, this has been accompanied by a steadily lengthening technological lag in those capital goods industries where the world frontier is advancing rapidly to larger scales, new techniques and products, greater automation, and the like. Thus, the user industries have been forced to adopt techniques which they may not otherwise have chosen, though a few have decided to set up captive units for their own use (TELCO, India's largest truck manufacturer, for instance, makes all its own specialised machine tools). To the extent that this has inhibited their own technological progress, the enforced reliance on domestic procurement has been harmful. In realisation of this, the government gradually liberalised on capital goods imports in the late 1970s, but no thorough evaluation of the impact of this is available.

HEAVY SALES TAXES ON SPECIFIC GOODS

There are a large number of products that are regarded as 'luxury' products in India and subject to punishing taxes in the final stages. These include several technology-intensive consumer durables like passenger cars, refrigerators, air conditioners, TV, audio equipment, etc. which in a country at India's stage of development would normally enjoy very high rates of growth. These are also the kinds of scale and skill-intensive activities that would provide the next burst of comparative advantage in manufactured exports. If these industries are deliberately held back by government policy, clearly very useful 'learning' opportunities are also lost to the economy.

PRICE CONTROLS

In contrast to the above there are a number of 'essential' commodities that are subject to strict price controls in order to make large supplies available at low prices (for example, drugs and, until recently, cement). The general effect is to so depress profitability that production, new investment and technological changes gradually dry up. This certainly happened in the Indian cement industry and is starting to happen in drugs. The government is aware of the problems and is adopting more pragmatic policies, but its response is generally very slow.

There are several other industrial regulation policies, concerning location, pollution, salaries, etc. which may peripherally affect technological development in India, but we shall not deal with them here.

SCIENCE AND TECHNOLOGY POLICIES

Science and technology policies affect technological development directly by stimulating R&D, setting up a scientific infrastructure and giving preference to the output of indigenous technology, and indirectly by regulating access to foreign technologies.

DIRECT EFFECTS

The Indian government has over the years since independence set up a massive scientific infrastructure to provide commercially viable technologies to manufacturing, mining, agriculture and defence. As far as manufacturing goes, the bulk of the effort is concentrated in the thirty-three national laboratories of the Council of Scientific and Industrial Research, which also covers such fields as experimental medicine, aeronautics, environment, oceanography and structural engineering. As noted in my study of Indian technology exports this network, operating through its commercialisation arm NRDC (The National Research Development Corporation), has not had much impact on technological development in large-scale organised industry, though it claims to have provided hundreds of technologies for use to small-scale enterprises. There is no assessment available of the cost and efficiency of these technologies.

As far as direct stimulation of major industrial technologies go, therefore, we must consider the incentives provided by the government to in-house R&D. The Department of Science and Technology, in collaboration with the Directorate General of Technical Development (DGTD), operates a scheme whereby 'recognised' R&D units of industrial enterprises receive fiscal concessions and other incentives.

The fiscal concession is currently at *125 per cent of current R&D expenditures,* together with customs duty exemption for imported R&D equipment, accelerated depreciation on this equipment, and special investment allowances (and licensing privileges) for units using local technologies. Other incentives relate mainly to liberalised and preferential import facilities for units setting up R&D laboratories. Royalties earned by Indian companies abroad are completely free of tax, and those earned within the country are given a 40 per cent rebate.

There is little doubt that the policy for stimulating in-house R&D by manufacturing units has been very successful. There are some 600 private-sector and 52 public-sector industrial units with recognised R&D facilities. Their R&D spending has risen from Rs 300m in 1972–3 to Rs 920m in 1977–8 and Rs 2000m in 1980–1. As a proportion of sales, the public-sector R&D performing units and the private-sector ones both spent 0.8 per cent in 1978–9. The main R&D spenders in the private sector (detailed data are only available for 379 recognised units for 1978–9) were chemicals, pharmaceuticals, electricals and electronics, and transportation equipment, while in the public sector they were electricals and electronics, telecommunications and chemicals. R&D personnel in these units totalled 17.8 thousand in 1978, of which 8.2 thousand were in the public sector and 9.6 thousand in the private sector.

The DST provides some data on the distribution of R&D expenditure, by firm size, as well as on the educational qualifications of R&D personnel. As far as firm size, as measured by total employment, is concerned, the distribution of R&D spending in the 379 recognised private-sector and 52 public-sector units together in 1978–9 is as follows:

Employment Size	No. of Units	R&D Per Firm (Rs. m.)	Total R&D Expenditure (Rs. m.)	% of total
Over 5000	46	14.9	683.1	50.5
3000–5000	25	5.5	138.1	10.2
1000–3000	95	2.5	234.5	17.3
400–1000	92	1.5	135.8	10.0
100–400	79	0.6	47.1	3.5
Under 100	94	1.2	13.9	8.4
Total	431	3.1	1352.5	100.0

Source: Department of Science & Technology, *Research and Development in Industry,* 1978–9 (New Delhi: 1981).

It is evident that there is a fairly high degree of concentration of R&D spending among the largest industrial firms. The top 46 firms (28 private and 19 public-sector) account for just over half of total industrial R&D, and on average spent Rs 15m (£1.9m) each on R&D in 1978–9. The large public-sector units dominated in this class: 19 public-sector firms spent an average Rs 79.3m ($10m) each as compared to Rs 6.3m ($0.8m) by 28 private-sector units.

R&D spending per firm declines consistently with size, though at the very tail-end the trend is slightly reversed, presumably because of high R&D spending by some small electronics firms.

As far as the educational qualifications of R&D personnel are concerned, 8 per cent of the total are Ph.D. holders, 21 per cent are postgraduates, 36 per cent are graduates, and the remainder diploma-holders. By branch of specialisation, 26 per cent are trained in natural science, 3 per cent in agricultural science, 65 per cent in engineering, and the remainder in medical and social science. The dominant presence of engineering in the sort of adaptive and assimilative technological work done in India is worth noting.

INDIRECT EFFECTS VIA ACCESS TO FOREIGN TECHNOLOGIES

The Indian government adopted a progressively more restrictive policy towards the import of foreign technologies from the mid-1960s, mainly in response to foreign exchange shortages. Controls were applied at several stages to access to foreign technology in the form of licensing agreements as well as direct foreign investments. The very first stage was to demarcate industries into three categories: those in which the government believed indigenous technology to be sufficient for the country's needs, and no foreign investment or licensing was to be allowed; those where some foreign technology was thought necessary but was not of a complex or tightly-held nature, so only licensing would be allowed; and those where both licensing and direct investment would be allowed. This list of industries was first issued in 1969 and updated in 1978. It would appear that after a period of growing stringency there has been some liberalisation, but we can imagine how this rather facile and static view of technological needs, coupled to a formidable bureaucratic and taxation apparatus, served to keep new technologies out of a large number of activities.

Recent policy statements tend to play down the rigidity of this primary screening. Thus:

Even in these industries in which foreign technology and foreign investment would not normally be allowed, import of technology

would be considered if the particular technology is so closely held or
it is required for updating existing technology to meet higher domestic requirements or to become competitive in export markets. There
is, therefore, scope for import of technology in almost all industries
open to the private sector.[14]

However, as with many other regulatory policies, a large area of discretion is left to the administrators, which makes for arbitrariness,
delay, political interference and ultimately corruption. In recent years,
procedures for screening have been streamlined and a 'single-point
clearance' scheme introduced, but by all accounts India still remains a
relatively difficult country to enter.

If a foreign technology qualifies to enter India, by way either of
licensing or direct investment, there are still a number of regulatory
hurdles and restrictions to be cleared. Up to 1977 all proposals for
technology import in any form had to run the gamut of every ministry
concerned with industry, finance, technology and the CSIR before getting approval. Objections could be raised (and lengthy delays insti-
tuted by recalcitrant bureaucrats) at practically any stage of the process. These objections could be based on the cost of the technology, its
appropriateness, the availability of local substitutes or even the long-
term building up of indigenous R&D capabilities. The strongest
pressures for restricting foreign technology imports came from the
DGTD and the CSIR *cum* NRDC nexus, the latter seeing themselves
very much as the guardians of indigenous science and technology.

Since 1976 a Technology Evaluation Committee (TEC) has been set
up, composed of members of the DGTD (which is under the Ministry
of Industry), the Department of Science and Technology, the CSIR
and NRDC. The TEC evaluates the technological aspects of every
proposed collaboration and the extension of existing collaboration
agreements. It then advises the Ministry or Department concerned on
the technical desirability of the import and the Ministry proceeds with
further action. If the Department itself is inclined to take a very narrow
view of technology imports, it can impose a far more restrictive policy
than recommended by the TEC – the prime example is the electronics
industry, where an extremely nationalistic Department of Electronics
has been able to so restrict technology inflows as to set Indian electronics firms back by over a decade in a very fast-moving technology.
What is more, the Department has persisted in this in spite of strong
criticisms from high-powered committees (for example, The Sondhi
Committee) set up to recommend means of improving electronics
technology in India.

Thus, even within sectors where foreign technologies are permitted, there has been a strong filtering mechanism which has a built-in bias towards protecting indigenous technologies and producers. The onus lay on the prospective technology importer to show that the technology was necessary (in terms of plan priorities), not available locally, and 'fairly' priced. The system probably deterred a large number of firms from seeking approval for technologies which may have improved their function but which were unlikely to pass through the filter. The approval process was long, cumbersome and expensive for the firms concerned (in terms of executive time involved in following through the application, if not actually illicit payments). The actual number of proposals turned down is therefore not a true indicator of the number of technical agreements that would have been entered under a more liberal system. As the figures stand, however, between April 1976 and December 1978 the TEC examined 919 proposals, of which it accepted 697 and rejected 222; of the latter, 46 were on grounds of availability of indigenous technology. [15]

As far as licensing is concerned, India has strict controls on the payments permitted and the life of the contract. Royalty payments are normally restricted to 3–5 per cent of the value of sales, and subject to a 40 per cent tax, so that the licenser receives, at the maximum, a 3 per cent royalty (though most rates are lower). Lump-sum payments are also permitted after thorough screening and bargaining. The life of a technology contract has been limited to *five years* for some time now. Exceptions are only permitted for export-oriented industries, though in the future a broader liberalisation may occur.

Both the payment terms and the duration of contracts are far less attractive than the norm for international technology contracts. Royalties of 5–10 per cent net of tax are common outside India and higher rates are also not uncommon (up to 30 per cent) for exceptionally valuable technologies. [16] Five-year contracts for transferring complex technologies would also be widely regarded as inadequate. Though Indian rules permit a renewal of the contract, the conditions are difficult and rather static (relating primarily to the absorption of the initial technology), that is, they do not take continuous technological change into account. Again, the wide degree of discretion accorded to the administrators provides scope for arbitrariness and delay.

As far as direct investments are concerned, the agreement has to go through the Foreign Investment Board, which is governed by the Foreign Exchange Regulation Act (FERA) of 1974, and by more general considerations which permit equity investment as the least-preferred means of acquiring foreign technologies. FERA rules lay down that foreign shareholding cannot exceed 40 per cent of total equity, but shares up to 74 per cent are permitted if 'high technology' is inducted for the home market, and up to 100 per cent if the project is wholly export-oriented. Despite these provisions, relatively few investments have qualified for the exception. In the interim, large numbers of existing foreign ventures have been forced to dilute their equity, and a few (notably IBM and Coca-Cola) have refused to conform and ceased operations in India.

In addition, the government lays down that technology contracts should not contain export-restriction[17] or import-tying clauses, that foreign brand-names cannot be used for domestic sales, that the Indian party should be free to sub-license the technology locally, and that the consultancy services needed should be provided by Indian firms or at least be under Indian prime consultants. Desirable though these requirements may be in principle, in practice they can serve to deter the transfer of new and valuable proprietary technologies.

The net result of these regulations is that a relatively constricted amount of foreign technology enters the country, and that, over time, the regulations may have forced importers to buy less expensive (and so less valuable) technology than they would otherwise have done. Foreign firms continuously complain that under the conditions laid down it is not worth their while to transfer their best technologies to India. Indian counterparts feel the same, and are always pressing the government to liberalise the regulations. The restrictions on equity participation and long-term agreements serve to cut Indian firms off from continuous technological developments abroad. The lengthy, complicated and expensive procedures worsen the impact of stated policy.

During 1957–79, the government approved 5,706 technical and equity agreements, a small number in view of the size and complexity of the industrial sector. In the eleven years from 1969 to 1979, out of 2,833 agreements, as many as 2,418 were only for licensing (without equity participation). The gross amount of new foreign equity which was approved by India in the remaining 415 ventures *over eleven years was Rs 571m*[18] *($70–80m* approximately) only. Compare this with the *net* direct private investment (that is, after subtracting profit remittances and equity repatriation) of $815m in Singapore, $873m in Malaysia, $668m in Mexico and $2,220m in Brazil, in *1979 alone.*[19] It appears also that the number of purely technical agreements entered into by India is far smaller (and, as noted, may embody less modern technologies) than those entered by Brazil, Mexico and much smaller countries like S. Korea and Taiwan.

Though the control of foreign technology imports was somewhat liberalised in 1980–1, and the signs are that further liberalisation is in the pipeline, the overall framework of FERA and TEC remains essentially the same. In any case, for the purposes of analysing the period in which most of India's technology exports (which are substantial) took place, it seems incontrovertible that India drew relatively little on direct imports of industrial technology.

The impact of this set of policies on the development of indigenous technological capability is complex and widespread, and only detailed cross-country comparisons would enable us to assess whether they inhibited, promoted or had no impact on such capability. The existing evidence suggests a mixture: large areas of Indian industry are technologically backward and growing increasingly so. At the same time, a number of Indian firms have assimilated a lot of basic technology and have improved upon it, but their innovations have left them far behind world frontiers. A few firms, however, have developed technological capabilities more or less on a par with world frontiers, especially in relatively slow-moving technologies. Both the latter two groups have the ability to export technology, the first where outdated technologies or products are actually a competitive advantage, and the latter where cheaper engineering manpower provides the selling edge.

It may be helpful at this point to refer to some of my earlier findings on technology exports by India and other 'newly industrialising countries'.[20] As noted at the beginning of this paper, one of the most interesting (and rather surprising) facts about Indian technological performance is that it is probably the largest, most diversified and sometimes the most sophisticated industrial technology exporter in the Third World. Though the value of exports of manufactured goods and capital goods (which are closely associated with technology exports) by India is well below that of other NICs like Korea or Taiwan, and though its domestic industrial sector (and capital goods manufacturing) is considerably smaller than Brazil, its international sales of industrial turnkey projects, consultancy services, licenses and general industrial know-how, and direct investment abroad by its manufacturing firms,[21] are greater and seem to embody a greater degree of local technological capability.

Its technological competence is particularly evident in the sale of industrial turnkey plant and direct overseas investments. Thus, by the middle of 1982, Indian capital goods manufacturers and engineering contractors had won some $2.0 to 2.5 billion worth of foreign turnkey contracts in manufacturing and power generation and distribution, while they had invested directly some $100m abroad, over 80 per cent of which was in manufacturing activity.[22] While these sums are tiny by the standards of world technology trade and investment, they are not unimpressive for a developing country. Even the sale of technical services and disembodied know-how fetched India's top 500 or so firms about $50m in 1978–9.

The great bulk of these technology exports by India has been directed to other developing countries at a lower stage of industrialisation. In each category of technology exports, a relatively small number of large firms account for most of the activity. Their competitive edge has resided in their mastery of the technology they employ in India, backed by the ability to design and reproduce it from scratch and to provide all or most of the capital equipment required. In some cases, the technology is practically identical to that offered by the developed countries (though the scales of production may be smaller); in others it may be modified to utilise different materials or to make products adapted to developing country conditions. There are no cases of 'major' innovations at the frontiers of technology. The most common cases were of a great deal of 'minor' innovation, or simply 'trouble-shooting', some distance behind the relevant international technological frontier. The specificity of the Indian experience and the relatively low cost of Indian engineers enables even these slightly outdated technologies to be sold in international competition.

However, while the achievements of India on the technology export front are not unimpressive, we cannot conclude on their basis that Indian technology as a whole is dynamic or competitive by world standards. It is apparent that indigenous efforts alone cannot bring large areas of Indian industry to internationally viable levels. What is more worrying, even the wholesale import of modern technologies may not enable Indian manufacturers to become competitive within the present framework of protectionist, inward-looking, anti-large-size, and highly interventionist policies. It is this overall thrust of industrial strategy that ultimately inhibits the country from fully realising and exploiting its technological potential.

CONCLUSIONS

The highly interventionist regime that has characterised the Indian economy since the 1950s has undoubtedly stimulated a great deal of technological effort. In particular, highly protectionist policies towards domestic production (especially of capital goods) and domestic technical effort have enabled the country to build up a diverse and fairly sophisticated base in industrial technologies. However, the same set of regulatory policies have fostered widespread areas of inefficiency and technological backwardness, and related policies (to promote public-sector enterprise, small-scale industries, egalitarianism and national ownership) have prevented a full realisation of the technological capabilities that have been painfully built up in the country.

A sensible technological policy clearly requires a very careful balance between the promotion of indigenous enterprises and institutions (in order to protect 'infant' learning) and the induction of the best technologies from abroad. Moreover, the full exploitation of a country's technological potential requires policies that enable growth and investment by innovative enterprises, and that enable its industries to compete in world markets on the basis of their comparative advantages. These obvious morals have been ignored by the Indian government, with the result that over-protected technologies and industries, hemmed in by a formidable battery of controls, are unable to sustain even moderate rates of growth. The government is acutely conscious of the need for liberalisation, but to a large extent finds itself caught in an ideological morass of its own making (and in the web of powerful vested interests that the system has created). It remains to be seen how much the various small moves towards a less restrictive economic framework add up to.

NOTES

1. I wish to acknowledge the stimulus provided by several discussions with Ashok Desai. This paper was written while I was Honorary Director of the Indian Council for Research on International Economic Relations, but it does not represent any views except my own.
2. See 'Developing Countries as Exporters of Industrial Technology', *Research Policy*, 1980; and *Developing Countries as Exporters of Technology: A first Look at the Indian Experience* (London: Macmillan, 1982)
3. See, in particular, J. N. Bhagwati and Padma Desai, *India, Planning for Industrialisation* (Oxford: Clarendon Press, 1970); J. N. Bhagwati and T. N. Srinivasan, *Foreign Trade Regimes and Economic Development: India* (New York: NBER, 1976); V. R. Panchmukhi, *Trade Policies of India: A Quantitative Analysis* (Delhi: Concept Publishing Company, 1978); and World Bank, *India: Export Performance, Problems, Policies and Prospects,* 1977.

4. Bhagwati and Srinivasan, *Foreign Trade Regimes*, p. 41.
5. Ibid, p. 245.
6. See A. V. Desai, 'The Origin and Direction of Industrial Research and Development in India', *Research Policy*, 1980.
7. See A. V. Desai, 'Technology Transfer and Development in the Indian Tractor Industry', National Council of Applied Economic Research, New Delhi, 1982 (mimeo).
8. These linkages are discussed for two auto firms in India in S. Lall, 'Vertical Inter-Firm Linkages in LDCs: An Empirical Study', *Oxford Bulletin of Economics and Statistics*, 1980.
9. See S. Lall, *Developing Countries as Exporters of Technology: A First Look at the Indian Experience* (London: Macmillan, 1982).
10. S. Teitel, 'Towards an Understanding of Technical Change in Semi-Industrialized Countries', *Research Policy*, 1980.
11. This acronym derives from the Monopoly and Restrictive Trade Practices Act on which the regulation is based. MRTP regulations are now being slightly relaxed in 'core' sectors and export-oriented activities, but still constitute a major restraint on overall growth of large firms.
12. Derived from the Foreign Exchange Regulation Act, 1974, which prescribed that all firms with foreign equity had to dilute the foreign share to 40 per cent over time if they were to expand within the country.
13. The most glaring example, of course, is the textile industry, where heavy controls on the organised sector have led to enormous loss of export markets, and technological backwardness.
14. Indian Investment Centre, *Foreign Investment in India: Opportunities and Incentives* (New Delhi: 1981).
15. DGTD, *Annual Report,* 1978–9, p. 19.
16. See A. V. Desai, 'Technology Import Policy in the Sixties and Seventies: Changes and Consequences', NCAER (Delhi: 1981) p. 3.
17. Though 'permissible restrictions' are accepted by the government for countries where the technology-supplier itself owns production facilities.
18. Indian Investment Centre, *Foreign Collaborations in India* (New Delhi: 1981) p. 17. Net foreign capital inflows into India were negative in this period.
19. World Bank, *World Development Report 1981,* Table 14, p. 160–1. Since Indian firms invested about $100m overseas during the 1970s, India has actually turned out to be a *net exporter* of direct investment – surely a unique case for a poor industrialising economy in modern history.
20. The preliminary findings have been published in Lall, *Developing Countries as Exporters of Technology;* more recent findings, based on a research project financed by the World Bank, will be forthcoming in a special issue of World Development edited by the present author. For a brief summary, see S. Lall, 'Indian Technology Exports and Technological Development', *Annals of the American Academy of Political and Social Science,* vol. 458 (November 1980) pp. 151–62.
21. See Lall, 'The Emergence of Third World Multinationals: Indian Joint Ventures Overseas', *World Development,* vol. 10, (February 1982) pp. 127–46.

22. Hong Kong is a larger Third World investor in manufacturing than India, but its investments are far more specialised in light manufacturing activities (which are the colony's major export strengths) than India's, and they embody relatively little indigenous technological capability. See note 21.

Achievements and Limitations of India's Technological Capability

Ashok V. Desai

As with all policy-oriented concepts, there is a risk of tailoring the definition of indigenous capability (ITC) to a conclusion: since ITC is obviously desirable, one is inclined to find in it an omnibus quality which brings all the luck in acquiring and using technology. Whether such a talisman exists or not, it is necessary to specify what precisely is required; and a closer familiarity with how technology actually changes in less-developed countries is necessary to understand how far the acquisition of ITC is feasible. In this paper we seek to set out what we understand by ITC, and to place it in the context of technological changes in Indian industry to get some idea of its feasibility and phasing.

In studying ITC we are handicapped by the fact that any statement about it is probabilistic. Capability can be proved by performance, but in LDCs its existence has often to be assessed without the proof of performance. If one goes by performance one risks underestimating ITC; relying on claims risks overestimating it. We shall go by performance; it should be stressed, however, that this is not due to any bias towards claimant groups but simply to come to conclusions that are more discussable and less controversial. Let us set out the components of industrial growth in which technological capability might assist.[1]

Purchase of technology	Price, terms, quality as judged by operation costs and quality of product;
Plant operation	Productivity of inputs, quality of product;
Duplication and expansion	Unassisted expansion or duplication of plant and transfer of concomitant technology;
Innovation	Marketable product or process innovations.

245

PURCHASE OF TECHNOLOGY

Is there some form of technological competence that gets the buyer better terms? Prima facie it seems that there must be. But this question should be answered in stages.

First, a buyer has to choose a seller. In our experience, Indian buyers, whether technologically competent or not, have seldom found the choice of preferred suppliers difficult. Most buyers of technology have some previous familiarity with the product, whether as importers or producers or their ex-employees, and know the world's major producers or technology suppliers. They can even rank them by the quality of technology, and where they cannot, they can work out a ranking from trade and technical literature.

Next comes the choice of technology. Generally it is settled by the choice of the supplier and what he is prepared to sell. The choices open to most Indian technology buyers are extremely limited. There are usually many more potential buyers than sellers; and most of them face a difficult task in convincing the sellers. In order to do so they have to show that they can build up production and sales rapidly; the major handicap, which is partly responsible for the excess demand for technology, is the smallness of Indian markets. Within the constraint of the market, how far and fast a technology buyer can penetrate it does depend on his technological competence, which would enable him to adapt the technology and overcome teething troubles.[2] But it depends even more on his size and access to finance. Big business houses have better access to imported technology (in the sense that they get more willing and better technology suppliers) not so much because they have greater technological competence – though they can buy it when they need to – but because they can exploit a market better and finance expansion more easily. Thus technological competence does increase the attraction of a buyer to a supplier, especially in technologically demanding industries like chemicals, but it is overshadowed by size and financial strength in the overall picture.

So, by and large, technological competence has only a minor effect on the terms of technology transfer. This is, however, true only as long as the interests of the buyer and the seller are complementary – that is, as long as they do not compete in the Indian or the international market. By restricting the access of foreign firms to the Indian market the government prevents conflict of interest as long as the Indian producer limits himself to selling in the domestic market. But once he wants to become a substantial exporter he is liable to run into the competition of potential technology suppliers (unless they specialise in different regional markets). He is then unlikely to be able to buy *major* technology outright, which would make a decisive difference to his competitive strength. Beyond this point he must take out licences and participate in market-sharing arrangements, or generate his own major technological advances.

A small number of Indian companies have come to the point where they can become serious exporters – TELCO for trucks and Bajaj for scooters are the best-known ones. They would find it difficult to buy major technologies if they tried. Some of them started as licensees of multinationals and continue to export within that framework; others are building up their own R&D. The two strategies are not mutually exclusive. A few business houses run a number of companies, some in partnership with a foreign licenser and others independently.[3] It is also possible for a licensee to build up his R&D capacity and generate his own technology, as many Japanese firms have done.

Thus we would argue that technological competence does not significantly improve the terms the importer of technology can get, and probably worsens them once he begins to compete with potential sellers of technology. But, for that reason, technological competence does reduce the need to purchase technology, and is essential to the winning of significant and stable export markets, at least for industrial products subject to technological progress.

PLANT OPERATION

Imported technology must frequently be adapted before it can be successfully put into operation. The most common form of adaptation is scaling down. It has not been required in all industries; in steel, oil refining and fertilisers, for instance, Indian plants have been more or less of the internationally prevalent size at the time they were built (these, incidentally, are also industries in which turn-key imports of plant and foreign principal consultants have been most common). But in most industries, the size of the market, the limited capital of entrepreneurs and the government's anti-concentration policy together led to small-scale plants, especially in the 1950s and 1960s.

The difficulty presented by scaling down varies with the degree of integration of the plant. In process chemical and metallurgical industries, considerations of speed, energy efficiency or logistics dictate plants in which a number of operations are undertaken in a rigid sequence. Here scaling down was applied to every operation, and often resulted in a plant that had to be custom-made, leading to high and unavoidable capital costs (Indian Chemical Manufacturers' Association, 1976). In those industries where plant-making capacity was set up, the government tried to offset the cost-raising tendency of small scale by standardising the size of plants. For instance, the capacity of locally built cement plants was standardised at 600 and later 1,000 tpd, of sugar plants at 1,000 and later 1,250 tcd, and of thermal power plants at 110 and then 200 MW. While this standardisation undoubtedly reduced costs, it also obstructed the inflow of technological improvements, and led to a periodic outcry from manufacturers with obsolete 'indigenous' technology when the technology for higher-capacity plants had to be imported. Thus the government took some agonised decisions to import technology in fertilisers, cement and steel in the late 1970s, and backed down in heavy electricals. In terms of costs, exports, supplies to domestic markets or technological change, the process industries have been relatively unspectacular and many of these plants have performed poorly.

This is in striking contrast to what we would call modular industries, where the scale and sequence of operations are not rigidly interconnected, chiefly engineering industries. Here there was considerable scope for the use of slower or more manual machines in individual operations. Imported technologies in this area were not readily scaled down; instead, product designs were imported, and small-scale production technologies were worked out with the help of less automatic machines than those in use in industrial countries.

Engineering firms also bought a high proportion of their components.[4] Their primary aim was to save their own capital. But this extensive trade in components ('ancillarisation' as it is known in India) had a number of other effects. First, it increased the capacity utilisation of component manufacturers and thus saved capital. Second, it encouraged the growth of small specialist firms, diversified their product pattern and increased their experience. Finally, it served as a conduit for considerable flows of technology within the country. The relatively large firms which imported the technology helped their suppliers to produce components of acceptable quality, and the trouble-shooting involved purchase departments in adaptive R&D in the guise of quality control.

Apart from providing scaled-down technologies, less automatic machines also employed more labour per unit of output, and thus promoted the use of a relatively cheap factor. Machinery production everywhere tends to be diversified, small-scale and labour-intensive; thus Indian firms were less at a disadvantage in it, and built up a range of cheap, sturdy, non-automatic machines.

There has also been some diffusion of technology within the country through formal technology transfer mechanisms, which has been actuated by two main factors. The excess demand for technology imports often led in the 1960s to the import of the same or similar technologies by a number of importers. Such 'repetitive' import of technology, which was believed to increase import costs, led the government from 1967 onwards to insist on a clause in technology import agreements giving the importer a right to transfer the technology within India. This clause did not lead to much diffusion since it was not in the importer's interest to pass on the technology to competitors; even government firms that were forced to transfer technology (for instance, Hindustan Machine Tools in tractors) did not do so with great enthusiasm or success. But another government measure had an unintended effect. Government restrictions on the growth of firms belonging to designated big business houses led some of them to pass on their old technology and plant, as well as to offer their managerial expertise to unrestricted firms and to modernise their own technology within the capacity constraints imposed.[5]

But far more widespread than these formal technology transfers was unauthorised duplication of products. Unauthorised imitators have penetrated a wide range of engineering product markets on the basis of lower prices, arising largely from lower wages. In competing on the basis of costs, they have cut corners in terms of materials, components and technology. For instance, diesel pumps produced by small manufacturers have notoriously low fuel efficiency; and the quality of electrical consumer goods produced by them is highly variable. But despite – or because of – dilution, engineering technology has been widely diffused into the economy.

We do not wish to imply that the technological difference between the integrated and the modular industries alone accounted for the relative success of the latter in adaptation to small scale; there are other differences also. Most of the integrated industries make a homogeneous intermediate product, and are subject to price control, which not only discourages cost reduction but is designed to subsidise high-cost at the expense of low-cost firms. They are also subject to revenue excise duties to which inefficient small firms are not subject. Many are entirely or largely owned by the government which imposes an inefficient form of management and absorbs the resulting losses; there is evidence that the government plants utilise at least capital less efficiently (Desai, 1981a). In a sense, the engineering industry has escaped the worst effects of government price and fiscal policies because its heterogeneous products have made its control difficult.

Apart from adaptation to scale, technology imports have also involved adaptation to local materials. The clearest cases of failure in technology transfer we have encountered involved failure to adapt processes to Indian raw materials. Conversely, a high proportion of the prizes given by the Indian Chemical Manufacturers' Association for technological excellence have gone to successful adaptors to local materials (Indian Chemical Manufacturers' Association, 1970). The supplier of technology has as little interest in adapting his technology to Indian materials as to Indian scales, so the burden of adaptation has generally fallen on the Indian buyer. Most of the corporate R&D also went into material adaptation, at least in the initial years.

Thus ITC was instrumental in making imported technologies applicable to India, but we should be careful about concluding that a high level of ITC led to successful adaptation. For one thing, the pattern of import-replacing industrialisation adopted in this country created a high demand for ITC by preventing the setting-up of plants of internationally common sizes and imports of raw materials; hence industrial growth might well have been constrained by the supply of ITC.[6]

Second, while the ITC build-up through adaptation will hopefully survive, many of its achievements will be scrapped as scales increase. Even now, tractor and truck plants which pioneered the use of general machine tools are installing CMC tools and robots in selected operations where the scales justify them. The technologies will not be junked precipitately; some will be transferred to low-wage areas, while others may be exported to countries with small markets. But it would be misleading to think that ITC has developed a specific range of technologies or path of industrialisation; it has simply marshalled technologies, often borrowed from an earlier generation of technologies in industrial countries, suited to a transitional stage in India's industrialisation.

Finally – and this is a point to which we shall return later – the type of ITC required for innovation is different from the type that has been developed. They are not unrelated, and it is not impossible for innovative ITC to emerge out of adaptive ITC. But innovative ITC requires something more; and if resources are constrained there might be a conflict between the two types of ITC.

EXPANSION

When a technologically innocent nouveau entrepreneur sets up a plant, he has to buy the whole plant and the technology with it. If a single plant manufacturer supplies the plant, he will also normally tell the buyer how to run it. In some industries, however, the plant manufacturers do not know all, or enough, about operation; and in Western countries it is quite common for plant manufacturers to specialise in parts of the equipment, so that none of them can supply a complete plant.[7] In such industries, a new entrant has to buy technology from either a manufacturer of the product or a consultant. By buying and using the technology, however, he acquires a capability which he can use in expanding production or transferring technology.

While building a plant a firm has to set up a skeleton organisation with a minimal technological competence to absorb the technology from the transferer. In India these initial organisations had a larger task arising from the government's policy of 'indigenisation'. When a new plant was proposed the Directorate-General of Technical Development went through the list of required equipment with a toothcomb and decided which items could be imported and which had to be bought within the country. Then the buyer of the plant had to chase the potential manufacturers of the items that could not be imported, persuade them to take orders, and ensure that they maintained performance standards and delivered on time. This task of procurement from an inadequately skilled and often overbooked engineering industry was an arduous one, and generated skills that the buyer would like to put to further use. So the initial procurement organisations were redesignated consultancy firms, and specialised in unpackaging plants as required by the Government and in domestic procurement.[8]

Consultancy firms of this type proliferated in the early 1960s, and there was not enough work for them in the industrial recession of the late 1960s. Their pressure led the government to decree that the principal consultant in all contracts should be Indian. This attempt at import substitution in technology has created problems ever since. Often foreign consultants refused to give performance guarantees when forced into a marriage with Indian consultants; the Soviet Union even refused at times to work with Indian consultants (Desai, 1972). Other consultants have tended to regard Indian associates as a necessary price for Indian contracts. But by the early 1970s Indian consultants had picked up enough contracts to do well and enough expertise to manage a high proportion of domestic contracts independently.

When massive investment programmes started from 1974 onwards in the Middle East, it was assumed that Indian consultancy firms, with their powerful accumulation of know-how, would capture a significant proportion of the market. While some of them did extremely good business, they failed as a group to penetrate the Middle Eastern market. The reasons are inadequately documented; the only firms for which we have some information are government consultancies. Apparently their major handicap was that they were expected to sell Indian equipment and Indian technology, which were found non-competitive. They also ran into alarming cost overruns.

Consultancy firms are traders in technology. There is no reason why they should not trade in the best or most appropriate technology wherever it is available. The Indian consultancy firms with the greatest success in the Middle East, for instance M. N. Dastur or Tata Consultancy Services, have been buying, or supervising the acquisition of, advanced Western technology. But success in trading depends on what a firm has to sell. In so far as the market is for Western technology, a Western or Japanese consultant who has sold and worked closely with such technology has an advantage over an Indian consultant.

The only market for technology that Asian firms have penetrated in the Middle East is construction. While India has captured a significant proportion of orders, Korean firms have captured a far larger share. The reason is the experience of Korean firms in large-scale, mechanised construction, first acquired in Viet Nam and then built up in Korea itself. India's own labour-intensive technology has relegated it to an exporter of labour, while the technology is supplied by others. Thus both the success of Indian consultancy firms in India and their limited and mixed performance in the Middle East stem from the fact that they grew up in the sheltered technology market of India and have no advanced technology to sell.

One might be tempted to contrast this with the rapid growth in the number of Indian firms that have invested abroad or exported technology. In our view, however, the Indian technology exports – which are generally accompanied by exports of capital or management services – arise from the same factors that account for the relatively slow growth of industrial output and exports. Under equal conditions, a centrally controlled firm would rather export goods than technology; a powerful force promoting technology exports is barriers against exports of goods in the form of import restrictions. The same force is behind the export of technology from India, except that what restricts the export of goods is not the trade barriers of other countries but the difficulty of expanding output and exports in India.[9]

So our total impression remains that while Indian firms and consultants have shown considerable skills in duplicating and adapting imported technology for the domestic market, they have neither absorbed innovations from abroad rapidly enough to keep pace nor made their own innovations on a large enough scale to generate distinctive saleable technologies.[10] This failure to innovate is what we turn to next.

TECHNOLOGICAL IMPROVEMENT

In economic literature, technical progress denotes growth in output that cannot be attributed to a growth in factor inputs. Kaldor (1961) measures it simply as the growth in the productivity of labour. Neoclassicals who believe in the measurability of capital take technical progress to be the growth in the productivity of an index of capital and labour. At a micro level one can bring more inputs into the analysis, vary the assumed functional relationship between them and output, and even get a normative measure of technical progress by giving the inputs normative weights (for instance, one who thinks that a rise in labour productivity is undesirable in a labour-surplus economy can simply remove labour from the production function). But technical progress in respect of some inputs at least is essential to a rise in per capita output and consumption, and we must ask how far, if at all, it took place in Indian industry.

Taking registered industry as a whole, it is reasonably clear that while labour productivity increased steadily, capital productivity fell after 1965, though there may have been a reversal of this trend since 1975 (Desai, 1981a). The rise in employment in private-sector registered industry after 1965 has been derisory, but its output has continued to expand. While industrial employment in the public sector has grown, the growth of total employment in registered industry has been slow. This poor contribution to employment, together with the rise in the capital–output ratio, has led to a widespread view that industrial growth has been contrary to India's factor endowment and therefore inappropriate; this distortion is held to have arisen from the import of advanced capital-intensive technology with little adaptation.

None of the primary evidence we are familiar with supports this view. Out of the thousands of industrial producers, less than four thousand imported technology; the rest either bought, borrowed or stole technology within the country. Many of the firms that imported technology adapted it to increase its labour-intensity, especially by using more labour in the handling and transport of materials. The small-scale plants imported were more labour-intensive (though not necessarily less capital-intensive) than larger plants abroad. And as we discussed earlier, the equipment market and production developed in a labour-intensive direction. The impression that technology develop-ment in India has been highly import-dependent has been nurtured by the fact that India *controlled* technology imports and generated fairly accurate (if rudimentary) statistics long before most other countries. Now that similar statistics are available for other LDCs there is no reason to persist in the myth of over-import of technology.[11]

Therefore, while we discount the overimport of inappropriate technology, we recognise nevertheless the slow growth of output, the still slower growth of employment and the rising capital–output ratio of registered industry. The slow recorded growth has been partly due to the competition of unregistered industry. Registered industry is sub-ject to industrial licensing, minimum wage laws, income tax, excise duties, and numerous regulations applicable to particular industries like textiles and sugar. Their evasion by avoiding registration can be highly profitable. There are certain legal exemptions: for instance, small-scale industry, whose definition has been progressively liberalised, is subject to lower excise duty; and co-operatives find it easier to get industrial licences (as well as to avoid the tax on profits by passing these on to members as costs). Apart from this, an unregis-tered firm has so much greater freedom and flexibility that many firms avoid registering and paying taxes as long as they can. Owing to the growth of this vast uncharted sector, official industrial statistics have become increasingly unrepresentative, until it is no longer possible to say how unrepresentative they are. But they still cover more-or-less adequately large-scale industries – integrated process industries – which cannot function independently of the official control network, and in their respect we must still answer the question: why have they become increasingly capital-intensive?

The rise in the capital–output ratios after 1965 occurred in most in-dustries, and capital–output ratios were higher and increased more in public-sector firms (Desai, 1981a). This is explained by the fact that all industry in India faced the pressure of employing more educated and semi-educated persons, that the consequent overmanning led to X-in-efficiency, and that government enterprises were less able to withstand the pressure. We now think that the pressure for employment is only one of the factors the managers have to reckon with. There are certain functions in integrated plants that have to be performed competently if they are to run well – for instance, the use of instruments, plant maintenance, inventory management of spare parts, continuous manning of key posts, etc. Every plant has to work out procedures for these functions. Indian plants, never having imported managerial expertise, had to work out the procedures themselves, and the practices they evolved leave something to be desired. Public-sector plants are at the double disadvantage of being bereft of outside expertise and also of being saddled with an inappropriate managerial tradition. That they suffer from X-inefficiency is suggested by the sudden, rapid increase in output they have achieved from time to time without the employment of more labour or capital, notably in 1976 and again in 1980.

Two other factors have contributed to the rise in capital–output ratios. One is a rise in the relative price of capital goods. Normally there would be no reason for capital goods prices to rise faster than the prices of the goods they produce. But in the most important integrated industries – coal, oil, electricity, steel, cement, fertilisers, base metals, sugar – the government operates price controls based on the historical cost of capital. As a result, their prices have lagged behind capital goods prices, and rates of return have declined to levels unattractive for new investment. In the industries owned by itself, namely coal, oil and power, the government invests irrespective of profit expectations. In the others it operates price and credit controls so as to cross-subsidise new plants. Either way, capital–output ratios are raised.

The second is progressive import substitution. Although import substitution began in 1956, for the next ten years it took place on a wide front: an increasing variety of goods was produced with a high import content. The components or functions that were indigenised initially were those that required less capital. After 1965, when the growth of industrial demand slowed down, the government stimulated it by compelling a progressive reduction in import content. As a result, more capital-intensive components were taken up for manufacture. Owing to limited experience, many errors were made in their manufacture, which both raised capital costs and reduced achievable capacity (see, for instance, Jethanandani 1971).

Thus we find ample reason for rising capital–output ratios in the government's policies on ownership, management, pricing, credit and trade, and little need to look further towards technology policy or practice.

TRANSFER OF TECHNOLOGY

Technology transferred is the difference between technology generated and technology absorbed. Its volume is small in relation to total
technology generated or used, since a great deal of technology is
generated for self-consumption. For efficient production, every firm
requires capability for trouble-shooting, material substitution and
adaptation, and quality and process control. It does not necessarily require a separate R&D establishment; depending on the range of technical problems encountered, training and experience can cope with a
large proportion of the problems. Miniature models of the production
process in the laboratory or the pilot plant are useful when problems go
beyond the experience of the technicians, and when it would be too
costly in terms of lost production, wastage or risks to experiment on
the main plant itself. Routine experimentation (for instance, the try-
ing-out of new weaves or patterns of cloth) can be accommodated on
the plant itself until its costs in terms of production loss justify separate
facilities. There is thus a maximum scale on which experimentation can
be done on the main plant without setting up a separate R&D establishment, which increases with size. There is also a minimum scale for an
R&D facility determined by the minimum number of technologists
and the resources they require, which will not be justified unless the
plant is large enough to generate enough work for them or unless they
have good enough leadership to generate usable technology on a
sufficient scale. Thus large plants tend to be more self-sufficient in
technology, whether they have separate R&D facilities or not. Small
firms are typically too small either to do much experimentation on the
plant or to afford an R&D facility. Thus separate establishments for
supplying production know-how – whether large firms, universities,
research institutes or consultants – are essential to service small firms if
they are to maintain technical dynamism.[12]

The dependence of small firms on external sources of technology
shows itself in a number of ways. For instance, most of the buyers of
technology from government laboratories are small firms (Desai,
1980). This source is not entirely satisfactory since, by policy, the
laboratories do not scale up their technology for commercial production. But there are two other sources. One is technology imports,
which are not accessible to very small firms, but which have enabled
many new entrepreneurs to set up production and expand it rapidly.
While large firms and business houses have undoubtedly imported
much technology, smaller firms and unestablished entrepreneurs have

been more crucially dependent on technology imports.

The other source is large firms. They have supplied technology to small firms through ancillarisation; that is, in the course of developing supplies of components. Some of them have sold their old plants to newcomers. Others, whose expansion was limited by government policy, took over small firms on management contracts, which included technological assistance. Finally, there has been considerable copying of large firms' technology by small firms, which either began by supplying components to the former and began eventually to manufacture the whole product, or which were started by technologists who had worked in big firms.

Large firms can afford better technicians, and can spend on R&D to tackle problems that require experimentation to solve. So they are more self-sufficient in production technology. But the quality of their technology will nevertheless depend on how far they experiment with it and how much they learn out of experimentation. And their ability to transfer technology will depend on how far they can standardise and codify their technology.

Within a plant, trouble-shooting can be done by in-house R&D and technologists. But if plants are remote from one another, the resulting loss of time and production would be costly. So multinationals that build a number of plants in different locations try to standardise a trouble-free design and to duplicate it, thereby minimising the need for localised trouble-shooting facilities. The tendency of multinationals to centralise R&D has been widely noted. By doing so they undoubtedly try to create a technology base for worldwide investment and trade. But they also try to save on research into day-to-day production problems by avoiding such problems through standardisation. Their concentration of R&D arises as much from their R&D-mix as out of their objectives.[13]

This is where Indian firms suffer from a handicap when it comes to taking turnkey orders and transferring technology. Their technology is not standardised, codified and written down. It is empirical technology grown out of and embodied in the experience of production technologists. Hence, when it is transferred, unexpected problems come up that have to be solved *ad hoc*. Indian firms try to internalise such problems by going in for subsidiaries and joint ventures rather than by selling technology at arm's length.[14] But while internalisation may avoid the adverse publicity arising from difficulties of commissioning, it cannot reduce the costs of slippage. This, in our view, explains the very mixed economic performance of Indian ventures abroad.

The transfer of technology requires its codification. It must be distilled out of the experience of technologists and documented as information that can be transferred without the movement of technologists. In so far as innovation entails an improvement in technology, the market for it is greatly extended if the improvement is codified. While innovation can be made at any scale of production, it is far more profitable if it is embodied into saleable codes and used repeatedly.

Codification, as embodied in designs, specifications, patent descriptions and other documents, is a record of a particular technology, and is an essential first step if a firm wants to go into the business of innovation. Innovation is the revision of the record on the basis of experience and experiment, and requires co-operation between the seller of technology, producers using the technology and equipment manufacturers. Two, or all three, may coincide, in which case problems of communication would be reduced. But, for innovation, storage, retrieval and revision of information are essential in a way they are not for building up a production technology on the basis of experience. While Indian firms have made much advance in the latter, they are still new to the former.

CONCLUSION

In an attempt to get closer to a definition of ITC, we would make a two-dimensional distinction. Among industries we would distinguish between modular and integrated industries, and suggest that while ITC has been built up to a great extent in the former, unfamiliarity with the methods of co-ordination required in integrated industries has led to a more mixed performance in those. Among types of ITC we would distinguish between ITC required for production, technology transfer, and innovation; while most of the ITC in India has been built up for, and in the course of, production, only the beginnings have been made towards ITC for transfer, and nothing beyond a glimmer is in evidence of ITC for innovation.

Finally, we would like to comment very briefly on the transferability of Indian experience. Four factors are particularly important. For historical reasons India has followed a nationalist policy and used its powerful industrial licensing mechanism to discriminate against foreign firms. Second, India's numerous traders have provided an abundant supply of potential entrepreneurs. Third, India's educational system produces a large output of low-grade technologists, and thanks to the generally low standard of living they are available on modest salaries. And finally, the stringent import substitution policy has led to the setting-up of small plants, import of non-standard technology and extensive manufacture of machinery. Of these, the policies are replicable, but the economic and social circumstances are not; where these are different, it is necessary to think afresh about what would work.

NOTES

1. Cf. Sanjaya Lall's (1978) classification of learning processes. Ron Dore's distinction between learning capacity and creative capacity, made elsewhere in this volume, corresponds to our last two categories. The fallacy in the argument for self-reliance lies, to our mind, in ignoring the large dose of ITLC that goes into ITCC: innovation is 90 per cent imitation.
2. This factor emerged clearly in Rajan *et al.*'s (1981) study of technology transfers from National Chemical Laboratory, Poona. But it refers mainly to investments under Rs 500,000, and does not take account of the influence of firm size and access to finance.
3. For instance, the Nandas have a tractor company producing adapted Ursus models and another joint venture with Ford, while the Lelbhais have a dye company as well as a joint venture with ICI to make dye intermediates.
4. Cf. Chaudhury (1980).
5. Thus Bajaj passed on its old scooter technology to a joint venture with the Maharashtra Government, and many textile firms began to have cloth woven by small-scale powerloom units, and processed by independent dyers and printers.
6. For instance, 244 out of the 270 pressure vessels required for a fertiliser plant were being made in India. Of the 19 manufacturers, only 6 had qualified metallurgists. Among 12 who furnished information, the average engineer-to-worker ratio was 21, and maximum 55, against 5 and 12 in the United Kingdom (Jethanandani, 1971).
7. In the steel industry, for instance, both the plants built with non-Soviet assistance, Rourkela and Durgapur, were built by consortia of German and British firms respectively.
8. Cf. the list of consultancy firms in Indian Credit and Investment Corporation of India (1972).
9. This point is treated more thoroughly and comprehensively in Sanjaya Lall's paper in this volume.
10. 'Self-reliance' was interpreted in terms of ability to duplicate and adapt technologies, which often could not be exported as they breached international patents. See Indian Chemical Manufacturers' Association (1977).

11. Between 29 January 1973 and 31 May 1975, 6,528 contracts were presented to the Mexican Registry – almost as many as approved to date in India.
12. It is noteworthy that technological improvements in OPS technology, held by Raphael Kaplinsky to be a major advance engineered in an LDC (see his paper in this volume), have come from a government research institute; also that this technology has not been commercially exported anywhere.
13. The difference in the international diffusion of R&D activities between US MNCs in process and in engineering industries found by Lall (1979) may be related to their R&D- mix.
14. The Federation of Indian Chambers of Commerce and Industry (1980) listed 197 subsidiaries and joint ventures, and 9 cases of technology export.

REFERENCES

Chaudhury, Shekhar (1980)'Acquisition and Assimilation of Technology in the Tractor Industry in India: the Strategic Perspective', Ph.D. thesis, Indian Institute of Management, Ahmedabad.

Desai, Padma (1972) *The Bokaro Steel Plant. A Study of Soviet Economic Assistance.* Amsterdam: North Holland.

Desai, Ashok V. (1960) 'Factors Underlying the Slow Growth of Indian Industry', *Economic and Political Weekly,* Annual Number 16 (10–12) 381–92.

Federation of Indian Chambers of Commerce and Industry (1980) *Report of Workshop on Indian Joint Ventures Turnkey and Third Country Projects.* 13 March 1980, New Delhi.

Indian Chemical Manufacturers' Association (1970) *Preliminary Survey on the Status of Research and Development in Chemical Industry.* Bombay.

Indian Chemical Manufacturers' Association (1971) *Proceedings of the Symposium on Import Substitution in the Chemical and Fertilizer Industry.* Bombay.

Indian Chemical Manufacturers' Association (1976) *Proceedings of the Seminar on the High Cost of Manufacturing Chemicals in India – Reasons and Remedies.* Bombay.

Indian Chemical Manufacturers' Association (1977) *Proceedings of the Seminar on Self-Reliance in Technology in Chemical Industry.* Bombay.

Industrial Credit and Investment Corporation of India (1972) Seminar on Consultancy Services in India. Bombay.

Jethanandani, H. H. (1971) 'Pressure Vessel Industry in India', in Indian Chemical Manufacturers' Association (1971).

Kaldor, Nicholas (1961) 'Capital Accumulation and Economic Growth', in Lutz and Hague (1961).

Lall, Sanjaya (1978) 'Developing Countries as Exporters of Technology, in Herbert Giersch (ed.) (1978) *International Economic Development and Resource Transfer.* Tübingen: I.C.B. Mohr, 589–616.

Lall, Sanjaya (1979) 'The International Allocation of Research Activity by US Multinationals', *Oxford Bulletin of Economics and Statistics,* 41(4) 313–31.

Lall, Sanjaya (1982) *Developing Countries as Exporters of Technology: A First Look at the Indian Experience.* Macmillan, London.
Lutz, F. A. and D. C. Hague (eds) (1961) *The Theory of Capital.* London: Macmillan.
Ministry of Industry (1980) *Guidelines for Industries (1979–80).* New Delhi.
National Council of Applied Economic Research (1971) *Foreign Technology and Investment.* New Delhi.
Peck, M. J. and A. Goto (1981) 'Technology and Economic Growth: The Case of Japan', *Research Policy* 10(3) 222–42.
Rajan, J. V. *et al.,* (1981) 'Transfer of Indigenous Technology – some Indian Cases', *Research Policy,* 1(2) 172–94.
Ramamurti, P. (1978) *Stop BHEL's dangerous truck with Siemens – an investigative analysis.* Centre of Indian Trade Unions, New Delhi.
Ramamurti, P. (1979) *For whom the BHEL tolls?.* Communist Party of India (Marxist), New Delhi.
Reddy, A. K. N. (1972) 'Basis of the Japanese miracle. Lessons for India'. *Economic and Political Weekly* 7(26) 1241–1245.

Insular and Open Strategies for Enhancing Scientific and Technological Capacities: Indian Educational Expansion and its Implications for African Countries

Thomas Owen Eisemon

The newly industrialised countries of East and Southeast Asia, first Japan and then in succession Taiwan, Singapore, and Hong Kong, have provided demonstrations of 'development' in what was once regarded as the capitalist periphery. Whether these countries are still considered to be appendages of international capitalism or examples of autonomous development is not an issue here. Irrespective of the interpretations given their economic performance, lessons are being drawn for the less developed countries of Africa and Asia. Typically and with much oversimplification the growth rates of the newly industrialised countries are attributed to a mix of economic policies favouring openness to foreign investment, to imported technology and to a collaborative relationship between government and the private sector especially in export industries. Predictably the economic strategies of these countries are favourably compared with countries that espouse scientific and industrial self-reliance. The insularity of the rhetoric of self-reliance is contrasted with the 'learning and copying' approach to scientific and technological development practised in Meiji and modern Japan and in other newly industrialised countries. (See, for instance, Ronald Dore's provocative essay in this volume.)

Educationally, most of these countries have emphasised high standards of scientific and technological training. Learning and copying have involved a careful step-by-step approach to the elaboration of university systems. Admission to universities is highly selective and pressures for expansion have been restrained in the interest of maintaining quality. Foreign study has been important in the development of an

263

educational infrastructure for scientific and industrial training. In this as well, the newly industrialised countries have been 'open' to foreign scientific and industrial influences.

African and Asian countries obtained independence at a time when science and technology had become explanations of the social and material progress of metropolitan countries and, conversely, for the 'backwardness' of colonial societies. Expansion of scientific training and research was embraced as necessary for the social and economic transformations that 'development' anticipated. Development of the capacity to train scientists and engineers is of special importance to African countries whose scientific institutions at independence were staffed mainly by Europeans (Eisemon, 1982). Plans for African scientific development organised by UNESCO in 1964, for instance, envisaged a five-fold increase in the production of scientific and technological manpower by 1980 (UNESCO, 1964). This was the preoccupation of African countries in the 1960s and 1970s, one consequence of which was the establishment of new universities that have played a key role not only in providing scientific training but as the locus of more pure and applied scientific research as well (Eisemon, 1982).

To achieve a measure of self-reliance, many African countries have relied on the scientific resources and expertise of North America and Europe in the development of their institutions for scientific training and research. In the colonial period, African institutions of higher education were typically affiliated to institutions in the metropolitan country which vetted academic appointments, monitored admissions and examinations and awarded degrees (Ashby, 1966).

Research stations, laboratories and scientific services functioned under the supervision of territorial and inter-territorial research councils, whose activities were in turn directed at the metropolitan level by a network of scientific offices and advisory bodies. In other words, the scientific and educational development of African countries emphasised gradualism and conformity to Western practices. The transition to self-rule did not bring about an abrupt departure in scientific and educational relationships to the former metropolitan country. Affiliating relationships with metropolitan institutions were terminated. But bilateral assistance agencies and philanthropic foundations stepped in to provide funds to cover the capital and recurrent expenses of the newly autonomous universities and, more important, to train African staff to replace expatriates. In East Africa, the regional network of agencies co-ordinating scientific research in the colonial period was retained in recognition of their centrality to the production of agricultural commodities for export. A regional approach to the development of higher education in East Africa was followed as well. International scientific and educational organisations have superseded the structures established for scientific and educational co-ordination at the metropolitan level. In recent years, regional approaches to scientific and educational development have fared poorly, as in East Africa, where bilateral or multilateral co-operation among states in the financing and administration of institutions was required (Southall, 1974). However, the dissolution of the University of East Africa and of the inter-territorial scientific institutes and services which functioned under the auspices of the East African community, did not result from the practical difficulties involved in international scientific and educational co-operation. Instead, the commitment of African states to developing their own scientific and educational capacities militated against forms of co-operation and postponed self-reliance.

India illustrates the limitations of an insular strategy of scientific and educational development, as Professor Dore suggests elsewhere in this volume. India was among the very first Asian and African countries to pursue a policy of import substitution, to restrict foreign investment and to monitor transfer of foreign technology. The adoption of national economic planning in the independence period, the promotion of state ownership in key industries, notably banking, energy, communications, steel and heavy manufacturing, and unrestrained expansion of scientific and technical education were the principal instruments for achieving self-reliance. They are now seen as important causes of sluggish economic growth and of a lack of significant scientific and technological innovation when India's actual performance is compared to the newly industrialised countries, or to its own scientific, industrial and educational potential.

India's development plans have clearly favoured entrepreneurship in the public sector, which has been relied on for scientific and technological innovation as well. But the low profitability and often substantial losses incurred by state-owned enterprises have been a serious drain on the country's scarce resources. In 1978–9, for instance, the *pre-tax* profits of these enterprises amounted to less than 2 per cent of the capital employed, compared with an average rate-of-return of nearly 60 per cent for the 200 largest private firms (Indian Institute of Public Opinion, 1980). There has been very little foreign investment in the Indian economy. In terms of direct foreign investment per capita in 1967, the last year for which comparative data are available, India ranked among the countries with the lowest foreign investment ($3.00 per capita) (Reuber, 1973, pp. 268–79), partly because of the size and management of state-owned foreign investments. Only some 6,000 proposals for foreign technical collaborations have been approved since independence (India, Ministry of Industry, 1978, p. 29). The largest number of proposals were in the period of 1960–5 (2,000), which can be attributed to India's second five-year plan emphasising growth of the manufacturing sector (Reserve Bank of India, 1968). Fluctuations in the number of foreign collaborations approved are the result of industrial growth and industrial policy, but the number of foreign collaborations has increased notwithstanding India's seeming preoccupation with inventing its own science and technology. The nature of these collaborations has changed in two respects, however. Whereas the collaborations entered into during the first and second five-year plans were mostly those that stressed import substitution and saved India much-needed foreign exchange, an ever larger number of collaborations have involved production of manufactures for export. Second, while the private sector, especially Indian firms with foreign equity, were once the principal importers of foreign technology, wholly owned Indian firms (and state-owned enterprises) have become major purchasers of foreign technology (Nayar, 1982, pp. 147–96).

While efforts to expand India's infrastructure for scientific training and research were initiated prior to independence, 1947 marked the beginning of massive expansion of this infrastructure. There were 102 research institutes established between 1947 and 1950. This pace continued in the 1950s when 257 such institutions were established (Rajagopalan, 1969). Opportunities for scientific and technical training increased exponentially as well. In 1947, a Ministry of Education survey of scientists and engineers drew attention to an acute shortage that would be exacerbated in the years to come (Mahanty, 1977; National Planning Committee, 1948). Expansion of the system of higher education in the 1950s, especially technical education (there were only ten engineering colleges at independence) quickly rectified this situation. Between 1950 and 1970, the annual output of scientists, engineers, agriculturalists and physicians increased sevenfold (University Grants Commission, 1979).

Expansion, legitimised as a development necessity, exacerbated weaknesses of the university system that had been the object of educational reform stretching into the colonial period: low standards, poor teaching, and inadequate facilities. More recently, reforms have sought to inoculate instances of academic excellence with a measure of significant autonomy and central funding against the parochial, populist influences that have shaped educational expansion. This was the approach of the University Grants Commission in 1961 when it identified a small number of post-graduate teaching departments in Indian universities as Centres of Advanced Study. The Education Commission of 1964–6, elaborating on the centres scheme, proposed that certain universities be designated as 'centres within the country for an academic community that is still on the periphery' (Heredia, 1979, p. 20). But government found the reform of the universities too difficult, politically, and established centres such as the Indian Institutes of Technology which operate outside the university system (Eisemon, 1974). The exam-ridden Indian university system, whose organisation and patterns of governance have changed little since the establishment of the first universities in the late 1850s, no longer provides the leadership it once exercised in science and technology (Basu, 1974). Though the governments of independent India have professed concern for the improvement of scientific and technical education and for fostering research in the university system, their preoccupation has been with expanding the network of national laboratories and institutes. These laboratories and institutes became the foci for investments in research and development and many have come to play an important role in post-graduate training as well (Eisemon, 1982).

If a restrictive attitude toward foreign technology and foreign investment contributes to India's ostensibly low rate of economic growth (between 3.5 and 4.0 per cent GNP in recent years), then India has been compensated not only by having itself to blame but, as I argue below, by the scientific, technological and political benefits it has derived from a strategy of self-reliant development. That India possesses the ability to make choices about how best to utilise indigenous capacities as well as those of other countries, is attributable in large measure to the unrestrained expansion of scientific and technical education, and to the nationalism embedded in its scientific development in the colonial and independence periods. The Indian experience has important lessons especially for African countries, which, like India a century earlier, are seeking to expand their facilities for training scientists and engineers in order to staff their own scientific institutions.

NATIONALISM AND SCIENTIFIC EDUCATIONAL EXPANSION IN INDIA

Pressures for political self-rule and for scientific self-sufficiency developed simultaneously in the late nineteenth century. The lack of sufficient facilities for scientific and technical education was the subject of constant complaint. The Indian National Congress, formed in 1885, took the position that 'the government be moved to elaborate a system of technical education' (Basu, 1974, p. 85). Believing that political agitation for scientific and technical education had little effect on colonial authorities, Indian philanthropy stepped in to provide such opportunities. In 1904 an association was formed in Calcutta for the Advancement of the Scientific and Technical Education of Indians. It supported the scientific studies of Indian students in Japan, the United States and European countries. In 1905, a conference sponsored by Indian nationalists and the Indian National Congress was held at Benares. The conference recommended that a national polytechnic institute be established as well as one engineering college in each state. In the absence of any initiative from colonial authorities on this proposal, industrialists and leaders of the independence movement started a college of engineering and technology at Jadavpur, Calcutta, in 1907. It was the first of many institutions founded by Indian philanthropy. Expansion of the country's educational, scientific and industrial capacity was resisted by colonial authorities. Viceroys pleaded insufficient funds and inadequate demand. More accurately, the interests of Indian nationalists and colonial authorities simply collided.

The First World War produced a momentary relaxation of the tensions. Politically, some concessions were made toward self-rule. Colonial authorities also recognised that India must become more self-reliant scientifically and industrially. The government established the Indian Industrial Commission in 1916 to examine steps that might be taken to lessen the country's scientific and industrial dependence on Britain. The scope of the resulting recommendations was broad, covering tariff policy, the need for import substitution and export promotion policies, as well as the establishment of mechanisms to advise government in industrial development and to expand scientific and technical education (Government of India, 1918). Although few of the Commission's recommendations were acted upon, they signified acceptance of the principle of self-reliance and marked the first step towards scientific and industrial planning.

Soon after it became evident to Indian nationalists that Britain conceded the inevitability of self-rule, the Congress set about preparing for this contingency. During the presidency of S. C. Bose in 1938, the Congress established a National Planning Committee under the chairmanship of Nehru. In the initial discussion of India's political and economic future there was some confusion as to whether national plan-

ning should seek to realise the Gandhian ideal of village self-sufficiency. Nehru put such romanticism to rest. The National Planning
Committee advocated large-scale industrial development (National
Planning Committee, 1940). Whereas Indian philanthropy provided
the initiative for much of the country's scientific and industrial development from the last quarter of the nineteenth century until the
1930s, this was not conceived as being the responsibility of the state.

The Second World War revived the interest of the colonial
authorities in the recommendations of the report of the Indian Industrial Commission. A national industry policy was needed if India was to
produce the war material necessary for its own defence. One important outcome of the adoption of industrial planning by colonial
authorities was the creation in 1942 of the Council of Scientific and Industrial Research (CSIR). CSIR was established to foster and co-ordi-
nate scientific and industrial research undertaken in universities, research institutions and in the private sector (Hill, 1945).

Science had an enthusiastic advocate in Nehru. On becoming prime
minister, Nehru agreed to be the president of the Council of Scientific
and Industrial Research which, along with the Indian Council of
Agricultural Research, the Defence Research and Development Organisation and the Department of Atomic Energy, have guided the
country's scientific development in the independence period. In 1958
on the advice of Homi Bhabha, physicist and initiator of India's nuclear research programme, Nehru piloted a policy resolution in favour
of 'cultivation of science, and scientific research in all its aspects [in-
cluding] according scientists an honored position by associating [them]
with the formulation of policies' (UNESCO, 1972, pp. 105–6).

Nehru's writings and speeches on science stressed the symbiotic relationship between independence and self-reliance, and the contribution of science to the achievement of both. Long before many science
policy-makers in Asia and Africa concerned themselves with the implications of technology transfer from industrial to industrialising countries, Nehru recognised that the scientific and technological interests of
developed countries did not always coincide with those of India
(Nayar, 1982).

Nehru, more than any other political figure in his generation,
grasped the implications of the divergence of political and economic
interests between the scientifically and technologically advanced countries of Europe and North America and the newly independent states.
Without enhancing its scientific and technological capacity, India, he
said, could not be economically or politically independent. National

security considerations were evident in Nehru's approach to expanding and organising India's infrastructure for scientific and technological research and development. The two principal innovations in the infrastructure inherited from the colonial period were the establishment of the Defence Research and Development Organisation (DRDO) and the Department of Atomic Energy.

India was the first developing country to explore the uses of nuclear energy. An Atomic Energy Commission was set up by Nehru in 1948 to apply atomic research to the generation of nuclear power. As controlling nuclear proliferation became a preoccupation of industrialised countries, Nehru warned that 'it might be to the advantage of [these] countries to retain and restrict the use of atomic energy to the disadvantage of a country like India'. The divergence between the interests of India and those of the industrial countries of Europe and North America in regard to the development of nuclear technology was brought into sharp focus in 1974 following the detonation of India's first atomic device.

One year after independence and partition (1948) Nehru created a defence science organisation, and in 1953 a defence science service was organised under the direction of Krishna Menon. These were later merged to form the Defence Research and Development Organisation (DRDO) which manages more than thirty research laboratories (Eisemon, 1982). In the Nehru years DRDO concerned itself with import substitution. It is now hoping to export some Indian military technology (light trucks and artillery to the Gulf States, for example). In 1963–4 India spent 38 per cent of its national budget on defence, about 1 per cent of that for defence research and development (SIPRI, 1972, pp. 10–19). This commitment increased after the wars with Pakistan in 1965 and 1971. In 1979–80 defence research and development expenditures were estimated to be Rs 590,000,000, or about 2 per cent of the defence budget and a large share of the country's research and development expenditures (India, Ministry of Defence, 1979). In the military/national security area India has been repeatedly rebuffed in its efforts to obtain advanced technology from Western countries. This has had an important impact on Indian thinking about developing its scientific and technological potentials. In the early 1960s India approached the United States for purchase of F104 aircraft and then for assistance in developing and manufacturing under license high-performance aircraft. The United States, which was supplying Pakistan with such aircraft, refused. By 1970 India was not only assembling a version of the Soviet MIG 21 but also an interceptor, the GNAT, manufactured under licence and significantly modified for the country's defence needs. However, Indian-produced military aircraft were no match for Pakistan's Mirages in 1971. When after the war India tried to purchase the Swedish Viggan fighter using an American engine it was again rebuffed. India purchased the British Jaguar licence instead after proposals from a number of Eastern and Western European countries. The lesson drawn from all of this was that though India might be unable to develop a self-sufficient aeronautics industry, it must have, as Nehru insisted, the manufacturing capability to make choices related to its security.

The importance of India developing scientific and technological capacities allegedly more appropriate for developed countries has been underlined by the reluctance of the latter to sell India sophisticated security-related technology or to allow India to acquire technology enabling it to compete in international markets. This is a recurrent theme in the testimony of American businessmen before Congressional committees, in the deliberations of various organs of the EEC monitoring technology sales to and manufacturing imports from countries outside the Community, and most explicitly in the practices of Japanese industrial houses toward less-developed countries of the Asian region (Nayar, 1981, 1982). Nayar recounts in this connection the unsuccessful efforts of Indian textile manufacturers to obtain modern spinning and weaving technology from their Japanese counterparts. The Japanese advised India to utilise more effectively its enormous labour resources, and discouraged it from acquiring more capital-intensive methods of textile production. Japan and Western countries have in the 1970s and early 1980s learned a great deal about the threat to their own economies of allowing imitation and competition from countries like India with significant industrial capacity.

SELF-RELIANT SCIENTIFIC DEVELOPMENT: AN ASSESSMENT

Few would claim that India has made the most of its scientific and industrial potential, but any critique must recognise the very real achievements. India is a scientifically developed developing country. Its scientific community is the world's third largest after the United States and the Soviet Union. There are more than one half million (697,600) Indian scientists and engineers, about 7 per cent of whom

(54,105) are engaged in research and development activities (UN-ESCO, 1980, p. 723). India has a very large infrastructure for scientific training and research, more than a hundred scientific societies and nearly a thousand scientific journals (UNESCO, 1972). In regard to the volume of scientific activity, India is one of the world's leading producers of science. It ranks among developed countries in the number of papers published in influential scientific journals (Frame *et al.,* 1977). In brief, India possesses the capacity for self-reliance in most areas of scientific training, a capacity to operate at the frontiers of many scientific fields, and, significantly, a capacity to apply basic science to manufacturing and agriculture. Some Indian scientific and technological achievements, such as the launching of a space satellite in 1980, may be dismissed as expensive public relations exercises, just as it used to be fashionable to criticise NASA's space programme prior to recognition of the impact of solid-state micro-circuitry on everyday life. Others are more difficult to dismiss. Through the atomic energy programme, for instance, India acquired capacities in a number of fields that use basic and applied research related to high-energy physics, including electronics, metallurgy, and medicine (India, Department of Atomic Energy, 1980). There have been some 'spin-offs' of this capacity locally, in cancer research and treatment, and radiation sterilisation of seeds, to take two less-well-known examples, and India has acquired some export potential as well (in radio isotopes and radio tracer technology, for which there is a large market in the Middle East and Southeast Asia) (Nayar, 1982).

In the world-economy it is India's strategy of self-reliance that has placed it between the nations at the centre and those at the periphery. In Gidengil's recent test of Galtung's theory of imperialism, in which she attempted to dichotomise countries in terms of level of development, income inequality and trade, India clusters with the OPEC countries (Gidengil, 1978). Its proximity to countries at the centre of the world-economy stems from the high degree of local participation in, and the productive capacity of, its economy, a consequence of India's strategy of self-reliance.

India has not fully realised its scientific and industrial innovative potential, in part for reasons related to the size and structure of the country's economy. India's domestic markets are very large despite its proverbial poverty. Export opportunities are often neglected in favour of expanded penetration of local markets, where returns on investment are typically greater than those prevailing in developed capitalist countries (Errunza, 1978, pp. 117–23). Notwithstanding governmental incentives for export production, Indian firms understandably prefer to exploit local markets where they have factor cost and marketing advantages and which are protected from overseas competition. The low-output/high-unit profit syndrome is attenuated by the monopolistic and oligopolistic character of most of the country's major industries. Firms have little incentive to invest in research and development, therefore compelling government to do so. Concern about the inadequacies of the technological innovation-to-production link which results from excessive reliance on government research and scientific services, cannot overlook the ill effects of monopolistic and oligopolistic conditions in an economy that by virtue of its size is not obliged to trade with other nations to a substantial degree.

The wastefulness and inefficiencies of investments in Indian higher education arise from processes of expansion whose implications for scientific and technical education are simultaneously deleterious and beneficial. Long before independence, India's system of higher education had become unmanageable. The autonomy and vitality of the university system were casualties of the struggle for control of higher education, which continued into the independence era, as caste, linguistic and communal groups demanded what the Congress leadership in the colonial period thought they were entitled to – access to higher education for those groups with the resources and political influence necessary to found colleges.

Unrestrained expansion of higher education in the independence period aggravated conditions that had been criticised by colonial authorities from the 1880s onward. Indian higher education was exam-ridden, instructional standards were low, and university authorities were frequent objects of student agitation to award grace marks to conceal the results of liberal admission and poor instruction (Basu, 1974). Despite the transformation of affiliating/examining universities established on the mid-nineteenth century University of London model into teaching institutions, and the assumption of instructional responsibilities at the post-graduate level, the studies offered in Indian universities remained much what they had been in the nineteenth century, institutions providing a humanistic education, the best of them providing opportunities for social, intellectual and moral development along the lines recommended in MacCaulay's famous *Minute* (Eisemon, 1982).

While efforts to reform Indian higher education, and to upgrade scientific and technical training particularly, have not enjoyed much lasting success due largely to the political causes and consequences of expansion, the country has none the less derived important benefits. Expansion of higher education has enabled India to become self-sufficient at the undergraduate and post-graduate level in most fields of scientific and technical training. It has enabled India to establish a large network of scientific institutions and services, to organise scientific societies and publish scientific journals in most fields; it has enabled India to have a scientific community in a meaningful sense (UNESCO, 1972).

CONCLUDING REMARKS

India's strategy of self-reliance placed importance on the development of scientific and technological capacities in fields ostensibly inappropriate to a poor rural society, and on unrestrained expansion of scientific and technical training. This is contrary to a great deal of the advice now given to African and Asian countries on their scientific and educational planning. Countries with limited scientific, industrial and educational resources, it is said, should concentrate on building capacities in applied sciences, especially export agriculture, and to carefully articulated expansion of scientific and technical training with anticipated manpower needs. Indian nationalists in the nineteenth century were rightly suspicious of such advice. When colonial authorities resisted nationalist pressures to expand scientific training and research and to accelerate industrial development, Indian philanthropists founded institutions for this purpose and Indian entrepreneurs set about providing the country with the industrial facilities needed for India to become a modern nation. Today Asian and African countries are being implicitly advised to rely on the international community for what Indians have obtained largely on their own.

There are, to summarise, two lessons to be derived from the Indian experience that have importance especially in so far as the scientific development of African countries is concerned. First, notwithstanding the sometimes deleterious efforts of expanding access to higher education, such expansion is necessary to create a scientific community. This is obvious, but not, because of that, unimportant. With the exception of Nigeria, Ghana and the Sudan, most African countries have sought to articulate expansion of scientific and technical training with anticipated manpower needs. India developed significant capacity for scientific training long before it discovered manpower planning, which, given the politics of educational expansion, it has never been able to employ. The growth of higher education in Africa has been restrained by recognition of the enormous investment expansion required as well as by concern that it would compromise the international standing many African universities have attained. Indeed, in India, such expansion was accompanied by stagnation and by parochialisation, relegating its universities to the periphery of the international scientific system and to the periphery of the country's scientific community as well.

Expansion of scientific training will entail considerable investment, much of it either wasteful or, from the point of view of development strategies emphasising equity and social justice, unjust and inegalitarian. Enthusiasm for higher-education institution-building has waned. It was once a priority of bilateral and multilateral assistance agencies as well as the governments of the newly independent African states. It is still a priority of African governments, notwithstanding the advice of donors to invest in primary and secondary education, especially in rural areas. Whatever may be the educational and economic merits of this advice, politically, pressures for expansion of higher education are growing as more qualified secondary-school graduates seek university entrance. Many African governments that have tried to deflect the demand for higher education through promotion of polytechnic education have encountered no more success in this than the colonial authorities who favoured education adapted to African needs. Moreover, as recent university student and professorial activism in Kenya and other African countries illustrate, governments that favour quality over quantity in higher education can neither expect gratitude nor loyalty. University expansion may intensify the politicisation of higher education and it may lead to an oppositional relationship between universities and government, as in India. However, these consequences may be politically less serious as university students and staff no longer see themselves as incipient or full members of the country's political leadership.

Second, the rhetoric of science for national development has in many African countries been interpreted very narrowly, to cover mainly the kinds of agricultural research and extension services that played a major role in the development of colonial society. Of course, applied scientific research now embraces concern for subsistence as well as for export agriculture, and the achievements of applied science in Africa are undeniable and have improved the lives of many Africans. Yet this should not preclude a small role for pure science, even if this is presumed to be more appropriate for scientifically advanced countries. The implications of the neglect of pure sciences for research and training in the applied sciences require study. It may well be that the science-based training and research in these professional fields characteristic of North America and Europe is inappropriate; but this requires demonstration rather than *ex-cathedra* pronouncement. More important, the neglect of pure sciences has serious implications for the capacity of African countries to develop sophistication in the applied sciences; to make choices about imported technology, to adapt and modify foreign technologies; to devise indigenous substitutes; or, to exchange their science and technology with other countries. Unless science planning in African countries embraces a concern for what is now regarded as inappropriate, gains made in indigenising institutions carrying out applied training and research may be offset by the new forms of dependency that this creates.

REFERENCES

Ashby, E. (1966) *Universities: British, Indian, African.* Cambridge, Mass.
Basu, A. (1974) *Growth of Education and Political Development in India.* Delhi.
Eisemon, T. (1974) *U.S. Educated Engineering Faculty in India.* Bombay.
Eisemon, T. (1982) *Science in the Third World: Studies from India and Kenya.* New York.
Errunza, V. (1978) 'Gains from Portfolio Diversification into Less Developed Countries', *Journal of International Business Studies,* pp. 117–23.
Frame, J. D., Narin, F. and Carpenter, M. P. (1977) 'The Distribution of World Science', *Social Studies of Science,* 7, pp 504–7.
Gidengil, E. L. (1978) 'Centres and Peripheries: An Empirical Test of Galtung's Theory of Imperialism', *Journal of Peace Research,* 15, pp. 51–66.
Government of India (1918) *Report of the Indian Industrial Commission 1916–1918.* Superintendent of Government Printing, Calcutta.
Heredia, R. (1979) 'Structure and Performance of College Education in India An Organizational Analysis of Arts and Science Colleges in Bombay'. Unpublished dissertation, University of Chicago.
Hill, A. V. (1945) *Scientific Research in India.* Government of India, Simla.
India, Department of Atomic Energy (1980) *Annual Report 1979–80.* Bombay.
India, Ministry of Defence (1979) *Report 1978–79.* New Delhi.
India, Ministry of Industry (1978) *Report 1977–78.* New Delhi.
Indian Institute of Public Opinion (1980) *Quarterly Economic Report, No. 98.* Delhi.
Mahanty, J. (1977) 'Science in the Universities', in B. R. Nanda (ed.), *Science and Technology in India.* Vikas, New Delhi (pp. 112–24).
National Planning Committee (1940) *Proceedings 1938–40.* K. T. Shah, Bombay.
National Planning Committee (1948) *General Education, Technological Education and Development Research.* Bombay.

Nayar, B. R. (1981) *India's Quest for Technological Independence*. Montreal.
Nayar, B. R. (1981) *India and Technological Self-Reliance: The Results of Policy*. Montreal.
Rajagopalan, T. S. *et al.*, (1969) *The Directory of Scientific Research Institutions in India*. New Delhi.
Reserve Bank of India (1968) *Foreign Collaboration in Indian Industry*. Bombay.
Reuber, G. L. (1973) *Private Foreign Investment in Development*. Oxford.
SIPRI (1972) *Resources Devoted to Military Research and Development: An International Comparison*. Stockholm.
Southall, R. (1974) *Federalism and Higher Education in East Africa*. Nairobi.
UNESCO (1964) *Outline of a Plan for Scientific Research and Training in Africa*. Paris.
UNESCO (1972) *National Science Policy and Organization of Scientific Research in India*. Paris.
UNESCO (1980) *Statistical Yearbook 1978–79*. Paris (p. 789).
University Grants Commission (1979) *University Development in India: Basic Facts and Figures*. New Delhi.

Sources of Technological Capability in South Korea

*Larry E. Westphal, Yung, W. Rhee and Garry Pursell**

This paper assesses the relative importance of contractual technology transfers and indigenous efforts in South Korea's acquisition of technological capability. It also evaluates the role of export activity. The period covered is from the early 1960s, when Korea experienced its 'economic take-off', to the late 1970s. For historical perspective and for discussion of related aspects of direct foreign investment and export activity, reference may be made to Westphal, Rhee and Pursell (1981), from which this paper is extracted.

DIRECT FOREIGN INVESTMENT

Direct foreign investment (DFI) has been relatively unimportant as a source of investment finance in Korea.[1] None the less, it is possible that DFI could have been important as a means of transferring technology. That would be true if DFI were concentrated in locally innovative ventures that subsequently diffused technology to other producers. The establishment of new lines of local production is the form of innovation relating to DFI most easily observed in Korea. In this respect, the evidence clearly indicates that DFI has been an important source of technology in only a few sectors, primarily in chemicals, electronics, and petroleum refining.

The first major foreign investments after 1960 were for import substitution in chemical fertilisers and petroleum refining. DFI has also been the principal source of technology for most of the electronics sector, but it should be noted that the sector was initially established by purely domestic firms engaged in what largely were assembly operations (Kim, 1980). Joint ventures played an innovative role in establishing facilities to produce basic petrochemicals and derivative synthetic fibres and resins, an important example being polyester fibre and yarn. But DFI has had no part in the production of many other chemical products of equal significance in Korea, such as rayon yarn and acrylic fibre and yarn. These products are all important exports, either directly or indirectly (that is, as inputs into textile exports).

* The views and interpretations in this chapter are these of the authors and should not be attributed to the World Bank, to its affiliated organisations, or to any individual acting on their behalf.

Other forms of innovation, particularly those leading sequentially to gradual improvements in production processes and product designs, are much more difficult to identify. But in so far as they represent minor adaptations, they are likely *individually* to be of much less significance. There is little direct evidence on which to base a judgement about the importance of DFI in relation to these forms of innovation. To our knowledge, the most relevant microeconomic information is that provided in studies of exporting firms by Cohen (1973, 1975) and more recently by two of us – Pursell and Rhee.

Cohen's study consists of a careful comparison of domestic and foreign firms producing ostensibly identical products. Foreign firms are those located in Korea and having some foreign equity participation. But the study has rather severe limitations: the period of comparison is relatively short; the sample size – twelve domestic firms, ten foreign firms, and six distinct products – is small; the range of information obtained is limited. Moreover, the study extends only to 1971, by which point Korea had received relatively little of its present stock of DFI. Despite these limitations, it is appropriate to quote Cohen's conclusion that 'neither the direct nor the indirect economic benefits of this [export-motivated] type of foreign investment are very great, if they exist at all. By most indices foreign firms resemble local firms' (1975, p. 119).[2] Thus Cohen was unable to uncover any evidence of technology diffusion from foreign to domestic firms for the sample of products he studied.[3]   Eighteen foreign firms were covered in the study of Pursell and Rhee (information regarding the scope of this study is given below in the section, 'Acquisition of Technology by Exporting Firms'). As would be expected, foreign parent or affiliated companies were an important source of technology for these firms. In contrast, foreign and domestic sources of technology were about equally important for domestic firms.[4]

To investigate whether foreign firms tended to be more or less innovative than domestic firms, the firms were asked whether they were the first to introduce any production technologies in Korea – and if so, to provide a brief description of the technology, the number of firms subsequently adopting it, the approximate time-lag, and the causal connection (if any) between its introduction by the firm responding and its subsequent adoption by other firms in Korea. Of the nine foreign firms that responded to this set of questions, six had introduced a total of ten new technologies in Korea; of the seventy-nine domestic firms that replied, twenty-seven had introduced a total of forty new technologies.

These results would seem to indicate that foreign firms on the average were somewhat more innovative than domestic firms. But the implication may not be generally valid; two-thirds of the foreign firms produced either synthetic fibres or electrical products. Moreover, a closer look at the responses suggests that Korean firms introduced important innovations even in these industries. In the electrical products industry, for example, televisions, refrigerators, elevators, and escalators were first produced in Korea by a Korean firm and were subsequently produced – after a time-lag of about two to five years – by both foreign and other domestic firms, which in some cases benefited by hiring away technicians employed by the innovating Korean firm.

Of course, a comparison of the frequency of innovation of foreign and domestic firms says nothing about the relative importance of the respective innovations. In this regard, the principal things of interest in the responses are the high incidence of innovation by both foreign and domestic firms and the apparent importance of many of the innovations. The six foreign firms introduced the following in Korea: the production of nylon yarn, a technique for manufacturing polyester staple fibre, a technique for dyeing and processing rabbit fur, a new technique for producing cement, the production of three electronic components, the production of small televisions, and techniques for manufacturing audio-speakers and home stereo systems. On the other hand, the twenty-seven domestic firms were responsible for introducing a wide range of products and techniques, including the following: acrylic fibre; rayon yarn and staple fibre; many techniques related to producing textiles, including various dyeing techniques and a technique for weaving high-quality Japanese kimonos; new techniques for manufacturing zippers and synthetic leather; a variety of techniques for producing pumps, ships, transformers, diesel engines, fork lifts, industrial machines, automatic looms, electric motors, and iron and steel products; and the production of radial tyres, aircraft tyres, tennis balls, golf balls, refined zinc, and canned mushrooms and asparagus.

Many of these innovations were subsequently adopted by other firms in Korea. According to the information provided by the innovating firms, twenty-nine of the fifty innovations, including four of the ten processes first introduced by foreign firms, were subsequently copied by other firms.[5] But only two firms indicated that there was any direct relation between their activities and the subsequent diffusion of the innovations they introduced; that relation consisted of the hiring away of technical staff by the new entrants. Thus it is possible that some of the later entrants would have established the new processes in Korea even without the example of the innovating firm. This further blurs the comparison of the importance of foreign and domestic firms in introducing new technology.[6]

TECHNICAL ASSISTANCE AND LICENSING

We now consider technical assistance from bilateral and multilateral sources, typically on concessional terms. We also examine formal licensing to obtain access to proprietary technology, for which royalty payments must be made, usually on a continuing basis over a stipulated period. The sum of both flows does not necessarily equal, or even come close to, the value of explicit payments made for technology. For example, payments made to engineering and management consultants of all kinds are not included, except in so far as they are financed by technical assistance.

Korea's expenditures on royalty payments abroad have until recently been small: the value of technical assistance exceeded that of royalty payments by a large margin through 1967–71. The cumulative value of technical assistance received from bilateral and multilateral sources from 1962 to 1976 was $243.8 million. The comparable figure for royalty payments to commercial sources of licensed technology is $113.5 million. But this comparison is somewhat misleading for industry alone: only 27 per cent of the inflow of technical assistance was directed toward the mining and manufacturing sectors, which were responsible for more than 90 per cent of total royalty payments. Moreover, even after making adjustments to reflect this difference, the degree to which these figures respectively measure comparable flows is questionable. Whatever the degree of initiative exercised by the Korean government in directing the flow of technical assistance to maximise the value of the resulting technology transfer – and there is considerable anecdotal evidence of a great deal of initiative – it remains that donor governments and agencies also exercised a significant degree of control.[7]

Japan has been Korea's principal source of licensed technology: nearly 60 per cent of Korea's royalty payments from 1962 to 1978 were made to Japanese entities. The United States, as the second most important source, received slightly less than a quarter of Korea's royalty payments. As would be expected, the composition of royalty payments by industry differs from that of DFI. Moreover, it is even more concentrated among sectors. There has been little licensing of technology in the textiles and apparel sectors, in which a sizable proportion of DFI was concentrated. The chemicals sector accounted for roughly 40 per cent of Korea's royalty payments; metal and basic metal products, 16 per cent; electrical and non-electrical machinery, 10 per cent each; and transport equipment and pulp and paper products, 3 per cent each.[8]

How do Korea's technology purchases compare with those of other countries? The comparative data are rather unsatisfactory because they include only royalty payments and express these in relation to the value of total commodity exports. It already has been noted that licensing is not the only means of purchasing technology. Moreover, comparisons in relation to the value of exports are difficult to interpret for two reasons. First, technology is also purchased in varying amounts by different countries for use in production for domestic sale. Second, exports differ in product composition across countries, leading to variations in the technology embodied in exports. The comparison none the less is of some interest.

For Korea, the ratio of royalty payments to the value of commodity exports ranged between 0.3 and 0.5 per cent from 1972 to 1976. This range is to be compared with ratios ranging from 1 to 3 per cent for other semi-industrial countries, such as Argentina, Brazil, Chile, and Colombia.[9] Only since 1977 have Korea's royalty payments reached comparable levels. In fact, combined royalty payments of $143.1 million in 1977 and 1978 exceeded the cumulative total for the preceding fifteen years. Increased reliance on licensing can in large measure be explained by increased emphasis on the development of technologically more advanced industries in recent years.

Aggregate data on royalty payments abroad reveal little about the importance of licensing as a source of technology for locally innovative undertakings. Although there is some information about how the initiators of new lines of production acquired technology, it is severely limited in detail and in the number of industries involved. It none the less indicates that some industries – those producing wigs, cement, and rayon yarn, for example – have been established on the basis of technologies acquired from overseas through means other than licensing. This result is not surprising, because not all technologies are proprietary. The information also gives a clear indication of extensive reliance on turnkey plant construction as a means of acquiring technology – sometimes involving licensing, though generally not.[10] Moreover, the second and subsequent plants typically were not constructed on a wholly turnkey basis, at least in those industries with which we are familiar.[11]

ACQUISITION OF TECHNOLOGY BY EXPORTING FIRMS

Given the importance of exports in Korea's industrialisation, the means by which exporters acquired technology are of particular interest. Here we can use the survey of 112 exporting firms that Pursell and Rhee undertook in 1976. The firms surveyed, on the average much larger than other Korean firms, were together responsible for slightly more than a third of Korea's commodity exports in 1975 and just less than 15 per cent of new contracts for construction services in the same year. The vast majority were 100 per cent locally owned.[12] Twenty-three of the firms had no domestic sales. Represented among 'traditional' Korean exports are processed-food products, fresh fish, cement, textiles, clothing, plywood, shoes, leather products, wigs, and toys, handicrafts and sporting goods; among 'non-traditional' exports are refined sugar, synthetic fibres and resins, tyres, basic metal products, tableware, electronics, non-electrical machinery, transport equipment, and construction services.

The firms were asked to indicate the importance of different designated sources of the technologies they currently used: that is, to distinguish among sources that were 'very important', 'important', 'of minor importance', and 'not important or not relevant'. Technologies were intentionally not specified; each firm determined the specific technology or technologies for which the importance of alternative sources was indicated. It is apparent from the survey results that the most frequent reference was to process technology, not to product design. Table 1 summarises the responses of eighty-eight firms that answered the question with respect to a total of 241 technologies. The figures given in the table state the percentage of responses in which each source was considered to have been either 'very important' or 'important'. The total of the percentages in each column is 100, the result of their being calculated with respect only to responses indicating that a particular source was either 'very important' or 'important'. The figures are thus to be interpreted as indicating the relative historical importance of different sources of technology. Sources of technology are shown separately for traditional and non-traditional exports, as well as for total exports.

Domestic sources transfer local know-how, which comprises technologies either developed indigenously or assimilated from abroad. (The accumulation of local know-how is discussed at the end of this section.) For all of the export industries surveyed, domestic sources were considered to be important slightly more often than were foreign sources.[13] As would be expected, domestic sources have had a more important role in the traditional than in the non-traditional sectors. But the difference is not pronounced. In a large number of cases, the respondents stated only that local know-how was important; they

TABLE 1   *Relative Importance of Sources of Process Technology*

	Percentage composition of responses indicating a source to be 'important'		
Source	Traditional exports	Non-traditional exports	All exports
Domestic			
Licensing and technical assistance	3.6	2.4	3.0
Experience acquired by personnel through previous domestic employment	12.3	8.7	10.5
Suppliers of equipment or materials	6.2	3.2	4.8
Buyers of output	3.1	5.0	4.0
Subtotal	25.2	19.3	22.3
Government-supported institutes	8.7	9.2	9.0
Local know-how	21.8	15.7	18.9
Total domestic	55.7	44.2	50.2
Foreign			
Licensing and technical assistance	11.8	20.7	16.0
Experience acquired by personnel through previous overseas employment	9.0	18.0	13.2
Suppliers of equipment or materials	12.3	8.9	10.7
Buyers of output	11.0	6.7	9.0
Total foreign	44.1	54.3	48.9
Unidentifiable	0.2	1.5	0.9
Total	100.0	100.0	100.0

Note: See the first paragraph of this subsection for the individual export product groups included under the categories 'traditional' and 'non-traditional'.

Source: Tabulated from a survey of 112 exporting firms conducted in 1976 by Pursell and Rhee.

did not distinguish among agents and mechanisms. On the basis of other information, however, it is highly unlikely that government-supported institutes had any substantial part in these cases.[14]

For domestic and foreign sources taken jointly, the sources of technology most frequently cited are buyers of output and suppliers of equipment or materials. Because suppliers can provide technology in both embodied and disembodied forms, it is not surprising that they are of somewhat greater consequence than are buyers of output; what perhaps is unexpected is the small difference between them. Next most important are employees with previous experience working in firms overseas – some as a result of turnkey arrangements – and in Korean establishments. Indeed the transfer of labour among firms counts for more than contacts with suppliers alone or with buyers alone.[15]

Formal mechanisms of licensing and technical assistance, of only modest importance overall, are of substantial consequence in the transfer of technologies from abroad.[16] Even so, though licensing and technical assistance is the foreign source of technology that most frequently is considered to be important, it was considered to be important only a third of the time that foreign sources were indicated.

For many industries it is important to distinguish between the mastery of production processes and the ability to design products that either conform to the structure of – or anticipate changes in – demand. Indeed, parallel questioning about the sources for product innovation – that is, for improvements in quality, additions to product lines, and changes in product design, styling, and technical specifications – revealed that Korean exporters, almost across the board, rely heavily on foreign sources for product-design technology, far more than for basic production, or process, technology. This is apparent from the information in Table 2, which summarises responses to a question about sources of information for product innovation.[17] Foreign sources have been by far the most important channels of information leading to product innovation, with buyers of exports being the most important single source.

Foreign buyers contributed to product innovation through the influence they exercised on the characteristics of exported products. Fully 74 per cent of the ninety-two firms that responded to this question stated that they either modified the characteristics of their product to accommodate buyers' requests or produced in direct accord with buyers' specifications. As is indicated in Table 3, some firms (fourteen, to be exact) produced all or nearly all (81–100 per cent) of their exports to buyers' specifications. But the majority of firms produced only some of their exports directly to buyers' specifications. The specifications most often influenced were product design and styling (forty-seven firms), followed by packaging (twenty-five), basic technical specifications (eighteen), and minor technical specifications (fifteen).

It also was apparent from the interviews with exporters that foreign buyers contributed importantly in other ways, most frequently as a result of periodic visits to inspect production facilities or of ongoing programmes to control and improve quality, through such things as suggesting changes in individual elements of the |production process and improvements in the organisation of producʌion within the plant and in management techniques generally, buyers helped many exporters achieve greater efficiency and lower costs.[18] It thus appears that the transfer of know-how from export buyers has been a major contributor to minor process innovations of the sort that sequentially lead to gradual improvements, the cumulative effect of which can be extremely significant.

TABLE 2 *Relative Importance of Sources of Information for Product Innovation a/(per cent)*

Source	Percentage composition of responses indicating a source to be 'important': for all exports
Domestic	
Parent firm	6.2
Sales staff	8.6
Buyers of output	8.6
Other firms, affiliated or not	1.6
Total domestic	25.0
Foreign	
Parent firm	1.2
Foreign publications	3.9
Overseas travel by staff	19.9
Buyers of output	26.2
Other affiliated firms	16.8
Total foreign	68.0
Unidentifiable b/	7.0
Total	100.0

Source: Same as for Table 3.
a/ Product innovation includes quality improvements, additions to product lines, and changes in the design, styling, and technical specifications of products.
b/ Includes production staff and 'other' sources.

TABLE 3 *Influence of Foreign Buyers on Design, Style, Packaging, and Technical Specifications of Exports*
(number of firms responding)

Outcome of influence	Influenced and details given	Details of influence: percentage of export sales affected						Influenced, but details unknown	Not influenced
		1–10	11–20	21–40	41–60	61–80	81–100		
Modified own design	47	11	4	8	4	8	12	21	24
Used design provided	52	6	12	10	4	6	14	16	24

Source: Same as for Table 3.

ACCUMULATION OF LOCAL KNOW-HOW

It is not surprising that exporters have depended extensively on foreign sources for product innovation. Such dependence is inevitable when technology is transferred to start new lines of production that serve export markets from their inception – as in much of Korean electronics and shipbuilding production, for example. But dependence can also occur if production has first been established to serve the local market, with exports following later, as is more typical of Korean experience. Here, mastery of technology is in the first instance often confined to achieving rudimentary standards of product design. These standards may suffice to gain entry into export markets, but continued growth of exports sooner or later requires that product standards be upgraded. Moreover, successful penetration of export markets frequently requires that product specifications be tailored to the different demands of individual markets. Until some experience has been gained in producing to meet differentiated demands, it undoubtedly is most cost-effective, and may even be necessary, to rely on export buyers for product-design technology. Not to be neglected in this regard is the fact that production for export thus provides a potent means of acquiring product-design technology through learning by doing, which spills over to product development in local markets as well.

The interviews with exporters clearly indicate that the acquisition of technological capacity by Korean industry in basic production processes has progressed further than in product design, at least in relation to product standards in developed-country export markets. In addition, given the high frequency with which domestic sources were said to be important, the interviews attest to considerable Korean mastery of process technology. Much of what was considered by the respondents to have come from domestic sources consists of technology originally developed overseas, subsequently transferred or brought to Korea, and then effectively assimilated and sometimes adapted by Korean industry. Some of this technology, particularly in the traditional export sectors, was part of Korea's inheritance from its colonial past.

The basic production technology for non-synthetic textile yarn and fabric is an obvious case: several leading textile exporters were established before independence, and many senior managers and technicians gained their initial experience in the industry during the colonial period. Plywood – also an important export, particularly during the 1960s – offers another example: the first plant to produce plywood was constructed in 1935. Plywood is equally an example of an industry that benefited from technical assistance provided under the US military's programme of local procurement during the 1950s. None the less, when queried about the sources of technologies in use today, producers of both textiles and plywood overwhelmingly indicated local sources.

The distinction between domestic and foreign sources thus has little to do with the locus of the inventions that originally created the technology. It has far more to do with the importance of the assimilation and adaptation of technology by local producers, and of the diffusion of technology through formal and informal contacts and through labour transfers among domestic firms. Further evidence of the importance of diffusion from domestic sources comes from the sizable number of exporting firms that indicated direct knowledge of diffusion to other firms of technologies they had introduced into Korea.

In industries for which process technology is not product-specific, mastery has frequently led to the copying of foreign products as a means of enlarging technological capacity. The mechanical-engineering industries, among others, afford many examples; such processes as machining and casting, once learned through producing one item, can easily be applied in the production of other items. One case that has been closely studied is textile machinery, particularly semi-automatic looms for weaving fabric (Rhee and Westphal, 1977). In this, as in some other cases, Korean manufacturers have not only been able to produce a capital good that meets world standards, albeit for an older vintage; they have, in addition, adapted the product design to make it more appropriate to Korean circumstances. (The adapted semi-automatic looms fall between ordinary semi-automatic and fully automatic looms in terms of the labour intensity of the weaving technology embodied.) In other industries in which technology is more product-specific, such as chemicals, mastery of the underlying principles has enabled greater local participation in the technological effort associated with the subsequent establishment of closely allied lines of production.

Recognition of the importance of local technological learning also is central to understanding how technologies initially introduced in Korea only very recently – within the past five to ten years – are now considered, in relation to subsequent undertakings in the same lines of production, to have come from local sources. Korea's very high industrial growth rate has permitted rapid rates of technological learning because of the short intervals between the construction of successive plants in many industries. In some industries, including synthetic resins and fibres, the first plants were often built on a turnkey basis and on a small scale, much smaller than either the size of the market or the size that would exhaust scale economies. Construction of the second and subsequent plants followed quickly, with Korean engineers and technicians assuming an increasing role in project design and implementation, and at scales much closer to or equal to world scale.[19] To the degree that local personnel undertook various functions involved in plant construction, Korea's technological mastery in these industries can be said to extend beyond operation of the production process to project design and implementation.

From all indications, Korea's technological mastery has developed rapidly. It is of interest to ask with what result, and to attempt an answer in the context of cross-country comparisons. We know of only one comparative investigation (Christensen and Cummings, 1979) of changes in total factor productivity that includes Korea among the countries studied, the rest of which are countries that belong to the OECD. The study relates to gross private domestic product in all sectors, not just in industry, which would be preferable for our purposes. The results, however, are consistent with the proposition that rapid development of technological mastery has been an important source of the fast rise in Korea's industrial output, more so than in most OECD countries. Between 1960 and 1973, aggregate output in real terms grew 9.7 per cent a year; total factor productivity increased 4.1 per cent a year, and thus accounted for slightly more than 40 per cent of output growth.[20] Of the OECD countries, output grew faster only in Japan (10.9 per cent a year); likewise, total factor productivity increased more quickly only in Japan (4.5 per cent a year). For all other OECD countries, the annual increase in total factor productivity ranged between 1.3 and 3.1 per cent.

Korea's technological mastery is further manifested in rapidly growing exports of industrial know-how – through turnkey plant construction, through direct investments to establish manufacturing facilities, and through licensing and the sale of various technical services, including engineering and management consultancy. Examination of the content of these exports provides additional and particularly valuable information about Korea's technological mastery. As is shown in Rhee and Westphal (1978), the know-how exported typically appears to be either the mastery of conventional production technology for industrial activities that are well established in Korea – such as cement and textiles – or the ability to organise and manage project implementation, plant operation, and marketing.[21] Except in a few instances, exports of know-how do not extend to project or plant design, this element having been separately secured by the project sponsor or sub-contracted to non-Korean firms.

This feature of Korea's technology exports highlights the fact that a number of industries have little mastery of the fundamental aspects of the underlying engineering know-how. As might be expected, these industries typically either are new to Korea or are experiencing rapid technological change globally. None the less, several of them are important export industries – as a result of exports by foreign-owned firms or, if by domestic firms, on a clearly subcontractual basis. Electronics is a notable example, not only because it is an important export, but because it illustrates that technologies for processes and product designs can be intimately interconnected. As of 1978, Korea's electronics industry lacked nearly all of the process technology required to implement newly developed product designs, with the result that there was virtually no indigenous product-design activity, except in the realm of copying technologically unsophisticated products.[22] In this industry, as in some others, mastery does not extend very far beyond assembly; only the technologically simpler components are domestically produced.

We conclude this section with a generalisation and a caveat. The generalisation is that Korea's technological mastery is much greater in production than in investment activity. Or, to put it another way, relative to world standards, Korea's proficiency in plant operation far surpasses that in product and plant design.[23] As with any generalisation, this one has important exceptions, some of which are apparent from the foregoing discussion. But it contains an important kernel of truth. Now, the caveat. The bias of Korea's technological mastery is neither unnatural nor a bad thing. It stems from the natural sequence according to which plant operation is learned before the capability for plant design is acquired. In addition, the continued use of foreign resources in investment activity has undoubtedly been necessary for the achievement of extremely fast production growth, for there are constraints on how quickly the requisite mastery can be acquired. What is significant in this regard is the evidence in many areas of gradually increasing use of domestic resources.

CONCLUSIONS

Korea's export-led industrialisation has overwhelmingly and in fundamental respects been directed and controlled by nationals. Although foreign resources have continued to make substantial contributions since the early 1960s, the transactions involved have typically been at arm's length. Thus, although Korea has relied rather heavily on inflows of investment resources, the inflows have overwhelmingly been in the form of debt, not equity. Except for industries established during the colonial period, technology has been acquired from abroad largely through means other than DFI. The purchase of technology through licensing has been of modest importance as the initial source of process technology; machinery imports and turnkey plant construction have been of much greater consequence in the transfer of technology, and a tremendous amount of know-how has entered with Koreans returning from study or work abroad. What is very important is the assimilation of technological know-how, which has been great. Moreover, Korean exports have critically depended upon transactions between related MNC affiliates or upon international subcontracting in only a few sectors, such as electronics.[24] None the less, though the organisation of export activity is in part locally managed, marketing is largely performed by overseas firms acting as middlemen. But what again is important is that the acquisition of marketing savvy is well under way.

Korea's strategy to gain industrial competence has thus relied heavily on indigenous effort through various forms of learning by doing, and emphasised transactions at arm's length in the use of foreign resources.[25] Several considerations arise in relation to extracting lessons from Korea's success in following this strategy. We will deal first with those concerning the nature of technology and product differentiation in the industries on which its industrial growth has crucially depended. This will permit us to gauge the likelihood that Korea can successfully pursue the same strategy in the future. Then we will consider whether Korea's past success in following this strategy has in any way depended on circumstances unique to Korea. This in turn will permit us to draw some conclusions relevant to programming the industrial development of other countries, particularly those at earlier stages of industrialisation.

Many of the principal industries in Korea's past industrialisation – such as plywood or textiles and apparel – use technologies that can be characterised as mature, in that the mastery of well-established and conventional methods embodied in equipment readily available from foreign suppliers is sufficient to permit efficient production.[26] Furthermore, the products of many of these industries are either quite highly standardised (plywood, for example) or differentiated in technologically minor respects and not greatly dependent on brand recognition for purchaser acceptance (textiles and apparel, for example). In short, for most of the industries that have been intensively developed to date, the technology for processes and for product design is not proprietary. With respect to acquiring technology or marketing overseas, there consequently are few advantages to be gained from either licensing or DFI, except in peculiar circumstances.

Electronics is an exception. It is an industry in which technology is changing rapidly worldwide, product differentiation is based on sophisticated technological know-how, and purchasers' brand preferences are evident. But it appears to be an exception that proves a rule, for electronics is precisely the industry in which Korea has extensively relied on DFI to enter production, particularly for export, and has so far failed to gain local mastery of fundamental aspects of production know-how.

In post-war Korea, however, electronics and certain chemicals perhaps are unique in their almost exclusive reliance on DFI for acquiring the very latest technology as well as market access. On the basis of licensing, Korea was able to acquire the most modern shipbuilding technology in the world, just as it was able to incorporate the most recent technological advances in its integrated steel mill. Other examples, which we will not cite here, further attest that Korean industry has been able to initiate, and in most cases successfully to operate, a variety of 'high-technology' industrial activities by means of licensing and turnkey arrangements. Moreover, even in electronics, an intensive effort is under way – through the current expansion and development of the Korea Institute of Electronic Technology – to obtain basic technological know-how and production capability by means of licensing.

What seems apparent from recent experience is that the shift toward promoting more technologically sophisticated industries implies greater reliance on licensing as the mode of acquiring technology. But this is not a matter of absolutes, for it remains possible to substitute for licensing by replicating foreign technology through local effort. The difference is simply that the cost of doing so is higher in the industries more recently promoted. What is not so apparent is whether firms overseas will license technology without restricting its use. They may impose severe restrictions on the sales of licensed products. They may prefer to give access to technology only through DFI. Or they may even deny access. Equally unclear is whether the shift also implies greater dependence on licensing and DFI for market access, if only to gain rapid consumer acceptance through the use of familiar brand names.

About all of these issues, the experience of the Korean automobile industry is instructive. Unlike such countries as Brazil and Taiwan, whose automotive exports take place through international subcontracting to subsidiaries of the large MNCs, Korea has started to export complete automobiles produced by wholly domestic firms with no involvement by the large MNCs. Korea's approach undoubtedly means slower growth of automotive exports and higher cost in the short run. It entails problems of gaining consumer acceptance not encountered under international subcontracting, and it requires the establishment of a network of overseas dealers and servicing facilities. But in the long run, having an independent sector under wholly Korean management may well pay off, just as the same approach continues to earn high rewards for the Japanese.

The example of the automobile industry suggests that Korea can and will continue to follow a strategy that emphasises local technological effort and control. But recent government pronouncements suggest that the emphasis may be changing toward greater encouragement of DFI. Whatever the case, the tradeoffs involved in acquiring competence become increasingly complex, the more technology-intensive the industry being developed. Based on Korea's record so far, strategies for particular industries are likely to evolve in a pragmatic manner as more experience is gained.

What, then, is the relevance of Korea's experience to other developing countries? If any element in Korea's past situation is unlikely to be widely duplicated, it probably is Korea's abundance of entrepreneurial resources, which in effect removed a major advantage of DFI: the possibility of substituting foreign for domestic entrepreneurship. Moreover, Korea's entrepreneurial talent has not been deployed only in industry; government also has benefited. Indeed, Korea's remarkable industrialisation would not have occurred without the design and implementation of effective government policies that have fostered industrial dynamism.[27] But rather than speculate about the universality of entrepreneurial ability and the prospect that other countries will adopt policy approaches to permit its productive deployment, we will concentrate on the lessons that apply in countries having entrepreneurial resources, even if those resources are latent, as they once were in Korea.

Korea clearly has not had to rely on foreign entrepreneurship to identify profitable ventures or to manage their operation. This fact has made it possible to 'unbundle' the package of resources that typically is made available by DFI, and has thus permitted the selective use of individual foreign resources. But, as we have argued, transfers of technology from abroad constitute only an initial stage in acquiring technological mastery. Of far greater consequence is local effort to master the technology that is transferred and to apply the mastery in other undertakings, thereby to reduce reliance on foreign technological mastery and to foster locally based innovative activity. In a similar vein, the organisation of export activity entails a variety of functions that must be learned if their performance is gradually to be taken over by nationals. Korea's industrial competence must therefore be considered as resulting primarily from indigenous effort.

It is very significant that Korea's experience in these respects runs counter to contemporary pronouncements about the shape of, and the constraints imposed by, the existing international economic order. In the context of calls for a 'new international economic order', it frequently is alleged that international markets are non-competitive and that developing countries either are denied access to technology and export markets in unbundled form or are given access only on highly unfavourable terms. It is often further asserted that foreigners necessarily play the leading role – through the transfer of technology – in the acquisition of technological capacity, and – through the initiative they exercise – in the organisation of export activity. If true, both characterisations imply a severe constraint on industrial development. But far from supporting these characterisations, Korea's experience shows them to be false for many of the industries whose development was important for its achievement of semi-industrial status.

These industries are not simply those producing labour-intensive products, such as textile fabrics or apparel. Also among them are various capital-intensive industries – cement and steel, for example – as well as a number of skill-intensive or technology-intensive industries – shipbuilding and certain types of machinery production, for instance. In these and in many other areas, Korean industrialists have been able to purchase technology on competitive terms, typically embodied in machinery imports and turnkey plant construction by foreigners, but sometimes disembodied in licensing and technical services contracts. Likewise, they have been able to sell their exports on competitive terms, typically to foreign middlemen, who none-the-less perform only some of the organisational functions, but sometimes directly to the final users.

In a number of industries, the initial acquisition of production know-how occurred during the Japanese colonial period. But this fact should not be ascribed too much importance. Korea has relied upon foreign suppliers to provide much of the capital equipment used in many of its industries and has only recently embarked on a concerted programme of import substitution in the capital-goods sector. In this connection, it is useful to recall a generalisation made earlier in the paper – to the effect that Korea's technological mastery has progressed much further in plant operation than in plant and product design. It thus appears that the know-how to operate production processes efficiently is, to a large degree, independent of the ability to use the underlying engineering principles in investment activity. But that is not to deny that Korean industry has acquired and exercised the capacity to select the technologies to be imported. Nor is it to deny that Koreans have become increasingly involved in various phases of project implementation. None the less, it is not too great an overstatement to say that Korea has become a significant industrial power simply on the basis of proficiency in production. There is an important lesson here: a high level of technological sophistication is not required to attain substantial industrial competence.

There is another important lesson about the tremendous efficacy of export activity as a means of acquiring industrial competence. Merely by their export activity, Korean firms have enjoyed virtually costless access to a tremendous range of information, diffused to them in various ways from the buyers of their exports. The minor innovations that have resulted have been significant in increasing production efficiency, changing product designs, upgrading quality, and improving management practices. Exporting thus appears to offer a direct means of improving productivity, in addition to the indirect stimulation that comes from trying to maintain and increase penetration in overseas markets. This beneficial externality of export activity has gone largely unnoticed in the literature on trade and development. But the Korean experience indicates that it is very real and is part of the explanation of why countries following an export-led strategy have experienced such remarkable success in their industrialisation efforts.

NOTES

1. During 1962–76 DFI contributed well below 10 per cent of the net inflow of foreign capital, excluding grant assistance. Roughly 80 per cent went into manufacturing, where its contribution to gross investment was in the order of 8 per cent. See Westphal, Rhee and Pursell (1981), pp. 16–24.

2. The quotation refers to comparison of foreign and domestic firms in Singapore, Taiwan, and Korea. But the conclusion is clearly meant to apply country-by-country as well as collectively.
3. The products are wigs, radios, transistors, cotton yarn, cotton cloth, and baseball gloves.
4. The difference between foreign and domestic firms in this respect is statistically significant according to the conventional chi-square test.
5. The six processes not imitated had been introduced a very short time before the survey.
6. In contrast with the Pursell–Rhee results, some recent surveys do not give any indication of significant innovations by foreign firms, but these surveys are even more limited than Cohen's. In a related area, though, Jo (1977) reports evidence – without giving any details – of considerable adaptation of technology to local conditions by MNCs. This does not necessarily imply that foreign firms use more innovative or appropriate technology than do domestic firms, but it certainly is consistent with either result.
7. Most technical assistance – more than three-quarters of the total – came from the United States and the United Nations. Of the total value received, slightly more than 30 per cent was for contractual services; roughly 25 per cent was for commodities, many of which were to equip such technical institutes as the Korea Institute of Science and Technology; another 25 per cent was for individual consultants who worked in Korea; and the remainder, roughly 19 per cent, was used to send Koreans overseas for training and education.
8. In addition to other chemicals, the chemicals sector here includes pharmaceuticals, fertilisers, and petroleum products. Payments for pharmaceutical technology have amounted to only 0.6 per cent of total royalty payments.
9. The percentage appears to be higher even in India, where it was 0.8 in 1973. Comparative data (also based on selected individual years for the other countries) are from UN Commission on Transnational Corporations (1978), p. 280).
10. Chung (1977) reached the same conclusion.
11. Particularly interesting in this regard are case studies under way by the Institute of Economic Research (1979); these show the progressive replacement of foreign by domestic technology suppliers in the construction of successive plants for the manufacture of steel, paper, petrochemicals, and nylon yarn and cord.
12. Only one firm was wholly foreign-owned; three had majority, and fourteen minority, foreign-ownership. These foreign firms were concentrated in the production of electronics and synthetic fibres. Because of their small number, separate figures are not shown for foreign firms in the tables that follow.
13. Hereafter, no distinction is made between 'very important' and 'important'. Both are considered to be 'important'.
14. The most commonly mentioned public or quasi-public institutes were the Korea Institute of Science and Technology and the Korea Science and Technology Information Centre.
15. The importance of labour transfer as a source of technology reflects high

labour mobility. Depending on the industry, between 33 and 51 per cent of the production workers recruited to individual firms in 1975 had previous experience in the job assigned to them. The importance of labour transfer from overseas reflects the relatively large number of Koreans who worked or were educated abroad before their employment in Korea.

16. Technical assistance here includes that for which the firm pays directly.
17. The different breakdowns of sources used in soliciting responses about sources of process technology and of product innovation explain the difference between Tables 3 and 4 in this respect.
18. Kawaguchi (1978) gives evidence from the (Japanese) buyer's side of the considerable efforts made in this direction. Further information from the exporter's side is provided by the survey research of L. H. Wortzel and H. V. Wortzel, sponsored by a World Bank research project under the over-all direction of Donald Keesing: 'Key Institutions in the Growth of Manufactured Exports from Developing Countries'. Morawetz (1980) also finds evidence of impressive contributions by foreign buyers to technological improvements of exporters.
19. The observed pattern of time-phased plant construction in these industries might be an optimal strategy, with small scales chosen for the first plants to minimise the costs and risks entailed in learning the technology. But it is not known whether these or other considerations were the controlling ones at the time the first plants were constructed.
20. As for all the other countries, the growth in total factor productivity is attributable to a variety of sources, including among others: changes in the composition of activity toward higher productivity sectors, increased capacity use, and improvements in labour quality due to rising educational attainments, in addition to 'pure' technological change, which is what concerns us here. For manufacturing alone, Kim and Roemer (1979, p. 90) estimate that 44 per cent of the growth in output (at 18.9 per cent a year between 1960 and 1973) was attributable to increased total factor productivity. But this contribution is reduced to 4 per cent if separate account is taken of increased capacity use and labour quality, with the former being by far the more important. While recognising the importance of increased capacity use, we are sceptical about whether its effect has been as pronounced as estimated by Kim and Roemer.
21. See Jo (undated) for an analysis of an extensive set of data on Korean direct investment overseas.
22. See Suh (1975) and Kim (1980). Kim documents considerable learning from the production of basic consumer products, such as televisions and tape recorders, as well as communications equipment and simple testing instruments. But critical elements of semiconductor technology are lacking none the less. Semiconductors, particularly in the form of integrated circuits, are the building-blocks of electronics production. Briefly, they consist of silicon wafers onto which impurities are introduced in pre-set patterns through the use of masks to obtain the desired circuitry. As of 1978 there was no domestic capacity to produce either the elemental wafers or the masks, as well as other important inputs for semiconductor production. Inability to produce masks is an obviously major lacuna, because they are the vehicle by which product designs are implemented.

Problems of communication make it practically impossible to purchase tailor-made elements from unaffiliated overseas firms.
23. The emphasis on plant design rather than on other aspects of capacity creation is intentional. It is meant to highlight that more is involved than simply the inability to produce certain capital goods, and to point to the relative lack of basic engineering know-how.
24. Korean exports thus conform to the hyphothesis advanced by Hone (1974) and Nayyar (1978) and further supported by Balassa (1979): the most important foreign influence on the growth of manufactured exports from developing countries is exerted by buyers in arm's-length transactions, and not – as suggested by Helleiner (1973, 1976) – by MNCs or firms engaged in international subcontracting.
25. That Korea was following, whether explicitly or implicitly, a consistent though evolving strategy having the elements stressed here is clearly indicated in various writings by Dr Hyung Sup Choi. A key figure in Korean science and technology policy, he served lengthy tenures as head of the Korea Institute of Science and Technology and then as Minister of Science and Technology. (See, for example, Choi, 1977.)
26. Note that this does not imply the absence of rapid technological change in the industry in developed countries. It simply means that developing countries can – at least for a while – maintain a comparative advantage, once established, based on mastery of conventional methods more appropriate to their factor endowments.
27. On the design of government policy, see Westphal (1978, 1981); on its implementation, see Jones and Sakong (1980).

REFERENCES

Balassa, Bela (1979) 'Intra-industry Trade and the Integration of Developing Countries in the World Economy', World Bank Staff Working Paper, no. 312. Washington, DC: World Bank.
Choi, Hyung Sup (1977) 'Role of Various Stages of Technology Relevant to Developing Countries', Keynote Address prepared for the Third Inter-Congress of the Pacific Science Association, Bali, Indonesia. Processed.
Christensen, Laurits R. and Dianne Cummings (1979) 'Real Product, Real Factor Input, and Productivity in the Republic of Korea, 1960–1973', Social Systems Research Institute Working Paper, no. 7918. Madison: University of Wisconsin.
Chung, KunMo, and others (1977) *Technology and Industrial Development in Korea*, Final Report of the Korean Science and Technology Policy Instruments Project. Seoul: Korea Advanced Institute of Science. Processed.
Cohen, Benjamin I. (1973) 'Comparative Behaviour of Foreign and Domestic Export Firms in a Developing Economy', *Review of Economics and Statistics,* vol. 55, pp. 190–7.
Cohen, Benjamin I. (1975) *Multinational Firms and Asian Exports.* New Haven and London: Yale University Press.
Helleiner, G. K. (1973) 'Manufactured Exports from Less-Developed Countries and Multinational Firms', *The Economic Journal,* vol. 83, pp. 21–47.

Helleiner, G. K. (1976) 'Transnational Enterprise, Manufactured Exports and Employment in Less Developed Countries', *Economic and Political Weekly,* vol. 11, pp. 247– 62.

Hone, Angus (1974) 'Multinational Corporations and Multinational Buying Groups: Their Impact on the Growth of Asia's Exports of Manufactures – Myths and Realities', *World Development,* vol. 2, pp. 145–9.

Jo, Sung-Hwan (1977) 'Direct Foreign Private Investment in South Korea: An Economic Survey', Korean Development Institute Working Paper, no. 7707. Seoul: Korea Development Institute. Processed.

Jo, Sung-Hwan (undated) 'Overseas Direct Investments by South Korean Firms: Directon and Pattern'. Seoul: Sogang University. Processed.

Jones, Leroy P. and Il Sakong (1980) *Government, Business, and Entrepreneurship in Economic Development: The Korean Case,* Studies in the Modernization of The Republic of Korea, 1945–1975. Cambridge, Mass.: Harvard University Press for the Council on East Asian Studies, Harvard University.

Kawaguchi, Yoriko (1978) 'Japanese Affiliates' Manufacturing for Export in Developing Countries', Washington, DC: World Bank. Processed.

Kim, Kwang Suk, and Michael Roemer (1979) *Growth and Structural Transformation,* Studies in the Modernization of the Republic of Korea. *1945– 1975.* Cambridge, Mass.: Harvard University Press for the Council on East Asian Studies, Harvard University.

Kim, Linsu (1980) 'Stages of Development of Industrial Technology in a Developing Country: A Model', *Research Policy.*

Morawetz, David (1980) 'Why the Emperor's New Clothes are not Made in Colombia', World Bank Staff Working Paper No. 368. Washington, DC: World Bank.

Nayyar, Deepak (1978) 'Transnational Corporations and Manufactured Exports from Poor Countries', *Economic Journal,* vol. 88, pp. 59–84.

Rhee, Yung W., and Larry E. Westphal (1977) 'A Micro, Econometric Investigation of Choice of Technology', *Journal of Development Economics,* vol. 4, pp. 205–38.

Rhee, Yung W., and Larry E. Westphal (1978) 'A Note on Exports of Technology from the Republics of China and Korea', Washington, DC: Economics of Industry Division, World Bank. Processed.

Suh, Sang Chul (1975) 'Development of a New Industry through Exports: The Electronics Industry in Korea', in Hong, Wontak and Krueger, Ane. *Trade and Development in Korea.* Seoul: Korea Development Institute.

United Nations, Economic and Social Council (1978) Commission on Transnational Corporations. *Transnational Corporations in World Development: A Re-examination.* New York: United Nations, E/C.10/38.

Westphal, Larry E. (1978) 'The Republic of Korea's Experience with Export-led Industrial Development', *World Development,* vol. 6, pp. 347–80.

Westphal, Larry E. (1981) 'Empirical Justification for Infant Industry Protection', World Bank Staff Working Paper No. 445. Washington, DC: World Bank.

Westphal, L. E., Rhee, Y. W. and Pursell, G. (1981) 'Korean Industrial Competence: where it came from', World Bank Staff Working Paper No. 469. Washington, DC: World Bank.

Some Hypotheses Regarding Indigenous Technological Capability and the Case of Machine Production in Hong Kong

Martin Fransman

INTRODUCTION

The aim of this paper is to investigate further a number of hypotheses that have been advanced in some of the literature on indigenous technological capabilities (ITC) in less-developed countries. The paper draws on a case study of a sample of machine-producing firms in Hong Kong.[1] Since the firm sample is relatively small, and since all the firms come from only one sector in one country, it is obviously not possible to reach very firm conclusions about the hypotheses. Furthermore, all the hypotheses are inherently difficult to examine since it is not clear in any concrete situation what would have occurred had certain crucial parameters been altered. Nonetheless, it is felt that Hong Kong is of particular interest in any discussion of ITC as a result of near-free-trade and minimal government intervention which are principal features of this country. In this respect Hong Kong is significantly different from all the other newly industrialised countries, including Singapore, with which it is often compared.

SOME ITC HYPOTHESES

A number of ITC hypotheses, for which the Hong Kong case has some relevance, have been advanced in the literature (although in what follows they might, for the sake of clarity, be expressed in bolder form that what was originally intended). These include the following:

(1a) The level of innovation is directly related to the degree of competition (for example, Ranis *et al.*, 1981).

(1b) The degree of competition determines the dominant form of technological change, for example, process technological change (see, for example, Stewart, 1982).

(2) Protection is a necessary condition for ITC – protection of learning and also possibly products (for example, Lall, 1980, 1981; Katz, 1978). (Clearly there is potential conflict between hypotheses 1a and 2.)

(3) Government promotion is a necessary condition for ITC – through the creation of incentives, provision of technological assistance, etc. (for example, Lall, 1980; Datta Mitra, 1979; Dahlman and Westphal, 1981).

(4) The establishment of a local capital-goods sector is a necessary condition for more advanced forms of ITC (for example, Stewart, 1977, 1982; Lall, 1980; Dahlman and Westphal, 1981).

(5) Inter-firm learning is an important source of ITC: for example, between users and producers, component-suppliers and producers, etc. (for example, Westphal, Rhee and Pursell, 1981; Corden, 1980; Dahlman and Cortez, 1982; and Cortez, 1978).

THE HONG KONG CASE

The industrial environment in Hong Kong – Little (1979, p. 16) goes so far as to refer to Hong Kong's 'perfect free trade regime' – enables us to throw some light on these hypotheses. Before doing so, however, it is useful to clarify some of the main features of this environment, distinguishing between policies relating to external economic relations and to the internal economy.

EXTERNAL ECONOMIC RELATIONS[2]

In general, no protection is extended to industrial firms in Hong Kong and there are only an insignificant number of import controls. 'As a free port, Hong Kong has no general tariff.' Furthermore, there are no export incentives. 'Virtually no restriction exists on the entry and repatriation of capital, nor on the conversion and remittance of profits and dividends arising from direct investments.' 'The government does not interfere with import trends and imposes no quantitative restrictions on any categories. It does not require prior deposits (for imports) or exercise any antidumping measures. Import of capital goods (new or used), components, and maintenance parts are free of government controls.'

THE INTERNAL ECONOMY

'The government does not attempt to channel investment, domestic or foreign, into particular sectors. Nor does it announce any "preferred projects".' (Cf. the 'pioneer industry' incentives given by the other Asian industrialised countries.) No selective incentives are given apart from the special industrial land policy to attract investment in capital and technology-intensive industries. However, company tax rates are low (with a corporate tax rate around 17 per cent). There are no local content requirements. There is no preferential treatment for either local or foreign firms. There are no restrictions on the proportion of foreign equity in an enterprise; enterprises can be completely foreign-owned or joint-ventures; no attempts are made to require foreign investors to make equity available to local investors.

Before going on to discuss the case study of machine-producing firms in Hong Kong, it will be necessary to be more precise about what is meant by ITC in this paper and to comment on the importance of the machine-producing sector.

ITC AND THE MACHINE-PRODUCING SECTOR

As Frances Stewart (1982) points out, 'Any successful industrial expansion is likely to be associated with some local technological activity, because adaption to local conditions is part of the process of successful industrial activity.' The only precondition, then, for less-complex forms of ITC is the production in sufficient quantity of the products associated with such forms of technological change. In order to capture relatively minor changes, some definitions of ITC have been broad in scope and have included activities such as the ability to select from available technologies (for example, Dahlman and Cortez, 1982) and the ability to master imported technology (for example, Westphal, Rhee and Pursell, 1981). These activities are significant and may have an important influence on profitability and the ability to compete, both at home and abroad. However, in the context of this paper, ITC is used in a narrower way to refer to the ability to introduce a degree of novelty in the production of products or processes. The degree of novelty, though, may be slight.

There are a number of reasons for focusing on the machine-producing sector. The main reason is that machine production lies at the heart of the processes involving the generation and diffusion of technological change. Most forms of technological change, as Rosenberg (1976) notes, whether they involve process or product change, require the production of new or modified machinery. With the sale of such machinery, technological change is diffused to other sectors of the economy. Some have argued (for example, Dahlman and Westphal, 1981) that a local machine-producing capability is also necessary for the production of more minor forms of technological change such as the modification and adaptation of products and processes. For these reasons a number of writers, as mentioned above, have argued for the protection and promotion of the machine-producing sector. Accordingly, a study of this sector has a particular relevance for the hypotheses enumerated earlier.

We turn now to the study of machine-producing firms in Hong Kong.

THE HONG KONG CASE STUDY

ITC IN MACHINE-PRODUCING FIRMS IN HONG KONG

Given the importance of the machine-producing sector, and in the light of the hypotheses noted above, it is of interest to ask: In this sector in Hong Kong under near-free-trade with minimal government intervention is there any evidence that firms have been able to produce a degree of novelty in their products or processes and, if so, how important is the capability that they possess? This question will be examined after a brief discussion of machine production in Hong Kong.

MACHINE PRODUCTION IN HONG KONG

Near-free-trade in Hong Kong has produced a narrow manufacturing base in terms of product specialisation. Four sectors contribute about 67 per cent to total manufacturing value-added: textiles and wearing apparel (about half of total manufacturing value-added), electrical machinery, apparatus etc., and plastic products. The machine-producing sector is not of great importance in terms of manufacturing value-added and employment. In 1980 this sector contributed 1.3 per cent to total manufacturing value-added and 1.7 per cent to total manufacturing sector employment. However, this understates the contribution of the sector in terms of the production and diffusion of technological change.

The bulk of the firms in the machine-producing sector are small. In 94 per cent of establishments employing 47 per cent of the sector's workforce, 1–19 persons were employed. In line with other newly industrialised countries, therefore, Hong Kong's machine-producing sector is dominated by small- and medium-sized firms. (See, for example, Cortez, 1978 for Argentina; and Amsden, 1977 for Taiwan.)

THE FIRM SAMPLE

In all, twelve firms were interviewed from a list of twenty-three supplied by the Hong Kong Productivity Centre and the Chinese Manufacturers' Association. The firms included in the list were biased in favour of the larger, technologically more dynamic enterprises. Total firm employment ranged from 6 to 260, although the bulk of firms employed between 25 and 55 people. Only one firm was started before 1949. Of the remaining eleven, four were established in the 1970s, two in the 1960s, four in the 1950s and one in 1949.

INTERNATIONAL COMPETITIVENESS OF SAMPLE FIRMS

One advantage of examining firms in Hong Kong is that it is valid to assume that these firms, operating in a near-free-trade environment with minimal governmental support, are internationally competitive. While other studies have had to look at exports of technology in order to gauge the efficiency and complexity of the local technology produced (see, for example, Lall on India and Dahlman on Brazil), in Hong Kong, all firms, by definition, possess an international competitive advantage. Empirical proof of this comes from the fact of their continued existence under these conditions and from the extent of their exports.

All the firms interviewed were engaged in exporting. The proportion of output exported ranged from 5 per cent to 80 per cent for the two most important products in terms of sales, and there was a positive relationship between size of output and proportion of output exported. With few exceptions the bulk of firms exported their machinery to South East Asian countries: Singapore, Indonesia, Thailand, Philippines and Malaysia. Other export markets included Korea, The People's Republic of China and Macau. In only a few cases were the most important markets in the highly industrialised countries. Export markets, therefore, tended to be in other Asian countries where the average size of firm was probably not very different from that pertaining in Hong Kong.

In most cases the firm's major competitor on both local and foreign markets was from Hong Kong or Japan although the People's Republic of China was important for two firms.

Sources of Sample Firms' International Competitive Advantage

Firm Product	1 a	1 b	2 a	2 b	3 a	3 b	4 a	4 b	5 a	5 b	6 a	6 b	7 a	7 b	8 a	8 b	9 a	9 b	10 a	10 b	11 a	11 b	12 a	12 b
a. Lower transport costs	U	U	U	U	U	U	F	W	F	—	W	W	F	F	NA	NA	U	U	U	U	U	U	F	F
b. Lower un-/semi-skilled wages	U	U	F	F	C	C	U	U	U	—	U	U	U	U	NA	NA	U	U	U	U	U	U	U	U
c. Lower skilled labour costs	U	U	F	F	C	C	F	W	U	—	F	F	W	W	NA	NA	W	W	U	U	U	U	U	U
d. Access to cheaper intermediate inputs	U	U	U	U	W	W	U	U	U	—	U	U	U	U	NA	NA	U	U	U	U	U	U	U	U
e. Access to cheaper new materials	U	U	U	U	W	W	U	U	U	—	U	U	U	U	NA	NA	U	U	U	U	U	U	U	U
f. Access to cheaper new machinery/equipment	U	U	U	U	U	U	U	U	U	—	U	U	U	U	NA	NA	U	U	U	U	U	U	U	U
g. Access to second-hand equipment	W	W	U	F	U	U	W	W	U	—	U	U	U	U	NA	NA	U	U	U	U	U	U	U	U
h. Production of cheaper/lower-quality machinery	C		C	C	C	C	C	C	C	—	C	C	C	C	NA	NA	C	C	C	C	—	C	C	C
i. Organisational/managerial production experience	U	U	U	U	W	W	U	U	U	—	U	U	U	U	NA	NA	U	U	U	U	U	U	U	U
j. Production in small batches of custom-built machinery	F	U	U	U	U	U	U	U	U	—	U	U	U	U	NA	NA	U	U	U	U	U	U	U	U
k. Other	F	W	U	U	U	U	U	W	U	—	U	U	U	W	NA	NA	U	U	W	W	U	U	U	W

Note: U = unimportant   W = very important

SOURCE OF INTERNATIONAL COMPETITIVENESS

Having established that Hong Kong machine-producers are internationally competitive, it remains to examine the source of this competitiveness. More specifically, can international competitiveness be related to the firm's ITC or is it more the result of factors unrelated to learning and technical change? In the case of Hong Kong the latter might include: favourable efficiency wages, excellent infrastructure including financial and transport facilities, proximity to other Asian markets, the importance of the 'ethnic connection' in exporting noted by Wells and others, and the availability of cheap and good-quality inputs as a result of near-free-trade. In order to examine this, firms were asked about the importance of various factors in accounting for their international competitiveness. The information collected is provided in the table opposite.

It is clear from this table that the 'crucial' source of international competitive advantage was seen to lie in the 'production of cheaper/lower-quality machinery'. The twofold nature of this source requires some elaboration. On the one hand there is the price element. Firms were very aware of the price-elastic nature of their markets and stressed that their product had to be price-competitive. It was suggested by the firms that the foreign competing product was anything from 60 per cent to 500 per cent more expensive (although it was not possible to collect independent confirmation of this). Since price was important, some of the other variables listed in the above table which also influence price were significant in determining the firm's international competitive advantage. On the other hand, however, the firm's competitiveness was also attributable to a quality dimension. In clarifying this aspect a few respondents compared the difference between an expensive motor-car and a relatively cheap one. In the case of machinery, the expensive model produced in a highly industrialised country (usually Japan in the case of Hong Kong) would be of better quality, more capital-intensive, perform more functions and produce a higher quality output than the Hong-Kong-produced model, but the latter would none the less adequately serve the needs of users. In view of the average income of using-firms, their desire for a relatively short pay-back period, and the quality of output required by their markets, the machine produced in Hong Kong was judged to be adequate and sometimes more profitable. Accordingly the sample firms were able to find markets both within Hong Kong and abroad.

Included in the quality dimension of the source of the firm's competitive advantage was also an 'appropriateness' aspect. Although, almost without exception, the firm's product was originally copied from a machine from a highly industrialised country, a substantial amount of adaptation and modification took place. Examples of this included: the performance of new functions by the machine, economising on raw materials and energy requirements, an increase in output per unit of time, a change in the source of power (for example, from diesel to electricity, to which most firms in Hong Kong have easy access), a change in the size and shape of the machine,[3] and a change in response to rising real wages in Hong Kong). Such product modifications and adaptations meant that the Hong-Kong-produced machine was at times more suited to the user's industrial environment.

Although the 'production of cheaper/lower-quality machinery' was felt to be the most important factor explaining international competitiveness, a number of the firms felt that other factors were also important. Six of the firms felt that the lower cost of skilled labour compared to the highly industrialised countries was 'fairly' or 'very' important, while five felt that the provision of local servicing and repair facilities was 'very' important. However, the latter does not explain success in export markets where servicing etc., was not provided. Three firms expressed the view that access to secondhand machinery through free-trade was 'fairly' or 'very' important. (These firms also stated that secondhand machinery constituted between 50 per cent and 100 per cent of the total value of their machinery and equipment.)

Accordingly, it may be concluded that it was the ability of the Hong Kong firms to introduce a degree of novelty in their products that was the major explanation for their international competitiveness. This 'degree of novelty' emerged in the production of simpler machinery using lower-cost inputs and at times incorporating adaptations and modifications that increased suitability to the local environment. Furthermore, we have an objective indication of the importance of the 'degree of novelty' introduced, since firms were able to survive, and expand, in a near-free-trade situation on the basis of the product innovations that they produced. It may therefore be concluded that the emergence of an indigenous technological capability which enabled the firms to make the product change referred to in the process of imitating, adapting and modifying, was necessary for the firm's entry into the local and export market and for continued survival.[4]

In the next section of this paper the firms' technological capabilities are examined in more detail.

ITC WITHIN HONG KONG MACHINE-PRODUCING FIRMS

Historical emergence of ITC
In most cases the sample firms had humble beginnings. Typically the owner/entrepreneur learned the art of production while employed as a skilled worker in another establishment. In forming his own enterprise he usually began by repairing and maintaining the machinery of other firms, or producing parts under subcontracting arrangements. These activities led to the production first of simple, usually manual, machinery, and then on to more complex forms of machinery. In most cases the owner/entrepreneur played a major role in product design, although in the case of the two largest firms the design function had become more specialised as the firm attempted to substantially improve the quality of its product and university-trained engineeers were employed. The firm, therefore, emerged organically from simple beginnings, and as experience was accumulated so expansion took place and increasingly complex kinds of machines were produced.

ITC and foreign technology
Direct purchases of foreign technology were limited to embodied purchases in the form of capital equipment. Substantial use was made of second-hand machinery. None of the firms entered into agreements for the purchase of technology, for example in the form of licensing, consultancy services, purchases of turnkey plant and equipment, etc. Nor were there any examples of even partial foreign ownership. However, firms did have indirect access to foreign technology and this was an important benefit provided by near-free-trade. Examples of such indirect access included the purchase of new or secondhand foreign machinery for the purposes of imitation (near-free-trade providing good sources of information), information (including requests for purchase) provided by other users in Hong Kong who had purchased such machinery, and information passed on as a result of maintenance and repair activities carried out by the firm. It would appear that this indirect access to foreign technology constituted an important input into the firm's product innovation, although it was not possible to gauge more precisely the relative significance of this input.

Complexity of ITC
With two exceptions, the technological division of labour in the sample firms was relatively simple, as has been noted in the case of some other newly industrialised countries (see, for example, Cortez, 1978, for

machine-tool producers in Argentina). Generally those involved in product design tended to spend the majority of their time in routine production activities. Skills were acquired through experience in production rather than through formal training. Production processes tended to be relatively simple and there was, for example, only one case where numerically controlled machine-tools and an assembly-line were used. This was in the case of one of the two largest firms, where, as mentioned, there were specialised design departments employing university-trained engineers who worked full-time on the design function. Furthermore, there were no important examples of process changes; technological change was confined to product innovation.

A further indication of the relatively simple nature of the technological capabilities existing in the sample firms is the absence of more complex form of technology export. In general, technology was exported in embodied form in the machinery that was sold. There was only one case of direct foreign investment (in Taiwan) and no examples of the export of turnkey projects, licenses or consultancies.

Having briefly considered the main findings of the Hong Kong case study, we are now in a position to examine the ITC hypotheses mentioned earlier and consider the relevance of the Hong Kong example.

ITC HYPOTHESES AND THE HONG KONG CASE STUDY

In discussing the hypotheses in the light of the Hong Kong study it is necessary to enter a note of caution for two main reasons. The first is that the case study is too narrow to allow the drawing of very firm conclusions. The second is that, while it may be possible to specify to some extent the technological capabilities that have emerged in the machine-producing sector under near-free-trade in Hong Kong, it is not possible to do more than speculate about what might have happened in the event of various forms of government intervention. With this caveat in mind we pass on to consider the hypotheses.

HYPOTHESES 1a AND 2 (COMPETITION, PROTECTION AND ITC)

It would appear from the case study that the near-free-trade situation in Hong Kong required product modification and adaptation as a condition of entry into the market and as a condition of survival. It would in most cases not have been possible to produce a machine that would compete with overseas producers (notably Japan) in terms of both quality and price. Accordingly, Hong Kong resorted to the production of simpler, cheaper machinery for what, in effect, was a different, lower-income, market. The competitive environment could, therefore, be viewed as contributing to this kind of product innovation.

However, it does not follow from this that the more competitive the environment (increased by the existence of near-free-trade) the greater the amount and rate of technological advance. The present study suggests that while the near-free-trade environment provided the benefits of an enhanced ITC, it also imposed costs. The benefits of near-free-trade included the requirement that ingenuity be exercised in modifying and adapting products, and the provision of channels of information-flow that constituted an important input into the product innovation process. But there are also costs, although these are far harder to specify. Some of the costs result from the prevention under near-free-trade of certain kinds of goods and services from being produced, and accordingly the inhibition of the attendant learning processes and technological change. Prevention may occur even where learning processes, with the passage of time, result in internationally competitive products, processes and materials. Under near-free-trade, if these cannot be produced efficiently from the point of view of international best-practice *in the short run,* then they may not be produced at all. This poses an important problem, since it is not at all obvious that longer-run costs will outweigh longer-run benefits where this is the case in the short run.

A concrete case of this, of course, arises with infant industries which, by definition, are internationally inefficient in the short run. Yet, as a result of learning and technological change, such industries may become efficient with the passage of time – although this is not always the case (cf. Bell *et al.*, 1980). Westphal (1981) suggests that it may not be exceptional for successful infant industries to register decreases in unit domestic resource cost of production (the indicator of increases in productivity) of around 10 per cent per annum during the first five to ten years of production, as a result of technological changes brought about by applying a newly-acquired technological mastery. He provides evidence from Korea to suggest that some of the infant industries which were accorded relatively high levels of effective protection ultimately, as a result of technological mastery, became internationally competitive. Yet such industries may be precluded under a near-free-trade regime which, like Hong Kong, does not extend protection to infant industries. Accordingly, the opportunity to reap the learning benefits that accrue from such industries may be forgone.[5]

Under near-free-trade, then, it is possible that some learning benefits will be inhibited. This is likely to be so in intra-firm and in inter-firm learning. The latter relates to Hypothesis 5.

HYPOTHESIS 5 (INTER-FIRM LEARNING)

A number of studies have suggested that inter-firm learning plays an important role in the acquisition of ITC. Westphal, Rhee and Pursell (1981), for example, point to the virtually costless flow of information to Korean exporters from sellers and users in export markets. Such flows, it is suggested, are a major source of technological change. Others, such as Lall (1981) and Dahlman and Cortez (1982), have pointed to the information flows between users and producer in the local market where there is greater degree of geographical proximity. Similarly, Cortez (1978) suggests, in a study of machine-tool production in Argentina, that information and assistance provided by the suppliers of components constituted a major source of technological change. Here too there was a geographical proximity. Inter-firm learning such as this may either be purchased or be the result of less-formal feed-back and feed-forward flows. Some form of inter-firm learning will, of course, be realised under near-free-trade. But others, particularly where close geographical proximity is necessary and where one or more of the interacting firms is internationally inefficient in the short run, will not.[6] In the Hong Kong case, the 'narrowness' of the manufacturing sector in terms of product specialisation and the high incidence of imported components and other inputs may have served to limit the potential gains from inter-firm learning. (This, of course, is not a very firm argument against near-free-trade since it is not possible to be sure about the benefits that would follow from inter-firm learning under a different trade regime.)

None the less, it seems reasonable to conclude that the high degree of competition provided by near-free-trade may prevent the realisation of various beneficial forms of inter-firm learning even where in the longer run these outweigh the corresponding costs.

HYPOTHESIS 1b (COMPETITION AND PROCESS TECHNOLOGICAL CHANGE)

The present case study does not provide support for this hypothesis. In the Hong Kong machine-producing sector, for the reasons outlined above, the dominant form of technological change was product rather

Stoplrecommon sense.

than process innovation. However, it may be that a different picture would emerge from a study, under competitive conditions, of larger firms with a more sophisticated technological capability.

HYPOTHESIS 3 (GOVERNMENT PROMOTION AND ITC)

The present study suggests that it is possible for somewhat more complex forms of ITC to emerge without any direct government assistance (that is, assistance given specifically to the sector or firm concerned). Certainly all the Hong Kong sample firms had developed their ITC without such assistance. However, the study also provides some evidence to suppose that there might, in some cases, be limits to the advance possible under these circumstances. In the case of the two largest firms which were attempting to move upmarket in terms of product quality, it was apparent that the most important operative constraint related to the firm's technological capabilities. While the one firm solved its problems by buying-in university-trained design engineers (including one from Japan and the other from the UK), the other relied on the technological input provided by the Polytechnic. However, both firms felt that technological assistance from government (or, presumably, the financial resources and incentives to purchase such assistance) would provide a significant boost. On the other hand, in the case of the smaller firms, who were not moving as far upmarket in terms of product quality, the technological constraint was less pressing and it was generally felt that the required technological capabilities existed for the firms to produce the kinds of products they wished. Other issues, particularly the shortage of factory space, were considered to be far more urgent.

Although the sample is too small to reach a firmer conclusion, it may be, therefore, that direct government intervention is required to facilitate the qualitative jump in ITC that is required for a firm to make substantial improvements in product quality. Significantly, despite the long standing taboo, the Hong Kong government has recently agreed, following the 1979 *Report of the Committee on Diversification,* to provide technical assistance and support facilities particularly in the metal processing and working industries. This report, which marked an important – though still rather limited – departure from previous practice, also acknowledged the relevance for Hong Kong's circumstances of the greater degree of government intervention in countries like Singapore, Taiwan and Korea. Certainly in these countries there is a far greater degree of government assistance given to the machine-pro-ducing sector. (See, for example, the substantial incentives provided to firms in Singapore in the machinery sector, which is regarded as a priority industry – Business International, 1979.)

HYPOTHESIS 4 (LOCAL CAPITAL-GOODS SECTOR AND ITC)

The existence of a local capital-goods sector in Hong Kong has cer-tainly provided substantial benefits. Perhaps the most important has been the capital-saving forms of product innovation that this sector has produced. These have resulted from the production, through imita-tion, of cheaper machinery coupled, in some cases, with modifications which have enabled further capital-saving. Examples of the latter in-clude space-saving changes and the use of cheaper energy inputs. The sector has also contributed to foreign-exchange earnings and has assisted in the process of skill-formation, as skills, built up through the experience provided in the production of machinery, have accumu-lated over time and become available to all sectors of the economy.

These are important benefits, but it is necessary to put them into perspective. Here it should be recalled that the machine-producing sector only contributes about 1.3 per cent to total manufacturing value-added, and, furthermore, that the technological capabilities of the sector are still rather limited. Evidence for the latter is provided by the relatively unsophisticated nature of technology exports – the ab-sence of exports of licenses, turnkey plant and equipment, consultancy services, etc. Lall (1980) has argued that a sizable local capital-goods sector is needed for the production of more sophisticated forms of technological change and export. Clearly Hong Kong machine-producers are a long way from achieving this. Nevertheless, it is pos-sible that a greater degree of government promotion would enable the machine-producing sector to substantially increase the contribution that it already makes. Obviously the kind of promotion that is given would be crucial, but the evidence provided by the present study would seem to suggest that the question of promotion merits further investigation in the case of Hong Kong.

NOTES

1. Further details of this study are to be found in Fransman (1982).

2. The quotations come from Business International (1979), a major reference for information on the relative advantages of various locations for investment in Asia.
3. One example was the redesign of a machine so that it was built vertically instead of horizontally, thus saving on factory-space, a critical constraint in Hong Kong. This is an example of capital-saving innovation, given the extremely high cost of factory-space.
4. Lest it be thought that imitation is an activity reserved for Third World countries, Pavitt (1982) referring to British and Canadian studies suggests that a quarter of major innovations recorded were 'imitations based on technology acquired from firms in other countries'. 'The Canadian study also showed that another quarter of the innovations were copies, in the sense that they were developed and commercialised in response to innovations already developed and commercialised elsewhere.' (p. 16)
5. We here refer to those cases where in the 'short run' there is enough uncertainty to deter entrepreneurs and financial institutions from providing risk capital.
6. See note 5.

REFERENCES

Amsden, A. (1977) 'The Division of Labour is Limited by the Type of Market: The case of the Taiwanese Machine Tool Industry', *World Development*, vol. 5, no. 3, pp. 217–34.
Bell, M., Scott-Kemis, D. and Satyarakwit, (1980) 'Limited Learning in Infant Industry: A Case Study'. Science Policy Research Unit, University of Sussex (mimeo).
Business International Asia/Pacific Ltd (1979) *World Sourcing Sites in Asia: Manufacturing Costs and Conditions in Hong Kong, Korea, Singapore and Taiwan*. Hong Kong.
Corden, W. M. (1980) 'Trade Policies', in J. Cody, H. Hughes, and D. Wall, (eds) (1980) *Policies for Industrial Progress in Developing Countries*. London: Oxford University Press.
Cortez, M. (1978) 'Argentina: Technical Development and Technology Exports to other LDC's'. Economics of Industry Division, World Bank.
Dahlman, C. J. and Cortez, M. (1982) 'Technology Exports from Mexico as a Starting Point in the Study of Technological Capability'. World Bank.
Dahlman, C. J. and Westphal, L. E. (1981) 'Technological Effort in Industrial Development – An Interpretive Survey of Recent Research'. World Bank.
Datta Mitra, J. (1979) 'The Capital Goods Sector in LDC's: A Case for State Intervention?', World Bank Staff Working Paper, No. 343, Washington DC: World Bank.
Fransman, M. (1982) 'Learning and the Capital Goods Sector Under Free Trade: The Case of Hong Kong', *World Development*, vol. 10, no. 11. (An earlier version of this paper appeared as EADI Working Paper No. 1, Tilburg, October 1982.)
Katz, J. (1978) *Technological Change, Economic Development and Intra and Extra Regional Relations in Latin America*, IDB/ECLA Research Programme in Science and Technology, Working Paper No. 30, Buenos Aires.

Lall, S. (1981) 'Indian Technology Exports and Technological Development', *The Annals of the American Academy of Political and Social Science,* vol 458.

Lall, S. (1980) 'Developing Countries as Exporters of Industrial Technology', *Research Policy,* 9, pp. 24–52.

Little, I. M. D. (1979) 'The Experience and Causes of Rapid Labour-Intensive Development in Korea, Taiwan, Hong Kong, and Singapore; And the Possibilities of Emulation', Working Paper No. 1, ILO Asian.

Pavitt, K. (1982) 'Some Characteristics of Innovative Activities in British Industry'. (mimeo).

Ranis, G. *et al.,* (1981) 'Summary of Scientific Progress – PRA–80–18867', mimeo, Economic Growth Centre, Yale University.

Rosenberg, N. (1976) *Perspectives on Technology.* London: Cambridge University Press.

Stewart, F. (1977) *Technology and Underdevelopment.* London: Macmillan.

Stewart, F. (1982) 'Facilitating Indigenous Technical Change in Third World Countries', (in this volume).

Westphal, L. E. (1981) 'Empirical Justification for Infant Industry Protection, World Bank Staff Working Paper 445. Washington DC: World Bank.

Westphal, L. E., Rhee, Y. W. and Pursell, G. (1981) 'Korean Industrial Competence: Where it Came From', World Bank Staff Working Paper 469, Washington DC: World Bank.

Foreign Technology and Indigenous Technological Capability in Brazil[1]

Carl J. Dahlman

Developing countries almost by definition have a vast pool of foreign technology on which to draw. However, that a country relies heavily on foreign technology does not necessarily mean that it does not develop indigenous technological capability (ITC). This paper focuses on the experience of Brazil, a country that has drawn extensively on foreign technology for its economic development, to illustrate some of the possible positive relationships between the importation of technology and the development of ITC. The first section provides a short background on the importation of technology and on government science and technology policy in Brazil. The second section presents case studies that illustrate how three different industries were developed in Brazil using different combinations of foreign technology and local effort. Finally, the last section presents some implications for the creation of ITC, investment analysis, and industrial and trade policy.

FOREIGN TECHNOLOGY AND GOVERNMENT SCIENCE AND TECHNOLOGICAL POLICY IN BRAZIL

Compared to other large and relatively industrially advanced LDCs such as India, Mexico, and Korea, Brazil appears to have relied more heavily on the use of foreign technology to achieve its economic development. Among these four countries Brazil has had the largest absolute inflows of foreign technology in the form of direct foreign investments (DFI), disembodied technology (patents, licences, and technical services), and capital goods. The higher absolute values for Brazil are in part due to the larger GNP of the country. When these values are scaled by an appropriate measure of the economic size of the country it is evident that DFI and, to a lesser extent, payments for licences and technical service have played a larger role in Brazil, particularly in

317

comparison to the two Asian countries. Brazilian policy toward foreign investment has been, in fact, one of the most open among developed countries. Brazil has relied on foreign investment both as a source of technology and as a source of capital to carry out large investment programmes as part of its national investment plans.[2]

But while Brazil has been heavily dependent on foreign technology it has also tried to develop local science and technology, although perhaps not as much, nor for as long as India. Among Latin American countries though, Brazil has given the most explicit attention to the role of technology in economic development and to the stimulation of technological development through government policy. Before 1968 most of the efforts in this area focused on institution building and human resource development. Beginning in 1968, scientific and technological development became a specific policy objective. The 1968–9 development plan defined an explicit policy for science and technology for the first time at the federal level. It proposed the creation of a National System of Scientific and Technological Development (SNDCT), of Basic Science and Technology Plans that would spell out the actions foreseen in the National Development Plans, and of a National Fund for Scientific and Technological Development (FNDCT) to finance the SNDCT.[3]

Brazilian technology policy has addressed the supply and the demand of local technology as well as the purchase of foreign technology. The main thrust on the supply side has been on the development of the country's physical and human R&D infrastructure. The supply effort has also included attempts to stimulate the development of technological capability in local firms, particularly by subsidised financing granted through FUNTEC and FINEP. The purchase of foreign technology has been controlled through the regulation of technology contracts by Institute of Industrial Property (INPI). On the demand side, the state has played an important role directly as a user of technology in autonomous state enterprises, and indirectly through a buy-local policy. The buy-local policy has been used vigorously to promote the development of the local capital-goods industry. The main instrument used to implement the buy-local policy has been subsidised financing for the purchase of domestic capital goods and a structure of protection which has been slanted in favour of capital goods.[4]

Unfortunately there is not enough information to evaluate directly the impact of these policies on Brazilian industrial development. It is clear that there has been an important build-up in the basic R&D infrastructure, but there is no current information on the relationship between R&D institutes and the industrial sector. While there is some information on the R&D activity undertaken or financed by the state, there is very little information on R&D activity by the private sector. Also lacking is any detailed analysis of the success of programmes such as those financed by FUNTEC and FINEP or of INPI's efforts to regulate imports of technology. Furthermore, while there has been a tremendous build-up of the local capital-goods industry, it is not yet clear to what extent such a build-up has been accompanied by local technological mastery in equipment design.

In this paper we shall look at the development in three industrial sectors. They are the automobile industry, the aircraft industry, and the steel industry. The *automobile industry* can be taken as an example of development based on the local activities of multinational firms. The *aircraft industry* can be taken as an example of development based on local R&D efforts, although it must be recognised that some of the elements were acquired through foreign licensing. In the *steel industry,* the focus will be on a specific joint venture because of the insights that can be learned about the successful combination of foreign and local efforts from the study of that particular case.

CASE STUDIES

THE AUTOMOBILE SECTOR

To a large extent the rapid development of the Brazilian auto industry over the past twenty-five years is a success story of infant-industry development. Through its backward linkages it played a key role in the development of Brazilian industry. In addition, it is the largest exporter of manufactured products in Brazil.

Brazilian automobile production started in the mid-1950s. Until then, Brazil had relied upon imports of completely-knocked-down kits (CKD). In the 1950s the government determined to establish a local vehicle industry as a key to Brazil's industrial development. Special incentives and conditions were provided to attract international automobile firms to set up production in Brazil, including: (i) duty-free import of capital goods and essential components; (ii) phased 'nationalisation' requirements to reach a local content of 95 per cent by 1960; (iii) prohibition of imported vehicles; and (iv) fiscal, financial and foreign exchange advantages to the firms who participated in the programme. The programme was implemented very quickly. By 1960, eleven firms were producing vehicles;[5] and, by 1962, the nationalisation content had reached virtually 100 per cent.

The growth of the industry can be divided into three cycles. The first cycle corresponds to the initial development of the industry, with rapid growth (1957–62) due to unsatisfied demand from strong import controls, followed by a period of relatively slow growth (1963–7). The second cycle of expansion of automobile production corresponds to the 'miracle growth' years of Brazilian industrialisation. Total vehicle production quadrupled from 225,000 in 1967 to 905,000 in 1974.[6] The third cycle corresponds to the period since 1974. During this period the expansion of the automobile production has been slow because of higher gasoline prices, gasoline rationing, a slower rate of economic growth, and a gradual contraction in credit for car purchases.

One of the most significant characteristics of the automobile industry in the past decade is the rapid increase in the percentage of production exported, which rose from 2.7 per cent in 1972 to 13.8 per cent in 1980.[7] While total vehicle production in 1980 was nearly twice that in 1972, exports grew nearly twelve times. An important question is to what extent the increasing amount and diversification of exports reveal increasing technological development and greater production efficiency, and to what extent they are the result of special subsidies.

The dramatic increase in exports can be partly attributed to an export incentive programme called BEFIEX,[8] and to a special subsidy equal to 26 per cent of the f.o.b. value of the export, called a *credito premio*. Strong incentives and subsidies offered for the exports of vehicles, however, does not necessarily mean that there has not been significant technological development and increasing efficiency in the industry. Although it was not possible to obtain direct cost data for the firms, there is strong indirect evidence that the Brazilian auto industry became increasingly efficient as it expanded. First, a study of direct price comparisons carried out during 1980–1 indicated that the prices of Brazilian vehicles are lower than those of similar foreign vehicles. (Tyler, 1981) The average implicit tariffs which result from the price comparisons indicate that internal automobile prices are, on average, 23.2 per cent lower than comparable international prices. The internal price of trucks and buses is even lower, with an average implicit tariff of −46.2 per cent. The magnitude of these price differences is surprising and contrasts with the findings of studies done in the late 1960s which showed that the price of Brazilian vehicles was significantly higher than US prices. (Baranson, 1969) The lower internal prices may be explained in part by the fact that the internal market prices were somewhat depressed during the period of comparison. In addition, local vehicles may not be strictly comparable to similar foreign vehicles, particularly in terms of quality and special features such as pollution control and safety mechanisms.[9] Thus, the real, quality-adjusted price differences may not be as large as suggested. The average prices for main components such as motors and vehicle parts, and tyres, are also lower than comparable international prices. To some extent, the lower vehicle prices may be traced to prices for iron and steel inputs, which are also lower than the international prices.[10]

Second, over time there has been a relative fall in the cost of Brazilian cars. An index of car prices deflated by the general consumer price index for the period 1961–78, shows that the relative price of a Brazilian car has been halved in that period.[11] In the earlier period, the fall in the average relative price closely parallels the movement in VW's price for small cars, because of VW's dominant share in the market. In the more recent period, when there is a larger diversity of models, there is more variation. However, two points stand out. First, all trends tend to show a flattening out after 1974 when the industry had a slower growth rate, which suggests that there may be a link with economies of scale. Second, the series for various types of automobiles manufactured by the three main producers show a strong downward movement. This probably reflects not only individual scale economies and learning-curve effects for each model as production increases, but also increasing technological development and cost efficiency among the local suppliers of machinery, parts and components for the industry in general.

To be able to increase the level of nationalisation of parts as required by law, VW and other automobile producers had to develop their local suppliers, including provision of finance, training, and technical assistance. In 1957, VW had 150 suppliers, increasing to 1,300 in 1965, 3,000 in 1970 and 4,330 in 1974 (only 900 of which were foreign). Many of the suppliers produce not only vehicle parts, but also machines, machine tools, castings, forgings, etc., which are used in other industries. The auto industry has thus helped to stimulate Brazilian technological development in industry through the backward linkages to such suppliers of parts and components and probably even further back to basic industries such as steel, glass, rubber, and plastics.

While the Brazilian automobile industry is an interesting example of the development of a sector based on foreign companies, a number of issues need to be examined to assess this strategy. The Brazilian automobile industry appears to be able to produce vehicles locally at prices equal to or less than international prices. However, it is not clear whether this has more than compensated for the high cost of local vehicles imposed during the initial period of import substitution. It is likely that forcing producers to achieve more than 95 per cent local content in only three to four years imposed unnecessarily high costs as compared to a more gradual increase in the nationalisation requirement. Also, it appears that the costs of achieving the last 10 per cent of nationalisation were very high because of the forced production of some components at very inefficient scales.

On the positive side, however, the development of the automobile industry has had great externalities in terms of stimulating the development of the parts, components, and input-supplying industries including machinery. These externalities are very difficult to quantify. They have involved not only the technical assistance and technology directly transferred to some of the suppliers, but also labour training and greater emphasis on quality control. The latter is likely to have led to greater cost consciousness and production control, which may have spilled over in some of these firms to other areas of production and led to an improvement in their overall efficiency.

A final issue that should be mentioned is that of control. As is pointed out by some, relying on foreign firms may be a quick way to set up local production, but foreign control means that national sovereignty may be limited. In addition, it is not always clear how much of the benefits of the ITC that is created accrue to the host country as opposed to the foreign companies. It should be noted, however, that the foreign automobile firms have shown some degree of technological adaptation to local needs, such as in complying with the government regulations to produce 100 per cent alcohol-powered vehicles. More generally it should be kept in mind that in some industries such as automobiles, the choice open to a country may often be between no industry and a foreign-controlled industry. In such cases, the decision should focus on what the country can expect to gain from the foreign industry, including externalities and spill-overs, and how they can be maximised.

THE AIRCRAFT INDUSTRY

Although the production of airplanes in Brazil dates back to 1910, when the first monoplane was built, the development of the airplane industry is essentially the development of Embraer. The creation of Embraer in 1969 was the culmination of a process of creating ITC in the aerospace sector which started almost thirty years earlier. The first step was the creation of a Ministry of Aeronautics in 1940, which was to become a great incentivator for research on aviation. The second step was the creation of the Instituto Tecnico de Aeronautica (ITA) in 1946 for training aerospace engineers. By 1980, ITA had trained more than 2,100 engineers at the college level and more than 300 at the graduate level. The third step was the creation of the Centro Tecnico Aero-Espacial (CTA) in 1954, an aerospace research centre mainly staffed with the engineers trained by ITA.[12] The final step was the transfer of the team that had designed the Bandeirante, from CTA (the research institution) to industry by creating a mixed state–private enterprise – Embraer – for the industrial production of the Bandeirante.

This process required large financial resources and was only possible through public-sector intervention. Because the private sector was sceptical about the feasibility of the enterprise and reluctant to make the large investments necessary, the government established that 1 per cent of the corporate income tax owned by companies in Brazil could be applied for the purchase of stock in Embraer.[13] In 1980 Embraer produced eleven different airplane models, and as of 1 January 1980 had an accumulated production of 2,071 military and commercial aircraft.[14]

Embraer's commercial aircraft category is centred around the Bandeirante and the Xingu, twin-engine turbo-props of local design, which were originally made for the Brazilian Air Force (FAB). In addition, Embraer produces two other commercial airplanes. One is the Ipanema, a Brazilian design which was made for agricultural uses. It can carry up to 680 litres of chemicals and is used for seeding, fertilising, and spraying. It accounts for 19 per cent of Embraer's cumulative production. The second type consists of four- to ten-seaters for general aviation, which Embraer produces as a result of a co-operation agreement with Piper. This type of plane accounts for 57 per cent of Embraer's output.[15]

The Bandeirante is basically an intermediate product developed for third-world conditions, which also found a market in developed countries due to the rise of fuel prices. The Bandeirante (which means 'pioneer' in Portuguese) was developed at the Institute of Research and Development of CTA at the request of FAB. In the early 1960s, FAB was worried that the old stock of DC3s, which formed the backbone of air travel to hundreds of small airports in the interior of the country, were wearing out, and that there was no product that could replace them. In the advanced segment of the market, the technological frontier was moving increasingly toward larger jets, which could not operate on the short and often unpaved runways characteristic of airports in the interior of Brazil; whereas in the small general aviation segment, the planes were too small. As a result, FAB commissioned CTA to design a plane smaller and faster than a DC3, but larger than the small four-seaters then available in the general aviation class. Since the idea was to produce the plane locally, it was also decided that the new plane should be a turbo-prop rather than a jet, because the latter was too ambitious a goal.

The original Bandeirante designed at CTA had its first successful flight in 1968. In 1972 two commercial Brazilian airlines, after studying the various models available internationally, ordered Bandeirantes for use on local routes, which had become uneconomical to operate because of lack of proper equipment. The success of this commercial model, which started operating in 1973 within Brazil, greatly encouraged Embraer.[16] It created a special group to try to launch the Bandeirante in the international market. By the end of 1979, 123 planes had been sold, including 66 to developed countries.

The success of the Bandeirante in the developed-country markets such as the USA is that as a small turbo-prop it found a perfect niche in short commuter runs where it is much cheaper to operate than jets. The success of the Bandeirante in the developing-country markets is that it is a very rugged aircraft that can take off and land in short and even unpaved fields and requires very low maintenance – the conditions it was originally designed for in view of Brazilian needs. Recently the competition has been getting much stiffer, particularly in the developed-country commuter market. Encouraged by Embraer's success with a thrifty turbo-prop, various large manufacturers are working on their own turbo–prop models. Embraer itself has designed a new 30–35-passenger model called the Brasilia which is aimed at that market. A mock-up of the Brasilia was presented in 1980, and, by July 1981, there were already 111 orders for this new model, even though the first was not expected to fly until 1983.[17]

A high percentage of the value of the airplanes produced by Embraer is of Brazilian origin. In part this results from the high labour share in the value of an airplane, which varies betwen 30 and 50 per cent of its total cost. In 1978 the nationalisation index for some of the planes produced by Embraer ranged from 75 per cent to 80 per cent for the Brazilian-designed airplanes such as the Ipanema and

Bandeirante, to 40 per cent to 45 per cent for planes in the Embraer/ Piper agreement. It is probably higher now for most models, as the local network of suppliers has been built up as part of the policy of increasing the participation of local firms in the manufacture of airplanes. Embraer has a Division of Nationalisation within its technical department, whose objective is to increase Brazilian participation. This has been very important in transferring technology to other local firms. In 1980 Embraer had more than 300 suppliers. Thus Embraer has played an important role in developing the local airplane-parts industry, which is now an important exporter in its own right. Moreover, the reputation that Brazil has achieved in foreign markets as a producer of airplanes is helping to open new doors for the export of the Brazilian airplane-parts industry.

The case of Embraer is an example of a successful local research response to specific and clearly articulated needs. It was possible only because there had been a long-term and carefully phased technological development effort. It should be noted, however, that this effort was not motivated so much by market forces, but by the desire to have local control over what was considered a strategic area. The identification and articulation of the product was also special, as it could only be made by a monopolist who could guarantee the market. That some of the airplanes originally designed for the internal military market appear to have become commercial successes seems to have been rather fortuituous. However, they have served to stimulate the newly created technological capability to seek a commercial outlet, and there appear to have been significant spill-overs into Brazilian industry both from CTA and from Embraer. It is not clear, however, whether the production of airplanes and the economic benefits of the externalities more than cover the economic costs involved, or that the creation of ITC in the aerospace sector was the best use of scarce human and material resources given the magnitude of other local development needs. Furthermore, it is not clear whether Embraer will be able to compete successfully in the commercial market with its new models. Nevertheless, the example is very important in showing that there can be successful research responses to local needs, if there is a sufficient local technological base, and the needs can be clearly articulated.

A FIRM-LEVEL CASE STUDY OF AN INTEGRATED STEEL PLANT

The final example is a firm-level case study of Usiminas, one of the three large state-owned integrated steel mills in Brazil. It is an illustration of a successful joint venture where the success was due in large part to the degree of technological effort put in by the local partner.[18]

Usiminas initially obtained the technology necessary for production by associating with the Japanese through a joint venture. The Japanese owned 40 per cent of the capital stock. The rest was owned by the state and the federal government. Founded in 1956, the firm started production in 1962 under the operational and administrative control of the Japanese. The plant reached the planned nominal capacity of 500,000 tons per annum (tpa) in 1966. Operational responsibility then passed to the Brazilians who had increased their share to about 80 per cent and had acquired the technical capability to run the plant themselves, thanks to training received from the Japanese.

The changeover of operational responsibility occurred in the midst of a contraction in the Brazilian steel market which was due to the simultaneous entry into production of Usiminas and of another equally large state-owned steel firm, almost precisely at the time that the economy entered into a recession. The only way Usiminas could break even was to expand output to at least a million tons per year. However, because of the market crisis and because of its poor financial shape, Usiminas was not able to obtain financing for the expansion. This forced the firm to stretch the capacity of its original equipment in order to get a better capital–output ratio.

Over the 1966–72 period, Usiminas was able to increase capacity approximately 140 per cent to nearly 1,200,000 tpa with basically the original equipment and very little additional investment.[19] Such capacity-stretching was the result of a systematic programme of local technological effort on the part of the firm, which involved the implementation of a standard cost system and an elaborate organisational infrastructure to study the firm's existing equipment, compare it with the best world performance of similar equipment, and then try to reach the same or higher levels of outputs. This required the expansion and specialisation of the technological support structure, which included the creation of departments of industrial engineering, metallurgy and plant inspection, and the development of an information organ which could search for and collect technological information external to the firm. Usiminas carefully studied the advantages and disadvantages of its own equipment, not just from what the manufacturers had suggested, but from its own experience and learning as well. The plant's personnel began to modify and adapt the equipment, to increase their control over the production process, and to streamline its operation in order to obtain the maximum performance from the original plant.[20] As this stage developed, a greater emphasis on technical support was necessary and led to the creation of a research centre in 1970.[21]

In the early 1970s when the market was once again booming, and the government was sponsoring, and in fact subsidising, large expansions, Usiminas responded by proposing a large capital-intensive expansion which would increase its capacity threefold in less than a decade. Also, in response to such massive expansion needs and the lack of sufficient national engineering capacity to meet those needs, Usiminas re-organised its internal structure to develop its basic engineering.[22] It first passed through an intermediate expansion plan, when its personnel worked very closely with foreign technical assistance to learn all the intricacies of designing an expansion plan, selecting the technology to be used, specifying the equipment, calling for bids, choosing the winner, negotiating the details of the specifications and controlling all the work of installation and start-up.

By 1975, Usiminas was in a position to do all the engineering work for its third expansion plan by itself. Rather than buying equipment and engineering mostly from the Japanese, as had been the case for the original plant and for the most of its first expansion, Usiminas could scan the technological frontier and draw up its own specifications for what it wanted to purchase. Equipment purchases now came from many different countries including Brazil, whose relative share has increased from less than 10 per cent to over 40 per cent. The latter was possible in part because Usiminas was able to provide engineering assistance to domestic capital-goods producers.[23] Technical assistance was also extended to other steel firms. For example, Usiminas provided basically the same type of technical assistance to a new 2,000,000 tpa Brazilian plant called Acominas as the Japanese had originally provided to it when the firm was first getting started.

Usiminas's success appears to be related to the emphasis it has given to the training of its personnel,[24] to the long period that it was under one management (which thus had a chance to implement a long-range technical capacitation programme),[25] and to the use of technical assistance contracts as learning experience.[26] The firm frequently contracted outside foreign technical assistance to help solve specific operational problems or to undertake particular studies. This purchase of technology did not involve the purchase of a patent or a licence, or the simple transfer of a set of blueprints, but an active exchange between personnel with regard to some specific problem or task. A large part of the technical change that took place at Usiminas was largely a dynamic process that involved the interaction of groups of people with respect to specific problems or situations. It is also worth noting that such interaction is also a large component of what is involved in embodying technology into new equipment purchased as part of a large expansion plan, in an industry such as steel where equipment has to be made-to-order rather than serially produced.

Overall the Usiminas experience suggests that successful local technological development depends on a relative long-term strategy of building systematically on experience as it is acquired. One of the elements that stands out from this case study is the tremendous amount of learning that took place. Such learning included much more than cost reduction with existing equipment. Allied to the further development of the firm's basic engineering capacity, the learning also extended to the selection, specification, and costs of new vintages of equipment, which can affect the cost structures possible through expansion plans. It included such externalities as the engineering assistance which the firm gives national equipment manufacturers through its expansions, and the training it provided for Brazilian workers in the firm. It also included the flexibility to adapt to changing conditions which might have otherwise led to increasing costs or even to production stops. Also, and even more difficult to measure, it was the basis of a change of attitude towards more self-confidence and self-reliance, which are essential for new indigenous technological developments.

The evolution of Usiminas shows a technological strategy that, rather than seeking to resist foreign technology, as was currently advocated by some, sought to pull itself up by it. Usiminas started by being completely dependent on foreign technology and using that as a base from which to selectively absorb more advanced technology, through which it progressively developed its potential. From a technologically dependent firm it has evolved to the point where it is developing technology of its own and selling technical assistance both nationally and internationally.[27] It is important to notice, however, that this was achieved as part of a long-term strategy, which involved development of the human element and a complex organisational structure to provide the technical support for such progress. While it may be the exception rather than the rule, it is an example of what is possible when the domestic partner pursues an aggressive technological strategy.

IMPLICATIONS FOR THE CREATION OF ITC, INVESTMENT ANALYSIS, AND INDUSTRIAL AND TRADE POLICY

The relationships between the importation of foreign technology and the development of ITC are many and complex. An important element in understanding the relationships between the two, however, is that there is a major distinction between acquiring technology and acquiring technological capability. It is possible, for example, to acquire foreign technology through direct foreign investment, licences, know-how and technical service agreements, and imports of capital goods. ITC, however, is acquired only through human capital formation, which involves formal education, on-the-job training, experience, and specific efforts to obtain, assimilate, adapt, improve, or create technology. It should also be noted that the actual use of a given technology is quite specific to local circumstances and that its successful operation in a particular context requires experience. In addition, since local circumstances (inputs, prices, markets, competition, government regulations, etc.) constantly change over time, and since there are competing technological developments and advances even within the original technology, ITC is needed to modify, to adapt, and to improve the original technology. ITC is also necessary to be able to screen and monitor foreign technological advances and to incorporate some of them for use in the local setting. Furthermore, since the technology required to meet particular local product or process needs may not exist even abroad, it is necessary to have some ITC to at least formulate what those needs are and to seek the appropriate solutions locally or abroad.

The above has important implications for investment analysis and for industrial and trade policies. First, it implies that in an investment project explicit provision should be made for the acquisition of ITC, particularly if local conditions are quite different, or if there are likely to be many changes in the local environment over time. A successful transfer of technology involves much more than the exact replication of the original technology. It also involves technological effort on the part of the recipient to learn to operate, and to assimilate, the transferred technology, and to be able to adapt it to changing circumstances.

Second, to the extent that different technology-suppliers may have different predispositions to provide elements necessary for the creation of ITC, it is important to examine these explicitly and to seek to evaluate trade-offs between cost of importing foreign technology from different sources and through different means, the contribution of each to ITC, and the expected benefits of the ITC that may be created. It should be noted, for example, that in some cases foreign technology may not be obtained except through direct foreign investment. In those cases the analysis of the desirability of that route should also focus on the extent to which technological externalities and spill-overs can be obtained, such as through the training of nationals and the transfer of technological information to local suppliers and buyers. Getting the maximum benefits from various forms of foreign participation implies the need for co-ordinating policies on foreign investment, on the importation of foreign technology, and on local technological development.

Third, since there are varying degrees of difficulty in building up ITC in different industrial sectors because of the nature and rate of change of the underlying technology, and because of the size of the physical and human capital investments required, careful thought should be given to which sectors should be promoted through various types of local and foreign participation. In addition, because technological capabilities in some areas may be prerequisite for successful developments in others, attention must also be given to the proper sequencing of the different activities.

Finally, it should be noted that industrial, trade, and technological policy interact in many ways, and that often hard decisions have to be made about some of the possible trade-offs. Some of these decisions, such as whether and how long to protect an infant industry in the expectation that it will develop local technological capability sufficiently to reach world levels of efficiency, are complicated by the dynamic nature of the problem and the inherent difficulty of measuring the benefits of possible externalities. Nevertheless, decisions such as those constantly have to be taken, and more has to be learned about the process of technical change and local technological development so as to provide better policy guidance than has been possible in the past.

NOTES

1. This is a shortened and revised version of a paper presented at the University of Edinburgh Workshop on Facilitating Indigenous Technological Capability, Edinburgh, Scotland, 25–27 May 1982. I gratefully acknowledge comments and suggestions on various parts of this paper made by Manuel Penalver, Larry E. Westphal, and Martin Fransman. (The author

is a member of the Development Research Department of the World Bank. The views and interpretations expressed here are the author's and should not be attributed to the World Bank, to its affiliated organisations, or to any individual acting on behalf of these organisations.)

2. For cross-country comparisons, including tables on the degree of reliance of these four countries on foreign technology, as well as of their technical and educational capital stocks, see the paper presented at the Edinburgh conference, 1982.

3. Since the creation of the SNDCT, three Basic Plans have been issued, covering the periods 1973–6, 1975–9, and 1980–5. The first plan promoted an increase in the volume of resources for science and technology by strengthening the FNDCT and other financial mechanisms. The 1975–9 plan aimed at broadening the supply of science and technology, and reinforcing the technological capabilities of national firms. The current plan differs from the previous two, in that rather than presenting government actions in the form of programmes, projects, and priority activities, it established a set of policy directions that are supposed to orient the actions of the public and private sector. Furthermore, it does not present any figures on planned expenditures.

4. For a fuller discussion of Brazilian science and technology policy, including policies to build up the capital-goods sectors, see the conference paper.

5. Simca, FNM/Fiat, Willys, Vemag, VW, Toyota (jeeps), Scania, Mercedes Benz, International Harvester, Ford, and GM (the last five only produced trucks). These included all eight firms that had been assembling vehicles in Brazil.

6. For an analysis of the development of the Brazilian automobile industry through these two cycles see Guimaraes and Gadelha (1980).

7. About one half of the value of the exports have been vehicles, and one half parts and components. Vehicles, either completely-knocked-down (CKD) kits or completely-built-up (CBU), have gone almost exclusively to other LDCs. The export of vehicles to other LDCs is partly related to similar low-octane fuel found in most of these countries. Also, to the extent that the vehicles have been adapted to rough Brazilian road conditions, they may also be better adapted to conditions in other LDCs. The types of vehicles that experienced the greatest relative increases in exports were precisely those (multiple-use pick-ups and utility vehicles) which are best adapted to rough use. Safety and antipollution regulations in most of the industrialised countries have been a barrier to entry into these markets. The only company that had significant exports to developed-country markets is Mercedes Benz, who exports CKD to its US assembly plant.

8. This programme, started in 1972, was primarily aimed at inducing multinational companies to produce at economic scales as part of an international investment strategy, with specialisation of production of different components across countries. The programme involved ten-year contracts between the firm and the government, with export commitments in exchange for duty-free importation of capital goods, parts, and components, for a total annual value up to a third of the value of its annual exports.

Other legislation also introduced in 1972 for the automobile industry established that the fiscal incentives for the imports of parts and components were conditional on exports of components, CBU units, and CKD kits of at least US $40 million annually for each firm during the next ten years, and that the value added in the country had to be at least three times the FOB value of the imports.

9. That Brazilian vehicles may not be of the same quality or as sophisticated as other vehicles, however, does not necessarily detract from their foreign sales appeal. In fact, they may be preferred if they are simpler and cheaper, because that may make them the most appropriate choice for buyers in other LDCs.

10. See price comparison figures in Tyler (1981).

11. These indices for car prices are presented in the statistical appendix of Guimaraes and Gadelha (1980).

12. CTA now consists of four institutes: ITA, the training institute; IPD, an institute responsible for R&D for aeronautical products; IAE, an institute responsible for R&D in activities related to space; and IFI, an institute responsible for co-ordinating and supporting activities to consolidate and develop the aerospace industry in Brazil. Among other areas, CTA has been very active in the energy-substitution programme, particularly the certification of alcohol engines and the search for a diesel fuel substitute.

13. As a result, Embraer is more than 90 per cent privately owned by almost 200,000 private firms.

14. The military category includes the Xanante, a single-engine jet trainer and ground-attack plane, whose manufacture was started in 1971 through a licence from Macchi Spa of Varesse, Italy. More than 150 of these planes built by Embraer were operating in the Brazilian Air Force in 1980, and ten had been exported to other developing countries.

15. The co-operation agreement is an illuminating example of how much a local company with strong government support can negotiate for better terms on technology transfer when there is a large domestic market to interest the foreign suppliers. Embraer decided to enter the four-to eight-seater market in 1973 after making a detailed analysis of demand. The Brazilian market was second only to the US market for aircraft of that type. Between 1964 and 1974, Brazil had imported 2,485 such planes. Embraer had three alternatives: it could develop its own models, it could manufacture foreign products under license, or it could negotiate an industrial co-operation agreement. It chose the latter in order to achieve rapid market penetration without excessive technological dependence. To obtain such a co-operation agreement, it made clear to the US companies that with the help of the government it was effectively closing off the Brazilian market to all foreign companies except for the one that entered into the agreement. Three essential features of the agreement were that: (1) there would not be any royalty payments, (2) Embraer would have the right to make modifications that it deemed appropriate to the imported models, and (3) there would be a progressive nationalisation of the components of the aircraft, which was expected to reach 70–75 per cent for all models. For more information see Baranson (1981).

16. By 1980, the regional carriers of Brazil were operating 43 Bandeirantes,

which had already flown 330,000 hours and carried more than 1,350,000 passengers.

17. Due to increased competition from other companies, Embraer was also trying to speed up the production of its new plane.
18. For a fuller treatment of this case see Dahlman (1979).
19. What little investment occurred was in small peripheral equipment such as sintering screens, roll crushers, minor modifications in major equipment units, etc. Technical change was disembodied in the sense of being complementary or based on the existing equipment rather than in equipment that substituted the original machines.
20. The capacity-stretching was achieved mostly through better selection and control of the physical–chemical properties and the preparation of the raw materials (particularly in the sinter and blast-furnace sections), and through better utilisation of the existing equipment units through changes in operational methods or useful volume (blast-furnace and steel sections). The problems with materials and their variations in quality (which was something beyond the firm's control) conditioned the technical-change path, and forced the firm to develop a whole series of homogenisation and uniformisation measures in its raw-materials receiving-and-preparation yard which were crucial for the improvement of the whole operation of the firm.
21. The research centre was initially oriented 100 per cent to technical support activities. Its implementation was gradual and it required an initial adaptation period. By 1978 the research centre had a staff of 314, and devoted about 40 per cent of its activities and 70 per cent of its budget to research.
22. As revealed by the thinking behind what high administrators in the firm called the 'technological prism', there was a growing concern for the necessary interrelationship between operation, research, engineering, and equipment manufacture, where the latter was closely tied in to the needs of firm's expansion plans.
23. In addition in 1972 it spun off Usimec, which became one of the largest producers of equipment for the steel industry in Brazil.
24. This has involved on average of 23 thousand man-courses per year in Brazil over the period 1972–76 and a total of 449 man-courses abroad between 1969 and 1976.
25. The company was under the same president since the planning stages in 1957 until 1975, a total of 18 years which permitted the systematic, long-term development of its technological capability.
26. For more details on these investments in technology see Dahlman (1979).
27. Usiminas in fact appears to be one of the principal technology exporters from Brazil, see Sercovich (1981).

REFERENCES

Baranson, Jack (1981) *Automotive Industries in Developing Countries.* World Bank Occasional Staff Papers, No. 8. Baltimore, Maryland: Johns Hopkins Press (for The World Bank).

Dahlman, Carl J. (1979) 'A Microeconomic Approach to Technical Change: The Evolution of the Usiminas Steel Firm in Brazil', unpublished Ph.D. Dissertation. New Haven: Yale University.

Guimaraes, Eduardo Augusto de Almeida and Maria Fernanda Gadelha (1980) 'O Setor Automobilistico no Brasil', Finep-CEP, Relatorio de Pesquisa, no. 2, Rio de Janeiro: Finep.

Sercovich, Francisco (1981) 'Brazil as a Technology Exporter', Washington, DC: Inter-American Development Bank (mimeo).

Tyler, William (1981) 'Implicit Tariffs and Implicit Nominal Protection', Ipea, Textos Para Discussoes Internas, No. 35. Rio de Janeiro: Ipea.

The Utilisation of Professional Engineering Skills in Kenya

Paul Bennell

While the provision of engineering manpower has, for obvious reasons, been consistently identified as being of crucial importance in the development of the indigenous technological capabilities of less developed countries (LDCs), relatively little detailed research has focused on the training and utilisation of engineering skills in these countries. This is clearly revealed by even a cursory review of the literature, which is overly preoccupied with analysing the adverse effects of technological dependence without considering in any systematic manner the engineering manpower aspects of this problem.

In this paper I propose to summarise some of the main empirical findings of my research on the utilisation of professional engineering skills in Kenya. This forms part of a wider study concerned with analysing the determinants of the structure of engineering labour markets in Kenya since the early colonial period and, in particular, the nature of the relationship between the supply of and demand for formally qualified engineers and engineering technicians and craftsmen.

The discussion will be structured as follows. In the first section the results of a tracer survey of engineering graduates from Nairobi University will be presented. The second section will be concerned to analyse the nature of the tasks undertaken by a representative sample of these engineers once in employment.

THE INTER-SECTORAL DISTRIBUTION OF ENGINEERS

Existing data sources on the distribution of university-trained engineers among the major sectors of the Kenyan economy are non-existent. It was decided, therefore, to undertake a tracer survey of the present employment whereabouts of all engineering graduates from the Engineering faculty, Nairobi University between 1964–79.

335

TABLE 6. *ISIC Sectoral Breakdown of Nairobi University Engineering Graduates 1964–1979*

Sector / Discipline		Agriculture	Mining and Quarrying	Manufacture	Water, Electricity	Construction	Finance Insurance, Real Estate	Transport and Communication	Finance etc. (inc. Engin. Services)	Community Personal & Social Services	Totals
Civil	No.	8	0	6	71	120	40	21	96	22	348
	%	2.4	0.0	1.3	20.5	34.5	11.0	6.0	27.7	6.4	100.0
Elec.	No.	2	0	35	42	21	13	59	10	26	208
	%	0.8	0.0	16.7	20.2	10.3	6.4	28.3	4.7	12.4	100.0
Mech.	No.	6	0	107	12	35	11	36	18	42	267
	%	2.1	0.0	37.8	4.8	13.0	4.2	13.4	6.7	15.9	100.0
All Disciplines	No.	16	0	148	125	176	28	116	124	90	823
	%	1.9	0.0	18.0	15.2	21.4	3.4	14.1	15.1	10.1	100.0

Source: EFTS.

TABLE 7. Present Employment of Engineering Graduates from Nairobi University, 1964-1979

Discipline	Central Government	Parastatals	African Industrial Entrepreneurs	Private Non-African	MNC and Joint Ventures	African Consul. Entrepreneurs	African Consul. Employees	Other Citizen Consultancy	Foreign Consultancy	Teachers and Students.	Migrated	Traced Total Reg.	Untraced	Traced % Total
Civil	166	56	0	10	9	9	13	22	52	10	12	359	36	91.1
% Traced	46.2	15.6	0.0	2.8	2.5	2.5	3.6	6.1	14.5	2.8	3.3	100.0	—	—
Registered	51/118	27/47	0	5/10	4/9	8/9	10/11	15/18	24/39	2/8	0	144/265	3/36	—
%	43.2	62.8	0.0	50.0	44.4	88.9	90.9	83.3	61.5	25.0	0.0	54.3	8.3	—
Electrical	34	105	1	6	38	3	2	2	5	12	10	218	22	90.8
% Traced	15.6	48.2	0.45	2.7	17.4	1.4	0.9	0.9	2.3	5.5	4.6	100.0	—	—
Registered	11/2	16/18	0/1	2/5	8/27	2/3	0/2	1/2	1/5	2/9	0	43/164	—	—
%	50.0	18.3	0.0	40.0	29.6	66.6	0.0	150.0	20.0	22.2	0.0	26.2	—	—
Mechanical	70	53	3	22	95	1	2	2	1	18	4	271	21	92.8
% Traced	25.8	19.6	1.1	8.1	35.0	0.4	0.7	0.7	0.4	6.6	1.5	100.0	—	—
Registered	14/48	23/39	0/2	9/18	16/60	1/1	0/1	1/2	0/1	5/13	0	69/186	3/21	—
%	29.2	60.0	0.0	50.0	36.7	100.0	0.0	50.0	0.0	38.5	0.0	37.1	14.3	—
TOTAL	270	214	4	38	142	13	17	26	57	40	26	848	79	91.5
% Traced	31.8	25.2	0.4	4.5	16.7	1.5	2.0	3.1	6.7	4.7	3.0	100.0	—	—
Registered	76/188	66/169	0/4	16/33	28/96	11/14	10/14	17/22	2/45	9/30	0	259/615	—	—
%	40.4	39.0	0.0	48.5	29.1	78.5	71.4	77.3	55.5	30.0	0.0	42.1	—	—

Source: EFTS.

The Engineering Faculty Tracer Survey (EFTS) was conducted over a nine-month period from July 1980. Since over 90 per cent of the graduates from all three engineering departments were traced, the great majority of whom with a high degree of certainty, the survey gives an accurate picture of inter-sectoral employment. In Table 6, graduate engineering employment is presented according to the International Standard Industrial Classification (ISIC). In Table 7 the data have been re-categorised into the major types of employers of engineering graduates as these emerged in the course of the survey, but which tend to be obscured if sole reliance is placed on the ISIC classification. Although the sectors are difficult to define rigorously, it is necessary to clarify briefly their specification for the purposes of this research. The public sector comprises central government, parastatal and teaching institutions. Central Government covers all engineers employed by government ministries. Parastatals include the Railways, Posts and Telecommunications (both local and international), the Ports Authority, marketing boards, the establishments that are genuine parastatals in the sense that they are not effectively managed or majority-owned by private capital. Local government employees have also been included since they enjoy a large degree of autonomy from central governmental control. Within the private sector, the major division is between industrial and consultancy enterprises. Since the extent to which African engineering graduates have become entrepreneurs in their own right is of particular interest, these invididuals have been separately delineated within the consultancy and industrial sectors. Multinational corporations (MNC) and joint ventures include all enterprises that are effectively owned and/or managed by foreign-owned corporate entities with generally widespread operations overseas. 'Non-African industrial' is essentially, therefore, a residual category comprising all non-African industrial enterprises, both local and foreign-owned, which cannot be considered to be MNCs. The consultancy sector has been divided into African (entrepreneurs and employees) and non-African (citizen and foreign).

THE INTERNATIONAL MIGRATION OF KENYAN ENGINEERING MANPOWER

The 'brain drain' is the most visible manifestation of the extent to which there exists an international market for skills. While considerable attention has been focused on the seriousness of this brain drain in frustrating manpower development in Africa, only meagre supporting evidence has been collected to substantiate these allegations. The results of the EFTS are, therefore, particularly interesting in that they provide concrete evidence of the magnitude of the out-migration of a major profession in an African country.

Well over 50 per cent of the 79 engineers who could not be traced were of Asian origin, and it seems likely that a large majority of them were no longer living in Kenya in 1979–80. This assertion is based firstly on the predominantly Asian composition of the 26 graduates who are known to have migrated overseas and, second, on the results of a tracer study of University College, Nairobi students who graduated between 1961–70, conducted by Sven-Erik Rastad[1] which found that of the 78 non-African engineering graduates 23 had already left the country and 14 could not be traced (47.4 per cent of the total). If it is assumed that at least the same proportion of the EFTS untraced graduates have also migrated, then the total 'brain drain' of locally trained engineers amounts to approximately 60–65 (7.5 per cent of total output between 1964–79). However, because most of these migrants were Asian who in the majority of cases left Kenya for political reasons (often as a result of their refusal to adopt Kenyan citizenship), this outflow of graduate engineers cannot be considered to be typical market-oriented brain drain. If only African engineers are considered, the amount of out-migration has been minimal – less than 10 of this group were discovered to be working overseas.

THE ENGINEERING CONSULTANCY SECTOR

The engineering consultancy enterprise has been identified as a key institution involved in the selection and modification of foreign technology which generally characterises the initial stages of the development of national technological self-reliance: 'The missing and crucial link in the process of generating domestic technology as well as making the best use of imported technology is the consultancy.'[2]

It is argued that the concentration of the most talented and experienced engineering manpower in this sector provides the basis for an indigenous capability to 'unpackage' foreign technology, thereby reaping considerable short-term advantages. The ability to utilise local engineering manpower in this way can lead to considerable cost saving by, for example, making greater use of raw materials, reducing reliance on proprietorial technology and dispensing with the payment of often substantial foreign consultancy fees. Roberts also emphasises the importance of several 'external' economies derived from planning and building projects using local engineers such as learning by doing, increasing the level of pre-investment information, and faster diffusion of technology. He argues that 'consultancy is a source of practical know-how about the realisation of projects in local conditions and hence can make a valuable contribution to economic planning'.[3] One would expect, therefore, that the emergence of a national industrial bourgeoisie capable of challenging the dominant position of foreign capital in key sectors of the economy must necessarily be linked in one way or another to the development of a strong engineering consultancy sector.

In spite of the proclaimed importance of the emergence and development of the engineering consultancy sector in LDCs, there is little detailed empirical research on this subject. It was decided, therefore, to undertake a short study of this sector in Kenya. A list of all enumerated enterprises (with, therefore, at least five employees) in the ISIC classification 'technical and engineering services' (ISIC 8324) was obtained from the Central Bureau of Statistics (CBS). From this listing, approximately thirty-five engineering consultancies in the Nairobi area were identified as being predominantly engaged in the design and supervision of capital projects in all sectors of the economy. Senior partners from thirty of these consultancies agreed to co-operate with us and they were personally interviewed in April–May 1980. A simple questionnaire was administered in order to obtain basic factual information about the main characteristics of each consultancy, but, in addition, a number of unstructured questions were included which covered areas of interest that were not particularly amenable to quantitative assessment, such as attitudes to appropriate technology, relations with major clients and other consultancy firms and the general structure of consultancy services and labour markets.

The rapid growth of the consultancy sector is one of the most important features of the pattern of development of engineering labour markets in Kenya since Independence. The share of the consultancy sector in total engineer employment rose from approximately 8 per cent in 1964 to over 20 per cent in 1979. But the most dramatic shift has been in the share of consultancy employment of civil engineers, increasing from 15 per cent of the total in 1964 to 50 per cent in 1979 whereas the corresponding increases for both electrical and mechanical engineers are only from 3 per cent to 6 per cent respectively. Although the CBS Annual Survey of Employment and Earnings does not disaggregate further than ISIC 8324 'technical and engineering ser vices', it can be reasonably assumed that the high employment growth rates that have prevailed in this sector also apply to the engineering consultancy sub-sector. Data from the interview survey on the year of establishment of each consultancy also indicate the extent of expansion during the post- Independence period: three pre-1960, one 1960–4, eleven 1965–9, eight 1970–4 and five 1975–9.

The thirty consultancies surveyed can be subdivided into the three distinct ownership groups already mentioned in relation to the EFTS, namely foreign, non-African Kenyan, and African. Foreign consultancies occupy a dominant position in the market for engineering services, although this is difficult to quantify precisely in financial terms given the reluctance of many respondents to disclose their annual fee income in 1979. But from what income figures are available coupled with the relative numbers of engineers employed, the dominant position of foreign consultancies *vis-à-vis* the other two groups clearly emerges. While most attention has focused on the global expansion of MNCs engaged mainly in manufacturing activities, the majority of foreign engineering consultancies in Nairobi are part of an extensive worldwide network of offices. These multinational engineering consultancies (MNECs) can be roughly divided into two groups, the first of which comprises mainly well-known British-based firms who developed their overseas work during the colonial period and have subsequently established a major position in the international engineering consultancy market, in particular in the civil engineering field in high-growth areas, notably the Middle East. Two of these British firms were the first to take advantage of the rapid expansion of this sector from the mid-1960s onwards. Both use Nairobi as a regional centre for their operations throughout East and Central Africa which accounts for the particularly large numbers of professional personnel employed by them. Another firm also has extensive overseas operations but only maintains a skeletal office in Nairobi, recruiting additional manpower on short-term contracts when required.

The second foreign group comprises mainly continental European consultancies who only started to undertake overseas projects during the 1960s, usually in an attempt to offset a generalised decline in the volume of work in Europe with the completion of major capital projects in the 1950s and early 1960s. Initially these overseas offices were essentially 'servicing points' with most of the design work being undertaken in the home country, but for most of them this is no longer the case today.

The non-African Kenyan sector comprises five consultancies headed by British engineers and six by Kenyan Asians. All are longstanding residents in Kenya and have adopted Kenyan citizenship. With the exception of one firm most of this group of consultancies were established between the late 1960s and mid-1970s.

The establishment of African engineering consultancies during the 1970s represents an important trend in the development of an indigenous technological and entrepreneurial capability in Kenya. Whereas there was only one genuinely African-run consultancy in 1970, this had increased to at least fifteen by 1979, the three largest being included in the survey. According to the EFTS, nearly 20 per cent of graduates within the consultancy sector are employed by the African consultancy firms, which is a sizeable proportion given their very recent establishment.

Of the six African consultancies in the survey, only one can be considered to be an attempt by non-citizen engineers to create 'an African front to satisfy the market'. The remainder have generally been founded by experienced African engineers who have held senior positions in the civil service, local government or parastatal sectors. This has enabled them to utilise extensive networks of personal relationships within the public sector, which, as has already been mentioned, is of considerable importance in accounting for many of these consultancies' impressive growth records. By the mid-1970s these young engineers had already reached the highest echelons of the public-sector employment hierarchy, and, while 'straddling'[4] activities are generally widespread at this level, there were severe logistical and legal constraints limiting their involvement in private income-earning activities. Realising the lucrativeness of the consultancy sector and aware of the generally low level of technological knowledge required in predominantly civil engineering design and supervision activities, these engineers decided to set up their own consultancies. Those who started before the mid-1970s were forced to rely mainly on private-sector clients, and given the extreme competitiveness of this part of the market and the relatively small size of the majority of projects, the position of African consultancies was very precarious. The turning-point came in 1975 with a series of government decisions actively to promote the localisation of engineering consultancy contracts, and it was the success of a small group of no more than five African consultancies in breaking into this much larger and stable market that allowed them to consolidate their position and begin to pose a real challenge to the middle-sized foreign firms. In order to make this challenge as effective as possible, the three main African consultancies have secretly formed an informal cartel where each has agreed to specialise in one major area of engineering activity and, at a more overt political level, they act together in applying pressure on government and relevant ministries for increased levels of localisation of contracts. There is, therefore, a high level of political consciousness in these attempts to counteract the 'economic money power' of the big, foreign consultancies. This is also reflected in their employment practices where maximum reliance is placed on the employment of African engineers in an attempt to prove conclusively that local manpower is as competent as much more expensive expatriates.

Engineering consultancies in Kenya, regardless of size or type of ownership, are heavily oriented towards civil engineering projects. This is reflected both in the type of engineering activities undertaken and in the pattern of employment of engineers by specialisation. In Table 7, it can be seen that while 96 civil engineering graduates from Nairobi University (26.7 per cent of the total) are employers or employees in the consultancy sector, the corresponding figures for electrical and mechanical engineers are only 12 (5.5 per cent) and 6 (2.2 per cent) respectively. Employment breakdowns according to engineering specialisation among the consultancy firms surveyed, indicate that over 80 per cent of engineers have been trained in civil and/or structural engineering. Over 85 per cent of these consultancies reported that at least 75 per cent of the work (measured as the total value of projects in progress) they undertook in 1979 related to three specific types of activity, namely roads, water-related projects and structures.

The virtual absence of engineering consultancies specialising in the design and implementation of industrial projects, in particular in the manufacturing sector, is symptomatic of the high degree of dependence on turn-key foreign technology acquired independently by enterprises themselves without resorting to outside technical assistance. Whereas production-oriented electrical and mechanical engineering consultancies are not required at this stage of the industrialisation process, the very nature of civil engineering activities necessitates a large-scale design input for each project, and this directly encourages the emergence of specialised engineering consultancies. Furthermore, the acquisition and utilisation of production engineering technology is heavily constrained both by limited local knowledge of the advanced technologies imported from abroad and by the legal barriers of patents. Civil engineering technology, on the other hand, is based on relatively easily acquired, non-proprietorial knowledge and skills, and hence in this important area of engineering activity many of

TABLE 8   *Employment Distribution of Engineers by Firm Size*
(percentages)

Sector	Firm Size (Employers)					
	0–50	51–100	101–200	201–300	301–550	550+
Manufacturing	5.5	10.0	19.0	5.7	22.1	37.7
Private Total	16.4	7.6	14.0	8.2	14.5	39.1

Source: CBS, 1980 Survey of Employment and Earnings in the Modern Sector, unpublished.

the conventional propositions underlying the concept of technological dependence are largely invalid. It is true, however, that among most engineering consultants in Kenya there is a marked reluctance to alter standard design criteria and construction techniques that have been developed in advanced industrial countries.

THE MANUFACTURING AND REPAIRS SECTORS

Private manufacturing enterprises comprise the second major employment sector for university-trained engineers in Kenya. ISIC sectoral employment totals for both Kenyan and foreign engineers, disaggregated according to public- and private-sector employers, are not available, but the EFTS revealed that private employers outside of the consultancy and manufacturing sectors accounted for less than 5 per cent of the total number of local engineers traced.

Excluding engineering consultancies (which in certain key respects can be regarded as extensions of the public sector), only 13 per cent and 15 per cent of the total populations of civil and electrical engineers are employed by private-sector employers. And among Nairobi University-trained engineers this figure is even lower. In the construction sector, for example, which employed over 60,000 people in 1980 fewer than seven graduates were traced (out of a total engineer population of at least 100–125), none of whom were construction entrepreneurs in their own right. While engineering consultancies are the principal employers of civil engineers in the private sector, manufacturing enterprises constitute a major source of demand for mechanical and electrical engineers in the private sector. However, only four (0.4 per cent) engineering graduates from Nairobi University have established their own industrial enterprises, and of these none employ more than ten people. Table 8 indicates the extent to which university

trained engineers are heavily concentrated in a small group of industrial enterprises which employ over 550 employees. In general, no more
than three or four enterprises in each sector account for a large proportion of engineers employed.

An interview survey of over forty manufacturing enterprises in the
Nairobi and Mombasa areas was undertaken in order to ascertain in
some detail the patterns of demand for formally qualified engineering
manpower. The following are the main conclusions that emerge from
this survey.

(1) Technically speaking, the pattern of import-substituting industrialisation in Kenya has not generated sizeable demands for formally
trained engineering manpower. Since virtually all production technology has been imported *in toto* from the advanced industrial countries,
there has been little need for high-level engineering manpower which
is generally heavily concentrated in research and development departments in the capital goods sector. Innovation activities were, with the
exception of only one company, completely absent. However, in
Kenya, there is little evidence to suggest that the large majority of
technology suppliers deliberately attempt to suppress knowledge concerning its operation, maintenance and repair from local manpower.
Most technology is purchased outright from suppliers in the advanced
industrial countries, and local companies are completely independent
from a manpower point of view once the technology has been installed
and production trials undertaken. Even where the technology is
owned by a parent company, the experience in Europe and increasingly in South America and South East Asia shows that this has not
prevented the complete localisation of engineering personnel. Simplistic expatriate conspiracy theories must therefore be discarded, since
the loss of monopoly control over patented technology exists in *all*
countries (and not just African or Third World ones), and juridical and
physical barriers preventing duplication have to be enforced regardless
of location. In Kenya, MNCs argue that the principal constraint frustrating engineering manpower localisation is the non-availability of
local manpower possessing the requisite technical and, more important, managerial competence (which it is frequently stated can only be
acquired after several generations of appropriate socialisation). In the
minority of cases where the head office wishes to maintain highly centralised control over the production/engineering activities of foreign
subsidiaries, this is still perfectly compatible with complete manpower
localisation, since modern communication and transport technologies
allow the parent company to monitor operations closely and provide

direct assistance (the 'fireman') when necessary. Where this type of close relationship does exist, it can, however, be regarded as a partial externalisation of the engineering function in the subsidiary which will dampen demand for local engineering manpower.

(2) The results of the case study are also consistent with the hypothesis that skill requirements are highly enterprise-specific majority of the enterprises do not require broad skill engineering personnel to undertake operational and maintenance activities since they utilise specialised imported technology. Instead they rely first and foremost on on-the-job acquisition of the necessary skills. The specificity of this internal training process for each enterprise gives rise to a complex pattern of recruitment criteria. Thus, whereas the conventional screening hypothesis argues that since employers associate education with productivity they will automatically impose higher 'minimum education qualification levels' as the numbers of increasingly well-qualified job applicants continue to increase, employers' views about trainability and formal educational attainment are, in practice, very varied, thereby considerably complicating the simple pattern of qualification that is normally postulated.

In the large majority of case-study enterprises, the main 'entry point' is at the bottom of a relatively flat, simply organised labour hierarchy. Enterprises recruit 'casual' workers who can be legally employed on a daily basis for a period of up to six months, although, in practice, this is frequently exceeded. At this level, there has occurred a straightforward process of qualification among the large majority of these enterprises who are able costlessly to select increasingly well-educated candidates from the rapidly growing number of job-seekers. The casual employment system allows employers to select out individuals who are considered to have particularly desirable attributes and place them on the permanent payroll, thereby minimising the risks normally entailed in more conventional job selection procedures. Since general educational achievement is high, these new workers are considered to be adequately trainable in order to undertake all operative and maintenance functions. Recruitment for higher employment positions is mainly internal, and is based on ability and seniority rather than on creating additional entry points and adopting credentialist selection criteria based on formal educational qualifications (as is generally the case in the public sector). Thus, among these enterprises, formal education above the minimum entry level for operatives is generally considered to be relatively worthless compared with the acquisition of experience on the job, and indeed there is a marked aversion to the use of educational qualifications to mark formal boundaries between different strata of employment positions within the labour process.

Among the minority of enterprises that do have formalised entry points higher up their labour hierarchies, the case studies indicate that there are still considerable differences in their selection criteria for engineering manpower. In a strict technical sense, it is generally agreed that the acquisition of higher engineering qualifications enhances the trainability of an employee required to perform technical tasks. However, this was frequently seen to be offset by the inappropriate values and attitudes of this type of recruit in relation to the managerial *and* technical tasks they are expected to perform. The result, therefore, is that enterprises make specific trade-offs in deciding which level of formally trained engineering manpower is most appropriate for each entry point, but these are not rigidly enforced, resulting in highly pragmatic and amorphous selection criteria. Many employers believe that the competitiveness of the educational system produces among those who graduate from the highest-level institutions unrealistically high expectations in relation to the managerial and technical requirements of the industrial sector. In the advanced capitalist countries, on the other hand, the inculcation of the appropriate employment attitudes and expectations is rooted in a well-established class structure which is more closely related to specific socialisation processes in educational institutions and the family. Given the low technical requirements of higher engineering positions in most manufacturing enterprises in Kenya, this tends to enhance the importance of the acquisition of the necessary managerial control skills, and this is reflected in the emphasis placed by many of the case-study enterprises on the screening of individual candidates not simply on the basis of their formal technical qualifications but, more important, on their overall attitudes and general amenability to a prolonged in-plant socialisation and on-the-job training process.

Another important factor constraining the process of qualification escalation for formally trained engineering manpower (and hence the overall level of demand) is that the recruitment of these individuals possessing 'general' skills will tend to enhance labour turnover. This could lead to an increase in training costs if the adverse effects of higher labour turnover are not offset by the greater trainability of formally qualified manpower. This disincentive is even greater in relation to the formal sponsorship of craft and technician apprentices, who receive (state-regulated) higher wages than their informally trained counterparts and are far more likely to leave once they are qualified.

(3) Marxist writers have emphasised the role of educational certification as a form of legitimation of increasingly stratified labour hierarchies characteristic of large-scale industrial enterprises in the capitalist metropoles. However, as an independent factor enhancing the demand for formally trained engineering manpower in Kenya, the enterprise case studies reveal that, given the generally simple labour hierarchy required to satisfy limited technical and managerial requirements, there is little need for the 'privileging' of mental over manual labour in order to provide the basis for the stratification of the working class within an enterprise.

THE PUBLIC SECTOR

Central government and the parastatal sector employ approximately 47 per cent of all engineers (40 per cent civil, 75 per cent electrical and 37 per cent mechanical). Among graduates from Nairobi University, however, it can be seen from Table 7 that these percentages are higher for civil (61.8 per cent) and mechanical (45.4 per cent) engineers. The proportion of engineers employed in the public sector is only slightly higher than its share of total employment (in 1979). Compared with many African countries, however, the proportion of engineers working in the public sector in Kenya is much smaller.

The distribution of engineers in the public sector is considerably more concentrated than in the private sector; the three Ministries, of Transport and Communication, Water Development and Works, account for over 90 per cent of civil engineers employed by central government (40 per cent of the total), and over 75 per cent of electrical engineers in the public sector are employed by three parastatal organisations – the East African Power and Lighting Company, the Post and Telephone, and the External Communications Corporation.

Unlike the private sector, higher-level manpower requirements in the public sector are much more intensive and continue to expand rapidly. This is due to a number of factors. First, public-sector establishments are responsible for producing, either directly through in-house capacity or indirectly by contracting work out to consultants, all the engineering requirements of the capital projects laid down in the development plans, and their subsequent maintenance. These are generally skill-intensive activities involving a substantial design input. Furthermore, the scope of government involvement has expanded considerably during the 1970s with increasing emphasis being placed on the provision of basic services in the rural areas. This has resulted in a greatly increased demand for engineers to design and supervise the construction of water, road-building and electrification projects.

The second important factor is that the organisation of engineering manpower in central government and most parastatal organisations is based on the rigid, hierarchical segmentation of engineers, technicians and artisans according to strictly enforced formal-qualification entry points. Among engineers, in particular, a strong sense of professional identity is fostered by making promotion to higher employment positions conditional upon registration as an engineer by the Engineers Registration Board.[5]

In contrast to the private sector, therefore, the place of the university-trained engineer in the employment hierarchy is formally defined and strictly enforced. In addition, it is widely argued that the public-sector engineering manpower pyramid is 'top-heavy', with too few engineering technicians compared with university-trained engineers.

THE NATURE OF THE EMPLOYMENT POSITIONS OF ENGINEERS

In analysing the nature of the demand for university-trained engineers in Kenya, it is necessary to determine not only the distribution of this manpower among the major sectors of the economy, but also the nature of the employment positions actually occupied. This will then permit an assessment to be made of the extent to which the conception of the engineer propagated by the engineering profession and supported by the Kenyan state (via its enactment of registration policies, its recruitment criteria as a major employer of engineers, and the structure and content of university courses) corresponds with the jobs undertaken by engineers once in employment.

In the absence of comprehensive job-evaluation studies in Kenya, information concerning the basic characteristics of employment positions was obtained from Kenyan graduate engineers using a postal questionnaire concerned with the characteristics of their present employment. This comprised the following questions: (1) Approximately how much of the engineering knowledge you learned at university do you now utilise in your present job (expressed in per cent)?; (2) What percentage of your working day do you devote, on average, to the following tasks: (i) routine administration (of a non-technical nature), (ii) managerial/supervisory duties, (iii) original design work

TABLE 9   *Utilisation of Formally Acquired Engineering Knowledge by Sector*

Sector	Discipline	0–24	% Utilisation 25–49	50–74	75–100	No. Respondents
Civil Service	Civil	17.3	56.5	17.4	8.6	35
	Elec.	14.2	57.1	28.5	0.0	7
	Mech.	33.3	33.3	33.3	0.0	12
Parastatal	Civil	11.0	55.5	33.0	0.0	9
	Elec.	31.4	42.8	20.0	5.7	35
	Mech.	29.0	53.0	18.0	0.0	28
Non-African Private	Civil	0.0	0.0	0.0	0.0	0
	Elec.	50.0	50.0	0.0	0.0	2
	Mech.	23.5	47.0	23.5	6.0	17
MNC	Civil	0.0	25.0	75.0	0.0	4
	Elec.	36.3	36.3	9.0	0.0	11
	Mech.	43.0	43.0	16.0	0.0	44
Consultancy	Civil	10.7	46.7	37.5	5.3	45
	Elec.	25.0	0.0	75.0	0.0	4
	Mech.	0.0	25.0	75.0	0.0	4
University/ Polytechnic	Civil	0.0	25.0	75.0	0.0	4
	Elec.	0.0	100.0	0.0	0.0	1
	Mech.	0.0	33.3	0.0	66.6	3
All Sectors	Civil	11.3	48.4	34.0	6.2	97
	Elec.	31.7	43.3	26.7	5.0	60
	Mech.	30.0	48.0	19.0	3.0	108

Source: Postal Questionnaire Survey.

(new projects; research and development), (iv) routine maintenance/ repair activities, (v) major maintenance/repair activities, (vi) routine production activities, (vii) other activities (specify)?; (3) How many people are you directly responsible for?

The extent to which formally acquired engineering knowledge is utilised within the main employment sectors is shown in Table 9. Extreme care must be exercised in interpreting these results since they are based on the subjective evaluations of each respondent. Moreover, even when the degree of utilisation is low (less than 25 per cent), it cannot be automatically concluded that a university engineering education is unnecessary in order to undertake these jobs satisfactorily. Given these important reservations, it can be observed that there are some interesting inter-discipline and inter-sector differences in the pattern of utilisation of university engineering skills. The overall median utilisation value for civil, electrical and mechanical engineers is in the 25–49 per cent region. However, the dispersion around this common median value is significantly different for each of the three disciplines. Just over 40 per cent of civil engineers claim to utilise more than 50 per cent of their university engineering knowledge, whereas for electrical and mechanical engineers the corresponding figures are 31.7 per cent and 30.0 per cent respectively. Conversely, 11.3 per cent of civil engineers utilise less than 25 per cent of their university knowledge. It would appear, therefore, that not only is the overall demand for university-trained engineers by the manufacturing sector much lower than is frequently asserted, but also that where university-trained engineers are employed, many do not undertake tasks that require the utilisation of a significant proportion of the engineering knowledge they acquired at university. Consequently, while their university education qualifies them for recruitment into much higher-paying jobs among a certain group of enterprises mainly in the MNC sector, it cannot be convincingly argued that this high rate of return to their education is directly attributable to their formal acquisition of engineering skills.

The standard EUSEC[6] definition of the professional engineer is based on a conception of the engineer as a problem-solver, and as someone who is engaged in tasks that are 'predominantly intellectual' and 'varied'. Considerable emphasis is placed, therefore, on the amount and degree of sophistication of design work undertaken by the young engineer seeking registration. For the profession, to design new engineering projects successfully signifies that an engineer has undergone the training required to translate the theory acquired at university into applied practice. However, in Table 10, it can be observed that only civil engineers spend a significant proportion of their time undertaking design activities. Given the variety of tasks undertaken by engineers, coupled with a large design input, they are generally able to satisfy the requirements laid down for full registration. In Table 7 it can be seen that 54.3 per cent of traced civil engineering graduates from Nairobi University are registered. However, in the case of electrical and mechanical engineering graduates, at least 50 per cent of whom spend less than 20 per cent of their time engaged on design activities, the corresponding figures are 26.1 per cent and 37.1 per cent (and in the MNC sector no more than 25–30 per cent of them are registered).

A closer analysis of Table 10 reveals that electrical and mechanical engineers are principally involved in routine administration and managerial and supervisory tasks, the remainder of their time being devoted to routine and major maintenance, repair and production

TABLE 10   *Task Analysis of University-Trained Engineers*

Discipline	Type of Task	Lower Quartile	Median	Upper Quartile
Civil	Design	10–19	50–59	70–79
	Managerial etc.	10–19	30–39	60–69
	Maintenance	0–9	0–9	0–9
	Production	0–9	0–9	0–9
Electrical	Design	0–9	10–19	30–39
	Managerial etc.	20–29	40–49	50–59
	Maintenance	0–9	10–19	40–49
	Production	0–9	0–9	0–9
Mechanical	Design	0–9	0–9	30–39
	Managerial etc.	10–19	30–39	50–59
	Maintenance	0–9	20–29	40–49
	Production	0–9	10–19	20–29

Source: Postal Questionnaire Respondents.

activities. In view of the generally low level of engineering knowledge required to undertake the latter tasks satisfactorily, in the majority of industrial enterprises in Kenya where engineering graduates are employed they are mainly managers-cum-technicians rather than professional engineers *per se*. As a result, employers frequently face a high degree of substitutability, in a technical sense, in choosing between engineering-degree and technician qualification holders. This tends, therefore, to enhance the importance of employers' assessment of the managerial (control) qualities of these two groups and, in particular, the extent to which these are seen to be correlated with the level of education attained. At a more general level, this relates to the extent to which recruitment criteria based on the structure of formal qualifications are important in legitimising the hierarchy of control within the labour process.

CONCLUSION

The aim of this paper has been to summarise some of the most notable features of the utilisation of professional engineers in Kenya. Civil engineers are concentrated in the three central government ministries and the engineering consultancy sector, and generally utilise a high level of their formally acquired knowledge in designing and supervising the construction of capital projects. Nearly 75 per cent of graduate electrical engineers are employed in the public sector. Although nearly 45 per cent of graduate mechanical engineers are employed in the private industrial sector, they generally utilise only a small proportion of their formally acquired engineering knowledge and do not engage in design and/or research and development activities. It is, therefore, among this group of engineers that the mismatch between the metropolitan, anglophonic conception of the professional engineer, which has formed the basis of training policy, and the subsequent utilisation of this manpower, is most apparent. This is reflected in the lack of liaison between the Faculty of Engineering and the industrial sector, the problems faced by young mechanical engineers in gaining full professional status (via registration) and the likelihood of increased underutilisation and possibly even open unemployment within the next ten to fifteen years.

NOTES

1. Sven-Erik Rastad, 'University Students and the Employment Market', *IDS (Nairobi) Staff Papers,* no. 74, June 1971.
2. UNCTAD, 'Technology Planning in Developing Countries', TD 238 Supp. 1, 1979, p. 29.
3. J. Roberts, 'Engineering Consultancy, Industrialisation and Development', in C. Cooper (ed.) *Science, Technology and Development* (London: Frank Cass, 1973) p. 48.
4. 'Straddling' is a term used to describe the widespread phenomenon in Kenya of public-sector employers engaging in extra-income earning activities in the private sector.
5. The Engineers Registration Board was established with the enactment of the Engineers Registration Act 1969. It lays down the formal educational and practical training requirements for registration as a 'professional engineer'.
6. The European and United States Engineering Conference (EUSEC) defines the professional engineer as follows: 'A professional engineer is competent by virtue of his fundamental education and training to apply the scientific method and outlook to the analysis of engineering problems. He is able to assume personal responsibility for the development and application of engineering science and knowledge, notably in research, design, construction, manufacture or management, or in education of the engineer. His work is predominantly intellectual and varied and not of a routine mental or physical character. It requires the exercise of original thought and judgement and the ability to supervise the technical and administrative work of others.'

Indigenous Technological Capability in Africa: The Case of Textiles and Wood Products in Kenya

*Steven Langdon**

This analysis examines indigenous technological capability (ITC) – its meaning, its origin, its impact, and the impediments to it – in two industries in Africa. Textile production and wood manufacturing are the industries under scrutiny, and the evidence reviewed is drawn mainly from Kenya. This evidence was gathered from field research late in 1980.

Overall, the study shows that ITC has developed in both Kenyan textiles and wood manufacturing – and has contributed to enterprise growth, profitability and external benefits in the country. But powerful impediments to policy shifts toward an overall ITC industrial strategy are also identified in Kenya, despite the evidence of how positive such shifts could be.

The analysis begins with a brief overview of the textile and wood industries being studied. The second section suggests indicators of ITC on which to focus, reviews the evidence from enterprise interviews, then probes the impact of ITC – looking especially at enterprise profitability and growth and at changing employment and linkage effects. The third section then shifts to what Stewart has called the 'political economy of creating local technology', by analysing the impediments to ITC in Kenya. A brief conclusion follows.

THE TEXTILE AND WOOD-PRODUCTS CASE

As a certain measure of industrialisation has taken place in Africa in the 1960–80 period, two of the industries that have expanded notably

* The research on which this paper is based has been funded by the Social Sciences and Humanities Research Council of Canada; this support is gratefully acknowledged.

355

have been textile production and wood-products manufacturing. The enterprises reviewed in this study were interviewed as part of a larger analysis of the changing structure of both industries in the context of European–African economic relations – a study that examined most significant textiles and plywood producers in France, the Netherlands, the Ivory Coast and Kenya, plus several European parent firms and African subsidiaries outside these four countries (see Mytelka, 1981; Langdon 1981b).

This analysis deals mainly with enterprises in Kenya. In the textile sector, ten firms there were interviewed, comprising the largest weavers and spinners in the country; Table 11 summarises certain basic data on these enterprises, dividing them into three categories according to ownership and origins. In the wood-products sector, eight firms were interviewed, including all three integrated plywood manufacturers in Kenya, a medium-sized chipboard producer, and four medium-sized manufacturers of such wood items as school furniture, doors, shipping pallets and brushes. All but one of these eight were domestically owned. Table 12 summarises data on these firms. In the wood case, this paper also draws on an interview with the largest plywood manufacturing subsidiary in Africa – Compagnie Forestière du Gabon (CFG) in which the largest Dutch plywood producer (Bruynzeel) has substantial shares; this is a useful comparison to the domestic-owned plywood manufacturers in Kenya. CFG in 1980 had sales of some US$50 million, 2,500 employees, and capital employed of US$25 million.

INDIGENOUS TECHNOLOGICAL CAPABILITY AND ITS IMPACT

Five indicators of indigenous technological capability were investigated in this study. First, the sources of technological knowledge in the development of the enterprise were traced – examining the original establishment of production facilities, and their pattern of expansion since that origin; the sources of machinery were reviewed as part of this analysis. Second, the extent of present dependence on formal links with technology sources abroad was probed; such links ranged from technology contracts with parent companies abroad to licensing agreements with independent foreign manufacturers to technical consultation contracts with overseas consulting firms. Third, the propensity of enterprises to undertake product or process initiatives in Kenya was investigated – by asking whether firms planned to manufacture new products in the immediate future, and testing whether any new product or process initiatives had been undertaken in the preceding three years. Fourth, the sources for technological knowledge to take such initiatives were examined – by asking on what sources enterprises would rely or had relied in undertaking such change. And finally, fifth, the emphasis of enterprises on formal research and development facilities was tested. These five areas represent a reasonable basis on which to determine the degree to which enterprises had absorbed essential technological knowledge for production in their industry and were able to use this knowledge to undertake new initiatives in their production.

If, on the one hand, an enterprise had itself organised the major inputs of essential technological knowledge for its own development, had no institutional reliance on foreign technology sources, was quite capable of confronting new product or process initiatives, and was able itself to organise the technological knowledge for such initiatives, then that enterprise clearly possessed indigenous technological capability in its sector. If, on the other hand, an enterprise had relied on foreign technology inputs for its development, continued to rely on institutional links with foreign technology suppliers, and felt product or process initiatives could only be undertaken via such foreign technology suppliers, then that enterprise as clearly did not possess indigenous technological capability.

Table 13 summarises data from Kenya for the eighteen enterprises interviewed, and suggests a number of points. First, in terms of the notion of ITC just suggested, there is a significant number of Kenyan enterprises in these sectors (three in textiles – L1, L2 and L3, and four in wood – P1, P2, M2 and M4) that clearly show the characteristics of indigenous technological capacity. This capacity is particularly significant in the wood-products sector, where two of the three large integrated firms with plywood facilities were based on ITC (although the expatriate presence in the most senior management of one of these firms may qualify this point somewhat). Second, as Mytelka (1978) has noted in her Latin American research, prior technological dependence does seem to generate continuing technological dependence; of seven enterprises that grew on the basis of foreign technology inputs and continued to have institutional links with foreign technology suppliers (that is, firms FT1, FT2, S1, S4, P3, M1 and FW1), six felt prepared to initiate new processes or products only on the basis of foreign technology inputs – and the seventh (S4) planned no such initiatives in any event (because of its desperate financial situation). Third, the insignificance of formal research-and-development facilities in shaping ITC

TABLE 11 *Kenyan Textile Spinners and Weavers Interviewed, 1980*

	Established as Foreign subsidiaries in the 1960s	Private Domestic Firms	Newly Established as European Subsidiaries in the 1970s
Number of Firms and Locations	3 (2 in Thika, 1 in Kisumu)	4 (Nairobi, Thika, Mombasa and Kiambaa)	3 (Nairobi, Nanyuki and Eldoret)
Total Sales Turnover (K.Shs.)	251 million	380 million	208 million
Employment	3730	4300	2343
Looms in Use	880	508	593
Spindles in Use	24,000	40,200	21,168* (covers only 2 of the 3 firms)
Products Manufactured and Sold	25–26 million metres of woven fabric (12 million cotton; 7 million blends; 6–7 million synthetics and nylon); some cotton yarn	19–21 million metres of woven fabric (11–12 million cotton; 7–9 million blends and synthetics); 1 million kg. of yarn; 3–4 million metres of knitted fabrics; some garments	18–19 million metres of woven fabric (13–14 million cotton; 5 million synthetics); thread and yarn

Source: Company Interviews, Kenya, November 1980; Interview with Industrial Adviser, Ministry of Industry, Nairobi, November 1980.

TABLE 12 *Kenyan Wood-Products Manufacturers Interviewed, 1980*

	Large Integrated Wood Manufacturers	Medium-sized Producers
Number of firms and Locations	3 (1 in Nairobi and Sokoro, 1 in Nairobi and Elgey in Eldoret)	5 (3 in Nairobi, 1 in Mombasa, 1 in Nakuru)
Total Sales Turnover (KShs.)	162 million	36–37 million
Employment	4220	500–515
Net Value of Assets (KShs.)	127 million	56–60 million
Products Manufactured and Sold	70 mil. sq. ft of plywood; 8 mil. sq. ft. of fibreboard; sawn lumber; doors; flooring; joinery	limited chipboard output; furniture; shipping pallets; brushes; doors; sawn lumber

Source: Company Interviews, Kenya, November 1980.

also seems evident. Given the size of these firms, the sectors they are in, and the sorts of product and process initiatives being confronted, formal R&D labs do not seem essential to ITC; indigenous technological capacity is being maintained, developed and deployed in other ways (although building ITC in enterprises previously dependent on foreign ties, such as S2, may require formal R&D facilities). Fourth, the data also suggest that technological independence is likely to encourage enterprises to innovate; of ten enterprises with no present technology links abroad, nine were undertaking new product changes, while of eight enterprises with such links, only five were initiating such changes.

Ownership was a factor in these patterns. It is clear that technological dependence is not simply the result of foreign ownership; P3 and M1 are local enterprises that were dependent on foreign technology ties. But it is striking that all three continuing subsidiaries (FT1, FT2 and FW1) remained dependent technologically – and that of nine enterprises with recent or planned initiatives, undertaken via their own technological inputs, seven were local firms in their origins, and all were local in present ownership and control. Of seven firms that were begun as subsidiaries, only two (S2 and S3) were moving toward ITC in 1980; of eleven that began as local firms, eight had no links with foreign technology suppliers and felt they could initiate changes on the basis of their own technological knowledge. The example of CFG, the Gabonese plywood subsidiary, seems to support this same perspective. Shareholding and technology links had been established with the Dutch wood MNC Bruynzeel in 1956, to try to build up the technological and managerial capacities of the firm. But by 1975–8 serious problems and large losses had emerged in the company, and a major reorganisation and production change had to take place – and could only be undertaken by making CFG even more dependent on Bruynzeel for shareholdings, technology and export marketing in Europe. Technological dependence bred yet more dependence in the enterprise, rather than greater ITC.

How did firms in Kenya develop the indigenous technological capability that many of them demonstrated? To analyse this question it is useful to focus on the seven local firms interviewed that had relied on their own technological inputs, had no formal technology links abroad, and were undertaking product or process changes based on their own technological knowledge (L1, L2, L3, P1, P2, M2 and M4 in Table 13).

What most characterised these ITC firms was their family-owned basis and their small beginnings. Six of the seven enterprises were owned by Kenyan Asian families, and five of these had been gradually expanded from very limited origins, as experience and expertise grew. The plywood facilities of the seventh enterprise (P2) had also been initiated on a small-scale basis, and were later meshed into the larger enterprise of which it was now part. Six of the seven had, in fact, begun with simple inexpensive secondhand machinery, and only after mastering that had expanded to more expensive and sophisticated technology. In the textile case, two of the enterprises (L1 and L2) had begun with simple saw mills, and then moved into plywood manufacturing with secondhand machinery; two others (M2 and M4) began by producing small and simple wood items (like ironing-boards and crates), and gradually expanded into more demanding wooden products. These seemed clear-cut cases of learning-by-doing – of the gradual accumulation of technological knowledge as enterprises expanded and entrepreneurial experience deepened.

The consequences of this gradual enterprise expansion, and another factor that undoubtedly contributed to growing ITC, was the unpackaged character of technological acquisitions made by the firms. All seven of them had machinery from a wide variety of countries and time periods in their factories. One plywood enterprise (P2), for instance, combined a secondhand UK hydraulic press, a new reeler from Taiwan, a peeler from Italy, and presses from Poland and three other countries; the other (P1) combined machines from Germany, Italy, Taiwan and Japan. This contrasted starkly with the technologically dependent plywood mill (P3) where 98 per cent of the machinery was from West Germany, and all of it was new. In textiles, one enterprise meshed knitting machines from Switzerland, Germany and Australia; another had spinning equipment from the UK, India, Germany and Italy, weaving machinery from Switzerland, India and UK, and processing machines from Germany and India. This contrasted with two enterprises begun as Japanese subsidiaries where virtually all the machinery was imported from Japan, and with two firms begun as German subsidiaries where most machines came from West Germany.

Unpackaging of technology, then, was certainly associated with ITC. But there were also additional mechanisms by which enterprises built up their technological capacity directly. Most useful seemed to be various direct forms of contact and experience abroad – not so much via formal educational experience abroad, which was rare in these firms, but via direct experiences with manufacturers overseas. One plywood producer (P1), for instance, had its manager work on a training/learning basis with Macmillan–Bloedel in Western Canada;

362

TABLE 13 *Technology in Textile and Wood Enterprises in Kenya, 1980*

Enterprise (Location, when first producing)	Main Source of Technological Knowledge in Development of Production Facilities	Present Institutional Technology Links Abroad	Recent or Planned New Products	Main Source of Technological Knowledge for any New Products/Processes	Present R&D Efforts Inside Firm
Textile Industry (Foreign Subsidiaries)					
FT1 (Thika, 1963)	Japanese Parent	Technicians from Parent	No	Japanese Parent	None
FT2 (Kisumu, 1965)	Indian Parent	Technology contract with parent; licence with input supplier; consultant agreement with British mnc	No	Indian Parent	None
(State Firms – All Previous Subsidiaries)					
S1 (Nairobi, 1973)	Former German Parent	Technology/Management contract with British mnc; trademark agreement with the same firm	Yes (continuous filament synthetics)	British Management/ Technical Contract mnc	None
S2 (Thika, 1965)	Former Japanese Parent	Technology contract with former parent, being phased out	Yes (new widths and fabrics)	Own R&D Lab	4 chemists in own lab; 8% of turnover
S3 (Nanyuki, 1976)	Former British Parent	None; expatriate management	Yes (garments)	Own enterprise	Beginning stress on this, via Indian processing manager
S4 (Eldoret, 1977)	Former German Parent	Licensing agreement for Sanforizing; license with Dutch mnc re designs	No	Own enterprise	None

(Local Enterprises)				
L1 (Thika, 1958)	Own enterprise	None	Yes (Polyester cloth)	Own enterprise	None
L2 (Nairobi, 1963)	Own enterprise	None	Yes (Filament yarns)	Own enterprise	No formal unit; only designers
L3 (Mombasa, 1964)	Own enterprise	None	Yes (Polyester cloth)	Own enterprise	None
L4 (Kiambaa, 1964)	Own enterprise	None	Yes (Printed cloth)	Dyestuff supplier	None
Wood Industry **(Plywood Manufacturers)**				
P1 (Elgeyo, 1971)	Own enterprise	None	Yes (New Plywood factory)	Own enterprise	None
P2 (Sokoro, 1967)	Own enterprise	None; expatriate management	Yes (Fibre board; prefab buildings)	Own enterprise (Make own conveyors)	None
P3 (Eldoret, 1973)	German Consulting firm	Technical agreement with German consulting firm	Yes (chipboard)	German consulting firm	None
(Medium-sized Producers)				
M1 (Nakuru, 1977)	German machinery suppliers	Technology contract with German trade partner	Yes (woodchip fuel bricks)	German trade partner	None
M2 (Nairobi, 1945)	Own enterprise	None	Yes (make own veneers)	Own enterprise (make some machines)	None
M3 (Nairobi, 1948)	Own enterprise	None	No	Own enterprise	None
M4 (Mombasa, 1961)	Own enterprise	None	Yes (use new horizontal lathes)	Own enterprise (make some machines)	None
(Foreign Subsidiary)				
FW1 (Nairobi, 1958)	Licensing from foreign firms; UK parent company; own enterprise	License with US mnc; UK parent supervises machinery choices	Yes (wood sailboats)	Licence from foreign firm	None

Notes: This table covers all firms interviewed in these sectors in Kenya in 1980. Dates of origin for P1, P2 and P3 indicate when each began plywood manufacturing.
Source: Company Interviews, 1980.

TABLE 14 *Enterprise performance in Kenya*

Enterprise	Average Annual Sales Increase	Average Annual after Tax Profitability (as Pct. of Turnover)	1980 Exports as Pct. of Sales	Average Annual Change in Employment	1980 Pct. of Inputs Imported	Linkage Investments Made
ITC – Textile Firms						
L1	25% (1975–80)	7.25% (1975–80)	0	13% (1975–80)	30%	No
L2	42% (1976–80)	'good'	11%	15% (1976–80)	60%	G, PFY
L3	40% (1979–80)	9% (1975, 1980)	0	9% (1976–80)	40–50%	T, C
Average	36%	8%	4%	12%	45%	
Non-ITC Textile Firms						
FT1	10% (1975–80)	3–4% (1975–80)	0	4% (1972–80)	25–30%	No
FT2	22% (1975–80)	1.25% (1975–80)	0.1%	12% (1975–80)	63%	No
S1	26% (1975–80)	–3.4% (1977–80)	5.9%	8% (1977–80)	42%	No
Average	19%	1%	2%	8%	44%	
ITC – Wood Firms						
P1	21% (1975–80)	7.5% (1975–80)	1%	13% (1975–80)	37%	CP
P2	12% (1975–80)	3.7% (1975–80)	14%	n.a.	n.a.	FB
M2	18% (1977–80)	4–5% (1980)	v. little	6% (1977–80)	50–60%	No
Average	17%	5.2%	6%–?	10%	46%	
Non-ITC Wood Firms						
P3	20% (1975–80)	4% (1979–80)	10%	22% (1975–80)	7–10%	FB, DP
FW1	12% (1975–80)	3.5% (1980)	10%	8% (1975–80)	35%	F
Average	16%	3.8%	10%	15%	22%	

Notes: Under Linkages, G = garments, PFY = polyester filament yarn; T = towels; C = carpet; CP = commercial plywood; FB = fibreboard; F = furniture; DP = door producer.

another (P2) had its management regularly participate in seminars in Western Europe on technology developments in the industry. One smaller wood firm (M2) organised a study-tour overseas for its managing director, during which he was able to tour various factories from which he derived technological adaptations to use in his own enterprise. One large local textile mill did utilise formal three-to-four year university courses in the UK and India in textiles technology; another large local textile manufacturer has guaranteed its contacts with process, product and design developments in Western Europe by taking over a UK firm as its subsidiary.

What difference did ITC make to enterprise performance? A definitive answer to this question would be complex. Both textile and wood industries in Kenya were marked by buoyant (if erratic) increases in domestic demand in the 1970–80 period, helped in the textile case by significant increases in import tariff levels and by tightened import quotas (see Langdon, forthcoming, for details). A definitive analysis would have to distinguish these market effects from technology effects; indeed, the considerable domestic competition that characterised this market expansion in Kenya may have been crucial in pushing many local enterprises to develop ITC to profit from these market effects. A definitive analysis would also have to take account of different dates of formation for enterprises, since one would not expect more recent firms to have had time to develop ITC. Nevertheless, it is possible to probe technology effects to some degree. This can be done by comparing a set of enterprises subject to essentially the same market effects. This is true of the enterprises in Table 14; none were established so recently (as with enterprises S3 and S4 in Table 13) as to distort the analysis unfairly; and enterprises have been excluded, especially in the wood industry, which experienced sharply different market conditions because of the pattern of their output or their date of establishment (such as M1 and M4 in Table 13. The remaining firms are divided between those that relied on their own technological knowledge and were initiating new moves using this (the ITC-firms), and those that relied on foreign technology sources (non-ITC-firms).

The average annual sales increases and annual after-tax profitability of the ITC firms in both industries were higher than those of the non-ITC firms – by a particularly high margin in textiles (17 and 7 per cent respectively), and by a small margin in wood manufacturing as well (1 and 1.4 per cent). This narrow wood margin underlines the fact, however, that ITC in the textile case seems to have had much more impact. The textile industry difference is even more dramatic when the performance of firms S2, S3 and S4 is considered – all of them dependent on foreign technology in their establishement and development. S3 and S4, in particular, were colossal disasters. S3 was based on machinery sold by one of its parents from an operation in Germany that the parent was shutting down – and never achieved operational viability; the enterprise was bankrupt less than two years after start-up and had to be rescued by the state at a cost of some 70 million Kenya shillings (US$7 million). S4 was sold very expensive new equipment, and provided a high return to its parent for inputs of technological knowledge, but also lost so much money (100 million K.shillings) that the state had to take it over in 1980. S2, meanwhile, had provided profits to its parent on input and machinery sales, but made minimal declared profits until it too was rescued by the state in late 1978. Technological dependence on foreign enterprise, then, had been extremely costly in the textile industry.

In export performance, the textile differences based on ITC seem less important – though it is worth stressing that the only enterprises that have penetrated the Western European market successfully are L1 (in the past) and L2 (as of 1980). Taking broader social effects into consideration, however, it is clear that other textile differences exist. Employment effects of ITC firms have been greater (12 per cent average annual increases versus 8 per cent); and while levels of imported inputs in textiles are virtually identical, ITC firms have shown much greater propensity to initiate linkage effects – with further indirect employment benefits.

Again, as with enterprise growth and profitability, the wood enterprises show a somewhat different pattern. P3 in particular expanded its employment faster than any of the other large firms in Table 14, had the lowest reliance on imported inputs, and had moved energetically on linkage investments – shifting first into plywood production from its saw mill, then later into manufacture of fibreboard and doors as well. In probing P3's technological capacities more closely, however, the nature of its technological dependence differs quite considerably from other dependent enterprises surveyed. The German firm on which P3 relied was an independent consulting group, not manufacturing itself, and not tied to any specific machinery supplier. The relationship had been a long one, starting when P3 first moved into plywood in 1973; it was a straight fee-for-service contract (at some £30,000 per year); and the technology link consequently involved no imposed constraints on P3 (such as tie-in input clauses or export restrictions), nor any incentives for the German consultant to oversell machinery in order to raise its fees or its returns from producing such machines. Indeed, when P3 expanded into its fibreboard production, the German consultant offered two options – a less expensive, more labour-intensive process, especially in handling, with 200 workers required per shift, or a much more expensive, highly automated process, requiring only 50 workers per shift. If anything, P3 management reported, the consultant inclined in its report toward the labour-intensive choice, but in the end P3 selected the more automated option because it wanted the convenience of fewer workers.

This was clearly a very different technology link abroad – quite a different dependence – from that involved in such cases as FT1, FT2, and S1, where the foreign parents or management agents entirely shaped Kenyan technology choices, rather than carrying forward consultations with a Kenyan management that clearly had some capacity itself to apply technological knowledge (as with P3). There are, then, variations in patterns of technological dependence that are important to recognise in analysing the impact of ITC. That impact tends to be especially significant, these cases suggest, in comparing ITC enterprises with enterprises that experience highly dependent technology links abroad.

The wood analysis may be supplemented by considering CFG's performance, since the Kenyan survey did not include any plywood subsidiaries. Plywood production levels and profits in recent years in CFG have run into problems – with output falling from 80,000 cubic metres in 1972 to 63,000 in 1975 and returning only to 74,000 in 1980; and profits falling from US$1.6 million in 1974 to losses of $0.7 million in 1976, $3.5 million in 1978 and only returning to profitability in 1980 (though at a healthy level of $3.2 million). These difficulties were not the results of technological problems within the enterprise so much as the consequence of rising South East Asian plywood exports which cut badly into CFG prices and markets in Western Europe. But the fact is that CFG did not have the capacity itself to reorganise and restructure to meet these challenges – but had to draw Bruynzeel more deeply into the operation and have it organise much of the restructuring that helped CFG recover. In the process, CFG reported no employment increases at all over the previous ten years – despite some diversification into blockwood and door manufacturing.

Overall, then, ITC is associated in the data from this study with better enterprise performance. On average, ITC enterprises increased their sales more and maintained higher levels of capital accumulation. In addition, in textiles in Kenya, and in comparison with CFG in

Gabon, ITC enterprises had significantly greater employment effects during the period analysed – and, at least in textiles, were more energetic at expanding linkage investments. Moreover, taking the two industries in Kenya, the most dynamic firms in each were ITC enterprises. In textiles, this was L2, with its high growth rates, investments overseas, capacity to penetrate the West European market and employment thrust; this enterprise showed its technological capacity in 1980 by reproducing on its own, and at a quarter the capital outlay, polyester filament yarn facilities which the government was building with foreign technology elsewhere in the country. In wood manufacturing, this was P1, with its high growth rates, consistent profitability and buoyant employment: as of the end of 1980, its sales were slightly higher than P3's, and its profits were much healthier, while its capital employed was one-third that of P3. This enterprise, moreover, had also shown its technological capability, by outcompeting foreign plywood enterprises who were negotiating with the Kenyan government to produce plywood from the Transmara forests: P1 persuaded the government it had the expertise in Kenya to do so on its own – and established a subsidiary, Veneers Kenya Ltd, which has successfully done so.

THE IMPEDIMENTS TO ITC

The previous section has documented the significant extent of ITC in two Kenyan industries, and has suggested the positive impact of ITC on enterprise performance. Yet Kenya, like most developing countries, remains dependent on foreign technology sources in most of its industrial sectors. Is there evidence from this research that helps explain the impediments to ITC that clearly exist in the country?

The survey results reviewed above indicated that the foreign subsidiaries in the textile industry, though they were among the earliest textile enterprises established in Kenya, remained highly dependent technologically as of fifteen to seventeen years later. The CFG in Gabon suggests the same point – overseas ownership by multinational corporations, precisely because it offers such easy continuing access to technology from abroad, inhibits indigenous technological development. Not only is such development usually unnecessary because products and processes are available via the parent, but the parent itself often imposes various controls and pressures that establish its dominance in all key technological decisions (see Langdon, 1981a, pp. 102–3).

This is, of course, a familiar argument by now – that a powerful mnc presence blocks indigenous technological development. But it might as easily be argued that the lack of ITC is what spurs the mnc presence. It is in assessing such counter-arguments that the material reviewed above can also be useful. For the evolution of the Kenyan textile industry shows that by 1970–3 there were growing and viable local enterprises, exhibiting considerable ITC, around which the Kenyan government could have organised a large-scale expansion in the industry. Instead, via a series of detailed negotiations, that government provided major concessions to foreign enterprises to set up three large new textile operations in the country. These were the three enterprises (S1, S3 and S4) that were such colossal disasters that the state had to rescue each of them and absorb large losses within a few years of their start-up. All this suggests that something other than bowing to the inevitable was involved in Kenya's continuing dependence on mncs – particularly since in the Transmara plywood case the government *was* persuaded to use local enterprise rather than draw in a foreign technology partner.

The interplay of a number of factors seems to be involved: pressures emanating from Western European enterprises themselves, based in turn on restructuring patterns affecting given industries there; efforts within developing countries to move painlessly to export manufacturing rather than import substitution; close relations that have developed between state personnel and foreign enterprises in Kenya; and domestic political economy relations that affect the role allowed certain local entrepreneurs. Each of these can be reviewed in turn.

Restructuring of production patterns was common in various Western European industries throughout the 1970–80 period; and these patterns set in motion different sorts of international investment and technology transfer pressures emanating from those industries. In the case of plywood manufacturing, for instance, import increases from South East Asia hit West European producers very hard; some, such as the major French manufacturers (Leroy and Rougier), simply absorbed large losses that made them weak and vulnerable; while others like Bruynzeel in the Netherlands restructured their production into more specialised and sophisticated plywood, modernised their equipment in a massive way, and shut down production of standard plywood. This restructuring opened opportunities for European enterprises to try to supply standardised plywood in other ways, and some enterprises accordingly drove ahead with new plywood investments in West African countries with excellent wood resources (such as

Liberia); other plywood multinationals, like Bruynzeel, followed a more careful strategy – getting some increased supplies of standard plywood from African investments like CFG, but also (in Bruynzeel's case) organising facilities to supply special veneers (from the Congo) to facilitate specialised production in Western Europe.

Thus, in the plywood case, restructuring in Europe accelerated European investment and technology transfer activities in the African wood manufacturing industry. But this pressure was concentrated in West Africa where good wood resources were available; it was relatively modest in its scope because the wood industry in Western Europe was relatively small, and few real wood mncs existed; and, in any event, since a firm like Bruynzeel was aiming through its investments to supply its crucial marketing and production needs in Europe, it had every incentive to select the most efficient and effective technology for its African associates. This incentive undoubtedly worked against the growth of ITC in those associates (as in the CFG case), but it also made unlikely the kinds of disasters experienced from foreign technology transfers in Kenyan textiles. As for the Kenyan wood industry, it was largely unaffected by this whole process, since abundant wood resources were not evident compared with West Africa. Thus one of the reasons the plywood industry in Kenya developed via local ownership and much ITC was precisely because there was no pressure from European enterprises to the contrary; the foreign alternative the government had been looking at in the Transmara forest case was an India-based enterprise, and it could clearly not mount much pressure to push its interests.

The situation was very different in textiles. The same restructuring presures hit the textile industry. But although a few French textile enterprises for a brief period saw a potential role for exports from their African subsidiaries back to Europe, and invested in certain Ivorian projects accordingly, that was not the general pattern that resulted. Rather, there was massive retrenchment of the textile industry in Western Europe, and the consequent emergence of considerable excess capacity – of textile machinery, of textile machinery manufacturing facilities, and of textile technical and managerial manpower.

This excess capacity was then marketed throughout Africa, some of it organised by European textile mncs (as in the case of Lonhro's David Whitehead group which set up S3 in Kenya, plus other enterprises elsewhere), but much of it organised by small-scale European entrepreneurs (as in the cases of S1 and S4 in Kenya). It is fair to say, in many of these cases, that the major incentive was to dispose of the most excess capacity possible, at the best price possible, earning returns that way, as public capital was pulled in to provide financing; of less concern was the long-run viability of the resulting enterprise as a key factor in ongoing corporate planning.

This is a recipe for the worst kind of foreign technological dependence possible, and it is not surprising that both over-building of facilities and disposal of inefficient older equipment should result. The key point to stress is that the whole pattern meant there was considerable pressure on Kenya to rely on Western European technological sources to expand the Kenyan textile industry in the 1970s – unlike the case for the plywood industry in the country.

But there was more to what happened in Kenya than that. For the Kenyan authorities clearly welcomed and encouraged this foreign interest. In part, this was for all the traditional reasons that developing countries commonly welcome foreign investment – expecting it to contribute foreign exchange, expand employment and supply missing managerial and technological knowledge; especially in the early 1970s, scepticism regarding foreign investment was uncommon in many African economies. Partly, too, there were mutual potential benefits that state decision-makers and overseas investors could share; in earlier research, I have stressed the symbiosis or mutual pattern of benefits that often emerged between African insiders in the Kenyan political economy and the mnc sector – oriented around regulatory privileges for the mncs, and minority shares, directorships and other favours for the insiders. There is no reason to believe such symbiosis was not a factor in the textile case in Kenya, too.

Another critical factor, however, was the Kenyan effort to develop export manufacturing in their industrial sector. As early as the 1974–8 Development Plan, this theme began to be stressed in Kenyan economic policy statements; and as export manufacturing became the new orthodoxy in mainstream development economics in the 1970s, the theme was emphasised more and more in Kenya. There are, though, several paths to such export industrialisation. One is to reduce import protection, enforce more efficiency on domestic industry, and provide aid and incentives for those firms that can achieve greater efficiency to expand their manufactured exports. This is a hard strategy to enforce in a political economy where protected domestic-based industry is politically powerful – and such was the case in Kenya. Again and again, Kenyan economic spokesmen have announced moves to cut protectionism – and again and again have had to retreat as the threatened forces mobilised to resist. So an easier route to export success has been sought. Kenya accepted the arguments of foreign enter-prises that they could be the shortcut to export success – and was accordingly prepared to give all manner of privileges to foreign entre-preneurs who promised to penetrate the European export market. This was a crucial leverage which the foreign textile entrepreneurs used in 1973–5 in Kenya to win their way in their detailed negotiations with the Kenyan state. All promised major exports in the European market – and the fact they were European-based added to their arguments that they could succeed.

This painless path to export success, of course, proved illusory. None of the three firms established achieved long-run export markets in Europe, and their ultimately massive losses were exceedingly painful for Kenya. But this interplay of attitudes and arguments was impor-tant in explaining why the Kenyan state relied on dependent technol-ogy instead of encouraging ITC enterprises in this industry. It might be argued that an export manufacturing strategy itself, then, is an impedi-ment to ITC. But the evidence from this case does not support that view; in textiles the only enterprises to achieve European market penetration successfully were L1 and L2, both ITC enterprises. Not only were export efforts and ITC not incompatible; but this example may even suggest that ITC contributes significantly to the success of such export efforts – by giving enterprises that capacity to vary pro-cesses efficiently to find lowest possible costs per unit, and to vary de-signs and product-mix quickly in response to demand shifts in that export market.

There remains one critical reality to stress in the Kenyan political economy. As noted earlier, six of the seven ITC enterprises identified in this study were Kenyan-Asian-owned – and the seventh was a public company without many Africans publicly involved in its direction. The non-African character of these enterprises inevitably was a factor, in a country with Kenya's past of racial differentiation of privileges, in the state's reluctance to rely on such firms and to turn instead to overseas alternatives. The evidence from this analysis suggests this course was costly for Kenya; and the reliance eventually on P1 for the Transmara plywood development suggests discrimination against Asian firms was not inevitable. But such discrimination does remain an impediment to ITC in Kenya.

CONCLUSION

This case study has examined ITC in two industries in Africa – textile production and wood manufacturing. ITC has been assessed in terms of freedom from overseas technology dependence, in past development and present operations, and of internal capacity to undertake new developments without such technology links abroad. And considered in this way, both industries in Kenya demonstrated such ITC in a number of enterprises – developed usually via learning-by-doing from small beginnings, and strengthened by direct managerial and technical experience overseas. This ITC, in turn, has been seen to shape higher growth rates and more consistent profitability in domestic enterprises – plus, on balance, a better record in employment and linkage effects.

This all suggests the possibility and desirability of developing ITC in a country like Kenya; and it suggests routes by which encouragement of ITC might be promoted – including support for small-scale domestic firms to learn-by-doing (rather than privileges for foreign technology projects), and mechanisms by which to support periodic enterprise learning experiences for Kenyan managers and technicians overseas. But, as section three suggests, such policy thrusts face many impediments in African countries. Pressures are powerful from overseas technology sources, both private and public; through relying on them the interests of some public policy-makers in Africa become entangled with those foreign pressures; the illusions of an easy route to manufactured exports contribute to such symbiosis; and the origins of local (Asian) industrialists may sometimes lead, as in Kenya, to state support for other foreign alternatives to them. This all suggests that movement toward an ITC industrial strategy in Africa, though feasible, requires major political shifts to make it likely. The growing economic crisis across the continent of Africa provides pressure towards such a movement, but the international and domestic forces threatened by this are powerful and effective, and change will not come easily – despite the evidence from studies like this that such changes could be beneficial to Africa's economic future.

REFERENCES

Langdon, S. W. (1981a) *Multinational Corporations in the Political Economy of Kenya.* London: Macmillan.

Langdon, S. W. (1981b) 'North/South, East and West: European Industries Restructuring in a Changing World Economy', *International Journal,* Autumn.

Langdon, S. W. (forthcoming) 'Industrial Dependence and Export Manufacturing in Kenya', in T. Shaw and J. Aluko (eds), *Africa Projected: from Dependence to Self-Reliance by the Year 2000?* London: Macmillan.

Mytelka, L. K. (1978) 'Licensing and Technological Dependence in the Andrean Pact', *World Development,* 6.

Mytelka, L. K. (1981) 'Crisis and Adjustment in the French Textile Industry', in H. Jacobson and D. Sidjanski (eds), *The Emerging Economic Order.* Beverley Hills: Sage.

Facilitating an Indigenous Social Organisation of Production in Tanzania

Jens Müller

INTRODUCTION

Twice within a time span of less than 100 years the Tanzanian social formation was drastically reorganised, and in each case an emerging indigenous technological capability was drastically reduced. The first setback was effected by the German colonisation (about 1890) which marked the start of a process of liquidation of the craftsmanship within the society. The second setback was brought about as a result of the post-colonial attempts at socialist transformation initiated in 1967 and formulated in the Arusha Declaration. A consequence of the latter overall policy change was that practically the whole entrepreneurial class (of Asian origin) was proclaimed an enemy of the workers and peasants and therefore restricted in many ways in its technological development endeavour.

This paper briefly analyses these two 'events' and their effects on the present technological capability of the society. It is demonstrated that the social carriers of the 'original' capability, that is the craftsmen and the entrepreneurs, are still at work, but diminishing in importance to a point where they may disappear. They are being replaced by a cadre of industrial managers and engineers within the state-owned or joint-venture enterprises which almost exclusively rely on imported technology.

The result is that the Tanzanian society is undergoing a process in which its indigenous technological capability is steadily declining. Instead of trying to adapt and modify the imported technology to the social and cultural requirements and norms, it can be argued that the society is being adapted and modified to the 'requirements' of the

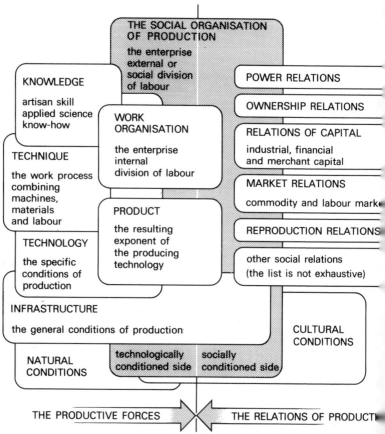

FIGURE 5   *Conceptual framework for the analysis of technology and society relations*

foreign technology, or as it turns out, to the requirements of the socia carriers of that technology.[1]

In this situation, therefore, the task of facilitating an indigenou technological capability appears to be almost insurmountable unles the process of liquidation of the existing indigenous capability i stopped. At best it is futile to facilitate something that at the same time is leaking away. The ancient Greek myth about the vessel of the Danaides tells us this.

The conceptual framework of this paper is for the sake of brevity illustrated in Figure 5. It can be seen that the social organisation of pro duction is placed as an intermediary concept which, so to speak bridges the gap between technology and society.[2]

LIQUIDATION OF THE VILLAGE CRAFT

Recent investigations and tests indicate that iron was excavated, smelted and forged in North Western Tanzania as far back as 500 BC,[3] which means that blacksmiths had definitely been at work before Arab and European intrusion. The early European explorers of East Africa tell of powerful and prosperous kingdoms where much of the reason for this power and wealth was their mastery of the technology of iron. A German lieutenant reported in 1892 that he had estimated the number of hoes annually traded at the Tabora market, the main centre for inland trading at that time, to be 150,000.[4] This corresponds to the production of the Chinese farm-implement factory in Dar es Salaam eighty years later! From the area on the East shores of Lake Victoria we are told that 20 hoes were traded for 35 pounds of ivory. Hoes were a regular means of barter around the lake. In fact the reports about iron smelting and forging are so numerous from practically all corners of the territory that it has been suggested that we should correct our perception of 'pre-colonial' being equated with 'pre-industrial'.

This suggestion probably takes the argument too far, since industrialisation usually relates to a stage where machines are replacing hand-tools. However, the observation remains that the pre-colonial social division of labour had reached a fairly high level, corresponding to a technology of the village craftsmen which seems to have been in a process of fairly rapid development. Not only had the iron trade been included in the territorial division of labour but also the cotton-weaving and leather-tanning trades as well as the exchange of pottery, baskets, mats and salt. A production of surplus food also took place, at least along the trading routes. In short we get a picture of an indigenous technological capability in a process of development, gradually facilitating a restructuring of the social organisation of production. An infrastructure of trading routes and markets was emerging and the population was probably on the increase.

Another impetus to this development was the Arab traders, who also brought in a demand for slaves from the emerging plantations in Zanzibar and elsewhere. This trade unquestionably brought some social disturbance to the territory, but not the social disaster and population decline we have generally been made to believe. The picture of the pre-colonial East African 'as either a violent, war-crazed individual or his hapless victim' has to be rejected.[5]

The real social disaster at the turn of the century was effected by the German colonisation and the British follow-up. Cattle and human diseases were perhaps the immediate cause of the population decline, but the simultaneous breakdown of the social organisation of production and the consequent arrest of the indigenous technological development also played a major and longer-lasting part.

In this paper I can give only a few examples of what actually happened.[6] All productive activities other than those of export crop extraction and strictly subsistence production were regarded as 'unproductive'. It was looked upon as a waste of labour to make iron tools, cotton cloths or domestic foodstuff for the neighbouring districts. Therefore, inter-district trade was banned, thus smashing the territorial division of labour. The bale of cotton spun for home consumption was not only regarded as waste of labour, but also of raw materials for the export market.

The German and later the British colonial authorities actually forbade the blacksmiths' trade in many districts of the country. In cases where the smiths defied the ban and were discovered for the second time by the district authorities, their tools were confiscated. By two independent sources in two different districts I was even told of the penalty of amputation of an arm in the case of a third discovery. The smiths were mastering the technology of gunmaking, which perhaps explains these sentences.

But these, largely administrative, measures to sabotage the trade of the blacksmiths were only partly successful. The smiths withdrew into hiding in the forests and swamps. Thus, to most observers later it looked as if they had completely disappeared. In a UN report of 1975 we read:

> At present there is no worthwhile village/small scale industry which can undertake manufacture of hand tools and manually operated machinery in appreciable numbers. Due to the conspicuous absence of the traditional artisans and basic workshop tools, with the existing skills and resources, only very limited quantities of crude hand tool of poor quality can be manufactured.[7]

Yet, piecing together bits of statistical and oral information supplemented by check-up survey trips in eight Northern and Southern regions of Tanzania in 1976 and 1977 gave reason to estimate the present number of rural metal-working craftsmen to be as many as 40,000 out of a rural population of 14 million. The survey also contradicted the last part of the above statement. The hand-tools, mainly hoes, that the blacksmiths turn out might be crude, but they are certainly not of poor quality. They are much preferred by the peasants to the mass-produced items, both for their durability and their suitability to the varying soil conditions and crops. The peasants often take the 'modern' hoes to the blacksmiths to have them modified and repaired. The output capacity of the blacksmiths in the 1970s was of the order of half a million hoes annually, still more than was turned out from the Chinese farm-implement factory in Dar es Salaam. Even today their repair capacity is still valuable, particularly in areas where ox-drawn agricultural implements are being introduced.

On the other hand, the number of blacksmiths in the UN report is now steadily declining to a point where the statement above is likely to become true. The snag is that there is a world of difference between the remedial action required to consolidate a trade that is already an indigenous part of the society, and the action required if you have to start from scratch. But whatever the assumption is about the present situation, it is imperative to understand what made the thing you want to promote disappear in the past.

Continuing to use the blacksmiths as a case in point the following questions have to be answered: (a) What made many blacksmiths continue their trade in spite of their illegal status during the colonial period? (b) What makes many blacksmiths disappear now they apparently have become legalised, or at least not illegal, after Independence, and in spite of a declared willingness to promote indigenous technology?

In answering the first question we should note that the blacksmiths' activities were so deeply integrated in and significant to the cultural life of the villages that the administrative ban by the colonial authorities couldn't stop them effectively. Further, the rural population was dependent on the supply of tools to subsistence agriculture for its survival. And finally, the technology of the smiths had not reached a point where it required infrastructural support. The smiths could still excavate and smelt their raw materials, their tools were completely 'homemade', and their marketing channels were not completely cut off in spite of the inter-district trading ban. On the other hand, the technology did not develop either: little development in agricultural technology took place; so little demand for improved products was at hand. We may also argue the other way round, that because the smiths were arrested in their development, little agricultural development could take place. However, either way, any further development of the technology of the blacksmiths would have required a change in the social division of labour, in a direction that could have supported innovations, supply of better tools and raw materials as well as better marketing facilities.

One couldn't expect the situation to change immediately after Independence. However, when some change did start to penetrate the rural scene it was in a direction that was directly detrimental to the requirements of the blacksmiths. For convenience I shall postpone the detailed explanation of this point and an answer to the second question above, since it ties in with the setback of the other indigenous technological development trend presented in the next section.

CHECKING THE INDIGENOUS INDUSTRIAL BOURGEOISIE

The arrested indigenous production activities of the village craftsmen in the early colonial period were superseded by another trend in what gradually was to become an indigenous technological development. This development was closely tied to the export crop sectors: cotton-ginning, sisal-decortication, coffee-pulping, sugar-refining, tobacco-curing, saw-milling, etc. The main direct agents of these processing activities were of Asian origin. Initially they were assigned the role in the social division of labour as trading intermediaries between the primary producers and the ports of exportation. They were not allowed to own land for agricultural production, so it became an obvious thing for these merchants to invest some of their surplus in primary processing.

The machinery for this processing was imported from Europe. It was of a type that could be run with some mechanical engineering insight and without very much infrastructural support. Moreover, the technology thus transferred was relatively easy to maintain, copy and adapt. The knowledge component was not based on 'high' science, but rather on accumulated empirical experience and simple know-how. The internal division of labour was straightforward, the owner being his own managing director and probably also production engineer commanding a couple of foremen who supervised the horizontally divided unskilled labourers. The socially conditioned side of this division went along racial lines, the foremen and upwards in the hierachy being Asians, the rest being Africans.

This setting fitted perfectly with the external division of labour imposed by the colonial government, and it developed over time to a point where the technology became indigenous seen from most angles and so did the social organisation of production. As the home market for consumer commodities gradually developed, the same Asian entrepreneurs were naturally the first to invest, sometimes jointly with European investors, until they grew in size and influence into being a veritable industrial bourgeoisie which to all intents and purposes could be labelled indigenous as well.

When the British at Independence in 1961 handed over the formal power to a government mainly based on the Tanganyika African National Union (TANU), it soon became apparent that much of the real power rested with the industrial bourgeoisie. An attempt was made to counteract this situation by formation of the National Development Corporation (NDC), which on behalf of the government was to either invest on its own or in joint ventures with foreign investors. For a number of reasons such investors did not come forward to a sufficient extent. This is probably part of the reason for the drastic policy change initiated in 1967 and formulated in the Arusha Declaration. The change was towards self-reliance and socialism. It implied nationalisation of banks and gradually of many industries, as well as establishment of state enterprises. The indigenous industrial bourgeoisie was proclaimed the class enemy of the workers and peasants, and where not directly checked through nationalisation it was restricted by a number of legislative means. Its indigenous technological capability was not facilitated any further. On the contrary, it was actively frustrated.

Whereas the number of medium-sized firms stabilised around 350, thus indicating that the indigenous entrepreneurs were still at work, the large-scale state enterprise sector grew by about 50 per cent to around 120 in 1972 before the world economic crisis also meant stagnation in this sector. In the period of expansion the social division of labour was changing in favour of the state sector, the most significant change probably being that the state took over much of the trading, through the State Trading Corporation and later the Regional Trading Companies as far as wholesale was concerned, and through promotion of co-operative retail shops. Other infrastructural arrangements were also directed towards the requirements of the large enterprises.

CONTRADICTIONS OF THE INTERNAL VERSUS THE EXTERNAL ORGANISATION OF PRODUCTION

In this section I shall briefly discuss and illustrate the contradictions that the state enterprise sector has experienced in its move towards a socialist-orientated industrialisation by means of an imported technology mainly of capitalist extraction.

First we have to note that TANU and the government, both at the ideological level and at the level of practical decision-making, of course had internal differences in interpreting what a socialist transformation is about. These differences were also mirrored in the group of directors and managers who were charged with building up the state enterprises. By and large suffices it here to look at this group and their civil servant colleagues, the state bureaucracy or state class, as divided into two factions, a progressive faction with an open outlook towards socialist reforms, and another, call it conservative, faction.

With a few exceptions, one of which I mention below, most of the technology employed in the nationalised and new state enterprises was transferred from the capitalist industrial countries. Incidentally, what is transferred is usually only the technique and the work organisation components of the technologies in question, whereas the knowledge component often remains either patented, embodied in the machines or rests with the foreign technicians. Here the transfer of work organisation is of interest, because when a whole plant is transferred both the technically conditioned side and the socially conditioned side of the internal division of labour are usually established in a similar form to that in its country of origin. As discussed earlier, there is not much to be done about the technically conditioned side, at least not immediately; if it is changed the technique stops functioning. But whether or not the manager wears a necktie, the production engineer a particular cap, the typist-girls high heels, or the floor-sweeper-girls low heels, etc., the technique will function.

This fact was originally recognised by the then most powerful, progressive faction headed by the president. In 1970 a presidential circular was issued on the construction of workers' councils, executive boards and boards of directors.[8] It was established that besides party cells and union committees, the workers through their councils should be represented in the various managements boards, thus participating in deciding the details of the work organisation and having economic planning insights. In other words, an attempt to break and restructure the vertical division of labour of capitalist design was made, with possible consequences for the horizontal division of labour.

The circular was followed up in 1971 with a set of more detailed guidelines from TANU. This contained a call for the workers to be watchful against mismanaging managers and discrimination. The guidelines resulted in a number of confrontations, strikes, factory occupations, of lock-ups of directors, etc. – and invariably in drop of production output. This gave the conservative faction the opportunity to intervene and counteract the progressive faction. Strikes in state-owned enterprises? Income loss in the very enterprises which had been instructed to show a profit? The press was filled with exhortative observations telling the workers that they had misinterpreted the guidelines.

Hereafter the conservative faction little by little took the lead. They could use the imported technology as a 'weapon'. The workers had so little grasp of the production techniques that most of them were dispensable. They had only secondary functions, the machines the primary function. It was relatively easy to divide-and-conquer and to dilute workers' influence back to the soap-and-towel democracy of the original plant designs.

Now it had been settled who was the boss of production another tendency could be observed – the sacking of inefficient managers. And their inefficiency was solely measured by the rate of profit or perhaps rather of loss which the enterprise would make. If someone was not capable of managing his firm according to strict businesslike principles, he was removed. One can sympathise with this tendency to some extent. However it completely cuts off the possibility of allowing for a change in the social division of labour in a direction where some enterprises are, for example, given the role of fostering an indigenous technological development.

The farm-implement factory in Dar es Salaam illuminates this argument. The name of the enterprise is Ubungo Farm Implement Manufacturing Company (UFI) and it was built and equipped by the People's Republic of China. The company became a member of the NDC group of enterprises in 1968, and soon after it had started production it was completely taken over by Tanzanian management.

The factory was fitted to produce a wide range of hand-tools, animal-drawn implements, and hand-operated processing machines. The production line was multi-purpose and versatile. Potentially, such a plant is conducive to the generation of innovations and adaptions for the ultimate benefit of the users of its products, but also for the workers, as they can gain useful experience and training. If allowed to exploit this potential, the plant could thus become more than just an import-substitution project: it could make a contribution to the technological capability of the country in general and to the agricultural development in particular.

The production capacity of the factory was announced to be equivalent to 800,000 hoes and 8,000 ploughs annually. This way of calculating the capacity may be appropriate in that the hoes could symbolise all kinds of hand-tools, and the ploughs all kinds of animal-drawn implements. However, UFI only did turn out standard hoes and ploughs, in trying to reach its capacity target. In other words, it was solely used as an import-substitution, mass-producing enterprise, not for innovations or adaptations or training, etc. Being an NDC subsidiary, UFI was primarily concerned with making a profit, and probably therefore turned to the production of products of highest and most secured exchange-value. Experiments in making other and perhaps improved use-values for agriculture were probably considered too costly.

UFI had many difficulties to begin with in getting anywhere near its capacity utilisation, but in 1975 it was announced that the enterprise would expand its capacity to 2.2 million hoes. In this connection it was said that the original lay-out of the factory would be changed. It was implied that the Chinese technology was 'wrong' and resulted in bottle-necks in the production flow. Now, with the aid of World Bank consultants, these bottle-necks would be removed. Interpreting these allegations of the inappropriateness of the Chinese technology the following may be deduced.

The Chinese had transferred their technology more or less directly. This technology used a knowledge, technique and work organisation, and turned out products, exactly as it would do in China. Let us call it a Chinese technology. This technology fitted the social division of labour in China where the profitability or exchange-value aspect of production is (or was) not in the forefront. The lay-out or the internal division of labour was not designed for import substitution and mass-production in the first place. Indentally, UFI was the first factory to establish a workers' council according to the before mentioned presidential circular, and was to form a model for the other state enterprises. However, as the NDC profitability criterion was imposed on the management, the originally intended product-mix was altered. The management thus changed the internal division of labour away from the original, but had difficulties with the technique. Therefore, when the expansion of the plant was planned, the technique was changed in accordance with the required division of labour and product-mix. We may say that the technology was changed from being Chinese to becoming a technology that fitted the external or social division of labour. Although caution is needed in labelling any types of technology, in a sense we may call the new UFI technology a capitalist technology.

THE DILEMMA OF FACILITATING AN INDIGENOUS TECHNOLOGICAL CAPABILITY

The village blacksmiths' trade is undergoing a process of liquidation, the entrepreneurial capability and 'spirit' of the industrial bourgeoisie is being checked, the state enterprises are blocking genuine workers' participation in production and an internal division of labour conducive to increased technological capability. In this situation, how can an indigenous technological capability be facilitated?

As stated in the introduction, I argue that a first step must be to liquidate, check or block the processes that de-facilitate an indigenous technological development. It may of course be decided to focus on only one of these processes and forget about the other two. However, as I conclude in this final section, it appears that the 'remedy' essentially is the same for all the three processes.

Let us take first the *blacksmiths* and the *village craft* and *small industries*. To stop their liquidation requires changes at three levels at least. Most of the required changes can be referred to as changes in the social division of labour.

(1) At the ideological level the blacksmiths' potential contribution to the technological development of the country has to be acknowledged. The state class at large must change their ideologically biased perception away from regarding the blacksmiths as inherently backward and lazy, and towards recognising them as skilled and industrious.[9] Only then can purposeful programmes for the consolidation of their trade be put into action. As it is now, only conventional top-to-bottom, direct support 'development programmes' are socio-politically feasible (although seldom economically feasible). For example, even simple tools and raw-materials assistance, which are the only immediate requirements of the smiths, cannot be 'given' without assignment of 'experts' to train the smiths in smithing, as if they didn't know that already, or to instruct them in product development, as if one knew better than the smiths (who are agriculturalists themselves) what shape of hoe or plough is optimal for the soils and crops of their home areas. The point is that only after the process of liquidation has been stopped, are training and product development required.

(2) At the industrial policy level, some of the market has to be assigned to the craftsmen, if for nothing else, to preserve their vital repair and adaptation capacity which should be regarded as an infrastructural element in support of agricultural technological development. The large industries may even have to provide the smiths with

semi-finished items, which the smiths can complete and give the shape of highest use-value in their respective areas. The large industries would thus become sub-contractors to the small industries.

(3) At the infrastructural policy level many more investments have to be made in the rural areas. As it is now, even the past levels of services seem to have deteriorated. At least, compared with what investments are directed towards the needs of the state enterprises, the gap in services provided to the small and the large industries is certainly widening. Apart from that, the case of the village blacksmiths has shown that they are already exploiting the local conditions to the fullest extent, and that no further technology of any noteworthy kind can make their productivity or output increase unless the local conditions are improved. And the craftsmen even have the capability of developing their technology if the local conditions should improve.

Perhaps it should be stated clearly that all the above suggested changes in the social division of labour are not argued for the sake of consolidating some 40,000 village metal-working people. The argument is that their indigenous technological capability is of vital importance for the agricultural production of the country, which is still mainly of the smallholder peasant farming type. Moreover, the changes proposed in (1) and (3) would be of direct benefit for the peasants themselves and would facilitate their technological capability as well as that of the village craftsmen.

A final question concerning the blacksmiths might need an answer: Why are they not able to withstand their present liquidation? They 'survived' the colonial harassment. Can't they once again hide in the swamps or forests? The answer is, of course, no. The economy seems to be penetrated by the state to such an extent that there is no hiding any more. Hiding means dying. Although subsistence farming prevails, it doesn't possess the same 'autonomous' properties and conditions of production as before. The socialisation of the production processes seems to have passed the point of no return.

As far as *the industrial bourgeoisie* is concerned, the way of re-employing their indigenous technological capability is more straightforward. They are still there in considerable number and all they need is an assured role in the social division of labour, one that will re-encourage their entrepreneurial 'spirit'. There are certainly signs of a new found awareness on the part of the government that the particular technology of the existing medium-sized enterprises could be a valuable asset. For example, it was announced in 1978 that the Industrial Licensing Act would be amended, so that it will be easier to get licences at the regional level. It has also been proposed by a high-powered governmental committee that a clarification of 'the owner-ship issue' should be considered. This issue is of course about the fear of nationalisation on the part of the Asian private capitalists. It may be expected that the issue will be solved by some kind of state assurance, that private capitalists will be allowed to operate within certain limits determined by size of investment, number of employed, and share in the national market. Talking to some Asians in early 1978 left me with the impression that their optimism indeed was growing.

So far we can only guess at what has brought about this change. Either the state class feels confident of being able to control the indust-rial bourgeoisie, or, being in a shaky, transitional position itself, might seek an alliance or even eventually merge with it.

Summing up, it is evident that the internal division of labour of pri-vate capitalist enterprises does not match very well with a socialist ex-ternal division of labour. Ultimately the contradiction will be solved by a change in either the former or the latter, and until such time we can expect a slow-down in technological development, either indigenous or otherwise.

As regards the *state enterprises,* the trend seems to be towards a con-tinuation of transfer of foreign technology, that is foreign knowledge, foreign technique and foreign work organisation, all of which amalga-mate in foreign products. These products, to the extent that they are used as input into subsequent production cycles, carry their charac-teristics of 'foreignness' with them into these cycles. In turn, the foreign technology requires or seems to 'demand' a social organisation of production which may be called foreign as well in the sense that it is matching the technology of foreign extraction. According to my thesis, the social organisation of production eventually 'actuates' the social relations of production, for example the power relations, ownership relations, market relations and ultimately the class relations.

This very mechanistic exposition of cause and effect should certainly not be regarded as a rigid technological determinism. We may get the impression that it is the foreign technology as such that causes the so-cial relations of production to change. It could be interpreted, as has been done by some development theorists recently, that import of capitalist technology invariably leads to capitalist relations of produc-tion.[10] The technology is thus inextricably connected with the relations of production of its country of origin. That is, if you want to facilitate a socialist transformation in the relations of production, don't import capitalist technology!

But I do not hold with labelling technology as either capitalist or appropriate or the like, precisely because it may lead to all kinds of deterministic interpretations or misconceptions. And I do not adhere to the thesis of contagious technologies.

In the case of the state enterprises of Tanzania, we have seen that an analysis of the class struggle at the particular period in question has to be superimposed upon the analysis of the technological development. It was demonstrated that the workers' attempt to influence the internal division of labour of the enterprises failed. Had they succeeded, the situation would have changed and the technology would have possibly been changed. Had the progressive faction had the power, the original internal division of labour of the Chinese factory would have possibly not been changed. In other words, the technology should be regarded as a means by which the most powerful social classes can influence the social division of labour and thus the relations of production according to their interests.

A change away from foreign influence on technological development, towards an indigenous influence, apart from a change in technology, would require a change towards establishing an indigenous social division of labour. The dilemma of Tanzania is that neither the indigenous nor the foreign-orientated potential carriers of technology are of socialist inclination. Everybody seems to be trapped – which may explain why the technological development in any direction appears to have stagnated.

In conclusion, I hold that until the class struggle has been decided in one or the other direction, very little will happen. The most expedient way of facilitating an indigenous technological capability at present seems to be to opt for a social organisation of production that is as 'indigenous' as possible. This implies a reorientation towards a true capitalist division of labour where the market directs the resource allocation. Most of the village blacksmiths would probably be totally liquidated, but a few could succeed and employ the others. Some of the medium-sized enterprises will grow bigger and perhaps merge with the state enterprises, others will remain at their stage of stagnation, and the rest will disappear. The conservative faction will merge with the industrial bourgeoisie and become part of it and possibly wrest the ownership and the control from the state. The progressive faction will either become conservative or 'die'. Over time, the technology of the country will become indigenous.

Perhaps the progressive faction and the industrial workers should wait until the above drama has matured. Perhaps the attempt to shortcut a period of capitalist accumulation is in effect not possible? One thing seems clear to me: a short-cut, should it succeed, is only practicable by establishment of such a strong socialist planned social organisation of production that it gradually forces the work organisation component of the technology to change towards a socialist division of labour. If this is done, the other components of technology, that is, knowledge, technique, and product, will eventually change in shape and contents.

There is a last observation about the village blacksmiths, who after all have been the focus of this paper. The social carriers of technology who at present are most susceptible to being integrated in a socialist transformation process, are these blacksmiths or village craftsmen. Evidence has shown that they are quite ready to change their internal division of labour into some type of collective producer groups, given the right incentives. We may also say that their internal division of labour is at such a low level of development that they are more open to radical changes in the social division of labour than both the medium- and the large-scale enterprises. In fact, almost the only way to effectively enlist their technological potential for development is a centrally planned and carefully assigned role in the social division of labour.

NOTES

1. The social-carriers concept is not discussed here. I refer to Charles and Olle Edqvist, *Social Carriers of Techniques for Development*, SAREC report R3, 1970.
2. For a more extensive exposition of this definitional exposition, see Jens Müller, *Liquidation or Consolidation of Indigenous Technology. A Study of the Changing Conditions of Production of Village Blacksmiths in Tanzania* (Aalborg University Press, 1980). (Distribution outside Denmark: Scandinavian Institute of African Studies, Uppsala.)
3. Peter Smith and D. H. Avery, 'Complex Iron Smelting and Prehistoric Culture in Tanzania', *Science*, vol. 201, no. 4361 (1978).
4. Much of the pre-colonial records of this chapter are quoted or inspired by Helge Kjekshus, *Ecology Control and Economic Development in East African History* (London: Heinemann, 1977).
5. Kjekshus, *Ecology Control and Economic Development*.
6. Müller, *Liquidation or Consolidation*.
7. Koka Kesava Rao, 'Report on Agricultural Implements and Machinery Production and Maintenance', FAO/UNIDO project URT/74/006/A/OL/12, Dar es Salaam, 1975,
8. The full text is in Henry Mapolu (ed.), *Workers and Management*, Tanzanian Studies no. 4 (Dar es Salaam: Tanzania Publishing House, 1976). Much of section 4 in this paper is inspired by this publication.

9. A fuller explanation of the ideological bias of the state class is in *Liquidation or Consolidation*.

10. See, for example, Samir Amin, 'The Transfer of Technology', UN African Institute for Economic Development and Planning, Dakar, March 1976 (reproduction/394) p. 5. Or see, A. G. Frank, 'Long Live Transideological Enterprise! The Socialist Economies in the Capitalist International Division of Labor', *Review,* I, 1 (1977) p. 124.

A Select Bibliography*

Sheena Johnson

Amsden, A. (1977) 'The Division of Labour is Limited by the Type of Market: The case of the Taiwanese Machine Tool Industry', *World Development*, 217–34.

Arrow, K. J. (1962) 'The Economic Implications of Learning by Doing', *Review of Economic Studies*, 29, 155–73.

Behrman, J. and Fischer, W. (1980) *Overseas R&D Activities of Transnational Companies, Part II, Case Studies*. Cambridge, Mass: Oelgeschlager, Gunn and Hain.

Bell, M. (1979) 'The Exploitation of Indigenous Knowledge, or the Indigenous Exploitation of Knowledge: Whose Use of What for What?', *IDS Bulletin*, 10: 2.

Bell, M., Scott-Kemis, D. and Satyarakwit (1980) 'Limited Learning in Infant Industry: A Case Study'. Science Policy Research Unit, University of Sussex. (mimeo)

Beranek, W., and Ranis, G. (1978) *Science and Technology and Economic Development*. Praeger.

Bhatt, V. (1979) 'Indigenous Technology and Investment Licensing: The Case of Swaraj Tractor', *Journal of Development Studies*, 15: 4, July.

Binswanger, H. P., and Ruttan, H. V. (1978) *Induced Innovation: Technology, Institutions and Development*. Johns Hopkins University Press.

Blumenthal, T. (1979) 'A Note on the Relationship between Domestic Research and Development and Imports of Technology', *Economic Development and Cultural Change*, 27: 2.

Brown, M. (1978) 'Some International Issues in the Development of Local Engineering Capabilities', Industry and Technology Occasional Paper No. 28, OECD Development Centre, Paris.

Canitrot, A. (1978) 'Method for Evaluating the Significance of Macroeconomic Variables in the Analysis of Technology Incorporation Decisions', IDB/ECLA/UNDP/IDRC Research Program on S&T, WP 12, Buenos Aires.

Chijioke, M. O. (1980?) *The Guidelines for a Modern Relevant Education Towards Self-Reliance in Technology*. AIHTTR, Nairobi.

Chijioke, M. O. (1980?) *The Higher Educational Resources for Industry*. AIHTTR, Nairobi.

Clark, N. (1982) Notes for Edinburgh Conference on Technology and Development. Science Policy Research Unit, University of Sussex.

For further references see the bibliographies of the individual papers in this book.

Clayden, T. (1982) 'Indigenous Technological Capability and the Changing Pattern of Industrial Skill.' Paper given to Edinburgh Conference Facilitating Technological Capability.

Cooper, C. (1973) 'Choice of Techniques and Technological Change as Problems in Political Economy', reprinted from *International Social Science Journal*, 25: 3.

Cooper, C. M. (1981) 'Policy Intervention for Technological Innovations in Developing Countries', World Bank Staff Working Paper 441, Washington, DC.

Cooper, C. and Hoffman, K. (1981) 'Transactions in Technology: Implications for Developing Countries' (mimeo) SPRU.

Cortez, M. (1978) 'Argentina: Technical Development and Technology Exports to other LDC's'. Economics of Industry Division, World Bank.

Crane, D. (1977) 'Technological Innovation in Developing Countries: A Review of the Literature', *Research Policy* 6, 374–95.

Dahlman, C. J. and Cortes, M. (1982) 'Technology Exports for Mexico as a Starting Point in the Study of Technological Capability'. World Bank.

Dahlman, C. J. and Fonseca, F. V. (1978) 'From Technological Dependence to Technological Development: The Case of the Usiminas Steel Plant in Brazil', IDB/ECLA/UNDP/IDRC Research Program on S&T, WP 21, Buenos Aires.

Dahlman, C. J. and Westphal, L. E. (1981) 'Technological Effort in Industrial Development – An Interpretive Survey of Recent Research'. World Bank, Washington DC.

David, P. A. (1975) *Technical Change, Innovation and Economic Growth.* Cambridge University Press.

Desai, A. V. (1980) 'The Origin and Direction of Industrial R&D in India', *Research Policy*, 9, 74–96.

Desai, A. V. (1975) 'Research and Development in India', *Margin,* Quarterly Journal of National Council of Applied Economic Research, 7: 2

Donaldson, W. (1980) 'Enterprise and Innovation in an Indigenous Fishery: The Case of the Sultanate of Oman', *Development and Change,* 11: 3.

Eisemon, T. (1982) *The Profession of Science in Indian and Kenyan Universities.* NY: Praeger.

Erber, F. S. (1978) 'Technological Development and State Intervention: A Study of the Brazilian Capital Goods Industry'. D. Phil Dissertation, Univ. of Sussex.

Fajnzylber, F. (1979) 'Mexico: Capital Goods Program. Conception, Content and Achievement'. UNIDO, Seminar on Strategies for Development of the Capital Goods Sector, Argel.

Fajnzylber, F. (1979) 'The Role of Technology in Planning the Capital Goods Industry'. UNIDO Symposium on S&T in Development Planning, Mexico.

Fidel, J., Lucangeli, J. and Shepherd, P. (1978) 'The Argentine Cigarette Industry: Technological Profile and Behaviour', IDB/ECLA/UNDP/IDRC Research Programme on S&T, WP 7, Buenos Aires.

Filices, E. (1978) 'Development of Local Engineering Capacity for Industry: Case Study of Peru', Industry and Technology Occasional Paper No. 24, OECD Development Centre, Paris.

Forester, T. (ed) (1981) *The Microelectronics Revolution: The Complete*

Guide to the New Technology and its Impact on Society. Oxford: Basil Blackwell.

Francisco, S. (1978) *Science and Technology for Development:* Main Comparative Report on the STPI Project. International Development Research Centre, Ottawa, Canada.

Fransman, M. (1982) 'Learning and the Capital Goods Sector Under Free Trade: The Case of Hong Kong', *World Development,* vol. 10, no. 11.

Fransman, M. (1984) 'Promoting Technological Capability in the Capital Goods Sector: The Case of Singapore', *Research Policy* (forthcoming).

Freeman, C. (1974) *The Economics of Industrial Innovation.* ch. 2. Harmondsworth: Penguin Books.

Ghosh, S. (n.d.) 'A Review of the Literature in Technical Change – with special reference to developing countries', IDB/ECLA/UNDP/IDRC Research Program in S&T, WP 17, Buenos Aires.

Godfredsen, E. A. and Godfrey, M. (1979) 'Technical and Industrial Education Review Committee: Background Paper', The Ministry of Higher Education of the Republic of Kenya.

Ghymu, K. I. (1980) 'MNEs from the Third World', *Journal of International Business Studies,* Autumn.

Granick, D. (1967) *Soviet Metal-Fabricating and Economic Development – Practice versus Policy.* Univ. of Wisconsin Press.

Gustafsson, H. (1981) 'On-the-job Learning and Resource Allocation in Developing Countries: A Measurement Problem in Project Appraisal and a Proposal on its Solution'. Sussex.

Harvey, R. A. (1979) 'Learning in Production', *The Statistician,* 28: 1, 35, 39–57.

Herrera, A. (1973) 'Social Determinants of Science in Latin America: Explicit Science Policy and Implicit Science Policy', in Cooper, C. (ed.), *Science, Technology and Development'.* Frank Cass.

Hirschmann, W. B. (1964) 'Profit from the Learning Curve', *Harvard Business Review,* 42, 125–39.

Hollander, S. (1965) *The Sources of Increased Efficiency: A Study of Du Pont Rayon Plants.* Cambridge, Mass: MIT Press.

Hoppers, W. H. M. L. (1982) 'Apprenticeship in the Urban Informal Sector'. Manpower Research Unit, University of Zambia.

IDRC (1975) 'Science and Technology Policy Implementation in Less Developed Countries: methodological guidelines for STPI project'. IDRC, Ottawa.

Jacobsson, S. (1981) 'Electronics and the Technology Gap – The Case of Numerically Controlled Machine Tools'. Research Policy Institute, Univ. of Lund, Sweden.

Jacobsson, S. (1981) 'Strategy Problems in the Production of Numerically Controlled Lathes in Argentina'. Paper from workshop on Comparative Methodology in Studies of Technical Change, Research Policy Institute, Univ. of Lund, Sweden.

Jacobsson, S. (1981) 'Technical Change and Technology Policy – The Case of Numerically Controlled Lathes in Argentina. Research Policy Institute, Univ. of Lund. Sweden.

Kamenentsky, M. (1979) 'Preinvestment Work and Engineering as Links

Between Supply and Demand of Knowledge', in Thomas, D. B. and Wionczek, M. (eds), *Integration of Science and Technology with Development: Caribbean and Latin American Problems in the Context of the United Nations Conference on Science and Technology for Development*. Oxford: Pergamon Press.

Kamenentsky, M. (1976) *Process Engineering and Process Industries in Argentina and Mexico*. Report funded by the Canadian International Research Centre, Buenos Aires.

Kamrany, N. M. *et al.,* (1976) 'Brazil: A Preliminary Analysis of the Machine Sector'. Centre for Policy Alternatives, MIT, USA.

Kaplinsky, R. (1981) 'The Impact of Electronics on the International Division of Labour: The Illustrative Case of Computer Aided Design'. IDS, Sussex.

Katz, J. (1980) 'Domestic Technology Generation in LDCs: A Review of Research Findings', IDB/ECLA/UNDP/IDRC Research Program on S&T, WP 35, Buenos Aires.

Katz, J. (1973) 'Industrial Growth, Royalty Payments and Local Expenditure on Research and Development', in Urquidi, V. and Thorp, R. (eds), *Latin America in the International Economy*. London: Macmillan.

Katz, J. (1982) A List of 'Main Issues' Emerging from Recent Research on Science and Technology in the Framework of the IDB/ECLA/IDRC/ UNDP Program, Buenos Aires, mimeo.

Katz, J. (1978) 'Technological Change, Economic Development and Intra and Extra Regional Relations in Latin America', IDB/ECLA/UNDP/IDRC Research Program on S&T, WP 30, Buenos Aires.

Katz, J. (ed) (1982) *Technology Generation in Latin American Manufacturing Industries*. Oxford: Pergamon Press.

Katz, J. and Albin, E. (1979) 'From Infant Industry to Technology Exports: The Argentine Experience in the International Sale of Industrial Plants and Engineering Works', IDB/ECLA/UNDP/IDRC Research Program on S&T, WP 14, Buenos Aires.

Katz, J. *et al.,* (1978) 'Productivity, Technology and Domestic Efforts in Research and Development', IDB/ECLA/UNDP/IDRC Research Program on S&T, WP 13, Buenos Aires.

King, K. (1977) *The African Artisan: Education and the Informal Sector in Kenya*. London: Heinemann.

King, K. (1974) 'Kenya's Informal Machine Makers: A Study of Small-scale Industry in Kenya's Emergent Artisan Society', *World Development*, 2: 4/5, April/May.

Kumar and Macleod (eds) (1981) *Multinationals from Developing Countries*. Lexington Books.

Lall, S. (1979) 'Developing Countries as Exporters of Technology: A Preliminary Analysis', in Giersch, H. (ed.), *International Economic Development and Resource Transfer*. Tubingen: JCB Mohr.

Lall, S. (1982) 'The Emergence of the Third World Multinationals: Indian Joint Ventures Overseas', *World Development*, Feb.

Lall, S. (1981) 'Indian Technology Exports and Technological Devlopment', *The Annals of the American Academy of Political and Social Science,* 458.

Lall, S. (1979) 'Transnationals and the Third World: The R&D Factor', *Third World Quarterly*, 1: 3.

Langdon, S. W. (1981) 'North/South, West and East: Industrial Restructuring in the World Economy', *International Journal.*

Lecraw, D. J. (1977) 'Direct Investment by Firms from Less Development Countries', *Oxford Economic Papers,* 29: 3.

Lecraw, D. J. (1981) 'Technological Activities of Less-Developed-Country Based Multinationals', *The Annals of the American Academy of Political and Social Science,* 458, 151–62.

Leff, N. H. (1968) *The Brazilian Capital Goods Industry: 1929–64.* Harvard UP.

McLaughlin, S. D. (1980) 'The Wayside Mechanic: An Analysis of Skill Acquisition in Ghana'. Centre for International Education, Univ. of Mass., USA.

Marulanda, O. (1982) 'An Analytical note on Indigenous Technological Capability', paper given to the Edinburgh Conference, Facilitating Technological Capability.

Mason, R. H. (1980) 'A Comment on Professor Kojima's "Japanese Type versus American Type Technology Transfer"'. *Hitosubashi Journal of Economics,* Tokyo.

Maxwell, P. (1979) 'Implicit R&D Strategy and Investment Linked R&D: A Study of the R&D Programme of the Argentine Steel Firm Acindar SA', IDB/ECLA/UNDP/IDRC Research Program on S&T, WP 23, Buenos Aires.

Maxwell, P. (1977) 'Learning and Technical Change in the Steel Plant of Acindar S.A. in Rosario, Argentina', IDB/ECLA/UNDP/IDRC Research Program on S&T, Buenos Aires.

Maxwell, P. and Tuebal, M. (1980) 'Capacity-Stretching Technical Change: Some Empirical and Theoretical Aspects'. Development in Latin America, WP 36, Buenos Aires.

Mitra, J. D. (1979) 'The Capital Goods Sector in LDCs: A Case for State Intervention?', World Bank Staff Working Paper 343.

Montano, A. E. (1981) *Exports of Technology from the Private Chemical Industry for Mexico.* Consultants Report of a Joint Inter-American Development Bank/World Bank Research Project, Washington, mimeo.

Morley, S. A. and Smith, G. W. (1979) 'Adaptation by Foreign Firms to Labour Abundance in Brazil', in Street, J. H. and James, D. D. (eds), *Technological Progress in Latin America. The Prospects of Overcoming Dependency.* Boulder, Colorado: Westview Press.

Mytelka, L. (1978) 'Licensing and Technical Dependence in the Andean Pact', *World Development,* 6, 447–59.

Nelson, R. R. (1979) 'Innovation and Economic Development: Theoretical Retrospect and Prospect', IDB/ECLA/UNDP/IDRC Research Program on S&T, WP 31, Buenos Aires.

Nelson, R. R. (1980) 'Production Sets, Technological Knowledge and R&D: Fragile and Overworked Constructs for Analysis of Productivity Growth', *American Economic Review,* Papers and Proceedings, 70: 2, 60–71.

Nelson, R. R. and Winter, S. G. (1977) 'In Search of Useful Theory of Innovation', *Research Policy,* 36–76.

O'Brien, P. (1981) 'The Argentinian Experience in Export of Technology: Retrospect and Prospect'. UNIDO, Vienna.

Ozawa, T. (1966) 'Imitation, Innovation and Trade: A Study of Foreign Licensing Operations in Japan'. Ph.D., Columbia Univ.

Pack, H. (1981) 'Fostering the Capital Goods Sector in LDCs, *World Development*, 9: 3, 227–50.

Parthasarathi, A. (1978) 'Electronics in Developing Countries: Issues in Transfer and Development of Technology'. UNCTAD, Geneva.

Pearson, R. (1977) 'The Mexican Cement Industry: Technology, Market Structure and Growth', IDB/ECLA/UNDP/IDRC Research Program on S&T, WP 11, Buenos Aires.

Phillips, D. Social Cost Benefit analysis and technological innovation, paper presented to Edinburgh Conference, facilitating technological capability, 1982.

Pursell, G. and Bhee, Y. W. (1978) *A Firm Level Study of Korean Exports:* Technology Research Report No. 2, World Bank, mimeo.

Rada, J. (1979) 'Microelectronics, Information Technology and its Effect on Developing Countries'. Paper prepared for the Conference on Socio-economic Problems and Potentialities of the Application of Microelectronics at Work, Netherlands.

Raju, M. K. (1979) 'Internationalization of Indian Business: some Missing Links', *Eastern Economist*, 30,11,79, 1066–75.

Ranis, G. (1979) 'Appropriate Technology: Obstacles and Opportunities', in Rosenblatt, S. (ed), *Technology and Economic Development: A Realistic Perspective*. Westview Press.

Ranis, G. *et al.,* (1980) 'International and Domestic Determinants of LDC Technology Choice: Contrasting Agricultural and Industrial Experience'. Economic Growth Centre, Yale Univ.

Ranis, G. *et al.,* (1981) Summary of Scientific Progress. PRA–80–18867, Economic Growth Centre, Yale Univ.

Rawski, T. G. (1978) 'Industrialization, Technology and Employment in the People's Republic of China', World Bank Staff Working Paper 291, Washington DC.

Rawski, T. G. (1980) *China's Transition to Industrialization: Producer Goods and Economic Development in the Twentieth Century*. Ann Arbor: Univ. of Michigan Press.

Rhee, Y. W. and Westphal, L. E. (?) 'A Note on Imports of Technology from the Republics of China and Korea'. Economics of Industry Division, World Bank, Washington DC.

Ronstadt, R. (1977) *Research and Development Abroad by US Multinationals*. Preager.

Rosenberg, N. (1976) *Perspectives on Technology*. Cambridge UP.

Sagasti, F. (1975) 'The INTIC System for Industrial Technology Policy in Peru', *World Development*, 3, 867– 76.

Sagasti, F. (1980) 'Science and Technology for Development: A Review of Schools of Thought on Science, Technology, Development and Technical Change'. International Development Research Centre, STPI Module 1, Ottawa.

Sagasti, F. (1980) 'Towards Endogenous Science and Technology for another Development', *Technological Forecasting and Social Change*, 16: 4, 321–30.

Sercovitch, F. (1978) 'Design Engineering and Endogenous Technical Change. A Micro-economic Approach based on the experience of the Argentine Chemical and Petrochemical Industries'. IDB/ECLA/UNDP/IDRC Research Program on S&T, WP 19, Buenos Aires.

Sercovitch, F. (1980) 'State-Owned Enterprises and Dynamic Comparative Advantages in the World Petrochemical Industry: The Case of Commodity Olefins in Brazil'. Harvard Institute for International Development, Development Discussion Paper No. 96.

Sercovitch, F. (1981) 'Brazil as a Technology Exporter', (draft) Inter-American Development Bank, mimeo.

Soete, L. (1981) 'Technological Dependency: A Critical View', in Seers, D. (ed.) *Dependency Theory: A Critical Assessment.* London: Frances Pinter.

Stewart, F. (1981) 'Industrialization, Technical Change and the International Division of Labour'. Institute for Commonwealth Studies, Oxford.

Stewart, F. (1979) 'International Technology Transfer: Issues and policy options', World Bank Working Paper 344, Washington DC.

Stewart, F. (1977) *Technology and Underdevelopment.* London: Macmillan.

Stewart, F. and James, J. (eds) (1982) *The Economics of New Technologies in Developing Countries.* Frances Pinter.

Stiglitz, J. (1979) 'On the Micro-Economics of Technical Progress', IDB/ECLA/UNDP/IDRC Research Program on S&T, WP 32, Buenos Aires.

Stoneman, C. (1982) Working Paper on Technology in Zimbabwe. Paper given to Edinburgh Conference, Facilitating Technological Capability.

Teitel, S. (1979) 'Notes on Technical Change Induced Under Conditions of Protection, Distortions and Rationing', IDB/ECLA/UNDP/IDRC Research Program on S&T, WP 34, Buenos Aires.

Teitel, S. (1981) 'Towards an Understanding of Technical Change in Semi-Industrial Countries', *Research Policy*, 10: 2.

Thomas, D. B. (1979) 'Building Scientific and Technological Capabilities in LDCs – A Survey of Some Economic Development Issues', in Thomas, D. B. and Wionczek, M. S. (eds), *Integration and Technology with Development: Caribbean and Latin American Problems in the Context of the United Nations Conference on Science and Technology for Development.* Pergamon Press.

UNCTAD (1980) 'The Capital Goods Sector in Developing Countries: Technology Issues for Further Research'. Study by the UNCTAD Secretariat, UNCTAD/TD/B/C.6/60. United Nations.

UNCTAD (1980) 'The Role of Small and Medium-Sized Enterprises in the International Transfer of Technology: Issues for Research'. Study Prepared by E. White with S. Feldman. UNCTAD TD/B/C.6164. United Nations.

UNDP/UNESCO (1981) 'Demand and Utilization of Technicians in Colombian Industry'. Ministry of National Education, UNDP/UNESCO, Bogota.

UNESCO (1981) 'Interaction between Education and Productive Work: A Bibliography'. Prepared by the IBE Documentation Centre, Geneva.

UNESCO (1980) *International Meeting of Experts on the Promotion of Productive Work in Education.* Secretariat working document, Final Report, UNESCO, Paris.

UNESCO (1980) 'Technical and Vocational Education in Asia and Oceania', *Bulletin of the UNESCO Regional Office for Education in Asia and Oceania,* no. 21, June, Bangkok.

UNIDO (1981) 'Technology Exports from Developing Countries – the Cases of Argentina and Portugal'. UNIDO/ICIS, March.

Van Rensburg, P. (1982) 'Technological Capability in Externally Controlled Societies – Botswana'. Paper given to Edinburgh Conference, Facilitating Technological Capability.

Watanabe, S. (1979) 'Technical Cooperation Between Large and Small Firms in Philippine Automobile Industry'. World Employment Program Research, ILO, Geneva.

Wells, L. T. (1981) 'Foreign Investors from the Third World', in Kumar and Macleod (eds) *Multinationals from Developing Countries*, Lexington Books.

Wells, L. T. (1978) 'Foreign Investment from the Third World: The Experience of Chinese Firms from Hong-Kong', *Columbia Journal of World Business,* Spring, 39–49.

Wells, L. T. (1977) 'The Internationalization of Firms from Developing Countries', in Agmont and Kindleberger (eds), *Multinationals from Small Countries.* Cambridge, Mass: MIT.

Westphal, L. E. (1981) 'Empirical Justification for Infant Industry Protection', World Bank Staff Working Paper 445, Washington DC.

Westphal, L. E. (1978) 'Industrial Incentives in the Republic of China'. Economics of Industry Division, World Bank, Washington DC.

Westphal, L. E. and Rhee Y. W. (1982) 'Korea's Revealed Comparative Advantage in Exports of Technology: An Initial Assessment', World Bank, Washington DC, mimeo.

Westphal, L. E., Rhee, Y. W. and Pursell, G. (1981) 'Korean Industrial Competence: Where It Came From', World Bank Staff Working Paper 469, Washington DC.

Whison, T. (1982) 'Changing Global Requirements', Paper Given to Edinburgh Conference, Facilitating Technological Capability.

World Bank (1980) *Brazil: Protection and Competitiveness of the Capital Goods Producing Industries.* World Bank Report No. 2488–BR.

Index

Abernathy, W. J.   115, 125
Ablin, E.   192
Acindar steel company, Brazil   327
Acominas steel plant, Brazil   327
Addis Ababa conference (1961)   37
Africa: science education in   47,
    264–5, 274–5; sub-Saharan   170,
    172. *See also* Addis Ababa;
    Arusha; Asians; Botswana;
    Congo; Ghana; Harare; Kenya;
    Lagos Plan; Liberia; Tanzania;
    Uganda; Zaire; Zimbabwe
agriculture   19–20, 32, 33, 48, 51, 70,
    76, 87, 89, 91, 92, 99, 101–2. *See
    also* CIGYAR; hand-tools; rural
    technology; Ubungo
aircraft industry   322–5
Amsden, M. A.   201–2, 305
'ancillarisation'   248
apprenticeship   32, 54, 218
Argentina   85, 86, 89, 192, 193, 197,
    283
arms exports and purchases   270–1
Arusha Declaration   375, 381
Ashby, E.   264
Ashok Leyland Co., India   231
Asians in Africa   12–13, 43, 44, 55,
    360–1, 372–3, 375, 380–1, 386–7
automation   117, 145–51, 153, 213,
    367
automobile industry   71–2, 117, 294,
    319–22

Babbage, Charles   175
Bajaj Co., India   247
Baranson, Jack   320
Baron, C. G.   152
Basu, A.   267, 273

Bell, R. M.   36, 54, 82, 187–206,
    215, 216, 311
Bennell, Paul   35, 37, 335–53
Bhabha, Homi   269
Bhagwati, J.   127–8, 226–9
BHEL Co., India   231
Bhilai steel plant   73
Bienefeld, Manfred   21–3, 157,
    161–73, 178–80
Biggs, S.   87, 89, 91
Binswanger, H. P.   90
blacksmiths   59, 101, 176, 378–9,
    385, 388, 389
Bose, S. C.   268
Botswana   42
brand names   85–6, 293
Brazil   19, 110, 283, 317–30. *See also*
    Acominas; Embraer; Metal Leve;
    Romi; Usiminas
Briones, G.   214, 217
Bruynzeel Co.   356, 360, 367, 369, 370

Cable, V.   154
Caillods, Françoise   36, 211–21
capital goods   5, 16, 17, 19, 21, 24–5,
    83, 100, 105, 302, 314, 317
careers   35, 50
cement industry   74, 75, 295
Cement Research Institute,
    Delhi   74
chemical industry   279
Chemical Engineering School, Santa
    Fe, Argentina   197
Chile   283
Chinese Manufacturers' Association
    of Hong Kong   305
Chinese People's Republic   84, 175,
    383–4

399

86, 176, 239–40, 249, 256–8. *See also* indigenous technological capability; scale; social relations of production; unpackaging
Teitel, S.   229
TELCO, India   72, 231, 232, 247
textiles   37, 103–4, 197, 288–9, 292–3, 355–73. *See also* cotton; Jacquard; rayon
Thailand   196–7
tobacco   380
tourism   176
tractor prices   92
trade. *See* exports; protection; technology
training   51–3, 87, 88, 196–7, 215–19, 266–7, 361, 356. *See also* learning
Transmara forests, Kenya   368, 372
Troussier, J. F.   213

Ubungo Farm Implement Manufacturing Co.   179, 383–4
Uganda   48
unemployment   37, 53, 165–7
United Nations: UNCSTD   34; UNCTAD   90; UNESCO   32, 37, 264, 271, 272, 274
United States of America   98, 100, 282

universities   32, 38, 48, 54, 79, 218–19, 266–7, 349–53, 365. *See also* Nairobi; Seoul
unpackaging   6, 36, 295, 361
Usiminas steel plant, Brazil   194, 198–9, 325–8

Veneers Kenya Ltd   368
vocational education and training   51, 215, 218

Wade, R.   171
Warren, B.   7
Wells, L. T.   307
Westphal, L. E.   10, 19, 20, 279–96, 302, 303, 311, 312
Winter, S. G.   8, 9
wood products   37, 42, 355–73. *See also* Compagnie Forestière du Gabon; plywood
work organisation   36, 211–16
World Bank   384
World Cement Report (1980)   87

Yawata steel mill   70

Zaire   48
Zimbabwe   54